INTERIOR STATES

NEW AMERICANISTS

A Series Edited by Donald E. Pease

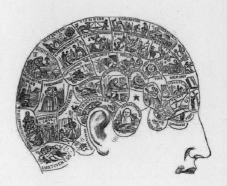

INTERIOR STATES

INSTITUTIONAL CONSCIOUSNESS AND THE INNER LIFE

OF DEMOCRACY IN THE ANTEBELLUM UNITED STATES

Christopher Castiglia

DUKE UNIVERSITY PRESS

Durham and London

2008

© 2008 DUKE UNIVERSITY PRESS

All rights reserved. Printed in the United

States of America on acid-free paper ∞

Designed by Amy Ruth Buchanan

Typeset in Minion by Keystone Typesetting, Inc.

Library of Congress Cataloging-in-Publication Data

appear on the last printed page of this book.

To the memory of my father,

Joseph A. Castiglia

* * *

And as ever, with love, to Chris

CONTENTS

ACKNOWLEDGMENTS

Fellowships from the National Endowment for the Humanities and the Loyola Center for Ethics and Social Justice, and a leave of absence from Loyola University Chicago, enabled me to complete research for this book. I thank the staffs of the Newberry Library, the Library Company of Philadelphia, and the Amherst College Robert Frost Library for their help in my research.

Versions of chapter 3 appeared in *Early American Literature* and *American Literary History*, a version of chapter 6 appeared in *In Search of Hannah Crafts* (Perseus), and versions of chapter 7 appeared in *The Cambridge Companion to Hawthorne*, *The Norton Critical Edition of* The House of the Seven Gables, and *The Blackwell Companion to Herman Melville*. I benefited from the thoughtful criticism provided by anonymous readers for those volumes and by their editors—David Shields, Gordon Hutner, Rick Millington, Robert S. Levine, Henry Louis Gates Jr., Hollis Robbins, and Wyn Kelley—and gratefully acknowledge permission to reprint here.

For inviting me to present portions of my work at conferences or at their home institutions, I am grateful to Steven Carl Arch, Gillian Brown, Pattie Cowell, Zabelle Derounian-Stodola, Teresa Goddu, Kristie Hamilton, Jack Kerkering, Robert Levine, Trish Loughran, Chris Looby, Ellen McCallum, Rick Millington, Dana Nelson, Sam Otter, Don Pease, Eliza Richards, Karen Sanchez-Eppler, Laurie Shannon, Frank Shuffelton, Eric Slauter, Tim Sweet, and Al Young.

My life in Chicago has been enriched by the friendship and conversation of George Chauncey, David and Lisa Chinitz, Lane Fenrich, Mary Finn, Verna Foster, Suzanne Gossett, Ron Gregg, Jay Grossman, Sharon Haar, Paul Jay, Tom and Noreen Kaminski, Jack Kerkering, Stephen Lapthisophon, Jules Law, Karen Lebergott, Mary Mackay, Jeff Masten, Gerry Reed, Mary Kay Reed, Harry Samuels, Moe Taylor, John Vincler, Wendy Wall, Joyce and Jerry Wexler, and Edward Wheatley. I owe a special thanks to Lynne Simon, who helped me escape the inner life and rediscover the pleasures of friendship. No aspect of my life during the writing of this book has been as stimulating as the conversations

I have had with students. Their wit, kindness, and startling intelligence have helped keep teaching a passionate calling for me. For that, I thank the graduate students at Loyola, particularly Krissy Egan, Danielle Glassmeyer, Doug Guerra, Nick Hurley, Shelly Jarenski, Zach Lamm, Carina Pasquiesi, Megan Pater Phillips, Rick Rodriguez, John Schlueter, and Gale Temple, and at Northwestern, especially Katy Chiles, Peter Jaros, and Sarah Mesle. Wes Whitlatch has been and is, in every way, a rock star.

I have also been fortunate to have an intellectual community that, over the past years, has supported and stretched my thinking. For this, I thank Bruce Burgett, Russ Castronovo, Zabelle Derounian-Stodola, Betsy Duquette, Leigh Gilmore, Teresa Goddu, Glenn Hendler, Richard Morrison, Ben Reiss, Augusta Rohrbach, and Priscilla Wald. Above all, I give heartfelt thanks to Bob Levine, Chris Looby, and Dana Nelson, who shared their homes, their keen intelligence, their wit, and their capacious generosity with me. They read drafts, discussed ideas, offered advice and encouragement, and improved my thinking at every turn. In every meaningful way, I wrote this book for and with them. Every scholar should be lucky enough to have fellow travelers like these.

The incisive intelligence, patience, and warm friendship of Ken Wissoker improved this book immensely. Working with Ken and his staff, particularly Mark Mastromarino, at Duke University Press has been an unqualified joy from start to end.

From the two men to whom I dedicate the book—my father, Joe Castiglia, and my partner, Chris Reed—I have learned everything I know about love. This book is small recompense, but I offer it with all my gratitude.

Is democracy a lost cause?

In past years, cultural critics in a range of fields have proclaimed the failing health, if not the imminent demise, of democracy.[1] By "democracy," these critics generally mean not the operations of electoral politics but citizens' capacity to organize themselves for collaborative negotiation and public action to rectify injustice and improve associational life in ways that take account of divergent expectations and experiences.[2] Citizens' democratic agency has been done in, according to such accounts, by a range of economic, ideological, and cultural forces that have led to a radically isolated, privatized, and depoliticized citizenry content, in Robert Putnam's phrase, to "bowl alone" rather than participate in the broad and eclectic public associations that Alexis de Tocqueville identified as the characteristic form of American life.[3] In some accounts, democracy is failing because of a host of contemporary causes, including the privatization of the economy, the erosion of the welfare state, increased xenophobia in the face of rapid globalization and the passing of industrial labor, and the failure of an intellectual left to think its way constructively beyond or, conversely, to effectively revitalize the "identity politics" of the 1980s. In other accounts, democracy was stillborn, done in at its inception by Whig elitism, the social polarization of the enfranchised and the disenfranchised, the absorption of local association into a bourgeois print public, the institutionalization of slavery, and incipient imperialism.[4]

As compelling as such postmortems are, they suffer from an unquestioning adherence to an uncomplicated interpellative model of trickle-down ideology. That is to say, just because an ideological apparatus seeks to generate a depublicized and individuated citizenry does not necessarily mean it produces one, or does so without unforeseen complications. Although the privatization of citizenship and the consequent loss of public and deliberative association and the pleasures and values it generates are certainly a central concern of the analyses that follow, *Interior States* argues that democracy is not dead or dying but misplaced. Citizens, I believe, still have a good deal of inventive energy and civic-mindedness that are ready to be given to the renovation and innovation of social life in the United States. The problem, however, is that we have been encouraged to misrecognize the location of the social, finding it, not in association with others, but in the turbulent and conflicted interiors of our own bodies. The bodily interior has become misunderstood as a social space, as *the* social space of modernity, and it is exclusively within that interior state that citizens are encouraged to develop democratic innovation and the skills of negotiation across differences.

To claim that human interiority is (mis)conceived as a social space may seem, to say the least, counter-intuitive, interiority being the sanctum of our most private sentiments and secret desires. It is a central argument of *Interior States*, however, that those sentiments and desires are conceived by the modern citizen, aided in that misconception by two centuries of public and psychological reform, in social terms. The increasingly discordant human interior (what I will call the *nervous state*), with its battles between appetite and restraint, desire and deferral, consciousness and unconsciousness, became, I will argue, a microcosm of the equally riven sociality of nineteenth-century America. As the inside became a reflection (and increasingly a displacement) of the ideological conflicts of the social world, citizens were encouraged to understand the incessant labor of vigilant self-scrutiny and self-management as effective democratic action. It is not, therefore, that citizens have lost the capacity to act democratically; they have misconceived the realm where that action can achieve its purported ends. While democracy may not be lost, then, it is certainly misplaced.

The reason for this misplacement may be found as much in what the interpellative model leaves out as in what it offers. When, in Louis Althusser's famous example, the police hail a citizen on the street and the citizen responds —thereby being interpellated into the rule of law, the order of the state, and the subject position of "citizen"—the metaphoric transformation obscures a historical process of self-conception that occurs not on the street or in the institutional spaces of the law, but in the mind, the emotions, the psychology, and the spirit of the citizen-subject. According to Althusser, those interior spaces are not themselves an effect of interpellation (Althusser insisted that the "unconscious" preexists history and hence ideology) but are the always already available arenas of psychosocial identification.[5] Attempting to analyze—and historicize—this gap, theorists of subjectivity from Michel Foucault to Giles Deleuze and Judith Butler have sought, in Fredric Jameson's words, "to reassert the specificity of the political content of everyday life and of individual fantasy-experience and to reclaim it from that reduction to the merely subjective and to the status of the psychological projection," which is "even more characteristic of American cultural and ideological life today than it is of a still politicized France."[6] Or, as Butler more succinctly states the problem, "It is a significant theoretical mistake to take the 'internality' of the psychic world for granted."[7]

The mistake of taking "internality" for granted characterizes much theorization of democracy, despite the fact that "internality" developed in tandem with democracy in the early national period. Among the first Enlightenment theorists to join deep interiority and civic order to produce what we might, following Foucault, call disciplinary democracy, the Founders, as chapter 1 argues, developed a philosophy of centralized *feelings* modeled on historically familiar modes of belonging (families, churches, and above all friendships) but newly conceived as metaphorical—rather than embodied and local—simulacra of the government. This new interpellative philosophy, which I term *federal affect*, helped to recast the bodily coercions of government as the apparently voluntary and internally managed orders of what Foucault calls governmentality, an interior state that is both consensual and self-managing.[8] The process of federalizing affect did not involve eliminating former and often highly volatile associations, but moving them *inward* into the privatized spaces of the new middle-class home and, more insistently, within the politicized spaces of the bodily interior.

In asserting that the bodily interior—the space of a newly conceived and self-managed "consciousness" and its unruly other, the unconscious realm of desire, appetite, and rage—became in the early United States a micro-state, I must be clear about what I am *not* claiming. First, I am not making a case for the origin of human interiority itself. Cultural historians have documented the existence of interiority in discourses of "character" dating from the late seventeenth century and early eighteenth century, while others have located nascent interiorities in the deliberations of Shakespeare's Hamlet or in the myriad affects of the Middle Ages.[9] Rather, I am making a claim for a development within the history of human interiority. During the late eighteenth century and early nineteenth century, I will show, the interior became a micro-version of the social, not simply as an individual's "private" realm of desires, affects, and appetites, but as a realm of disruption and attempted order that, mirroring the often tense struggles between popular demand and juridical control, may be called an *interior state*.

Central to this understanding of antebellum interiority, then, is a different conception of the subject not as a being interpellated or disciplined into unitary subjectivity or a single "performative" but, rather, as overpopulated and—as any large population will be—riven by conflicting demands and aspirations. In the late eighteenth century and early nineteenth century, after all, the United States was anything but an ordered reflection of federalist design. Rather, that society was diversified and at times disrupted by the often colliding ideological regimes—and the resulting social associations—of slavery, immigration, industrialization, urbanization, imperialism, market capitalism, and liberal humanism, to name but a few. If antebellum society became an arena for contests between the demands of ownership and labor, farmers and urbanites, Catholics and Protestants, free citizens and slaves, immigrants and nativists, then its interior simulacra equally became sites of divisions and conflicts that were, in their origins, not psychological or behavioral but *social*.

The interiorization of the social in the antebellum United States did not produce disciplined subject positions in the image of state ideology, then, but generated a site for negotiating the contradictions and conflicts of the state's myriad ideologies—as well as models of association and social interaction beyond the interests of the state—in ways that belied the coherence of national or market interests. The human interior was, in important ways that *Interior States* addresses, beyond the state's power to regulate. What the invention of a social interior did produce, however, were modes of vigilant and habitual self-management, the first step in the ideological production of the modern security state.

It is worth noting, however, that this self-management was necessarily a *failed* endeavor, a failure essential to the security state, perpetuating in the very moment of failure the continued need for ever greater security. Few seemed to believe, in the antebellum period, that the divided interiors of the antebellum citizen could be integrated once and for all into an orderly and unified whole, a psychic *e pluribus unum*. On the contrary, the relentless production of the "unconscious," as representative of forces of social demand that perpetually threatened the orders of the state no less than the integrated harmony of self-regulated and unified personhood, demonstrates that the goal was neither to regulate once and for all the unruly interiors of the citizen nor to keep citizens from developing skills of negotiation, but to give those skills a virtual arena in which to operate, the divided and conflictual space of the interior. If moving such negotiations inward protected them, on one level, from state intervention, it also made democracy an essentially mobile phenomenon in ways that served state interests. No longer relying on local relations between people engaged in negotiated association, democracy could now travel with the body, crossing the borders of localities—even nations—without sacrificing the sensation of social continuity. In a period when citizens traveled with unprecedented frequency, the mobile sociality provided by antebellum interiority became a necessary check on disorientation and alienation and, in the process, enabled the state's expansion across national borders without sacrificing the *feel* of a still intact democratic integrity.

While interiority enabled increased mobility, the semblance of permanence was generated by a corollary public discourse, what *Interior States* addresses as the emerging social theory of *institutionalism*. Distinct from the material practices of particular institutions, the discourse of institutionalism asserted its power to carry current social interests unhindered into the future. Orienting citizens from present negotiations to a perpetually receding horizon of futurity, institutionalism, as chapter 2 demonstrates, deferred temporally what interiority displaced spatially. While interiority left citizens no need for public spaces of association, institutionalism left no present in which to associate. Splitting time into an undemocratic past and a democratic future, institutionalism not only made a democratic *now* nearly impossible to conceive, it assisted in the divisions of *types* of people depending on whether they were oriented toward the future (biologically and ideologically reproductive) or the past (those "stuck" in their memories by an underproductive nostalgia or melancholy).[10]

The continuous future promised by institutionalism does not encourage labor today for a glorious democracy tomorrow, however, but naturalizes the immobility of de-historicized stasis. Institutionalism does not imagine a better future, but one that will exactly replicate the present. This projective fantasy has three dangerous effects for democratic citizenship. Most obviously, it denies the very possibility of historical change. Deferring democracy into a future when our always cited grandchildren will enjoy the freedom we willingly for their sake forswear for ourselves, institutionalism assures citizens that, for all our melting-pot, rags-to-riches fictions of generational improvement, our grandchildren will want exactly what we want *for* them. This promise not only denies future generations of citizens the capacity to negotiate needs, values, and aspirations that differ from the present, it also naturalizes the idea of a democratic paternalism: that "we" should make institutions for "them" and not that they should do so for themselves.

Even granting its paternalistic premises, however, institutionalism's promise of a self-same future is not as altruistic as it at first appears. Rather, it flatters "us" with a pleasing image of a *currently* coherent and unified society. That is, if the future is a projection of "us" and that future is a place of democratic harmony, then it follows that we, too, enjoy unity, if only imminently. Our capacity to negotiate difference and generate a different future—the anti-institutional work of democracy—is thus mooted by institutionalism's elimination of the very appearance, material circumstances notwithstanding, of social division and conflict. To accept institutionalism's future, in other words, is to deny the nature of the social and, hence, of democracy.

What is most disturbing, however, is that institutionalism's appeal comes not despite but because of its cancellation of the needs and capacities for social negotiation and historical change. The power of institutions arises, according to antebellum theorists, from their capacity to outlast the mortality of constitutive members. To believe in the self-perpetuating "life" of institutions is to credit them with an agency of their own, separable from the embodied agency of participants and therefore unanswerable to their demands and visions. Separated from the various and often passionate participation of citizens, according to antebellum theorists, institutions operate impartially, disinterestedly, abstractly. It is precisely through antebellum theories of institutionalism (themselves responses to the popular uprisings of the French and Haitian revolutions), in fact, that the idea arises that democracy *should be* impartial, without conflict or passion. More dangerously, institutionalism imagined citizens, partisan and potentially passionate, as the subjective and therefore threatening others of "the political." While this contrast of citizen and institution in antebellum theory appears as a necessary balancing act, it in fact generates the interiority of citizens as intrinsically "passionate" and hence antipolitical and conversely conceives politics as a realm without conflict (the result of which is the idealization of "nonpartisan" centrism in the political discourse of our own age). Institutionalism thus "cleanses" the agency of partisan negotiation through the supposedly "impartial" operations of the institutionalized state. Even as interiority became the means to alienate citizens from the institutions they supposedly authorize, however, it was perceived as compensation, democracy's door prize. No longer entitled to exert agency *over* institutions, citizens were given the responsibility of regulating and managing the turbulent interiors that supposedly made them unfit for civic participation. Citizens became administrators, in short, of themselves.

The supplemental relationship of institutionalism and interiority produced what Marx in *The German Ideology* called "estrangement," the "consolidation of what we ourselves produce into an objective power above us, growing out of our control, thwarting our expectations, bringing to naught our calculations." This "objective power" Marx identified as the state, an "illusory form of communal life," which citizens believe comes about naturally, "not as their own united power, but as an alien force existing outside them, of the origin and goal of which they are ignorant, which they thus cannot control, which on the contrary passes through a peculiar series of phases and stages independent of the will and the action of man, nay even being the prime governor of these." In return for our estranged power, Marx wrote, we are given our "particular interest," which prevents us from seeing our "communal interest." As interiorized self-management became the primary form of "particular interest" in the antebellum United States, institutionalism became the corollary "estrangement" of citizens' agency, supposedly supplementing but in fact appropriating the capacity of citizens to act for themselves.[11]

In focusing on the state as a series of interconnected institutions, I mean to displace the restrictive focus of so many recent studies of early-nineteenth-century U.S. literature on the nation and on nationalism. One finds, in the writing of antebellum political theories such as Lyman Beecher and Francis Lieber, less talk of *nationalism* than of the *state* as a network of civil institutions, of which nationalism is perhaps a late sedimentation. (Hence, as the second chapter shows, in times of "national" crisis the government defends seemingly apolitical institutions such as marriage.) Although *Interior States* is primarily interested in the emergence of a social interior in the antebellum United States, then, it does not make a claim for national particularity, not only because the discourses of reform, self-management, and institutionalism arose in other national contexts and traveled transnationally, but also because those very concepts mooted the efficacy of nationalism, relegating the "social" to the bodily interior and the ever expandable estrangement of that body in institutions, neither of which was bound by geopolitical borders.

Perhaps it was this extranational capacity that linked interiority to the network of tracts, newspapers, fiction, lectures, and material culture that made up what became known collectively as "social reform." In the first decades of the nineteenth century, movements sprang up to reform almost every aspect of public and private life in the United States, including efforts to liberalize religion, abolish slavery, encourage temperance, ease the condition of the urban poor, renovate education, establish the vote for women, popularize "free love," and institutionalize the teachings of the French socialist Charles Fourier in agrarian communities such as Brook Farm, Oneida, and Fruitlands.[12] Reformers saw structural inequalities arising from the coercion of labor, the unequal distribution of profit and opportunity, the legal disenfranchisement of classes of citizens, and the stultifying aridity of conventional domesticity. In response, they called for the overthrow of what Ralph Waldo Emerson decried as "a system of distrust, of concealment, of superior keenness, not of giving but of taking advantage," and sought to establish instead ways of life one might consider with "joy and self-approval in his hour of love and aspiration."[13]

The popularity of these reform movements suggests how tenaciously citizens held on to the promise and pleasures of associational life, even as the "societies" they joined, invested in the institutional circulation of social interiority, transformed local associations into what Michael Warner identifies as America's first mass public.[14] The 527 U.S. antislavery societies in 1836 more than doubled to 1,300 by 1838, claiming 109,000 members, while in 1835 an estimated 1.5 million Americans belonged to temperance societies.[15] Through these societies and their vast networks of publications and lectures, reformers helped generate the concept of "public opinion," over which they maintained an unshakable hold. "We rarely see the Reformer," Henry David Thoreau commented, "who is fairly launched in his enterprise bringing about the right state of things with hearty and efficacious tugs, and not rather preparing and grading the way through the minds of the people."[16]

My interest in *Interior States* is not in reform's role in generating a static mass public, however, but in the significant changes in the objects of reform—in what we might call *reformability*, a set of recalcitrant predispositions rather than of correctable actions—in the antebellum period. Initially, abolitionists in the 1820s and 1830s imagined those predispositions in highly valued terms, as an inclination on the part of African Americans toward hard work, civic order, and emulation of virtuous teachers. Not only were African Americans capable of citizenship, abolitionists argued, they embodied what, in chapter 3, I call the *citizen form*, a compendium of virtues emanating from a *civil interiority*. So exemplary was this interior state, chapter 3 shows, that white abolitionists imagined themselves as black in order to assume a civic depth that white citizens, passionate and prejudiced, were assumed to lack. If such constructions took from African Americans the right to define values and social arrangements that might compete with the citizen form, they nevertheless granted a core civility that contrasts starkly with the gothic interiorities of the 1840s.

During that decade, reform moved from a focus on structural injustices such as slavery to individual vices such as drinking, gambling, masturbation, eating spicy foods, smoking, reading trashy novels, and wearing tight corsets. As increasing numbers of everyday leisure activities—eating, dressing, sex, recreational reading—became conceived as reformable vices, nearly any non-laboring citizen could be said to possess reformability. The dissemination of reformability dramatically extended reform's reach into the middle-class institutions of marriage and family and, in the process, obscured the *systematic* injustices borne by slaves, the poor, or the disenfranchised, locating the cause of their suffering in individual flaws of character that everyone potentially shared. The shift from structural to individual reform turned the institutions of privacy into sites of surveillance and habitual correction. Parents were encouraged to spy on children and servants, spouses to inspect one another for signs of disloyalty, children to watch for alcoholism in parents. Ultimately, however, it was not the responsibility of parents or employers to maintain a vigilant watch over unruly natures. Rather, it was each citizen's civic obligation to manage himself or herself.

In the end, however, no amount of self-management could decisively change one's nature, as the interior remained divided and conflictual, out of sight and beyond reach. Because of this resolute irredeemability, interiority became visible not as discrete dispositions, but as their sedimentation into what we today call identities. Reformers sought to codify and regulate identities, conceived as a mass of reformable inclinations and drives, the new language of interior unrest. One could not take a drink without becoming a drunkard or engage in "solitary vice" without becoming a masturbator. Reformers coined terms such as "addict," "alcoholic," "psychopath," "con man," "hoodlum," and "pornographer" to turn actions into identities that were, despite their emergence in reform contexts, ultimately inalterable ("incorrigible," "intransigent," "recalcitrant," and "irredeemable" were also reform coinages).[17] In an age of increased economic speculation, the irredeemable lacked a contractual frame of mind, characterized in terms of ephemerality, immediate gratification, nostalgia, and recklessness, and were incapable of evaluating consequences or of sexual, social, or economic reproduction. By the end of the nineteenth century, such traits would divide and solidify a host of recognizable social identities: the violent and shiftless black, the loose and frivolous female, and ultimately the narcissistic and pleasure-seeking homosexual. Before settling into recognizable population types, however, the attributes that marked citizens as reformable floated promiscuously, attaching to a range of diverse and shifting social bodies and their new literary corollaries—the whore, the swindler, the libertine, the gambler, the social climber, the drunkard—whose natures, like those of their real-world counterparts, were composed of unnatural appetites and desires. In both fictional and sociological accounts of degradation, reformability became the habitual state of groups who were, ironically, the *most* biologically and economically (re)productive: immigrants, slaves, Jews, workers, and urbanites whose bodily acts became the expressive indices of their interiors rather than the other way around. Addicted, licentious, vulgar, and gluttonous, devoted to hedonism rather than productive labor, nostalgic and melancholy rather than forward-looking, trafficking in ephemera rather than building permanent structures, the reformable in effect became the normative modern citizen, whose wayward inclinations could be countered only by the institutional disinterest of the state.

Beyond defining individual identities, however, reformable predispositions came to characterize clusters of bodies—what became known as *cultures*—that were social extensions of those bodies and their interiors, not the other way around. Cultures, no less than individuals, became characterized, judged, and regulated on the basis of reformable interiority. In so doing, antebellum reformers normalized or vilified forms of sociality depending on whether they affirmed or challenged the values and arrangements of emerging middle-class privacy. Throughout the 1840s, reform targeted modes of sociality that were public, collective, nostalgic, pleasurable, and unproductive (although they often involved the sharing of material goods and information) and that therefore countered the middle-class values of futurity, privacy, self-restraint, generational productivity, and competitive individualism. These adjudications between valuable and reformable socialities were made in the name of health rather than economics or social power (masturbation was said to waste reproductive energy needed to generate children, for instance, while eating spicy foods over-stimulated the nervous system, unfitting one for work). In popular fictions of the 1840s and 1850s, as chapter 4 shows, barrooms were depicted as sites of a raucous sociality that became the primary target of temperance reform, more than the consumption of alcohol itself. Despite the fact that most people in the antebellum United States drank at home rather than in barrooms, the home became alcoholism's other in this fiction, promising health and an orderly productivity by nurturing the values—what I call the inner life of capital— necessary to participate in the competitive market.

As I have already suggested, however, the goal of reform was not self- or collective management but *failed* management. While abolition and temperance reformers might depict conflict between people or groups characterized by clear interiorities (the addicted drunkard versus the self-restrained teetotaler, the licentious overseer versus the chaste slave), reform literature increasingly focused on the conflicts that raged in the interiors of each and every person. As chapter 5 argues, despite reform's production of clear and easily distinguishable "types" of interiority (good or bad, licentious or pure, productive or unproductive, self-indulgent or self-restrained), no one lives in either of these positions. They are impossible endpoints that exist only hypothetically, off the scale of human experience. Rather, citizens possessed of riven interiorities shuttle perpetually *between* self-control and appetite, desire and deferral, wait and want. That shuttling—the condition I analyze in the fifth chapter as nervous citizenship—is the necessary result of the interiorization of social division.

There is, then, an obvious contradiction in reform literature, a tension between promised resolution and perpetual self-management. On the one hand, reform espoused self-management as achievable through habitual exercise and continual vigilance. On the other, the perpetual presence of a multiply divided interior meant that the forces of addictive appetite were never entirely conquerable, any more than the borders of any given social unit could ever be effectively closed. It is precisely the tension between these two views of interiority that made reform a self-authorizing and self-perpetuating enterprise. More troubling, the two views generate in citizens an endless (and endlessly failed) effort to achieve a goal that is, to say the least, illusory. Struggling continually to achieve an absolute state that existed only as a fictional possibility, shuffled between states of degradation and purity, the reformable subject became the nervous citizen, caught in the tense contradictions between two equally impossible epistemologies in ways that could serve only to escalate the fretful vigilance and failed self-managements of the individual subject. The failures of nervous citizenship ensured the ongoing effort that made an increasingly de-socialized citizenry feel nevertheless active.

* * * * *

Whether the intended outcome of nervous interiority was the benevolent uplift of degraded populations or the production of self-managed social order and productive labor, the results were unforeseen in the period's political theory and reform literature. Encouraging citizens to work at internal integrity rather than to struggle with social negotiation, discourses of interiority produced consequences that filled the flamboyant pages of popular fiction. Those unforeseen yet powerful deployments of interiority make up the counter-narrative of the first five chapters of *Interior States*. Such counter-narratives—made of unruly affects, mental waywardness, and inventive extravagances—took the form of persistent and seemingly unmotivated melancholy (as in Hannah Foster's *The Coquette* or Washington Irving's "Rip Van Winkle," discussed in chapter 1) or of sadomasochistic intimacy (as in Maria Monk's *Awful Disclosures*, discussed in chapter 2). Often they took the shape of irrepressible appetites and errant desires (as in the temperance fictions of Timothy Shay Arthur and Walt Whitman or in George Lippard's gothic masterpiece, *The Quaker City*, discussed in chapters 4 and 5). The desires, appetites, and longings that evade reform, that refuse integration into the mandated orders of self-management, I argue throughout *Interior States*, become an archive of democratic aspirations that have been discredited or foreclosed, the visions of citizens who are socially dead yet living—often persistently and even ragefully so—in the interior state.

Although such demands and aspirations were sometimes discredited as unhealthy, illicit, addictive, even monstrous, they were most often simply trivialized as *imaginary*. It might stand to reason that when social relations became the stuff of interiority, imagination, in turn, became intrinsically *social*. And yet it was the capacity of the imagination to see what has not already been seen, to imagine narratives of social interaction unaccounted for by discourses of the "real," that the antebellum period denigrated as fantastic and trivial, too big and too small to be properly "social." In the fictions of the period, the work of imagination became screaming dissent and murmured epiphany, the manias, reveries, neuroses, and daydreams that fill the pages of popular fiction. Those fictions were frequently themselves the target of reform efforts, decried in the same terms that characterized the people deemed reformable: ephemeral, seductive, impractical, unhealthy, selfish, and unproductive. The assault on imagination drove a wedge between invention and politics that became one of our most destructive inheritances from the period of popular reform. When antebellum phrenologists analyzed the Great Men of the Republic (John Quincy Adams, Daniel Webster, Andrew Jackson), using portraits, death masks, and busts, they found them rich in Enlightenment virtues that make public order possible: common sense, reason, civic responsibility, self-control. Yet in every case, the statesmen were lacking in one trait: marvelousness, the capacity to see what is not empirically observable, to think beyond precedent, to imagine. The public orders of the state had no need for the capacity to marvel—to be surprised out of the expected and the already known, to see the unimaginable as if it were real—but the loss for democracy, as the fiction of the 1840s and 1850s demonstrates, was heart-rending.

To denigrate imaginative acts—to place them outside the orders of the state —was not, of course, to shame them out of existence but simply to deny their public status as social theory, as democratic participation. Made unpublic, imagination, like other forms of discredited sociality in antebellum America, became an interior state. *Interior States* demonstrates how the forms of inner labor—nervousness, desire, appetite, fantasy, the language of estranged personhood—became in antebellum fiction articulations of democratic strivings that, however trivialized, refused to disappear. If fantasy is a poor substitute for revolution, as I argue in chapter 6, it is nevertheless a tool available to citizens of the interior state, one that, working in a sanctioned and (seemingly) safely depoliticized register, survived the material normalization of middle-class values in the antebellum United States. Viewed in this light, imaginative fiction is not a mere reflection of social values and mores, handy documents of more immediate historical and cultural forces. Rather, imaginative fiction is the archive of the socially possible, an archive of alternatives to the historically or sociologically "real." To study literature of the antebellum period, then, is to find not what "was" but what might have been, what citizens aspired to in an age when public aspirations were disappearing before the interiorized self-managements of reform. The aesthetics of antebellum fiction are not simply transpositions of European literary conventions; they are blueprints of social negotiation and associational empowerment that the socially "real" refused to credit as anything other than neurotic or whimsical. The ongoing work of interiorized democracy, that is to say, can be found in the products of the imagination, which can be read not only in the explicitly social narratives sponsored by reform, but also in the aesthetic conventions—and even more so in the frequent disruptions of those conventions—that constitute antebellum U.S. popular fiction.

As a case in point, the final two chapters of *Interior States* focus on the emergence of the romance as a particularly fantastic refusal of both reformist interiority and middle-class institutionalism. African American authors faced a particular challenge in narrativizing interiority, as enfranchising discourses of racial "uplift" mandated the simultaneity of civility (public order) and identification (interior order). In taking up the inventive strategies of romanticism, black authors assailed that alignment by dismantling the necessary orders of civility and the coherence of identification. Martin Delany's *Blake* and Hannah Crafts's *The Bondwoman's Narrative* undertake this effort, demonstrating how (white) civil order is maintained through discourses of self-regulatory uplift that result not in the public enfranchisement of African Americans as citizens, but in the interiorization of a de-socialized "blackness." While Delany views that "blackness" as a unifying counter-force to social alternatives that he denigrates as superstition or fantasy, Crafts shows the process of identification (no matter the race or gender of the supposedly unifying imago) to be the disabling work of romantic civility and offers fantasy and superstition as potent alternatives to identification. Although these works counter each other in their strategies, they are alike in demonstrating the disastrous consequences of separating public and interior life, showing public civility to be the enemy of imaginative revolution. Romanticism falls short of revolution in both works, the allure of private civility overcoming the demand for structural justice. It is the imaginative work of romanticism, however, that holds open in both novels the revolutionary potential for sociality without either identity or civility.

Most frequently, romances challenged interiority by denying the power of precedent—the pre-given rules that characterize, classify, and hierarchize interior traits in ways that make the disciplinary imperatives of those categories seem like the innocent naming of interiority's inevitable conformity. A whimsical example of how romanticism challenged this fictional alignment is found in the "Cetology" chapter of *Moby-Dick*, in which Herman Melville ridicules the "systemized exhibition" of interior traits that will produce a clear taxonomy of whales.[18] Instead of aligning interiority with law, Melville insists, whales' "internal parts" reveal "peculiarities . . . indiscriminately dispersed among all sorts of whales, without any regard to what may be the nature of their structure." If "a rabble of uncertain, fugitive, half-fabulous whales" can defy "right classification," he continues, surely human interiority contains the social possibilities of an "almost frantic democracy."[19] For Melville, the illusory and elusive borders between desire and world making, aesthetics and empiricism, fantasy and freedom, make interiority a realm not of regulatory taxonomy, but of what Michael Rogin names subversive genealogy.[20] Revealing not identity but variety, not compliance but deviation, interior states for Melville are intrinsically *queer* places, in the nineteenth-century sense of unpredictable, unusual, and unconventional.

Melville's description of the "rabble" of "half-fabulous whales" suggests that the conditions of queerness—of the "uncertain" and the "fugitive," the ephemeral and the contingent—do not foreclose sociality but may be its most promising opportunities. As chapter 7 shows, the "half-fabulous" qualities of contingency and ephemerality are the basis of queer sociality in the most imaginative romances of the antebellum period: Hawthorne's *The House of the Seven Gables* and Melville's *Pierre* and *Clarel*. Those romances undermine interiority by taking it too much at its word, making it so deep, so opaque, so *interior* that its operations can no longer be made public and hence reformed. Throughout these works, the aspirations and desires of characters are so powerful that they pass beyond the regulatory precedents of the law, generating forms and objects of passionate attachment that refuse to conform to normative and institutionalized conventions. Despite their radical inscrutability, however, these forms of attachment are extraordinarily generous, opening to include strangers in a queer sociality built on ethics of mutual responsibility and affection that is not predicated on shared histories or identities. The democratic queerness of *The House of the Seven Gables*, *Pierre*, and *Clarel*—frail, contingent, alienated, but also richly inventive, respectful of mystery, obliquely eroticized, and persistently public—echoes the ephemeral and contingent socialities of the disenfranchised in barrooms, dens of iniquity, and licentious boudoirs throughout the pages of popular fiction. If the appetites, desires, and fantasies generated in these spaces were themselves the productions of interiority, they were also, as the romances of Delany, Crafts, Hawthorne, and Melville show, interiority's most imaginative protest.

* * * * *

While *Interior States* suggests that romances often deploy imagination to counter the imperatives of interiority, it does not seek to romanticize interiority per se. Quite the contrary. In the contemporary world, interiority has become ubiquitous in public discourse (such as it is), serving as the grounds of conviction ("That's just how I feel inside"), satisfaction ("I felt all warm inside"), and even identity ("I have to be true to who I am deep down"). Deployed as a final determination of meaning, the grounds of adjudication, interiority brings democratic negotiation to an end. While interiority is now ubiquitous—Hayden White goes as far as to declare that interiority has rendered it "not only impossible but also undesirable even to aspire to the creation of full-blown sciences of man, culture, and society"[21]—I do not believe that it is inevitable. The epilogue posits the possibility of post-interior sociality based on debate and negotiation without the interior states of desire as agency or emotions as adjudicative grounds. Unlike other theories of post-interiority that propose the necessary abandonment of humanism, I suggest that a humanist vocabulary, divorced from the adjudicative grounds of interiority, might prove a productive means for generating social associations of citizens skilled in negotiating differences among strangers. This state of social negotiation without the forms of adjudicative interiority that have come to define modern personhood I call *humanism without humans*.

The work of making a post-interior democracy must be local and ad hoc, contingent and creative. It must begin now, among people who have reclaimed their estranged powers, not deferred to a generational future or abstracted to the agency of institutions. As Emerson wrote in "Experience": "I settle myself ever the firmer in the creed that we should not postpone and refer and wish, but do broad justice where we are, by whomsoever we dwell with, accepting our actual companions and circumstances, however humble or odious, as the mystic officials to whom the universe has delegated its whole pleasure for us." Undeferred, local, pleasurable, and inventive, made among strangers who may be odious and still be treated as companions, democracy may yet transform "the true romance the world exists to realize" into "practical power" and a "victory yet for all justice." This is the promise of the post-interior world, for, as Emerson also cautioned, "the world is all outside; it has no inside."[22] Taking up the possibilities of humanism without humans, a romantic sociality beyond the reformable interiorities that, in turn, are the grounds of contemporary public life, we may find that democracy is not dead but ready to emerge in unprecedented possibilities for social action. The power of post-interior sociality is the democratic possibility Tocqueville saw in Americans' proclivity to association. "There is no end which the human will despair of attaining," he wrote, "by the free action of the collective power of individuals."[23] If interiority has become the shadowy archive of that power, then it is time to leave the archive and reenter the world.

1

"MATTERS OF INTERNAL CONCERN":

FEDERAL AFFECT AND THE MELANCHOLY CITIZEN

Responding in Federalist 27 to anti-federalists such as William Findley, who cautioned that the new system of centralized governance was "not merely (as it ought to be) a Confederation of States, but a Government of Individuals,"[1] Alexander Hamilton unexpectedly turned his attention to the interior lives of citizens:

> Man is very much a creature of habit. A thing that rarely strikes his senses will generally have but a transient influence upon his mind. A government continually at a distance and out of sight, can hardly be expected to interest the sensations of the people. The inference is, that the authority of the union, and the affections of the citizens towards it, will be strengthened, rather than weakened, by its extension to what are called matters of internal concern; and that it will have less occasion to recur to force, in proportion to the familiarity and comprehensiveness of its agency.[2]

The "more the operations of the national authority are intermingled in the ordinary exercise of government," Hamilton continued, "the more citizens are accustomed to meet with it in the common occurrences of their political life; the more it is familiarized to their sight, and to their feelings, the further it enters into those objects, which touch the most sensible chords, and put in motion the most active strings of the human heart; the greater will be the probability, that it will conciliate the respect and attachment of the community."[3] Hamilton understood that turning people into citizens required reaching them where they live, which was not yet in a nation but in churches, families, and communities where the affective bonds of loyalty and affection already existed. Those familiar locations of feelings held structures of hierarchy that, if reoriented toward federal affiliation, would render coercive power obsolete. Hamilton saw that education in social feelings precedes the law, rendering its dictates palatable to citizens who might otherwise see little profit in consenting to its restrictions or in answering to its interpellative naming.[4]

In turning the social feelings into "matters of internal concern," Hamilton makes clear that at the close of the eighteenth century, citizenship was becoming an interior state in which individuals were being encouraged to recognize the interests and disciplines of the state as originating not in coercive legalisms or competitive capitalism, but in their "deep" selves. That Hamilton's phrase "internal concern" can signify the interior of both the nation-state and the citizen's body suggests how interconnected the two were becoming in the federal imaginary. The nation-state's future as an imagined community required, as Hamilton recognized, a federalization of affect: the creation of metaphors of "innerness" to serve as sites of correspondence between individual bodies (character, personality, even biology) and state interest. Although purportedly immutable (beyond the possibility of collective, public redefinition and change) and instinctual (beyond the reach of volitional self-control), federalized affect resulted from collective discourses learned, as Hamilton suggests, through rituals rehearsed to teach citizens that affect determines social order in ways that preexist "the social" itself. This belief that civic life arises from a self-contained depth, and not the other way around, had the effect of limiting citizens' public participation within prescribed forms of "private" life while promising, through the management of their interior states, a phantom social volition.

Despite Hamilton's confidence, however, participation in the federalization of affect appears to have been less than universal. The literature of the early republic registers citizens' resentment at their loss of control over powers to associate, much less to *feel*, as they saw fit. As several critics have noted, early national literature is saturated with a profound melancholy that marks the impassable boundary between sanctioned forms of "private life" and the divergent affects and attachments that animate citizens' progressive imaginations.[5] Melancholy marks the border not only between public and private spheres but, more urgently, between a "public" that is increasingly inaccessible to a privatized citizenry and a realm of interactive sociability that is marked as much by disorder and dissent as by the managed "character" of sanctioned citizenship. The latter, characterized within the federalized public as the trivial and self-indulgent "fantasies" of the disenfranchised, moved increasingly into the never entirely subterranean space of the human interior, where it became archived as the losses manifested through melancholy. While melancholy seems to preserve a material loss, it is important to note that, rather than archiving an ideal sociality that existed in historical time, melancholy more often preserves the power of social imagining itself, the inventive potential that makes social alternatives not merely imaginable but attainable. Read in this way, melancholy is not an involuntary reaction to irretrievable loss, but a productive act of democratic imagination through which citizens safeguard their social aspirations by situating them in history (what is lost must once have existed) and in human interiority (melancholy disguises social visions as involuntary convulsions of emotion). While seeming to concede to calls for citizens to understand the social *as* affective, then, melancholy reveals the tense but constitutive relationship of history and interiority, of the social investments in interior states, and of a consequent "loss" (which is also an aspiration) that is necessarily both deeply personal and inexorably collective. The literary works discussed here—Hannah Webster Foster's *The Coquette*, Washington Irving's "Rip Wan Winkle," and Caroline Dall's *The Romance of the Association*—depict the diminished public participation brought about by citizens' education in sanctioned interiority while simultaneously showing how affective redaction allowed the unruly interiors of citizens in the making to contest federalization by preserving in their melancholy interiors the hopes for a different—and better—social world.

Federal Affect

A critical problem for the new nation, as Michael Warner has shown, arose from the contested sovereignty of law: having delegitimized British rule, denying the representativeness of law (if the American people were not represented in Parliament, they had no obligation to honor British laws), the Founders could not simply declare the legal authority of a new federal constitution. At the same time, to leave unfettered the revolutionary dispersal of social agency was to legitimize a radically democratic state in which people agreed to rules only when convinced, by demonstrable outcomes, that laws were necessary. The danger faced by the Founders was the unpredictable lines of local affiliation and the unrestrained modes of social imagination they produced. To contain this danger, Warner argues, the Founders reinstated the sovereignty of law through the detachment of writing: by granting agency to the abstract trope "We, the People" that stands as a non-reciprocal substitute for local assembly, "writing became the hinge between a delegitimizing revolutionary politics and a non-revolutionary, already legal signification of the people." Republican beliefs about the disinterestedness of print further "elevated the values of generality over those of the personal. In this cognitive vocabulary the social diffusion of printed artifacts took on the investment of the disinterested virtue of the public orientation," Warner notes, "as opposed to the corrupting interests and passions of particular and local persons."[6]

Warner's powerful analysis of print's role in redirecting local presence into the abstract and, hence, non-negotiable sovereignty of law, however, fails to account for why Hamilton, instead of arguing against "the corrupting interests and passions of particular and local persons," encouraged those "passions" in managed channels. A crucial question for the interpellative theory of legal sovereignty, in other words, is why, if local assembly was as satisfactorily participatory as Warner contends, citizens invested in the abstract simulacra of the Constitution. How did a people skeptical of the law know to "listen" for their name in its print proclamations? The answer to these questions lies in the rhetorical production of "feelings" that enabled people to believe, affectively, in their federalized name, "citizen," or to take affective belief *as* the grounds of acceptable naming. The shift in post–Revolutionary America was not simply from local assembly to legal print, then; it was a circulation between those entities carried out through the federalization of affect.

Such circulations were enabled largely through one of the prevailing fascinations of political and literary discourse in late-eighteenth-century America: friendship. In the movement toward constitutional law, friendship linked local speech and abstract print, making the abstract interpellations of law emotionally satisfying and hence believable to the citizens of the new nation. The role friendship played in interiorizing federal law into the affective orders of "social feelings" can be discerned in the emergence of the Constitution from its predecessor, the Articles of Confederation. While the Constitution asserts a unified national entity ("the People") established prior to the interpellation of print, the Articles located juridical power among bodies assembled in a particular space and time: "whereas the Delegates of the United States of America, in Congress assembled, did, on the 15th day of November, in the Year of Our Lord One thousand Seven Hundred and Seventy seven, and in the Second Year of Independence of America, agree to certain articles of Confederation." Through the primary authority of locally and historically situated individuals, the states take on the qualities nominally possessed by autonomous citizens, each state maintaining "its sovereignty, freedom, and independence, and every Power, Jurisdiction and right, which is not by this confederation expressly delegated to the United States, in Congress assembled." Having figured the states as autonomous citizens ("in Congress assembled"), the Articles set forth their association as the affective give-and-take of friendship: "the said states hereby enter into a firm league of friendship with each other, for their common defense, the security of their Liberties, and their internal and general welfare."[7] By figuring the confederation of state power through a metaphorical equivalence with the negotiations of friendship, the Articles bridged the widening gap between local assembly and abstract legality.

In the Articles, furthermore, affective affiliations took precedence over the abstract categories of law, even while their suturing, through the transfer of friendship to abstract state personalities, became what Warner calls "the site where all lesser collectivities are evacuated."[8] Having established this affective rationale, the legal apparatus no longer required its metaphorical equivalences: the primary purpose of law in the Constitution is no longer to guarantee friendship but to ensure its own jurisdiction. The language of rights and immunities, of juridical purview, therefore carried over from the Articles to the Constitution, but the affective rationale of "friendship" was removed.[9]

There is, of course, a tension inherent in the transformation of friendship from a local affiliation with historically and spatially localized subjects into legal sovereignty and abstract affinity. In the *Federalist Papers*, for instance, friendship sometimes describes the peaceful coherence of secular division into national unity (as in Hamilton's papers 8 and 11) and the already proposed nation's entrance into international commerce (as in Jay's papers 4 and 5). At other times, however, friendship figures as a counter-federal force arising from the competing loyalties of still localized citizens. In Madison's paper 46, for instance, the "superintending care" of federal government is a corrective to the "ties of personal acquaintance and friendship, and of family and party attachments."[10] In arguing for a single president over a corporate leadership, Hamilton asserts in paper 76 that a president "will have *fewer* personal attachments to gratify" and therefore "will be so much the less liable to be misled by the sentiments of friendship and of affection."[11] The tension in these conceptions of friendship—which serve both as a guarantor of peaceful cooperation and the cause of rancorous discord and disunity—is veiled by the narrative sequence of the papers themselves: having channeled local affection into federal coherence, that coherence, over the course of the papers, serves to eradicate the competing claims of unruly affection and its local affiliations. The theory of constitutional interpellation notes the second step, but not the first, and by ignoring the first— the ways in which citizen-subjects were shaped to guarantee the orderly management of a federalized civil sphere—readings of early American constitutionality miss the opportunities that existed for alternative forms of social configuration and citizenship.

Although scholars have recently investigated early American sympathy and other forms of social feeling, the federalization of affect has nevertheless escaped critical attention, perhaps because it stayed *federal* for a relatively brief period of time.[12] Hamilton's call for a national pedagogy of orderly affect was quickly translated into—and found its broader fulfillment in—the social "uplift" movements that flourished in the 1820s and 1830s, forerunners of the institutional reforms that subsequent chapters examine. "Legislature may enact laws, but education must originate their conception, and interpret their meaning," Jonathan Blanchard told the American Institute of Instruction in 1835. "Government may check and restrain, but duty and obedience are the result of instruction. The hopes of our country depend on the bias which the minds of our children and youth receive."[13] Blanchard surpassed Hamilton in placing national pedagogy in the hands of civil institutions that precede law in making acceptable to citizens social orders whose goal is not the enhancement of liberty but its constraint. Those constraints, Blanchard frankly noted, become palatable through the promise ("hopes") of an abstract national association ("our country") deferred to the horizons of futurity.[14] If that future never arrives, citizens can prepare for it, in Blanchard's program, by training themselves in proper feelings, which are presented as the fundamental human desire for social relationships such as friendship:

> Desire of society is as truly a part of our nature, as the dread of anguish or the love of life. This simple original desire, finds its gratification in the exercise of those natural affections, which interest us in the welfare of our kindred, our friends, our acquaintances, and our race; and, together with these affections, it forms that complex class of emotion, which we call the social feelings; and these, again, being constantly excited by the circumstances and relations of life, grow into a permanent habit, and become the all-pervading, master-feeling of the soul. (3)

Without explicitly proscribing a citizen's affiliations (which might take forms other than an abstract and exclusionary "race") or prescribing the modes of participatory consent (the family, which is based on non-consensual relations of obligation and hierarchy, becomes the affective original of which the civil sphere, nominally based on more evenly distributed consent, is simply a reflection), Blanchard yokes public order and private affect in a way that is seemingly consistent with democratic rhetorics of self-determination. At the same time, the privileging of the private realm as a prior yet equivalent source of "social feelings" promises citizens civic participation while limiting the scope of identification and action. What drops out of Blanchard's equation of the affections of the private realm and the abstract associations of "race" is precisely the *social* itself, the interactions of people who are perhaps unknown to one another but nevertheless invested in a collectively conceived design for shared opportunity and mutually satisfying justice.[15]

Blanchard does not disguise his efforts to naturalize social relations into the private and bodily confines of the human interior. On the contrary, he self-

consciously, if counter-intuitively, locates the "natural" in the disciplinary pro-
cedures of training, habit, and mastery—the social technologies that will produce the natural affects that in turn guarantee the orderly operations of society.[16] The initial divergence of feeling and law enables Blanchard to divert
attention from the constraints of juridical prohibition by locating the language
of coercion ("master-feeling") within the self-contained human interior. That
gesture both permits the naturalizing of constraint in the language of desire
(the law's powers are simply an extension of what the body already craves) and
maintains the illusion of democratic consent by giving citizens control not over
the law, but over the law written in their own natures. As Blanchard recognizes,
social order without habitually trained affect lays bare the potential dispersion
of a supposedly unified "race," the members of which feel no instinctive investment in the managed orders of its law. "Strike out the social feelings,"
Blanchard declares, "and a mere intellectual skeleton is all which you leave" (6).
The connection between an "intellectual skeleton" and affective satisfaction
comes in the priority accorded feelings cast as habitually restrained social order;
for democracy to work, that is, sentiment had to supersede legal classicism.
With the dissemination of federal affect through the growth of social reform in
the 1820s and 1830s, in other words, the Enlightenment era of "legal sovereignty" ended in the United States and the romantic period of interiorized
sociality began.

Due in large part to this transition, Blanchard could appear not, like Hamilton, as an architect of federal power, but as an agent of progressive change who
believed that "the rules laid down for cultivating the social feelings are such as,
if children once thoroughly imbibe, they could not but shrink with horror from
all war, spiritual despotism, slavery, intemperance, and impurity—the head
evils under which the world at present groans" (25). Moving as it does from war
and slavery to drunkenness and illicit sexuality, from structural injustice to
bodily illness, Blanchard's list predicts the increased privatization of reform
in the following two decades. While his articulation of the "uplift" available
through civic education would seem to proclaim a new phase in civil liberty,
in which citizens educate themselves in ways distinct from the juridical imperatives of the state, viewing his program alongside Hamilton's call for federal affect demonstrates the continuities between legal sovereignty and private
affect—what I am calling *interior states*—in ways that complicate formulations
of the civil sphere as a site of independence from and contestation of state
interests.

The fact that the federalization of affect sought to manage and limit citizens'
affiliations does not mean, however, that citizens surrendered their capability to

imagine competing forms of social relationship, of "friendship," as Washington Irving's "Rip Van Winkle" and Hannah Foster's *The Coquette* demonstrate. Both texts show that friendship remained a concept through which early Americans struggled to understand competing models of sociality and alliance. On the one hand, friendship was a negotiated relationship between proximate people who insist on their autonomous status *prior to* the law. On the other hand, the Constitution's subsuming of "friendship" into a print circulation that establishes the law prior to human interaction—that establishes consent to a rule-bound model of civil relationship as fundamental to human interaction—places citizens in a privacy severely proscribed by social conventions. If the former asserts the citizens' entitlement to shape public life in accordance with their particular, localized needs and desires, the latter imagines a civility built on the traits of an abstract and liberal character, serving the interests of the emergent public orders of governmentality (unity, loyalty, self-sacrifice) and capital (openness, diligence, organization).

Central to the ways Irving and Foster wrestle with these competing definitions of friendship is the relationship, in federal rhetoric, between affective alliance and mobility. In the Articles of Confederation, for example, most references to the friendship between states occur in the first three articles. Article IV, however, yokes friendship to the imperative movements of commerce: "the better to secure and perpetuate mutual friendship and intercourse among the people of the different states in this union, the free inhabitants of each of these states, paupers, vagabonds, and fugitives from justice exempted, shall be entitled to all privileges and immunities of free citizens in the several states; and the people of each state shall have free ingress and regress to and from any other state, and shall enjoy therein all the privileges of trade and commerce, subject to the same duties, impositions and restrictions as the inhabitants thereof respectively."[17] Friendship gives way to mobility—the movement between states—tied not only to a growing market economy, but to the presumed *stability* of private life. The vagabonds, paupers, and fugitives from justice who shape friendship's outer boundaries establish an ideal citizen who is economically engaged, situated in a definable home, and willing to believe that laws sufficiently ensure justice. While privacy becomes apparently more stable, public life, tied to commerce, is structured by mobility, the site where no citizen has a time or place. Suturing the asserted, only ever imaginary, split between localized privacy and mobile publicity is the law, which maintains the local and affective dynamics of "friendship" in the face of growing physical and economic distances generated by an increasingly federal (and, quickly, global) market. Caught between law and commerce, "friendship" holds the space of negotiation, contingency, and dissent—of citizen participation—in a discursive structure that is already designed to play both ends off the middle.

Even in such a seemingly well-ordered legal structure, however, citizens' dissent often took the form of unruly, ungainly, and unpredictable interiority. As Blanchard acknowledges, "When, from neglect of cultivation, the social feelings sink into selfishness or sensuality, the imagination becomes introverted or polluted, and the heart thenceforth a festering centre of uncomfortable emotions," creating "the volcanic eruptions of furious anger, mad enthusiasm, or unbridled licentiousness" (8). Just as the hopes of the republic can be read, Blanchard suggests, in the properly cheerful, sympathetic, and benevolent emotions that suggest the proper installation of legal "bias," so its threats can be traced in the darker, more volatile emotions that suggest an interiority resistant to civil order: "ill regulated social feelings produce nearly all the fretfulness and repining, melancholy and dejection, so common in society" (8).

Blanchard moves quickly to contain such expressions of social dissent, deploying the shame that would become, in the reform rhetorics of nineteenth-century America, the prison door on the private locations of identification and alliance constituting the everyday lives of citizens. "Few, indeed," Blanchard contends, "are those, who if their hearts were letters, would dare to have their nearest friends read them" (15). The epistolary misgivings of Foster's heroine are just such an open text, in which one may read not just legal abstractions, but the melancholic, licentious, and petulant longings for proximate and negotiable connections—friendships—that held open the space of a more radically contingent democracy within the abstract legal simulacra of national affinity.[18] Friendship, for Eliza, is not the second-best relationship it has become in contemporary America (and was already becoming for the Founders). Rather, friendship was for Eliza something akin to what Foucault describes as a way of life, a mode of self-conscious invention beyond the interior prescriptions of civil institutions.[19] Citizens living in the wake of the war might well have hoped, as Eliza does, that new freedoms, new virtualities, could be opened by a network of equally inventive citizens who would decide among themselves the ethical shape of their lives, with all its flexible pleasures, loyalties, and responsibilities. That, after all, is what democracy promises.

The Republic of Intercourse and the Supplemental Citizen

If the flexible intimacies of friendship rigidified into the abstract sovereignty of law, codifying local negotiations of social life into the abstract jurisdiction of the state, modern discipline required the opposite movement: the rules of civic order needed to find expression in the local domain of the citizen's interiority, a task accomplished through discourses of "character." As Blanchard notes, the "social part of our nature is the scale of character upon which different degrees of excellence are marked down in heaven" (10). Absorbing local interactions ("social feelings") into something both more universal and more ordered, Blanchard makes character a sign of self-determined consent (what one has cultivated in oneself) and of identifications with abstract conventions of social behavior. "You may inform the intellect, in many things, by precept alone: but teaching the affections by precept is a flat absurdity," Blanchard states. "There is a chameleon habit in our nature, which makes our feelings change their colors to those we behold" (20). Having used "social feelings" to locate civic participation in the limited realm of one's affective training, Blanchard deploys "character" to put affect in the identificational thrall of social convention, a realm in which the citizen need no longer take an active part, affective satisfaction being the consolation for lost participation. For Blanchard, it is precisely the subject's willed and multiple identifications (one's "chameleon habit") that are stabilized by the abstract order of character.

Such notions of character grow from late-eighteenth-century endorsements of liberality that, like metaphors of friendship, yoked local affiliation to national identification. Needing to preserve the values of social interaction while severing citizens' local allegiances, the Founders (and the reformers who adapted their rhetoric) reconceived the affective qualities of local communities— sympathy, benevolence, tolerance—as functions not of relations *between* persons, but of something both larger and smaller: autonomous and abstract character.[20] Self-possessed character was measured not by empirical effects on other people, but on its likeness to definitions made familiar to citizens through circulation in newspapers, pamphlets, and manuals. Public and private, abstract and heartfelt, character emerged in dialectics of affect and alienation that promised freedom to those who were willing to reshape themselves along the lines of sanctioned character.[21] Character thus assumed both an interpellative and a disciplinary function in the new republic, as pressures to exhibit conventional character became paradoxically recognized as "freedom."[22]

Rhetorics of national belonging are rarely—if ever—constituted without the aid of an imagined "other," however, and character, despite its inclusive universality, is no exception.[23] The traits deemed "illiberal," character's constitutive other, became synonymous with those allegiances whose discrediting helped incorporate citizens as affective members of an abstract union: the prejudice of families, the narrowness of church and parties, the provincialism of small communities. Allegiances that competed with what Dana Nelson has aptly called the imagined fraternity of national manhood were denigrated as constraining and coercive, the enemy of freedom. As discredited local formations lost their instructive authority over citizens, liberalized discourses of etiquette, manners, and health became civic preoccupations, preserving the order risked by the evacuation of localized sociality and attaching the discipline of individual bodies to increasingly generalized allegiances.[24] Beyond constituting local assemblies as inherently illiberal, the guides to early national character defined a series of traits and activities—anger, boisterousness, gossip, sensuality, intemperate desire—as illiberal, the unruly interiority not just of individual subjects who were the targets of antebellum reform, but of categories of identity that were *collectively* disenfranchised on the basis of their illiberal characters: women, African and Native Americans, the poor, the insane, prostitutes, drunkards, immigrants, bachelors and spinsters, children.

At the same time, character bore traces of the discredited affiliations it supplemented and supplanted. If Americans supposedly possessed an unusually high degree of exemplary virtue, character's alleged universality simultaneously threatened jingoistic claims to national exceptionalism. Especially as character became central to international commerce, its global circulations challenged the nation-state's self-contained and autonomous status, while international trade brought about cultural exchanges that highlighted character's composition in language and, hence, its deep ties to cultural ambition and prejudice. Regularly revealing its origins in language rather than deep selfhood, character further opened the vexed question of interpretation, the tendency of words to circumvent conventional meaning. Moved increasingly to the "soul" or the "heart," where language allegedly played no part, character attempted to stabilize the diversity of linguistic invention—and the subsequent multiplicity of local allegiances—by insisting on a solidity of virtue at the citizen's core while discrediting competing cultures and their linguistic practices. Yet those very practices—passion, temper, gossip, sensuality, fretfulness, boisterousness— continued to constitute other affiliations that contested the natural status of federal affect and the national character it allegedly cohered.

Character's ambitions and its attendant contradictions become apparent in a commencement address delivered in 1846 at Miami University in Ohio by the eminent political theorist Francis Lieber. In the widely reprinted address, "The Character of the Gentleman," Lieber articulates the transition from revolutionary concepts of social liberty to reformist insistence on orderly character.[25] "Liberty, which is the enjoyment of unfettered action, necessarily leads to licentiousness," he states. While "liberty offers to man, indeed, a free choice of action, it cannot absolve him from the duty of choosing what is right, fair, liberal, urbane, and handsome" (254–55). In one sentence, Lieber removes "liberty" from the realm of unfettered actions, which lead citizens into potentially unsanctioned social affinities ("licentiousness"), and places it instead in an interior state, where citizens deliberate *about* action. More importantly, Lieber transforms interiority from a locale of desire (that which "leads") to one of restraint (that which "binds"). Returning to this point later in the address, Lieber draws the line even more sharply. Asking whether one may have bad character provided one continues to obey the laws, he demonstrates the degree to which the sovereignty of law had become by midcentury an obsolete apparatus. "To put this question shows the utmost confusion of morals and politics," Lieber insists, "of the righteous and the legal, of the law written in our heart and the statute printed in the book" (245). "The greater the liberty which we enjoy in any sphere of life," he asserts, "the more binding, necessarily, becomes the obligation of self-restraint, and, consequently, the more important become all the rules of action which flow from the reverence for the pure character of the gentleman" (264). The social subject—what Lieber calls "the gentleman"—is left with less and more than he starts with. Having had "greater . . . liberty" in "any sphere of life," the "gentleman" finds his greatest freedom in freedom's negation, liberty giving way to obligation not to others or even to oneself, but to the abstract principle of self-restraint. In compensation, the gentleman learns that such restraint is "more important" than liberty itself. If interiority becomes the site of self-government, the incorporation of the state into one's being drains him of any "passions" that might compete with that identification.

Yet passion cannot be entirely drained. It is repeatedly produced by the very discourses of character that check its wayward promptings. If the citizen's continual policing of his own interiority is necessary because the law has lost its ability to monitor an increasingly mobile and privatized citizenry, it is *justified* by the continual failure to master passion. The desired outcome is not good character per se, then, but constant vigilance in citizens instructed to fix their attention not on the operations of the statehouse or the market, but on the unruly workings of their own hearts. Character thus exists in the interstices between the interior ("passions") and the exterior ("laws"), circulating without acknowledged authorship in a continually unstable manner. One's only reliable volition—abstract character's power to restrain—is thus perpetually alienable, leaving citizens holding on precariously to identifications with normative conventions without which they will be ruined by their illiberal passions. As interiority gains importance as the site of citizens' vigilance, the social realm correspondingly shrinks. In Lieber's catalogue of the inner law's purview—"the duty of choosing what is right, fair, liberal, urbane, and handsome"—citizens begin with deliberations about what is "right and fair," the stuff of public democracy, but end by passing judgment on the relatively shallow realms of fashion and fastidiousness.

Although citizens were encouraged to think about their activities in increasingly banal terms, interiorization was anything but trivial. On the contrary, character rationalized the most potent social hierarchies based not solely on distinctions between "good" and "bad" character, but also on types and classes of people who possessed certain social affinities and pleasures. Lieber begins with a definition of character consistent with liberal discourses of his day: "I believe the word gentleman signifies that character which is distinguished by strict honor, self-possession, forbearance, generous, as well as refined feelings, and polished deportment" (229–30). Soon, however, he resorts to negative definition. A true gentleman shows "a character to which all meanness, explosive irritableness, and peevish fretfulness are alien; to which, consequently, a generous candor, scrupulous veracity, and essential truthfulness, courage both moral and physical, dignity, self-respect, a strenuous avoidance of giving offence to others or oppressing them, and liberality in thought, argument, and conduct, are habitual and have become natural" (229–30). Meanness, irritation, fretfulness, deceptiveness—all traits one might associate with the frustration and anger citizens might well have experienced as the promise of the Revolution gave way to "the urbane and the handsome"—characterize, for Lieber, types of people, especially "the clown, the gossip, the backbiter, the dullard, coward, braggart, fretter, swaggerer, the mob, the flunkey, the bully, the ruffian, and the blackguard" (230). Despite Lieber's grand claim that the "character of the gentleman produces an equality of social claims, and supersedes rank," establishing "a republic of intercourse, as we speak of the republic of letters" (232), then, certain forms of intercourse—gossip, frivolity, anger, resentment—move beyond the republican pale. Only those who take on the attributes with which Lieber supplements that nervous, belligerent, unproductively sociable citizen are worthy of "power, physical, moral, purely social or political, [which] is one of the touchstones of genuine gentlemanliness" (271).

The derogatory names Lieber gives the illiberal—blackguard, dullard, bully —seem to justify their elimination from social power. Quickly, however, Lieber makes clear that these "ruffians" and "gossips" are simply the discredited parties in virtually all hierarchies ordering everyday life. Among those hierarchies, Lieber includes the power of husbands over wives, fathers over children, teachers over pupils, the old over the young, the strong over the weak, officers over servicemen, masters over hired hands, magistrates over citizens, employers over employees, the rich over the poor, the educated over the uneducated, the experienced over the confiding, keepers of secrets over whomever those secrets concern, the gifted over the ordinary, and the clever over the silly (271–72). The discourse of character organizes virtually every social relationship of antebellum culture, both by ensuring that those possessed of "gentlemanly" virtues maintain power over those with competing social values and by insisting that disenfranchised citizens put their energy not into challenging dominant social structures or pursing alternatives, but into managing themselves so as to produce the character that will make them members of an abstract national alliance. Considering that most Americans fell into at least one of the discredited categories of the illiberal, character's ability to generate a publicly disempowered, inwardly gazing, and self-governing citizenry becomes clear.

If Lieber's pedagogy of character attempted to dismantle local allegiances in order to foster identifications that were more abstract and therefore more mobile, however, the irony was that the resultant order was destabilized by the very forces—expansive nationalism and competitive capitalism—that character served. At moments, Lieber, himself an immigrant and a staunch defender of international trade, seems quite optimistic about the compatibility of global flows of people and capital with national stability and hierarchical order. "The character of the gentleman passes the bounds of states and tongues," he asserts, "and, without enfeebling our love of country (did it so we would repudiate it), gives a passport acknowledged through the wide domain of civilization" (232). Establishing the "freemasonry of a liberal education, of good manners, and propriety of conduct" (232), character becomes for Lieber the sine qua non of "all international transaction with sister nations of our race, and even with tribes which follow different standards of conduct and morality" (267). At the same time, noting that "large numbers are constantly rolling westward, and changing their dwellings, neighbors, and associations," while "a degree of success, in a worldly view, awaits almost with certainty health, industry, and prudence, without necessarily requiring the addition of refinement of feelings or polish of conduct" (276), Lieber acknowledges that, even as character unmade local attachments in favor of self-management and national allegiance, nationalism's own expansion and the restless desires generated by competitive capitalism simultaneously threatened character's jurisdiction.

In the face of such threats, Lieber, like most reform advocates of his day, stresses the importance of habituation. "If repeated and constant acting upon that truth has not induced a habit or grown into a virtue, it may be sufficiently strong to produce repentance after the offence, but not to guide before the wrong be committed," he advises. "Apply yourselves, then, sedulously at once to act habitually by the highest standard of the gentleman, to let a truly gentlemanly spirit permeate your being" (275). Acknowledging character's reliance on habituation, Lieber opens the possibility that such rituals, enacted in local cultures with differing histories and patterns of socialization, will generate divergent manifestations and comprehensions of the very virtues he wants to present as universal. In response to that risk, Lieber places character in a developmental model, in which universality (conformity) marks a maturity that transcends "peculiarity" (local determination). "Each of the various constituents of this character," he asserts, "required peculiar social conditions to come to maturity" (238). Given this association of maturity and identifications with abstract virtue, it is not surprising that reformers took on the status not just of teachers, but of surrogate parents, while the illiberal subjects who became the object of organized reform were repeatedly characterized as immature (and most of the traits Lieber lines up on the side of illiberality—the drive toward immediate gratification, anger, all sorts of unproductive interests and modes of discourse—are still considered "childish" or, after Freud, "infantile").

Yet the developmental model could not fully stabilize the danger localism opens in the rituals of character, as becomes evident in the hesitant start of Lieber's address. After thanking the graduating class, Lieber admits, "I find difficulties of no common character surrounding me at the moment. My foot treads for the first time the soil of your sylvan state; I am unacquainted with what may be peculiar to your society, or characteristic of your institution. I thus may stand in danger of losing myself with you in unprofitable generalities" (225). Lieber's telling phrase—"difficulties of no common character"—sums up the dilemma nicely, for if it is true that different cultures, in adapting the pedagogy of character to local needs and customs, will make virtue itself subject to a particularized hermeneutic, then "generalities"—the abstract icons that attempt to bind graduating men to the disciplinary orders of the managed state and of competitive capital—will indeed prove "unprofitable" and identities grounded in them will result in a lost self. Like all pedagogues, Lieber faces the possibility that what he says and what the audience hears may turn out to be very different, for his audience retains the power of interpretation, shaped by local habits of understanding. This risk becomes interestingly pronounced when Lieber attempts to move character into the service of nationalist modernity. Claiming that character is "peculiarly Anglican" (235) and "of modern development" (236), he immediately confronts the problem of an increasingly multiethnic nation and what he characterizes as a "rootless" modernity, forms of *in*coherence that he understands as divergent interpretation. "You will, of course, not misunderstand the point I have advanced, that the present type of gentleman is of modern development and Anglican origin, as if I could mean that there are no true gentleman in other countries, or that there have been none in antiquity. All I can wish to convey is that with other races, and other periods, the character of the gentleman has not developed itself as a national type, and as a readily understood and universally acknowledged aggregate of certain substantial and lofty attributes" (236). Reducing interpretive difference to the "readily understood" and "universally acknowledged," and yoking both to a national "type" understood now as only one of many, Lieber forestalls rather than resolves the risks of difference.

In a world of difference, the real threat to good character is not illiberality, however, but counterfeit character. Antebellum reformers became obsessed with counterfeiting, and Lieber was no exception. "All noble things have their counterfeits," Lieber warned his audience, "and every great idea or exalted type has its caricature in history. So is the saint's counterfeit the hypocrite; the patriot is caricatured in the demagogue; the thrifty husband in the miser; the frank companion in the gossip; the chaste in the prude; the sincere reformer in the reckless Jacobin, and the cautious statesman or the firm believer in the necessity of progressive improvement, disturbing abrupt changes, in the idolator of the past and the Chinese worshipper of the forefathers" (242). Faced with such fakery, Lieber insists on the authenticity of character—"But these reflections from distorting mirrors do not detract from the real worth and the important attributes of the well-proportioned original" (243)—that the supplementary discipline of habituation belies. The tension between the supplementary and the real becomes especially troubling when Lieber turns to "national types" and "distinct classes of characters, clearly stamped by an imprint known and acknowledged by the whole people" (237). Lieber's assertion that national character will come through from the interior despite the apparent differences of race or class allows him, without irony, to offer as a gentlemanly exemplar "an old, and departed, negro slave . . . whom I have never seen other than obliging, polite, anticipating, dignified, true, and forbearing—in short, a gentleman in his lowly sphere" (231). Lieber's example not only demonstrates the impossibility of "national character" in a society that makes whole classes of people inherently counterfeit (his description of the "obliging, polite, anticipating, . . . true, and forbearing" slave is precisely the Uncle Tom–like performance that African Americans from Lieber's day onward have revealed as trickster counterfeits), it also hints at the relationship between self-management and servility, both of which produce and rely on the same catalogue of traits.

Despite his bravado claims to universal comprehension (and hence, consent), Lieber opens the linguistic can of worms from which character, now a text prone to interpretation rather than an inevitable outgrowth of universal interiority, cannot be fully rescued. His lecture on character quickly turns to the waywardness of language:

> The different meanings of words branch out in different directions, and their derivative and cognate terms branch out for themselves. It frequently happens, especially in the English language, that the adjective form of a noun receives an additional meaning or one widely different from that which we would have had a right to expect did the grammatical relationship alone furnish us with a sure guidance. These topics do not lie within the limits of our inquiry. Our endeavor is to ascertain and dwell upon the noblest and purest meaning which, consciously or unconsciously, is given to the term; an adaptation which has legitimately developed itself in the progress of the race to which we belong. (232)

Lieber becomes caught in a circular logic—character is composed of language, and yet the meanings of words can best be determined by character—that was by no means his alone. Rather, the corner into which he backs himself is typical of the dangers reformers found themselves in generally over the vexed question of cultural relativism. If cultures ("races") exist on a scale of development that makes the superiority of some peoples "naturally" determined, the danger is that residual ("unconscious") understandings that preexist one's interpellation into an abstract "race" may assert their unruly influence through unregulated linguistic/interpretive practices. From attempting to regulate character, then, Lieber moves to regulating the uses of language: "dealing in superlatives, substituting extravagant figures of speech for arguments or facts, and interweaving our discourse with words of the gravest import used as profane expletives, while it shows want of taste, proves also a consciousness of weakness" (246).

In the end, though, the only check on the extravagant tendencies of language (and of those like braggarts and gossips, who use it inappropriately) is interiority. Only by taking character out of the realm of ritual and placing it in the affective realm of deep personhood can Lieber seemingly stop linguistic play: "all language, except in mathematics, is but approximation to the subject to be expressed, and affection is the readiest and truest interpreter of the ever-imperfect human world" (275). Character ends up, then, both in the body and outside it, the product of affect and that which governs affect. Circulating between interiority and generality, character sutures the memory of local attachments to the increasingly mobile circulations of abstraction, generating a supplemental citizenship that seeks to reform the memory stock that produces the affective core of each citizen. In a world in which the print public sphere is always threatening to dissolve back into localism through the interactive and inventive exchanges of embodied people—what Lieber calls "the republic of intercourse"—only the supplemental citizen can stem the spread of interpretive division and dissent. Local affiliations uncontained by the interiorized order of character continued to pull on citizens' imaginations, however, producing rips in the social fabric of the early republic through which some of its most haunting literature emerged.

Liberal Rip

As Lieber's speech suggests, nationalism is an ongoing vanishing act in which citizens are asked to relinquish local attachments in favor, on the one hand, of a nation whose borders, given the flows of global capital, are at best difficult to discern, and, on the other, of an interiority compressed within the confines of the body.[26] The troubling location of federal affect between the nowhere and the narrow animates Washington Irving's "Rip Van Winkle" (1819), which begins with a wry depiction of the supposed source of the story, the antiquarian Diedrich Knickerbocker. In what might be considered a tableau vivant of historicism, Irving presents the good-natured Knickerbocker posed atop a "hobby," representing the historian's quirky interests. Riding off, Knickerbocker kicks up dust "in the eyes of his neighbors and grieve[s] the sprit of some friends, for whom he felt the truest deference and affection" (37). In presenting Knickerbocker's journey from specious oral folklore to the supposedly more reliable facticity of print, Irving mocks the federalizing project of creating creditable history from the discredited fictions of the colonial past.[27] Yet beneath Irving's humor lies a dark insight: the movements of localism into the abstract circulation of print "kicks dust" at the bonds of "deference and affection" represented by neighbors and friends, whose contingent identifications will thereafter be trivialized as the fictional (romantic, fantastic, and counter-intuitive) "past" that is never entirely supplanted by the factual (and nationalized) mediations of print.[28] At stake, then, in this mobility of the print record that will extend and perfect Knickerbocker's slapstick journey away from his local connections is the modern nexus of identifications shaped by the redaction of traditional associations (church, workplace, and family) into a single, predominant one based on character. Those modern discourses of character are, for Irving as for Lieber, essentially mobile, figured both by Knickerbocker's departure at the opening of the preface and, later in the tale, by Rip's own flight and by the Dutch "explorers" Rip encounters. Even while the preface figures "Rip" as a national tale, then, the story itself expands mobility into the realm of the individual narrative (Rip's journey) and into imperial expansion (the Dutch invasion), making the nation-state an always already destabilized and surpassed mode of identification. At the same time, just as fiction persists to trouble the presumed facticity of national historiography, so affective bonds live on in mournful memory (his neighbors remember Knickerbocker "more in sorrow than in anger"), a trace of a more idiosyncratic social past. Despite Irving's decidedly tongue-in-cheek tone, grief persists in "Rip Van Winkle" as a relational supplement, the affective localism created among neighbors, that refuses to be subsumed by the movements of stories into print and hence into federal affect.

The fate of the local seems set in "Rip Van Winkle" by the illiberal provincialism that was so often localism's defining feature in the early republic. Freedom increasingly meant freedom *from*, with counter-freedom defined in terms of improvisational socialities that in the late eighteenth century became labeled narrow, prejudicial, and constraining. The federalizing of affect generated a desire for a life beyond the constraints of the local and familiar, an affiliation with the broader border crossings begun with the Revolutionary War. This is the setting for Irving's tale, an apparently cynical picture of the freedoms the war brought to citizens' everyday lives. Describing George Washington's clothes painted over a portrait of George III hanging at Jonathan Doolittle's Union Inn, Irving suggests that the drag of representational democracy will produce little improvement over imperial sovereignty. In either case, the citizen will be expected to "do little" in the management of the nation.[29] Indeed, the electoral factions and superficial debates that occupy the citizens at the end of the tale show the distressing ways in which the illusions of participation offered by electoral democracy cover the comically limited options for inventive freedom provided in the wake of the war.

If it fails to provide significant freedom for Rip and his neighbors, however, the Revolution *does* represent a watershed, providing a mobility that can be satisfactorily misrecognized as freedom. In the tale, the war coincides with a moment of physical—and ultimately metaphysical—mobility for Rip. Although for much of his life he has been famously henpecked by the shrewish Dame Van Winkle, Rip seems incapable of escaping her "petticoat government" (5). Like the later narrators of Hawthorne's romances, Rip is held to his place by the local myths and histories—of ghosts, witches, and Indians—that shackle him to his vituperative wife, even as they provide a momentary respite in entertaining his equally place-bound neighbors. With the Revolution and Rip's physical mobility into the mountains, however, comes a move from identification with the victims of imperial conquest (ghosts, witches, and Indians) to a new identification with the agents of imperial expansion—in this case, the Dutch settlers of

New York. The Revolution apparently provides Rip with modes of identification that take him beyond the prejudicial local (his tales are dismissed as
superstitious) into a new nationalism marked less by electoral politics than by
an expansiveness tied to both the past (the haunting history of Dutch invasion)
and the future (a manifest destiny that will take many, like Rip, into the wilderness to escape the stifling provincialism of "civilization").

The story suggests, however, that Rip's new mobile identification is at odds
not only with the past provincialism represented by Dame Van Winkle, but
with the electoral democracy of postwar America. When Rip returns to town
after his twenty-year absence, he initially feels alienated by the changes he
witnesses. But the change the town's citizens have undergone is perhaps not as
unlike Rip's transformation as he initially imagines. One of the surprising
aspects of Irving's story is how quickly Rip and the newly democratic town, at
first so strange to one another, become mutually accommodating. When the
citizens, listening to Rip's new tale of expansive mobility, embrace him as one of
their own, they suggest that his extraordinary experiences are familiar to them
as well. What Rip learns through the haunting history of imperialism, the
townspeople learn through a spirit of open-minded tolerance, an expansive
sympathy that enables them to embrace Rip for the good character they recognize, more than local history or electoral participation, as the true marker of
civic belonging.

Given that the community into which he is welcomed is predicated on
abstract virtue rather than familiar history, however, Rip's return, not surprisingly, remains haunted by dissatisfying isolation. Irving's description of Rip's
reactions might fit any number of displaced Americans who found themselves
in locations undergoing rapid population growth following the war: "the very
village was altered; it was larger and more populous. There were rows of houses
which he had never seen before, and those which had been his familiar haunts
had disappeared. Strange names were over the doors—strange faces at the
windows—everything was strange" (47).[30] As he inquires after his former associates and learns that they were killed during the war or have moved to Philadelphia to participate in the new government, "Rip's heart died away at hearing
of these sad changes in his home and friends, and finding himself thus alone in
the world" (50). Rip does not connect his isolation to social changes, however,
but to a more individualized cause consistent with the interiorized sociability of
postwar America. "The very character of the people," he observes, "seemed
changed" (48). Cannily cognizant of the new language of "character" that has
gained prominence during his twenty-year absence, Rip proves adaptive to his
new neighbors and consequently is not alone for long. Almost immediately, he

is surrounded by an audience willing to suspend their election to enact the more important ritual of self-disclosure. As Rip repeatedly tells his story, he gains greater civic prominence, until in the end he is hailed as a "patriarch of the village" (52). That Rip's tale seems largely fictional does not detract from its function as self-narrative. Indeed, it adds to is efficacy, making Rip's "self" a creation (now, in Irving's story, a print commodity) that can circulate as *any-one's* story.

At the same time, Rip's self-disclosure is perceived not as a collective fiction but, rather, as the fulfillment of what Rip always already was: a composite of liberal values. From the beginning of the tale, he is described as "kind" (39), full of "patience" (39), tolerant, and above all sympathetic. " 'Poor Wolf,' he would say, 'thy mistress leads thee a dog's life of it; but never mind, my lad, whilst I live thou shalt never want a friend to stand by thee!' Wolf would wag his tail, look wistfully in his master's face, and if dogs could feel pity, I verily believe he reciprocated the sentiment with all his heart" (42). Although Irving takes to its absurd extreme the power of liberal sympathy to reproduce itself on its object, turning even a difference in species into an imagined sameness, the tale affirms that America's liberality, like Rip's, was not a new phenomenon but a nascent potential, its articulation not a disciplinary ritual but a fulfillment. The land Rip returns to is therefore not "strange" at all, as he first thinks, but is now free to show what it always was: liberalized and affective, an interior state. After he has disclosed his "true" self—or, rather, after he has learned to tell his "self" in ways consistent with the values of his audience—Rip is integrated into the community. As one of the townswomen says, " 'Welcome home again, old neighbor' " (51).

The assertion that the town has not changed, that it is still the "home" Rip left behind, is enabled by the insistence that Rip himself has not changed. Irving states of his title character, "the changes of states and empires made but little impression on him" (52). Confessions of stasis thus conceal the dramatic mobilities—emotional as much as geographic—undertaken by citizens in the new republic. Rip's tale generates an affective sphere that distinguishes the town from its previous ties to the provincial past (represented by Dame Van Winkle), the national present (represented by the elections), and the imperial future (represented by the imperial "ghosts" that hover around the yet uncolonized wilderness). The new social sphere, in other words, is little *but* mobility, un-anchored from any of the ethical orders that reside outside the affective control of the liberalized citizen.

All of these competing orders are characterized in terms of their lack of lib-eral affect. Dame Van Winkle and the election officials are twins in intolerance, while the Dutch, although "evidently amusing themselves, yet . . . maintained the gravest faces, the most mysterious silence, and were, withal, the most melancholy party of pleasure he had ever witnessed" (45). Unlike these illiberal forces, the town, in its response to Rip, can conceive itself as an affect-dense and liberal "home," while its citizens imagine themselves as satisfactorily relational and mobile, present and abstract, without accruing the unpleasant responsibilities of the economic and political orders their identifications serve. Irving's tale thus demonstrates that two modes of expansive identification—one interiorizing (governing the town's incorporation of Rip) and one imperial (Rip's newfound knowledge of the nation's imperial past and future)—form a partnership: if the latter allows the nation a form of territorial power to compete with its European forebears, the former cloaks that power in a mantle of benevolence that distinguishes the "new imperialism" from the foreign sovereignty disavowed by the Declaration of Independence. Both forms of mobility merge in a hybridized and interior civic construction—"character"—that becomes the safeguard of national expansion while apparently preserving the virtues of local relationships.

"Rip Van Winkle" ends happily, with Rip and his fellow citizens in a state of universal satisfaction. Yet Irving's story complicates this satisfaction. For one thing, whereas before the Revolution the characters in the town, although largely emblematic, nevertheless possessed distinguishing characteristics—the erudite if droning Derrek Van Bummel, the sanctimonious Nicholas Vedder, not to mention the Van Winkles themselves—after the Revolution the townspeople are denied distinctive identities, interchangeable in their reactions to Rip. If, as Benedict Anderson has argued, the abstractions enabling imagined national communities generated the bland homogeneity that deadened local distinctiveness, the location of the state inward—into imagined interiorities—locates the deadness of regulated life in the affective space of the citizen's character. While Rip claims that the new civic character of the town rescues his dying heart, then, he misrecognizes the extent to which that "rescue" is itself mortifying.[31]

But Rip's is not a complete misrecognition. When he surveys his ruined home, he has a fleeting moment of grief: "This desolateness overcame all his connubial fears—he called loudly for his wife and children: the lonely chambers rang for a moment with his voice, then all again was silence" (48). Dame Van Winkle's despotism notwithstanding, she represented not the abstract comforts of a civil "home," but the local satisfactions of his abode. The absence of that attachment—connected by the narrator to the "dying heart" produced by the changed character of the town—is the source of Rip's despair. While universal interiority was heralded, in Irving's story and in the culture more broadly, as a freedom (the only freedom, in fact, that the Revolution enabled), then, "Rip Van Winkle" suggests that it was also experienced, in more or less conscious ways, as a moment of death.

Rip's mourning for his wife's passing is short-lived. Representative of conservative impulses in a newly liberalized nation, her virtues appallingly retrograde, Dame Van Winkle is left unmourned at the end of the story, having receded into a past that was always her proper place, one that she, unlike Rip, cannot transcend. But Rip's initial grief, his heart dying at the sight of changing character, suggests that at least some *did* weep—if not for the shrewish Dame, then for the conventions, attachments, and social orders that passed with her. Certainly, there was no end of weeping in the federal novel, although, as Julia Stern demonstrates, most cried for dead fathers, not for passing wives and mothers. Stern argues that the tears drenching the pages of the early nation's novels register the painful passing of democracy, as increasing numbers of Americans —women, workers, children, African Americans, Native Americans—found themselves without the freedoms promised by the revolutionary rhetoric.[32]

Yet this brief reading of "Rip Van Winkle" enables us to ask whether citizens were mourning the loss of democracy or mourning other losses caused *by* democracy. For those associated with the particularities of illiberal character (Rip's shiftlessness and lack of sympathy for his wife, for instance), the disavowals necessary to reform into the abstract virtues of liberal character were not simply a matter of taking to the hills; they meant the loss of one's communities, one's strategies, one's life. Rip's momentary grief over the loss of his family and friends—of his whole familiar way of life—may rightly be called mournful, for, as Freud tells us, the person who mourns quickly finds a new object (an abstraction as well as a person or object) on which to cathect his libido, as Rip apparently does when he relocates his pleasure at the end of the story in the narratives necessary to liberal self-imaginings.

If Irving, who wrote thirty years after the ratification of the Constitution, could easily suspend Rip's grief, hailed into the mobile community defined by abstract character, others writing closer to the events Irving described found their loss—and the anger that lies behind persistent loss—harder to resolve. The early national period is haunted less by mourning than by melancholia. For Freud, melancholia is the result of an unresolved anger or sense of betrayal— what he characterizes as ambivalence—that cannot be appropriately expressed in regard to the lost object and is therefore directed at aspects of the loved one incorporated into oneself. In a historical moment in which the passing of a way of life marked as illiberal could not be properly mourned, we might well expect ambivalence toward the simulacra of those social orders maintained within the self. Indeed, the transformation of interpersonal relations into the individualized and interiorized orders of abstract character—a civic dynamic of identification and mournful incorporation—lends itself to Freud's conception of melancholia, in which the lost loved one, usually "found among those in his [the melancholic's] near neighbourhood," is transformed into "a cleavage between the criticizing faculty of the ego and the ego as altered by the identification."[33] The suffering of melancholia is produced not just by the interiorization of a previously interpersonal relation (a near neighbor), but also by the insistent misrecognition of a difference (an autonomous person) as an affective simulacrum of oneself (identification) that produces irresolvable interior schisms, making melancholia the dark twin of sympathy. This melancholy is, perhaps, what haunts the soon-to-be equally mobile townspeople, a more persistent if submerged legacy that, refusing to diminish, disrupts the pleasures provided by the new national parties (now electoral rather than "of pleasure").

While curing melancholy might seem to require re-exteriorizing the social, Freud also characterized health in terms of mobilities similar to Rip's: "when the work of mourning is completed the ego becomes free and uninhibited again."[34] This perverse metalepsis, which posits the cause of melancholy as its cure, haunts both Irving's and Freud's social imaginary. The death of social relations and their relocation in an interior space creates a psychic unrest that disquiets the pleasure of presumed normalcy; at the same time, the health of "uninhibited" freedom might seem to ensure, not resolve, the dissolution of connections to "near neighbors" that created melancholy in the first place. The next section explores the effects of this double bind on one of America's best-known early melancholics: Eliza Wharton, heroine of Hannah Webster Foster's epistolary novel *The Coquette* (1797). Unlike Rip, who quickly resolves his loss and thereby resists ambivalence, Eliza Wharton wrestles loss throughout the novel, expressing her ambivalence, as Freud tells us melancholics will, in a process of suicidal self-revilement and self-denials. Eliza's struggles with and through melancholy suggest that the fleeting grief that Irving registered was just the diminished trace of a deeper cultural ambivalence about the emergence of the interiorized social orders made possible by liberal character.[35]

At the same time, critics have persistently read Eliza's ultimate demise as a sign of failed resistance to the regimes of "good character," a reading that Freud's account of melancholia partially corrects.[36] Freud tells us that the melancholic labors under the "delusional expectation of punishment," but Eliza's punishments are far from delusional, since the social ostracism of unwed mothers and those who participated in promiscuous social fantasies were material and often extreme.[37] If Foster's novel suggests caution in accepting Freud's assertion that the punishment feared by the melancholic is purely delusional, it might also lead us to wonder whether the victories Freud attributes to the melancholic are entirely imaginary. In melancholy, Freud writes, "the sufferers usually succeed in the end in taking revenge, by the circuitous path of self-punishment, on the original objects and in tormenting them by means of the illness, having developed the latter so as to avoid the necessity of openly expressing their hostility against the loved ones." Melancholia thus becomes a lesson, for Freud, in "what the conflict of ambivalence by itself can achieve." While the victory Eliza's death poses may indeed appear pyrrhic, her fantasy world holds open the space for an alternative communal relationship. Normalcy is restored to the melancholy ego, Freud concludes, when reality "passes its verdict—that the object no longer exists—upon each single one of the memories and hopes through which the libido was attached to the lost object, and the ego, confronted as it were by the decision whether it will share this fate, is persuaded by the sum of its narcissistic satisfaction in being alive to sever its attachment to the non-existent object."[38] Again, freedom, which Freud repeatedly associates with normalcy, involves a severing, a liberal rip, that promises the subject satisfaction even while it leaves her in the figurative state of criminality. Eliza's melancholy, never resolved in *The Coquette*, forestalls the juridical force of this social imaginary, suggesting in the process that relations that apparently die in Irving's tale may have only gone inside, into a melancholic state that preserves the historical specificities of the local.

Alienated Affections and Melancholy Hopes

Lauren Berlant's important insight into intimacy's plight might stand as a defense of Eliza Wharton's melancholy: "desires for intimacy that bypass the couple form and the life narratives it generates have no alternative plots, let alone few laws and stable spaces of culture in which to clarify and to cultivate them. What happens to the energy of attachment when it has no designated place? To the glances, gestures, encounters, collaborations, or fantasies that have no canon? As with minor literatures, minor intimacies have been forced to develop aesthetics of the extreme to push these spaces into being by way of small and grand gestures." If Eliza is forced into the small gestures of coquetry or the larger ones of melancholy to challenge the primacy of the couple and to maintain the minor intimacy of friendship, the stakes are high enough to warrant the risk. "To rethink intimacy," Berlant asserts, "is to appraise how we have been and how we live and how we might imagine lives that make more sense than the ones so many are living."[39]

When Foster wrote *The Coquette*, the association of normalized intimacy and civic order ("laws and stable spaces")—of federal affect and character—was more than theoretical. As Fredrika Teute and David Shields document, in the unquiet times following the Revolutionary War, when mutinous soldiers, already demoralized by internal disputes and insolvency, surrounded the Continental Congress and forced its leaders to flee Philadelphia and reestablish headquarters in rural Princeton, New Jersey, civil order was restored only through the promulgation of national manners manifested in properly federalized unions not of states, but of bodies.[40] The dissolution of civil order, as Thomas Jefferson observed to George Washington, resulted from the very abstraction of friendship into public civility necessary to the legal apparatus of the Constitution. "Where in privacy friendships had taken shape," Jefferson noted, those affective unions were now breaking down in "public assemblies" under the pressure of "difference of opinion, contradiction & irritation."[41] To repair such rifts, Annis Boudinot Stockton gathered at her Princeton estate the political and economic elite of the colonies. Counseling these men about manners, taste, and, above all, affairs of the heart, Stockton (and the women who followed her lead, including Elizabeth Willing Powel, Mary White Morris, and Sarah Livingston Jay) encouraged affective alliances between leaders from diverse—and increasingly antagonistic—regions and economies and lined up these alliances behind the man who would lead the new federal government and the woman who would continue Stockton's strategy by holding regular salons as First Lady, George and Martha Washington. The so-called Confederation Court worked, Teute and Shields argue, by insisting that the nation's future relied on "dynastic marriage, not flirtation or adultery." While at Princeton, "Benjamin Hawkins of North Carolina courted Miss Livingston of New Jersey; James McHenry of Maryland wooed and wed Margaret Caldwell of Philadelphia; [James] Madison affianced and lost Kitty Floyd; Jacob Read of South Carolina dreamed of Miss Calvert in Annapolis." Surrendering the cavalier sexuality of the war period, the leaders of the new republic, through properly civil marriages, gained national unity. "By the time the Federal Convention convened," Teute and Shields conclude, "there was a core of men and women whose horizons had expanded and their outlook broadened to a continental vision."[42] What was lost in the death of friendship, then, was resurrected in the nationalization of marriage. When Foster's female characters insist that marriage "renders us more beneficial to the public,"[43] then, they are not simply engaging in the false consciousness of an emergent separate spheres ideology. Rather, they are participating in a public imaginary that sought national coherence through the bodily economy of self-governing manners and normative intimacy that made inviolable "unions"—the institutionalized manifestation of federal affect—the metonymic safeguard of national oneness.

Not all citizens, however, were among the elites invited to the Stockton salon. What happened to the rage of the soldiers, the randy sexuality of the patriots, the urban sophistication of the city girls left behind when the Congress fled? Did their expectations for a more just distribution of power (or for the minimum justice of their wages), their extravagant experimentation with the body's pleasures, their nostalgic adherence to European culture and manners, their investments in what Jefferson called private friendships simply evaporate in the face of federal affect and national character? Or did the "losers" in the Revolution—among whom were those who took seriously the Declaration's call to pursue happiness in its myriad forms—begin to write their histories as novels such as *The Coquette*, which allowed those who survived "freedom" to "imagine lives that make more sense than the ones so many are living"?[44] To imagine such lives, such non-federalized intimacies, Foster had to show the imaginative powers of melancholy, which held tenaciously to the possibilities of friendships as alternative forms of public imagination and commitment.

While several critics have noted Eliza's friends' exercise of surveillance and disciplinary judgment over the heroine, none accounts for why Eliza continues to turn to her friends for support and guidance, even when their advice proves so disastrously ill-suited. Taking up this question, I will argue that *The Coquette* is not, as critics have assumed, a novel of loss, but one that deploys loss to hold open the space of social imagination among a people who increasingly were being interpellated into the nationalizing order of federal affect. If, that is, friendship became the interpellative metaphor that allowed local attachment to become national belonging, *The Coquette* maintains a range of possible friendships, the multiplicity of which denies the hegemonic status of a single sanctioned union.

Eliza's longing for lost friends, then, can be read not only as a romantic nostalgia for an idealized past of uncomplicated, harmonious friendships, but also as a *productive* mode that continues to imagine forms of sociability squeezed out of the social imaginary by the abstract relationships necessary to federal belonging. Viewed this way, *The Coquette* is a doggedly optimistic book that preserves—in the ironic guise of loss—the hope of social relations that might yet be.[45] In a society in which life was conceived through the managed narratives of normative affect, the alternative plots of intimacy required the counter-life gestures of loss and melancholy. Through those gestures, Foster's heroine discovers what Walt Whitman would note sixty years later: "All goes onward and outward, nothing collapses, / And to die is different from what any one supposed, and luckier."[46]

The Coquette begins and ends with scenes of death that occur, as it were, offstage. The novel starts shortly after the death of Haly, an older man to whom Eliza was betrothed at the behest of her parents and friends. Feeling newly liberated, Eliza begins a series of visits to her friends, the recently married Mrs. Richman and Lucy Freeman, who also marries and moves away in the course of the novel. During these visits, Eliza is courted by the Reverend John Boyer, a man of indisputable character but, to Eliza, a stuffed shirt. Her attention is drawn instead to the libertine Peter Sanford, whom she mistakenly believes is quite wealthy. When Boyer discovers Eliza secluded in the garden with Sanford, he breaks off their engagement in a rage and promptly marries another woman. Shocked and dismayed, Eliza turns to her friends, who are either preoccupied or give her bad advice. Eventually, Eliza succumbs to Sanford's persistent advances (although he has married another woman for her money) and becomes pregnant. Eliza flees her home and dies, along with the baby, leaving behind only "scraps of paper" to console her mournful friends.

Despite the centrality of death to this plot, however, Eliza's melancholy does not start with anyone's demise. In fact, the death of her fiancé releases Eliza, she declares, into new experiences of pleasure. Without the death of a character to precipitate it, Eliza's melancholy would appear to arise from the loss not of a near neighbor but of the abstraction "near neighbor" itself. Whereas Rip Van Winkle can accommodate the paradox of expansive interiority, however, Eliza, confronted by the particularly dire consequences for women of federalized affect, enacts an agonized struggle to imagine social networks that are the prerequisite for a democratic way of life. As Eliza watches her friends grow more distant, ideologically as well as geographically, she, like Rip, experiences an intense grief. Unlike that of her male counterpart, however, Eliza's grief is prolonged and suffused with the ambivalence Freud puts at the heart of melancholy. Nor does Eliza's melancholy remain static. It evolves from an initial shock and betrayal into a social critique justified by extremes of emotion, into a silence that becomes Eliza's refuge in a world that is increasingly invested in the dynamics of confession and criminality focused on the regulation of inner life. While Freud presents melancholy as an involuntary falling away from normalcy, then, Foster presents it as the result of and response to coercive normalcy and offers a willed deployment of the mandatory rhetorics of feeling to create a space, however limited, of social invention for the citizen bereft of friendship. That space, in Foster's novel, takes the form of death as a register not of failure, but of the citizen's willed withdrawal from circulations of character in print.

Throughout *The Coquette*, death is profoundly pedagogical.[47] Following Haly's death, Eliza writes to Lucy, "He lived the life, and died the death of the righteous. O that my last end may be like his! This even will, I hope, make a suitable and abiding impression upon my mind, teach me the fading nature of all sublunary enjoyments, and the little dependence which is to be placed on earthly felicity."[48] Yet Eliza begins the letter by crowing to Lucy, "An unusual sensation possesses my breast; a sensation, which I once thought could never pervade it on any occasion whatever. It is *pleasure*, pleasure, my dear Lucy, on leaving my parental roof!" (107). Why Eliza needs to report a death Lucy has herself witnessed is unclear, but it suggests that she writes not to impart new information, but to situate Haly's "righteousness" as a contrast to her statement of determined pleasure. The letter also suggests a disavowal of Lucy's authority as witness, a word that prefigures her panoptical presumption throughout the novel.[49] If Eliza's "sensations" diverge from Lucy's witness in this case, why would they not in other cases, as well? Eliza's first letter thus establishes itself as a commentary on the text of righteous character: if the latter requires the end of pleasure, the former takes death as the birth of pleasure, as a state that permits Eliza the wiggle room of discrepancy between decorum and desire that she exploits throughout the novel.

Of course, Eliza's female friends, as Stern notes, dutifully "keep the voices of dead male authorities alive" (82), and true to form, Lucy responds to Eliza's assertions of pleasure with a series of "monitorial lessons" (109). Rather than repenting, however, Eliza immediately expresses doubts about the "correspondence," in the sense of both "agreement" and "letter-writing," between herself and Lucy: "is it time for me to talk again of conquests, or must I only enjoy them in silence? I must write to you the impulses of my mind; or I must not write at all" (109). In this epistle, Eliza draws a contrast not between silence and pleasure or agency, but between silence and monitory pedagogy. Her silence, as she understands it, allows her to indulge the pleasures of her fancy unmolested by the circulatory scrutiny of her epistolary "correspondence."[50] Eliza deploys silence and withdrawal, then, as textual strategies, resisting imperatives to, as she puts it in the characteristically conflated language of character and criminality, "confine virtue to a cell" (114). "I am not so happy to day in the recollection of last evening's entertainment," she later writes to Lucy, "as I was in the enjoyment" (118). Eliza's refusal to relate her enjoyments forestalls Lucy's ability to censure them. Withdrawing from the civil circulations of print appears to Eliza as the best means to avoid the circuit of surveillance, confession, and adjudication that occupies her friends.[51]

Eliza's experiments with the potential freedoms of silence bring her close to an alternative understanding of death, as Boyer seems to recognize. Following their breakup over her flirtations with Sanford, Boyer writes to Eliza, "The regard which I felt for you was tender and animated, but it was not of that passionate kind which ends in death or despair. It was governed by reason" (188). If reason is the antidote to passion coded as death, then might not death be the antidote to the kinds of reasonable self-managements espoused by Boyer? Eliza suggests as much when she writes to Boyer of the "pleasing remembrance of your honorable attention [that will] preside, till death, in the breast of Eliza Wharton" (187). Eliza's final third-person appellation suggests a distinction between sensation and signature that, as Cathy Davidson notes, is true as well of her inscription on the tombstone that ends the text.[52] In this instance, that distinction allows Eliza to predict an endpoint to Boyer's influence on her heart, an impact that, her politeness notwithstanding, Eliza has experienced as anything but pleasing.

To understand Eliza's withdrawal, even to death, from the judging scrutiny of her beloved friends, one must first recognize the potential freedom Eliza believes friendship will deliver, and the regulated pleasures it comes to represent. Eliza begins the novel, like Rip Van Winkle, believing that freedom comes through mobility, that pleasure can be purchased simply by leaving a restrictive home: "A melancholy event has lately extricated me from those shackles, which parental authority had imposed on my mind. Let me then enjoy that freedom which I so highly prize. Let me have opportunity, unbiased by opinion, to gratify my natural disposition in a participation of those pleasures which youth and innocence afford" (113). Eliza's location of desire in the nexus of mobility and pleasure will become painfully paradoxical, as the same faith in movement that takes her beyond parental control takes her friends away from her and begins the print circulations of character against which she struggles. At the outset, however, declaring, "I wish for no other connection than that of friendship" (108), Eliza distinguishes that relationship, a network of proximate intimacies unmediated by law and unrestricted by discourses of property or propriety, from the "other connections" that would stabilize and contain friendship's inventive negotiations. Eliza seems to imagine, not irrationally, that friends will provide her with the freedoms denied by supervision while still maintaining the support, affection, and intimacy familiar from her local relations. Misrecognizing the ways friendship was becoming a technology for managing public "character" through the circulation of federal affect, and trusting that intimacy could be maintained despite the mobilities she believes are the condition of freedom, Eliza views friendship as a viable mode of social inventiveness.

Almost immediately, however, Eliza discovers that social revision is difficult to materialize in the face of the normalizing belief in autonomous and normalized privacy. Eliza's friends do not see, as she does, that the "private" intimacies of marriage and family limit the options for inventive freedom in the name of virtues that make managed intimacy a primary location for disciplinary interiority. Smarting with disappointment as her friends settle down and move on, leaving her feeling more abandoned than any libertine could possibly do, Eliza bitterly writes:

> I hope, said I, that my friends are not so weary of my company, as to wish to dispose of me. I am too happy in my present connections to quit them for new ones. Marriage is the tomb of friendship. It appears to me a very selfish state. Why do people, in general, as soon as they are married, centre all their cares, their concerns, and pleasures in their own families? former acquaintances are neglected or forgotten. The tenderest ties between friends are weakened, or dissolved; and benevolence itself moves in a very limited sphere. (123)

Eliza's contention that the more people share the responsibilities ("cares" and "concerns") and pleasures that constitute public intimacy, the more functional and widespread the operations of benevolence, seems consistent with the democratic rhetoric of the new republic.

Yet Eliza also suggests her growing awareness of the managed privacy that "dissolves" friendship and removes intimacy from the public sphere, making it the contained property of the isolated and increasingly mobile family. Eliza's friends encourage her not only to conform to norms of good character and sanctioned intimacy, but also to put herself in circulation, which Eliza resentfully regards as a form of disposal. Eliza's counter-intuitive conflation of circulation and conventional intimacy reveals a persistent pattern in the novel (and in the culture the novel chronicles). The joining of consensual adults into autonomous couples is always accompanied in the novel by a geographic move: since families safeguard the public virtues of trustful responsibility, public character can circulate in the mobile unit of the private family. While "character" may be safeguarded by the apparent autonomy of the family circle, however, circulation erodes contact *between* such circles, "disposing" of friendship as a way of life just as Eliza suspects her friends wish to dispose of her personally. Associated with the minor intimacies represented in the novel by friendship,

Eliza understandably describes marriage, which most in the novel credit with the beginning of life, as a state of death, suggesting the inversions of life and death that characterize Eliza's bids for freedom throughout the novel.

Against this charge, arising as it does from a social imaginary that competes with the interiorizing rationales of federal affect, Mrs. Richman responds by casting her "very limited sphere" as the nursery for democracy:

> True, we cannot always pay that attention to former associates, which we may wish; but the little community which we superintend is quite as important as others, and certainly renders us more beneficial to the public. True benevolence, through it may change its objects, is not limited by time or place. Its effects are the same, and aided by a second self, are rendered more diffusive and salutary. (123)

While republican liberality promised that casting wide one's loyalties would guarantee the intimacies familiar from family and neighbors, here the opposite is true. By confining her affection to husband and children, Mrs. Richman believes, she is unlimited by time or space, her affections perpetually transferable through an unspecified chain of public objects. When a male admirer declares Mrs. Richman "truly republican," he suggests not only that her civic concern makes her a good citizen, but also that there is something "republican" about the location of the affairs of the common weal in the affective interior. Mrs. Wharton echoes this sentiment in response to Eliza's complaint that a clergyman's wife is too dependent: "Are we not all links in the great chain of society, some more, some less important; but each upheld by others; throughout the confederated whole? In whatever situation we are placed, our greater or less degree of happiness must be derived from ourselves" (136). Unlike Eliza's desire to create intimacy with actual people in a contextual public, her female mentors encourage her to purchase an abstract "association" through the severe limitation of her affective investments. Eliza is thus encouraged to locate her expansiveness within the confines not only of her husband and children, but of her individual body ("our happiness . . . must be derived from ourselves").

Ironically, although Eliza's friends deploy the political rhetoric of their day to decry her social inventiveness as coquetry, her faith in friendship appears consistent with their assertions of the mobilities of federal liberality, in which the attachment of one's loyalty to a promiscuously substitutable chain of what Mrs. Richman calls "objects" might characterize intimate as well as civic expansiveness. Generating a geographic mobility that disrupts the mutual knowledge of intimate communities, liberality produces libertinism, which it then purports to fix through the mobile circulations of character (a circulation disguised by its own claims to locations within social customs that, in a geographically mobile society, are far from stable). Yet Eliza differs from the productive circulations of liberality and libertinism by insisting that her friendships are compensation for other structural inequalities. Expected to adopt the customs appropriate to her class, Eliza defies social status by denying the inevitable certainties of character. "Fortune, indeed, has not been very liberal of her gifts to me," she declares, "but I preserve a large stock in the bank of friendship" (110). Locating her "objects" of affection within a localized network that she wishes to maintain despite the imperative to abstract attachment, Eliza, taking a rare look inward, states, "At present, the most lively emotions of my heart are those of friendship" (129).

If Eliza, looking inward, finds her investments in friendships, her friends see only good character. Lucy Freeman counsels Eliza, "As to fortune, prudence, economy, and regularity are necessary to preserve it when possessed" (150). These character traits are imperatively, if paradoxically, yoked to—and strictly contain—the ideals of freedom that pervaded post–Revolutionary public rhetoric: "Act then with that modest freedom, that dignified unreserve which bespeaks conscious rectitude and sincerity of heart" (125). The authenticity promised by character, however paradoxical, becomes the best guard against the libertinism (false character) that lurks everywhere in *The Coquette*. Of Eliza's friend Julia Granby, who "unites the liberal sentiments, with a benevolence, and candor of disposition" (212), Sanford acknowledges, "the dignity of her manners forbid all assaults upon her virtue" (218). Giving this rectitude a disciplinary twist, Boyer tells Eliza, "Your own heart must be your monitor," guarding her against "an aversion to the sober, rational, frugal mode of living" (171).[53]

Against the disciplinarity of republican character (Eliza and Sanford use the word "character" twenty-one times, twice more than everyone else combined, suggesting that "character" is a concept wrestled with primarily by those who would escape its normative confines), Eliza maintains her skepticism about the value of interiorized manners. For one thing, it is striking, given her propensity for romance, that Eliza resolutely turns the language of nature against the logic of interiority, declaring, "such have been my situations in life, and the natural volatility of my temper, that I have looked but little into my own heart" (126). Nor does Eliza wish to limit her pleasures to the prescribed sphere of either a family or her own body. "I am a poor solitary being, who need [*sic*] some amusement beyond what I can supply myself. The mind, after being confined at home for a while, sends the imagination abroad in quest of new treasures," she claims, "and the body may as well accompany it, for ought I can see" (115).

Despite her faith in friendship, however, Eliza soon finds herself separated from her friends by their insistent participation in heteronormative social conventions justified in the name of "character." Reporting on Lucy's wedding, Eliza acknowledges the discrepancy between her responses and those of the other guests: "Every eye beamed with pleasure on the occasion, and every tongue echoed the wishes of benevolence. Mine only was silent. Though not less interested in the felicity of my friend than the rest, yet the idea of a separation; perhaps, of an alienation of affection, by means of her entire devotion to another, cast an involuntary gloom over my mind" (168). In response to Mr. Richman's directive on the birth of his daughter, "Mrs. Richman expects to receive your congratulations, in a letter by the next post" (159), Eliza's gloom takes on a sarcastic edge: "From the scenes of festive mirth, from the conviviality of rejoicing friends, and from the dissipating amusements of the gay world, I retire with alacrity, to hail my beloved friend on the important charge which she has received; on the accession of her family, and, may I not say, on the addition of her cares" (159). For a time, Eliza maintains the belief that inventive friendship can survive, as when she agrees to accompany Lucy to Boston after her wedding: "I have agreed to accompany her, and spend a month or two in her family. This will give variety to the journey of life" (161). Yet mobility soon leads to distance, which in turn necessitates the epistolary forms that provides a simulacrum of intimacy that betrays the relational inventiveness Eliza craves. The fixity of character and the rendition of pleasure in print become simultaneous in these epistolary relationships, and refusing the former, Eliza comes in time to refuse the latter: "I am too much engaged by the exhilarating scene around, for attending to a subject which affords no variety. I shall not close this till tomorrow" (160).

Once her friends realize that Eliza has no intention of settling into the patterns of virtuous privacy, their calls for self-disclosure become more imperative, their diatribes against nonconformity more starkly juridical, as Eliza registers when she refers to "those friends who pretend to be better judges of my happiness than I am myself" (174).[54] Pressuring Eliza not to "diverge too far from her present sedateness and solitude," but to let "her passions . . . vibrate with regularity" (202), her friends baldly place their benevolence in the service of convention. "Slight not the opinion of the world!" Lucy warns Eliza: "We are dependent beings, and while the smallest trace of virtuous sensibility remains, we must feel the force of that dependence, in a greater or less degree. No female, whose mind is uncorrupted, can be indifferent to reputation" (212). Ever able to see through her friends' rhetoric, Eliza recasts their assertions of benevolence— Julia demands, "Answer my question sincerely; for, believe me, Eliza, it is not malice, but concern for you, which prompts it" (220)—in terms of crime and punishment: "I plead guilty . . . to all your charges" (221). Although by the end of the novel Eliza apparently concurs with the normalizing judgments of her friends, claiming "my conscience is awakened to a conviction of my guilt" (234), her "conviction" comes only in print. In conversations with her proximate companions, Eliza continues to reject the terms of public justice: "My friends, she [Eliza] said, are very jealous of me, lately. I know not how I have forfeited their confidence, or incurred their suspicion" (209). Their insistence on the transparent overlay of character and justice causes Eliza a new ambivalence about the presence of her friends. "I anticipate, and yet I dread your return," she writes to Julia, "a paradox that, time alone can solve" (214).

Ambivalence ("paradox") is at the heart of melancholy, and with Eliza's doubts about her friends comes her angry mournfulness, a function not of thwarted romance, but of failed friendship. "I am extremely depressed, my dear Lucy" (183), Eliza declares, moving into a period of severe self-reproach. "I am pleased with nobody; still less with myself" (214). While Freud claims that the melancholic's self-revilement is the anticipation of an imaginary judgment, Eliza's appears to be the internalization of the oft-repeated reproaches of her friends: "If I indulge myself in temporary enjoyment, the consciousness or apprehension of doing amiss destroys my peace of mind" (214). Eliza moves from believing "some evil genius" governs her actions to blaming "my own imprudence" (192). In explaining her acquiescence to Sanford, Eliza becomes a classic melancholic: "Grief has undermined my constitution. My health has fallen a sacrifice to a disordered mind. But I regret not its departure! I have not a single wish to live. Nothing which the world affords can restore my former serenity and happiness!" (222–23). Friendship no longer holds the promise it once did for Eliza, who acknowledges, "In the society of my amiable friends at New-Haven, I enjoyed every thing that friendship could bestow; but rest for a disturbed mind was not in their power" (189). Distance is not compensated for by the abstract fusion of character, the simulated intimacies of print, or even the physical negotiations of a short visit. "Oh that you were near me, as formerly," she writes to Lucy, "to share and alleviate my cares! to have some friend to whom I could repose confidence, and with whom I could freely converse, and advise, on this occasion, would be an unspeakable comfort!" (190).

Rather than providing that comfort, Eliza's friends increase their distance by accentuating the print basis of their relationships to her. Lucy responds that Eliza's is a "truly romantic letter," which "would make a very pretty figure in a novel," filled with the "*et ceteras* of romance" (190). Indeed, Eliza's friends perversely treat melancholy as they do "character" and "friendship," detaching it from its embodied context and attaching it promiscuously to a variety of objects, often explicitly textual. In the closing pages of the novel, they refer to a "melancholy story" (224, 231), a "melancholy discovery" (226), a "melancholy intelligence" (235), "the melancholy story of Eliza Wharton" (241), a "melancholy tale" (240), and even to a "fatal paragraph" (236). If her friends treat Eliza's melancholy like an open book, she responds by consigning her inventive hopefulness ("unspeakable comfort"), counter-intuitively, to the inscrutable domain of silence. Of her mother, Eliza declares, "I dare not converse freely with her on the subject of my present uneasiness, lest I should distress her. I am therefore, obliged to conceal my disquietude" (190). Although Eliza's silence here takes on the benevolent cast of filial concern, she also uses it to avoid the juridical scrutiny of her prying peers. Crying to Boyer that "my motives were innocent, though they doubtless wore the aspect of criminality" (178), Eliza refuses to participate in the dynamic of confession and adjudication: "I had no inclination to self-defense. My natural vivacity had forsaken me, and I listened without interrupting him to the fluency of reproachful language, which his resentment inspired" (179).

Given her friends' drive to place intimacy solely in the domain of print (creating what we might call printimacies), Eliza's silence is most powerful when it involves her withdrawal from the circulation of letters, which might be understood not as a failure of fortitude or a collapse into depression, but as an effort to maintain her inventive faith apart from the abstract righteousness of disciplinary self-inscriptions. "You must excuse me," she writes to Lucy, "if my letters are shorter than formerly. Writing is not so agreeable to me as it used to be" (207). Later she writes to Julia, "Writing is an employment, which suits me not at present" (213). If her friends speak to Eliza in one united voice, she responds in turn, denying them the variety they would deny her, and writing one letter to two friends. Claiming that "nothing remarkable has occurred in the neighborhood, worth communication" (213), Eliza draws a distinction between her unworthy experiences and their print circulations. Denying their altruistic solicitations of more letters, Eliza warns her friends that if they continue to write, "Your benevolence must be your reward" (214). When Lucy disingenuously defends herself to Eliza, claiming, "Marriage has not alienated, or weakened my regard for my friends. Come, then, to your faithful Lucy" (212), Eliza never again writes to her. Eliza's silence allows her to remove herself from the circulations of conventional intimacy and the "gloom" it causes her, leaving her an enigma to her friends, "like patience on a monument, smiling at grief' " (216).

Eliza's friends immediately interpret the enigma, however, as a conventional narrative of shame. Eliza, they contend, has fallen (away), asserting that she has left their circle for the false charms of romance. By telling this story, they assert that she has undergone a change. They, by contrast, gain a gratifying sense of their own constancy, a satisfaction that requires the fiction of Eliza's change. The tale of Eliza's "departure" (now mobility rooted entirely in the affective discourse of character, as a journey from virtue to shame) has been encouraged by Eliza's friends from the outset. Egging Eliza on every time she seems about to take their advice to settle down, her friends produce the temptations they then congratulate themselves for predicting. From the beginning, Mrs. Richman knowingly arranges for Eliza to meet Sanford, leading Eliza, when she then learns that Sanford is a libertine, to rightly ask, "O, why was I not informed of this before?" (119). When, after Boyer breaks off their engagement, Eliza ceases what her friends consider coquettish behavior, Mrs. Richman reignites her ambitions, saying, "Heaven, I doubt not, has happiness still in store for you—perhaps greater than you could have enjoyed in that connection" (182), while Julia urges her "to revisit the scenes of amusement and pleasure" (192). Although Lucy congratulates Eliza on avoiding Sanford, she also tells Eliza that Sanford has bought an estate near her mother's home (128), thereby planting the seed that takes Eliza directly into harm's way. When Eliza resolves not to see Sanford, Julia intervenes, claiming, "I see no harm in conversing with him" (199), and then, when Eliza is closest to seduction, Julia abandons her, even while acknowledging to Lucy: "I regret leaving Eliza! I tremble at her danger! She has not the resolution to resist temptation, which she once possessed" (211). Modeling the voyeuristic pleasures—and distance—of the novel's readers, Julia declares, "My heart thrilled with horror at the sacrifice of virtue" (219). Eliza is the marker of the proximate and embodied pleasures of intimacy that her friends—signed on, as they are, to the abstract virtues of circulating character—cannot enjoy except as a print commodity, which they need to ensure for themselves the compensatory pleasures of judgment and reason. While character relies on the continual mobilities of print, then, it produces the affective satisfactions of stability and stasis.

Although Eliza negatively defines the virtues that constitute the discourse of liberal character, she also continues as a deconstructive uncertainty within that discourse. Her friends' mobile association, sutured by abstract character, can be fully achieved, therefore, only when Eliza is gone.[55] Ironically, it is Sanford who begins this work, neutralizing Eliza's melancholy critique of her friends' severe judgments. "I have, at last, accomplished the removal of my darling girl, from a place where she thought every eye accused, and every heart condemned her," he writes to his friend Deighton. "She had become quite romantic in her notions" (232). With Eliza's challenge neutralized as "romance," her friends claim full confidence in their benevolent grief, as Julia does when she writes to Lucy,

"How sincerely, my dear Mrs. Summer, must the friends of our departed Eliza, sympathize with each other" (235). As Sanford's scornful deployment of romance suggests, Eliza's friends recover from their grief by cathecting their pleasures not on a person, but on a text. As Claire Pettengill succinctly notes, "It is as if, in the eyes of her friends, Eliza's confessional letters, as well as the scraps of writing which mark her final days, redeem her by permitting her again to become the subject of examination and judgment by the female circle, fulfilling her function as a woman and a sister."[56] The novel suggests, then, that we as readers should similarly cathect onto the printimacies of the novel, thereby normalizing a "fated" loss of presence. Julia says as much to Lucy: "These valuable testimonies of the affecting sense, and calm expectation she entertained of her approaching dissolution, are calculated to sooth and comfort the minds of mourning connections. They greatly alleviate the regret occasioned by her absence, at this awful period" (236).

Against the assertion that print will successfully suture the inventive intimacies of friendship ruptured by normative character and geographic mobility, Eliza goes on valuing friendship, even unto death. Declaring that she remains "still feelingly alive to the power of friendship" (194), Eliza proclaims, "It is an ill-natured, misjudging world and I am not obliged to sacrifice my friends to its opinion" (204) and resolves to "seek shelter among strangers, where none knows, or is interested in my melancholy story" (231). For Eliza's friends, death takes on the meaning of fated failure, shame's inevitable trajectory. Yet if her emotional state at the end was not, as her friends assert, shamed repentance for her fall into romance but a dedication to nondisclosure as the way to keep alive the social imaginary of friendship, then death, at least for Eliza, becomes a place beyond guilt (Eliza tells Julia that she flees her mother's home so "that her displeasure may not follow me to the grave" [221]), beyond criminality (Eliza urges Julia "to bury my crime in the grave with me" [231]), and beyond memory (Eliza predicts that "in the grave there is no remembrance" [234]). Guilt, criminality, and memory are the constitutive elements of the cohering normalcy predicated on a print cathexis, of the movements of intimacy from interpersonal inventiveness to abstract character, which has pushed Eliza into silence from the beginning of the novel. Death might be understood, then, not in its literal sense as closure or finality but, rather, as a holding place for those aspirations denied by civic character, the ultimate mystery in a society that makes full visibility a necessity of civic "life." If Eliza has entered *that* space, then she has indeed "made a happy exchange of worlds" (236).[57]

In the end, *The Coquette* shows that the imagined communities established through printimacy relied on a death-in(to)-character that gave rise to constructions of apparently viable sociality (such as those Eliza's friends construct at the novel's end through their "healthy" management of grief and desire) that require the death, if not of otherly desiring and non-consenting bodies, then of their social imaginations. Unlike Irving's tale, however, which quickly mends the rip in the social fabric of citizens' everyday lives through the abstract associations based on liberal character, Foster's heroine clings tenaciously to the possibility of inventive intimacy, despite the social transformations of her age. Friendship, for Eliza, involves a self-conscious invention beyond the interior prescriptions of federal affect and the civil institutions it generated. There are no laws governing friendship, few financial contracts, even a relatively small number of informal rituals to give it shape. In the absence of abstract patterns, friends, as Foucault observes, "face each other without terms or convenient words, with nothing to assure them about the meaning of the movement that carries them toward each other. They have to invent, from A to Z, a relationship that is still formless, which is friendship: that is to say, the sum of everything through which they can give each other pleasure." What is troubling to society about friendship, what makes Eliza's friends rush to prioritize the more ritualized relationships of the romantic couple and the nuclear family, is its enactment of "everything that can be uncomfortable in affection, tenderness, . . . fidelity, camaraderie, and companionship, things which our rather sanitized society can't allow a place for without fearing the formation of new allegiances and the tying together of unforeseen lines of force." Generating alliances based not on the abstract character traits tied to productive labor and hierarchical social order, but to the inventive pleasures negotiated—and renegotiated—in a spirit of historical contingency, "an historic occasion to re-open affective and relational virtualities," friendship holds the potential power to "yield a culture and an ethics," even ones that compete with nationalism itself.[58] Yet friendship, in Eliza's lifetime, was already being consigned to nostalgia, a live feeling visible only through a dead convention, by the abstract traits of character and the supposed joys of broad affiliation that subsumed the more hands-on negotiations of communal intimacy. It was not just marriage, as Eliza claims, but managed interiority itself that was the tomb of friendship.

As writers of gothic tales a half-century later well knew, however, tombs do not always contain their dead, who continue to speak, through the mourning bodies of their survivors, where the lingering rage of melancholia (which Eliza's friends report even as they dispute it) disrupts the settled character of national-normative life. That dissent is incorporated into the bodies of the living. In mourning Eliza, after all, her survivors engage in the very acts of wayward desire and identification—with her, of her, in place of her—that her death is meant to foreclose. No wonder the censorious Lucy writes to Eliza, apropos of *Romeo and Juliet*, "Death is too serious a matter to be sported with!" (195). It is tempting to say that democracy was dying from the moment it was born. That would certainly explain why we practice so little of it today. Yet even as her friends gather to mourn her loss, they enact the intimacy she always hoped for. Eliza's death becomes not the end of her story, then, but a threshold metaphor between the civil sphere regulated by federal affect and some more fantastic space, where democracy is crafted from the stuff of intimate life. This is Eliza's legacy to the ongoing drama of democracy in the United States.

Melancholy Associations

Eliza's death produced its own ambivalences in her readership, producing in turn a melancholy visible in the repeated resurrection of "Eliza Wharton" as the ungrieved possibility for different social configurations in nineteenth-century America. That persistent melancholy, I will argue in the last chapter, became the queer emotions of the American romance. For now, suffice it to say that melancholic disruptions of abstract association constitute a potent counter-narrative to Irving's sanguine tale of grief resolved, asserting a lingering hope for networks of responsibility and pleasure generated by people who are willing to negotiate, among themselves, relationships beyond the bounds of abstract character. When this vision competes with the managed privacies of federal affect, Eliza Wharton is dead but not forgotten.

Eliza's legacy may be most explicit in Caroline Dall's bizarre *The Romance of the Association; or, One Last Glimpse of Charlotte Temple and Eliza Wharton* (1875), in which the unnamed narrator purports to discover and transcribe Eliza's posthumous "scraps of writing."[59] Mostly addressed to the eighteenth-century poet Joel Barlow, these found letters reveal that Eliza was never seduced by a libertine but married a foreigner "of rank and distinction, probably some man younger than herself."[60] Dall redeems Eliza not only from charges of coquetry, but from melancholy as well. While Foster's novel "plunges Eliza into dejection and despair," Dall's shows her "cheerful, industrious, and useful" (67). While the former "represents her as confessing her guilt, confiding in her friends, and writing to her mother," the latter insists that "no confession passed her lips, no confidence was ever given, no letter was ever written by her, for the simple reason that all the circumstances of her departure were open and natural" (67). Defending Eliza against "parental tyranny, fraternal censorship, and social abandonment" (10), Dall returns her from the dead in a victorious confirmation of "the strength and beauty of Eliza's character," which "have kept her memory green under the suspicion of great error" (13).

Ironically, Dall redeems Eliza using the very terms that Foster's heroine disavows: a print-confirmed character generated by consensual conformity to the private life of marriage. Open and natural, fully visible and legible, Eliza loses the resistant silence through which she escapes circulation in *The Coquette*. Nevertheless, Dall uses Eliza to generate the imaginative intimacies that federal affect disabled but did not kill. In Dall's recounting, Eliza maintains her imaginative fortitude, writing to her unnamed husband, "Expect every thing, hope every thing, and *do* every thing to make your circumstances agreeable" (88), adding, "Keep up your spirits, and be certain of the constant affection of your friends" (94). Dall's Eliza privileges near neighbors, not distant correspondents, in maintaining affections that are explicitly public in their benefits. In a letter to Mrs. Barlow, she writes, "I have always thought myself very public-spirited, and know that the riches of a community consists [*sic*] in the number of its inhabitants" (99). The narrator begins as a resistant reader of Foster's novel: "Of course, I was too young to take in the whole meaning of her story: still I detected its inconsistencies: I wondered over its stilted sentiment, the severe rebukes she received, and the almost idolatrous love she inspired; and the older I grew, the more perplexed I became" (31). The narrator's ambivalence— toward Eliza (could she have been so perfect as to inspire idolatry?) as well as toward the stern rebukes and stilted sentiments attributed to her friends—leads her to challenge her own inherited knowledge. When she asks her grandmother about her memories of reading *The Coquette*, the old woman's irritable reply launches the narrator's revisionary labors:

"There is only one lesson for *you* to learn from 'The Coquette.' *You* are to mind your mother. If Eliza Wharton had done as her mother bade her, she would have died quietly in Hartford, and nobody would have called her hard names."

"But, grandmamma, was she a bad woman? If she was, what did you go to her grave for, and why do the young lovers like to talk of her?"

"I don't think she was," my grandmother reluctantly admitted. "She said she was a married woman with her dying breath, and her ring was buried with her. Her husband must have been a cruel man. She was always expecting him, but he never came. If he had loved her as he ought, she would not have died alone. But, whatever *he* was, *she* was true to him: she never gave the least hint of his name; she burned all her papers, and kept his secrets, and so perhaps some woman loved him after she was dead. Her faithfulness was what the young lovers liked. Why, child, your own grandmother came home in tears from her grave the night she was promised to your grandfather!"

"Then the book can't tell the truth!"

"Can't it?" It was an old story to my grandmother, and she would not pursue it. But I thought of it all through my maiden life, never once accepting the conclusions of the novel, and always wishing that I could go to Danvers and stand upon her grave. (32–33)

The narrator and her grandmother conspire to recast Foster's heroine as the virtuous wife that was the ideal of Eliza's friends in the earlier novel. The explicit goal of the narrator's resistant reading is to redeem Eliza's "character," not to continue her critique of heteronormative privacy.

Dall's framing narrative extends Eliza's message, however, deploying a skeptical inventiveness made possible by local and nonconforming negotiations of sociality. If the narrator cannot imagine Eliza freed from the imperatives of proper character, the act of reinterpreting Eliza takes the narrator herself beyond convention. The search for Eliza's story brings the narrator into contact with a variety of people—Eliza's surviving nephew, the foster sister whom he loved in childhood, tavern owners and antiquarians with evidence about Eliza, and so on—who have all, in various ways, resisted conventional social arrangements. (Most are single, invested in professions, memories of vaguely incestuous love, or same-sex friendship rather than marriage or child raising.) In part because of the freedom provided by their unconventional lives, these strangers can come together physically to provide the comfort Eliza's friends denied. "When we parted," the narrator reports, "it was to meet once more to read over Eliza's letters. We were all tremulous with a strange delight when we remembered that she who had waked up yester-morn, friendless and poor, shorn of all the natural results of a most useful life, could now lie down in peace, sure that a friendly hand would compose her to her rest" (61).

In the end, the intimacy generated by the narrator's search for Eliza's story represents a nostalgic wish for a way of life reminiscent of Irving's "Rip Van Winkle." "If I am asked for proofs," Dall writes, "I have none to give, but I do not doubt that they exist in some of the inedited [*sic*] manuscripts hidden at the moment within the sheltering roofs along the Connecticut River" (112). Buried in those neighborhoods is a communal memory placed beyond the reach of nineteenth-century Americans by the yoking of science and reform that, as I discuss in later chapters, interiorized social orders that Eliza saw as dire threats to the intimacy of near neighbors. Ironically, the "Association" of Dall's title refs not to the confederation that pieces together Eliza's counter-narrative, but to the American Association for the Advancement of Science, a group to which the narrator belongs, among whom she discovers Eliza's nephew, and to whom she presents her narration. As the next chapter will show, the transformation of "association" into "Association" accurately reflects the widespread institutionalization of affiliation in the years between Foster's novel and Dall's. In the midst of institutional reform's determined mapping of the interior's regulated orders, however, Dall's counter-narrative suggests the unpredictable ways inner life may generate resistant socialities protected by—even as they are unaccounted for within—the normative formations of privacy. If such faith is largely untenable ("If I am asked for proofs, I have none to give"), its melancholic persistence is still productive of the social skepticism and imaginative reformulations that Dall rightly characterizes as "romance."

2

BAD ASSOCIATIONS: SOCIALITY, INTERIORITY, INSTITUTIONALISM

Objecting to the Massachusetts Supreme Judicial Court's 2003 ruling that gays and lesbians may legally marry, U.S. President George W. Bush asserted, "Marriage is a sacred institution between a man and a woman." Bush might have said, "a sacred bond" or "union," but he chose "institution" because, as Malcolm Gladwell reasons, "nobody imagines that the court's decision will actually jeopardize the personal bond between any particular man and any particular woman."[1] In addition, however, Bush's remark expresses something important about the role of institutions in cultural politics. While Gladwell describes institutions as "place[s] to hide when we can't find our principles,"[2] it is more accurate to say that institutions erode our capacity for principled public action. As this chapter will show, asserting the authority to define private good while strategically blurring the lines between public and private life (to make the private management of interiorized "character" appear as public participation), institutions separate "principles" (now the individual business of managed privacy) from "public action" (now the responsibility of abstract authority) in ways that make unthinkable the ethical behaviors Gladwell invokes.

But why should debates about institutions arise in the specific context of queer intimacy? Institutions, Gladwell notes, offer citizens the impression that "there is some abstract thing out there . . . that is bigger than them and will long outlive them all, and that it needs to be nourished and protected with socially approved behavior."[3] Promising futurity (they will outlive any constitutive member), institutions assume social responsibility and distribute socially accepted behavior ("character"). Attributing these qualities to institutions, however, requires locating their opposing traits somewhere else. If we take those other traits to be an interest in undeferred gratification and a disregard of "normal" social principles, we can see how queer people, who reportedly surrender a self-regulating (and self-sacrificing) commitment to social and biological reproduction in favor of an unprincipled hedonism in the present, become institutionalism's other.

The final question we might ask of Bush's "misspeak" is how gay marriage brings about a panic over institutional security—or, to ask the question differently, why gay-marriage debates crop up concurrently with concerns over other forms of social unease and dissent. Marriage, I would argue, is the privatized theater in which dramas of national security are made comprehensible to a radically de-publicized citizenry. Paranoid claims about the institutional threat posed by queer demands to be included in social normalcy localize the spread of global dissent across the purportedly impenetrable borders of the nation, permitting politicians to resuscitate a failing nationalism in the name of "domestic institutions" (the not-quite-nationalism of the "homeland"). Here is Sandy Rios, president of Concerned Women for America, calling for a constitutional amendment to prohibit gay marriages: "if you don't do something about this [gay marriage], then you cannot [complain] in 20 years—when you see the American public disintegrating and you see our enemies overtaking us because we have no moral will."[4] Rios links the futures of generational reproduction, civic responsibility, and social normality in opposition not only to the enemy without, but also to the more potent one within, sexuality, which requires continual self-scrutiny and self-management, privatized anti-terrorism.[5]

Before dismissing Rios's absurd equation of foreign enemies and married gays and lesbians, however, note her assertion of a public sphere where citizens are free to "do something." Even as Rios asserts the possibility of action in such a sphere, the twin assertions that underlie the marriage controversy—that private life (marriage) is equivalent to public life (making privacy virtually public) and that the public is threatened by reimaginings of what social affinity might comprise in the present (not in twenty years)—require properly patriotic citizens to defend institutions by remaining private and normatively immobile. Rios's proposition—that citizens can "do something" in "public"—is thus a trace fantasy that supplements the erosion of civic agency by the very normative institutions she wishes citizens to defend.

If, as the previous chapter argued, Eliza Wharton's story suggests a struggle within the intimate rhetorics of federal affect, her posthumous "resurrection" within the American Association for the Advancement of Science allegorizes intimacy's management within a public sphere that has been newly constituted as a network of institutions. While some institutions in antebellum America (as in our own day) enhanced citizens' quality of life in beneficial ways (one could think of lending libraries, public schools, or abolition societies, for instance), the *theory* of institutionality diminished citizenship and democratic participation in crucial ways. It is this theory, a discursive meta-institution, rather than particular institutional practices, which I refer to here as "institutionalism."

While particular couples may engage in the "institution" of marriage to organize their intimate lives in creative ways, for example, the discursive uses to which marriage is put in the public sphere serve the interests not of those couples, but of a less inventive, more normative conception of citizens' roles in the nation and the world. Institutionalism dominated the social theory of antebellum America's most influential thinkers, men such as Alexis de Tocqueville, Lyman Beecher, Ralph Waldo Emerson, William Lloyd Garrison, and, above all, Francis Lieber, antebellum America's most eminent political theorist. Placing institutions at the center of America's social, political, and territorial growth, these men purported to manage the sociality through which strangers, left to their own resources, might engage in the contingent and inventive productions of what, following the Declaration of Independence, we might call happiness.

In return for the deferred happiness demanded by institutionality, citizens were offered a horizon of immanent satisfaction, a "future."[6] Since citizens see that future only as a receding horizon, institutionalism also generated a realm of private management—the human interior, home of unruly and insistent appetites—over which to enact the agency that was short-circuited in the public sphere by the deferrals of futurity. As the potential for public satisfaction became internalized as the demand of unappeasable appetite, the pleasures of public action became internalized as self-inspection and self-correction. Although Jürgen Habermas asserts that the civil sphere "assumed the peculiar ambivalence of public regulation and private initiative," the history of antebellum institutionalization suggests the opposite.[7] Civility's ambivalence arose from public initiative and private regulation. "Initiative" became the drive toward a horizon of always receding futurity (institutionalism), while privacy, now the realm of consumption ("appetite"), was granted the not quite corollary agency of self-government, the regulation of appetites. How this rather unappealing version of interiority became naturalized as the common sense of American democracy is intrinsically tied to the growth of institutionalism in America.

That story of institutionality's rise is indistinguishable, in the United States, from the popularity of social reform. The transformation of relatively disorganized tract and foreign-mission societies into the vast national networks of the American Temperance Society and the American Anti-Slavery Society apparently instantiates the Habermasian narrative of private virtue turned to public debate through an impressive mobilization of "publicity" (newspapers such as Garrison's *Liberator*, for instance) that engaged "public opinion" in critical opposition to the state. This account has much to recommend it, but its depiction of power is flat, showing how public opinion moves the state but neglecting how state discourses shape private character. If institutions as instruments of critical debate facilitated the development of reform, they also served as an apparatus of civil discipline, establishing the at times tense relationships between universality and particularity, order and outrage. Antebellum reform, in turn, granted institutionalism its most characteristic features: apparent benevolence, the assurance of untroubled futurity, and the promise of civic depth. These constitutive traits—affect, futurity, and interiority—are the topic of the sections that follow, which together challenge the location of interpellative abstraction at the level of the nation and suggest that the civil sphere is itself the primary realm not of "free" critical debate, but of restricted sociality.[8]

Struggles over the institutionalization of the civil sphere are evident, however, in the haunting presence of Catholicism within antebellum institutional theory. Anxious narratives of the Pope's plot to undermine American democracy by having priests, in the secrecy of confessionals, tell Catholic parishioners how to vote proliferated in the 1830s (the very moment organized reform emerged in the public sphere). These tales, centered on the power of the Catholic church as a monstrous institution, were often set forth by institutionalism's strongest proponents. As such, they represent both institutionalism's guilty conscience and its most effective diversionary tactic, undermining the proximate intimacies (priests and congregants) and private indulgences (the confessional) of citizens generally. It is possible, therefore, that grotesque tales of convent atrocities such as Maria Monk's *Awful Disclosures of the Hotel Dieu Nunnery in Montreal* (1836) became bestsellers not only because they were proto-pornography, but also because they offered an early critique of institutionalism to a citizenry that was beginning to feel its power over public participation.

Nobody Rules

While the shift from association to Association might appear innocuous, citizens lose something substantial in the change. That something, according to Hannah Arendt, is the possibility of political action necessary to democratic society. What makes a citizen a political being, for Arendt, is the active capacity "to get together with his peers, to act in concert, and to reach out for goals and enterprises that would never enter his mind, let alone the desires of his heart, had he not been given this gift—to embark on something new."[9] Political freedom, for Arendt, rests on the conditions of proximate and negotiated invention —"to get together with [one's] peers" in order "to act in concert" to create "something new"—that Eliza Wharton struggles to realize in *The Coquette*. Freedom, for Arendt as for Hannah Foster, bears a close kinship to intimacy: the desires of the heart are a collective invention (desires arise from social mingling, not the other way around) that, in turn, enables new social imaginaries, the exercise of freedom.

The greatest threat to political freedom, then, is not brutish tyranny but, as Eliza's story dramatizes, geographic mobility and its subsequent bureaucratization, which abstracts power beyond contestation. "In a fully developed bureaucracy," Arendt writes, "there is nobody left with whom one can argue, to whom one can present grievances, on whom the pressures of power can be exerted."[10] Denied the possibility of action in response to rules, citizens lose the capacity for freedom, by which Arendt means the ability to identify and respond collectively, responsibly, and at times conflictually across differences of perspective and opinion to the conditions of social organization. As citizens lose the capacity to gather, to negotiate, and to act, bureaucracies absorb the authority to speak and act in the name of those citizens, so that power becomes exercised on behalf of a nominal agent, but only to the degree that the named agent ("the people") surrender their capacity to create and to act for themselves (the process that Marx, in *The German Ideology*, calls "estrangement").[11] When citizens no longer feel responsible for and to each other, a condition Arendt calls "the bureaucratization of public life," they experience severe frustration, leading to the violence endemic to modernity.[12]

For Arendt, "bureaucracies" are intrinsically tied to state government. "Bureaucracy is the form of government in which everybody is deprived of political freedom, of the power to act," she argues, "for the rule by Nobody is not no-rule, and where all are equally powerless, we have a tyranny without a tyrant." Although Arendt maintains the centrality of the state, the "transformation of government into administration, or of republics into bureaucracies, and the disastrous shrinkage of the public realm that went with it,"[13] required a more significant, although (because) less visible transfer of power, not from government to bureaucracies, but from bureaucracies to institutions. If bureaucracies are governments without identifiably powerful figures ("tyrants"), institutions are bureaucracies without the identifiable structures of governmentality—they are administrations that can pass, that is, as direct agency. At the same time, because institutions, as I will show shortly, bear a close relation to the proximate intimacies they surrogate, they seem to compensate citizens' loss with an aura of benevolent promise, the compensation of affective interiority and of generational futurity. The transformation from association to Association, then, requires that institutions, while gaining control over the always deferred horizons of social action ("futurity"), grant citizens the interiorities that are the trace of lived social affinity in the here and now.

In his 1835 *A Plea for the West*, the influential theologian and educator Lyman Beecher warned readers that "the conflict which is to decide the destiny of the West will be a conflict of institutions for the education of her sons, for purposes of superstition or evangelical light, of despotism, or liberty."[14] While Beecher locates manifest destiny in the imperial spread not of military nationalism, but of civil institutions, he also acknowledges the contested nature of those institutions (or, rather, the cultural contest that is covered over by what he presents as a choice between kinds of institutions, thereby foreclosing any potential debate over the desirability of institutionality itself). Dangerous institutions are brought to the West, in Beecher's account, by "foreign emigrants . . . unaccustomed to self-government, inaccessible to education, and easily accessible to prepossession, and inveterate credulity, and intrigue, and easily embodied and wielded by sinister design" (51). Beecher lumps together this hodgepodge of credulous, embodied, intriguing behaviors as "superstition": old-world beliefs passed orally among those denied formal education. Beecher subtly transforms immigrants' geographic displacement (from one nation-state to another) into temporal displacement (from the past to a more modern present) and therefore renders their beliefs always already lost, hardly worth defending. At the same time, Beecher acknowledges superstitions' lingering power to attract, characterizing their hold over the credulous as "despotism," both populist and commanding. In contrast to backward-looking superstitions, home-grown "evangelical" institutions are forward-looking, tied by Beecher's appeal on behalf of "our sons" to generational futurity. Because Beecher has pushed the realization of "liberty" into the (always deferred) generational future, he can posit institutions as liberty's fittest instruments.

While Beecher may well have imagined institutionalization as being *for* the people, however, he certainly never conceived it as being *of* them. In fact, institutions are valuable precisely because they prevent the danger that "our intelligence and virtue will falter and fall back into a dark minded, vicious populace—a poor, uneducated, reckless mass of infuriated animalism" (39). Not surprisingly, given this Hobbesian view of a degraded populace, Beecher saw institutions, not "universal suffrage" (42), as the safeguard of democracy. Only when "republican institutions" (42) have brought about "the education of the head and heart of the nation" (42) so as to imbue them "with intelligence and virtue" (42) could people be trusted to rule themselves.

If the unschooled masses could not be trusted with democracy, however, neither could the nation-state, which, attempting order only through "effort at arms-length" (38), necessarily fails to reach the "heads and hearts" of the people. Civil institutions obviate the need for a state without challenging the state's drive toward ordered expansion. In establishing proper civil institutions, Beecher assured readers, the "government of force will cease, and that of intelligence and virtue will take its place; and nation after nation cheered by our example will follow in our footsteps till the whole earth is free" (38), institutions having generated "the power to evangelize the world" (10). Between the "mob rule" of the people and the coercive force of the state, institutions seemingly generate consensual order, voluntary labor, and domestic and foreign expansion, all with the benevolence that only an agency without agents (what Arendt calls "rule by Nobody") can achieve.

To accomplish this goal, however, Beecher had to project an abstract middle ground representing a disciplined conformity of "public sentiment" that apparently sutures the geographic distance brought about by territorial expansion. "And so various are the opinions and habits," Beecher lamented, "and so recent and imperfect is the acquaintance, and so sparse are the settlements of the West, that no homogenous public sentiment can be formed to legislate immediately into being, the requisite institutions" (16). Institutions, Beecher imagined, would turn multiple populations with diverse customs and beliefs into a single entity, "the public," capable of abstracting and hence supplanting previous cultural systems. Beecher's association of such institutions with "liberty" becomes troubled, however, when one asks—as Eliza did of her friends—whose authority (whose definition of virtuous sentiment) will establish such institutions (if, that is, the people are themselves too base and the nation-state is too distant to conceive of virtuous institutions). Beecher dodged this problem with a paradox: the people will call forth institutions, which in turn will ensure (not coercively, but through the benevolence of the passive voice) that public sentiment is to "be formed" (38). But the troubling question of responsibility arises again when the public sentiment formed by evangelical institutions "legislates." Institutions, for Beecher, are separable from the too-distant state (necessarily so in territories), yet they carry out the labor of the state—to legislate—in the state's absence. Having posed institutions as the surrogate of the state (the state made more effectively disciplinary because more local in its effects on "our sons") and supplanted the operations of local community (more effective because regimented and coordinated into an abstract "public"), institutions can both bring "sentiment" into being and arise as its desired object. Beecher guards from scrutiny the paradoxical yet constitutive yoking of "systematized" and "voluntary" by placing institutionalism's agency under erasure, within the sphere of "nowhere" (the place where "Nobody" rules) that Arendt locates at the core of antidemocratic bureaucratization.

Freed (at least, grammatically) from the embodied agency of constitutive members, institutions become seemingly immune as well to the vicissitudes of history, attaching instead to a realm of pure—if opaque—futurity. Institutions, Beecher asserted, run by "a perpetual self-preserving energy." It is not the past, not "anniversary resolutions and fourth of July orations," but the future, guaranteed "by well systematized voluntary associations" (43), that makes social and biological reproduction imperative. If the promise of democracy is endlessly deferred into a future when our always cited grandchildren will enjoy the freedom we forswear, we need the guarantee not only that there will be grandchildren, but also that, for all of our fictions of generational improvement, those descendants will want or be able to enjoy the same political and social structures we bulwark in their names today. Change and stasis, progress and permanence, choreographed in this unsteady promise, are seemingly stabilized through a paradoxical futurity I have been calling institutionality: an abstract structure that apparently guarantees a stasis of order across and despite the historical changes endemic to generation. What allows us to believe, evidence to the contrary, that biological reproduction will correspond to social reproduction, that "our" way of life has a future, is the presence of institutions that are supposedly free from the vicissitudes of fashion and ideology (that is, of history) and of will or whimsy (that is, of agency).

While institutionalism seemingly guarantees the nation's future, it also generates certain apparent compensations for citizens who must now wait for democracy's fulfillment. Those compensations—interiority and its traces of affective sociability or collaborative agency—along with futurity, are what distinguish institutions from what Arendt calls bureaucracies. If entrance into institutions requires the suspension (if not the surrender) of memory and mutual responsibility, institutions offer in return agency in the form of self-management, the maintenance of one's qualification for membership in institutions. We become, that is, administrators not of social relations or even of institutions per se, but of ourselves. For this to happen, we need to be given interiority, an "inner" and often unruly domain (the simulacrum of the social), over which "management" is necessary. The growth of institutions relies on the deepening of interiority. (It is significant, for instance, that Beecher quickly substitutes the affective phrase "public sentiment" for the more cerebral "opinion.") This is why institutionality makes such sharp—and often absurd—appearances in discussions of intimate relationships where institutions play no obvious role. Such moments of conflict offer insight into the function of institutionalism in cultural politics (or, rather, into the role institutionalism plays in rendering politics "cultural"), as well as into the characterization of certain forms of association and the people who practice them (how, Beecher might say, such people become "embodied and wielded") as abnormal, unhealthy, and nonproductive, institutionalism's others. The hinge that binds progress and permanence, intimacy and institutionalism, embodied abnormality and abstract publicity, as the cultural skirmishes around marriage suggest, is love.

Love's Future

The most obvious opposition to association in antebellum America might be thought to come not from institutionalism, but from its apparent opposite: individualism. The two ideologies—individualism and institutionalism—share more, however, than might at first appear, not least their opposition to an ethics of communal life. Individualism's most eloquent and consistent advocates were, of course, the Transcendentalists, particularly Ralph Waldo Emerson and his friend and student Henry David Thoreau. By tracing their attacks on association and by examining Emerson's theories of love, however, we can see that transcendental individualism derived from and supported the institutional promises of abstract futurity and self-managing interiority that animated the institutional theory of men like Beecher.

Nineteenth-century reform, I suggested earlier, played an instrumental role in transforming the public sphere into a network of interrelated institutions that supplanted, rather than enhanced, citizens' participation in public life. It is nevertheless true that within the circle of New England reformers, hope persisted that reform might regenerate associational life, manifested in the rural communities—Fruitlands, Brook Farm, and Hopedale, most famously—begun by reformers such as Charles Lane, Adin Ballou, and Charles Dana in the early 1840s. The complex response of social reformers to collective social life became most evident, however, in Boston's 1844 Amory Hall lectures on the topic of "Association." Those lectures created an apparent choice between a solitary individualism understood as private and a publicity conceived in the organizational logics of benevolent institutionalism. Corollary to this split was the citizen's apparent choice between a privatized and individualized interiority and an abstracted public character. If reform privileged the public by casting the private as the site of errant, sinful, and unhealthy impulses, transcendentalism privileged the private by casting the public as the outcome of impersonal and ineffectual rhetoric.

For twelve Sundays between February 4 and April 21, 1844, many of New England's best-known social reformers addressed audiences on topics such as slavery and the annexation of Texas, women's rights and the limitations of bourgeois marriage, and temperance and the neurological health of the body.[15] Organized by a committee headed by William Lloyd Garrison, the lectures met with general enthusiasm from "the spell-bound audience" composed, as Garrison put it, of "disturbers of the peace" committed to "irreverently exposing the corruptions of the Church and the State."[16]

Some of the speakers chose to disturb the peace of the reformers themselves, however. On March 3, Emerson accused his audience of attempting to fix in society defects they were unable—or unwilling—to cure in themselves. Emerson warned that "society gains nothing whilst a man, not himself renovated, attempts to renovate things around him: he has become tediously good in some particular, but negligent and narrow in the rest; and hypocrisy and vanity are often the disgusting result."[17] Focusing his criticism particularly on the obfuscations required by institutional reform, he continued,

> I have failed, and you have failed, but perhaps together we shall not fail. Our housekeeping is not satisfactory to us, but perhaps a phalanx, a community, might be. Many of us have differed in opinion, and we could find no man who could make the truth plain, but possibly a college, or ecclesiastical council might. I have not been able either to persuade my brother or to prevail on myself, to disuse the traffic or the potation of brandy, but perhaps a pledge of total abstinence might effectually restrain us. The candidate my party votes for is not to be trusted with a dollar, but he will be honest in the Senate, for we can bring public opinion to bear on him. Thus concert was the specific in all cases. But concert is neither better nor worse, neither more nor less potent than individual force. (17)

It turns out, however, that "individual force" *is* better, in Emerson's opinion. "Every project in the history of reform, no matter how violent and surprising," he told the audience, "is good, which is the dictate of a man's genius and constitution, but very dull and suspicious when adopted from another" (13).

The following Sunday, Henry David Thoreau, a stranger to most in the hall, struck a similar chord, albeit with more pointedly sour notes. Seeming to praise his audience, Thoreau began by contrasting reformers, who "are no doubt the true ancestors of the next generation," to conservatives, who "naturally herd together for mutual protection. They say We and Our, as if they had never been assured of an individual existence. Our Indian policy; our coast defences [sic], our national character. They are what are called public men, fashionable men, ambitious men, chaplains of the army or navy; men of property, standing and respectability, for the most part, and in all cases created by society."[18] Despite their superiority to conservatives, however, reformers, according to Thoreau, are sick with "tradition and conformity and infidelity" (181), projecting as social evil "some obscure, and perhaps unrecognized private grievance" (184). The "ills" of reform, for Thoreau, are comically literal. "Now, if anything ail a man so that he does not perform his functions," he claimed, "especially if his digestion is poor, though he may have considerable nervous strength left; if he has failed in all his undertakings hitherto; if he has committed some heinous sin and partially repents, what does he do? He sets about reforming the world" (183).

While the Transcendentalists certainly underestimated the generous motives that brought many reformers to their efforts to improve society, they nevertheless exposed an important aspect of antebellum reform, which, as Thoreau notes, popularized human character as inherently frail (prone to temptation from drink, urban squalor, or sensuality) or depraved (prone to seduce others into drink, urban squalor, or sensuality). Pointedly criticizing reform's gothic vision of a degraded and corrupt humanity, Thoreau denounced "the death that presumes to give laws to life" and accused his auditors of "affirming essential disease and disorder to the child who has just begun to bathe his senses and his understanding in the perception of order and beauty" (192). As Thoreau curtly put it, "It is rare that we are able to impart wealth to our fellows, and do not surround them with our own cast off griefs as an atmosphere, and name it sympathy" (191). Antebellum reformers, as Thoreau suggested, often made pain and degradation the keys to authorized personhood in their salvation dramas. To gain public notice, one needed to become the object of popular sympathy, not the subject of social demand, and therefore one needed to project an interior stuffed with suffering injustice. As more and more citizens became the objects of reform movements—from the relatively contained populations of the heathen or the enslaved, reform expanded to tipplers, masturbators, workers, bad eaters, housewives, romance readers, and corset wearers—the condition of degradation spread, becoming by the mid-1840s nearly normative. Not only did this displace the structural suffering of slaves, the poor, or the disenfranchised, locating the cause of their suffering in individual flaws of character that everyone potentially shared, but it obscured the potential for politics—modes of collective organization and social demand—based on anything other than degradation, pain, or suffering. Targeting sensuality and appetite of various kinds and the forms of sociality based on them (the enjoyment of brandy, of rich foods, of fine dress, of non-reproductive sex), reformers can even be said to have misrepresented the pursuit of happiness *as* the experience of degradation, thereby alienating citizens from their capacity for pleasure. Against this tendency, Thoreau urged the audience, "Be green and flourishing plants in God's nursery, and not such complaining bleeding trees as Dante saw in the Infernal Regions" (191).

Despite their cogent criticism, however, Emerson and Thoreau mostly faulted social reformers for their propensity toward small-"a" association. Accusing reformers of the same rigidity and conformity associated with church and state, Emerson and Thoreau claimed that the kinship between "institutions" and the "reliance on Association" (Emerson, 16) accounted for the pyrrhic outcomes of most reform endeavors. While reformers begin by making institutions their target—"With the din of opinion and debate, there was a keener scrutiny of institutions and domestic life than any we had known" (13)—they end, Emerson asserted, by demanding the same "destructive tax in my conformity" (14). Here Emerson was repeating his claim in "Self-Reliance" (1841) that he was "ashamed to think how easily we capitulate to badges and names, to large societies and dead institutions."[19] Representing his audience's purported difference from conventional institutions as vain posturing, he declared, "No one gives the impression of superiority to the institutional, which he must give who will reform it" (16). Thoreau went further, declaring, "I know of few radicals as yet who are radical enough, and have not got their name rather by meddling with the exposed roots of innocent institutions than with their own" (183). Lampooning the bureaucracy of associational reform, Thoreau claimed, "There have been meetings, religious, political and reformatory, to which men came a hundred miles—though all they had to offer were—some resolutions!" (187).

In opposition to their associational auditors, Emerson and Thoreau insisted that successful reform could come only through radical individuality. A true reformer, Thoreau claimed, "must not rely solely on logic and argument, or on eloquence and oratory for his success, but see that he represents one pretty perfect institution in himself, the centre and circumference of all others, an erect man" (184). Claiming to hold "no objection to action in societies or communities, when it is the individual using the society as his instrument, rather than the society using the individual," he nevertheless insisted, "The great benefactors of their race have been single and singular and not masters of men" (186). "Consider, after all," Thoreau urged his audience,

> how very private and silent an affair it is to lead a life—that we do not consider our duties, or the actions of our life, as in a caucus or convention of

men, where the subject has been before the meeting a long time, and many resolutions have been proposed and passed, and now one speaker has the floor and then another, and the subject is fairly under discussion; but the convention where our most private and intimate affairs are discussed is very thinly attended, almost we are not there ourselves, that is the go-to-meetings part of us. It is very still, and few resolutions get passed. Few words are spoken, and the hours are not counted! (187)

Thoreau subordinates what he perceives as the institutionalism of public reform to the interiorized state of the private heart, far removed from the noisy, crowded, animated publicity of gatherings such as the Amory lectures. Yet he also maintains the sensation of rich sociality, of discussed affairs and actions.

The claims made by Emerson and Thoreau notwithstanding, however, individualism and institutionalism were not as distinct as they might appear. To begin with, they share a firm belief in an unruly interior that necessitates continual vigilance and self-management. While Emerson famously declared, "an institution is the lengthened shadow of one man,"[20] he might more accurately have identified institutionalism as the lengthy shadow *in* one man, the dark space of interiority that counterbalances the transcendent pull of the Oversoul. If he would leave the reformer alone with his heart, Thoreau also granted him a compensatory inner depth. "Most whom I meet in the streets," Thoreau told his audience, "are, so to speak, outward bound, they live out and out, are going and coming, looking before and behind, all out of doors and in the air. I would fain see them inward bound, retiring in and in, farther and farther every day, and when I inquired for them I should not hear, that they had gone abroad anywhere, to Rondont or Sackets Harbor, but that they had withdrawn deeper within the folds of being" (194). Resisting reformers' drive toward association, Thoreau made private interiority the site of all properly conceived reform: "Is not our own interior white on the chart? Inward is a direction which no traveller has taken. Inward is the bourne which all travellers seek and from which none desires to return" (193). By describing the human interior as an alluring social and geographical landscape, Thoreau suggested that, with such a "world" inside, there was no need to engage with fellow reformers to confront social problems that for him were only the dead abstractions and gothic horrors of reformist rhetoric. In their critiques of reform, furthermore, both Emerson and Thoreau blamed ungovernable affects and appetites—bad stomachs, indigence, "cast off griefs"—that were also targeted by social reformers as the sources of social disorder. Just as many reformers began to blame not structural injustice but unruly character for social disorder, so Emerson and Thoreau turned institutional reform from a symptomatic instantiation of broader cultural change (the push for institutionality articulated by Beecher, for instance) into the disastrous consequence of flawed self-monitoring and self-mastery. When Thoreau urges each reformer to be a "pretty perfect institution in himself," he comes close to acknowledging the shared investment of institutionalism and individualism in the rhetoric of interiority.

If Emerson and Thoreau saw associational reform as sacrificing the inventive possibilities of human relationality by turning collective innovation into institutional rhetoric, transcendental individualism risked the same loss by sacrificing not innovation, but collectivity. This potential sacrifice becomes most clear when Emerson takes up Eliza Wharton's favorite topic. "Friendship and association are very fine things," he declared, "and a grand phalanx of the best of the human race, banded for some catholic object: yes, excellent; but remember that no society can ever be so large as one man. He in his friendship, in his natural and momentary associations, doubles or multiplies himself; but in the hour in which he mortgages himself to two or ten or twenty, he dwarfs himself below the stature of one" (17).[21] The best friends, Emerson insisted, "live in different streets or towns. Each man, if he attempts to join himself to others, is on all sides cramped and diminished of his proportion; and the stricter the union, the smaller and the more pitiful he is" (18). "The union," he concluded, "must be ideal in actual individualism" (18).

Despite Emerson's claims that individualism can replace sociality without loss, however, removing "union" from other people and relocating it in the interior enables the same investment in institutional disciplinarity for Transcendentalism as it did for Eliza's conventional cohort. George Ripley's letter of resignation from the Purchase Street Church, for instance, demonstrates how transcendental love justifies the institutional structures at the center of nineteenth-century social order. Ripley told his congregants, "If society performed its whole duty, the dominion of force would yield to the prevalence of love, our prisons would be converted into moral hospitals, the schoolmaster would supersede the executioner, violence would no more be heard in our land, nor destruction in our borders. Our walls would be our salvation, and our gates praise."[22] In Ripley's vision, bodily resistance becomes unnecessary, as the school and the hospital—two of the institutions Foucault credits with installing new regimes of disciplinary order within the individual—take over from the forces of physical punishment. These are also, significantly, interpretive institutions, training pupils to locate "deep" meaning emanating not from institutional sources, but from the interiorized spaces of the spirit (in the case of the schoolroom) and the body (in the case of the hospital).

Despite the apparent differences between the nonconforming individualism of Transcendentalism and the intimate normativity of Eliza's republican cohort, then, both might agree that love, prone to wander into unproductive, public, and ephemeral connections, is in need of institutional control. Emerson's essay "Love" gives that control its transcendental cast. The essay begins by drawing a distinction between love for proximate people and for the abstract virtues those people purportedly represent. "Every thing is beautiful," Emerson wrote, "seen from the point of view of the intellect, or as truth. But all is sour, if seen from experience. Details are melancholy; the plan is seemly and noble."[23] In a counter-intuitive inversion, Emerson makes embodied particularity representative of an abstract "plan" that is superior to its tangible manifestations. He argues that one must look at love as he does to believe in its magic at all, for the local love object quickly irritates and disappoints. Time, bringing blemishes and decay, is the enemy of local love; only eternal love can produce happily ever after.

Before the future saves the day, however, local love serves an important purpose for Emerson. Having fallen in love, the smitten "no longer appertains to his family and society . . . ; he is a person; he is a soul" (101). Emerson described falling in love as a dual process: on the one hand, one becomes increasingly individuated (a "person") and interiorized (a "soul"); on the other, one's interiorized individuality is not simply a supplement to but a supplanting of previous forms of social relation ("family and society"). "But things are ever grouping themselves according to higher or more interior laws," Emerson claimed. "Neighbourhoods, size, numbers, habits, persons, lose by degrees their power over us," and "even love, which is the deification of persons, must become more impersonal every day" (105). Love as a broad social affect—the tie that binds one family member to others or, more important, one member of a society to others—is thus sacrificed in favor of the romantic couple, but that romance plot, for Emerson, is only a vehicle for the interiority that is ultimately solitary. The latter ("soul") compensates for the losses—of family, of friends, of social relations—that for Emerson is the price of admission to the Tunnel of Love.

Having removed the lover from the entanglement of competing social relations ("she extrudes all other persons from his attention as cheap and unworthy"), however, the beloved, herself an imperfect embodiment of passing time, must metamorphose into a series of abstractions, "carrying out her own being into somewhat impersonal, large, mundane, so that the maiden stands to him for a representative of all select things and virtues" (102). Love, Emerson wrote, arouses itself at last from these endearments, as toys, and puts on the harness, and aspires to vast and universal aims. The soul which is in the soul of each, craving a perfect beatitude, detects incongruities, defects, and disproportion in the behaviour of the other. Hence arise surprise, expostulation, and pain. Yet that which drew them to each other was signs of loveliness, signs of virtue; and these virtues are there, however eclipsed. They appear and reappear, and continue to attract; but the regard changes, quits the sign, and attaches to the substance. This repairs the wounded affection. (106)

Involving not embodied agents in history (corrupting time) but passive representatives of an unchanging abstraction, love, occurring "wholly above [lovers'] consciousness" (107), not surprisingly brings a loss of agency: "what we love is not in your will, but above it" (103). Tellingly, the scene of agency evacuation reflects grammatically what Emerson described as the scene of love: a shift from a collective "we" to an individuated "you." It is as if in squeezing the world so tightly around the subject, the excess sociality flies out into the realm of abstract virtue. Transcendentalism might therefore be called the after-image of evacuated sociability, leaving only the residual compensation of interiority (the soul capable of love). But interiority (selfhood) and transcendence (universalism) are in a necessary state of tension: Can the self rooted in the material world achieve the transcendent? Can the transcendent make itself known through the material forms apprehensible to the senses? These are the questions that animate most of Emerson's work.

In "Love," however, Emerson, lacking the metaphor to close the widening gap between the rhetorically advisable and the socially feasible, opted for an imprecise relay between interiority and transcendence:

If, however, from too much conversing with material objects, the soul was gross, and misplaced its satisfaction in the body, it reaped nothing but sorrow; body being unable to fulfill the promise which beauty holds out; but if, accepting the hint of these visions and suggestions which beauty makes to his mind, the soul passes through the body, and falls to admire strokes of character, and the lovers contemplate one another in their discourses and their actions, then they pass to the true palace of beauty, more and more inflame their love of it, and by this love extinguishing the base affections, as the sun puts out the fire by shining on the hearth, they become pure and hallowed. (103–104)

Here Emerson describes what Foucault calls "spirals of pleasure and power": from bodily sensation, the soul passes into a realm of abstract truth.[24] That passage is never complete, however, since the soul remains housed in the body and therefore can never be distinguished from "base affections." The call to transcendence, therefore, is an injunction to failed vigilance and a guarantee that the sensations of social and bodily attachment, never fully disavowed, remain only as irritants and hindrances, not as the sources of pleasure or creative social action.

Through love, which takes one from sociality to interiority, then from interiority to abstraction, Emerson achieves love's future. But at what cost? Emerson assured readers that "we need not fear that we can lose anything by the progress of the soul. The soul may be trusted to the end. That which is so beautiful and attractive as these relations must be succeeded and supplanted only by what is more beautiful, and so on for ever" (107). Despite his claim that we lose nothing in generating abstract futures ("so on for ever"), when one considers the catalogue contained in the disavowed "finite," the loss necessary to love's abstraction is staggering. In particular, one loses not only what is "beautiful and attractive" in bodily pleasure, the carnal that Emerson dismissed as "prowling in the cellar" (104), but, more important, the initial realms of attachment—neighborhood, family, and society—and the agencies they enable. Faced with such losses, what keeps love alive? The answer, for Emerson's contemporaries, was institutionality. Emerson would shudder at the suggestion that he endorsed institutions, but his portrait of Love—as the thing that stands above time, assuming the agency that individuals surrender, supplanting social relations with universal traits of interiority that, by virtue of being "timeless," are beyond the constitutive negotiation of actual persons—is precisely what characterized nineteenth-century institutionalism. Institutions, then, become love's future.

Emerson's love is not quite what motivated the associations advocated by many of the reformers gathered at Amory Hall, who might well have listened to Emerson and Thoreau—or later read "Love"—with growing bewilderment. History proved kinder to those who espoused individualism, such as Emerson and Thoreau, or who built institutional networks, such as Garrison, than it did to the founders of alternative communities whose work the Amory lectures were organized to publicize. The three lectures framing Emerson's and Thoreau's were delivered by founders of reform communities at Fruitland (Charles Lane), Hopedale (Adin Ballou), and Brook Farms (Charles Dana). Lane's "The True Life; Association; and Marriage" (February 18), Ballou's "Association" (February 25), and Dana's "Association" (March 17) advocated collective life based on shared principles and pleasures. By all accounts, such communities were far from ideal, reproducing the gender and class inequalities of the mainstream culture. Yet without idealizing these "utopias," we can nevertheless recognize that many in Amory Hall were trying to keep collective democracy thinkable, even as they were being cast (as Hawthorne would later write them into literary mythology) as the prematurely nostalgic advocates of an always already defeated hope. If embodied association was becoming democracy's past, institutional liberty was emerging as its future.

Institutional Liberty and Self-Government

If individualism and institutionality jointly rendered other social models unthinkable, they also posed important challenges to one another. In particular, if institutions are to govern the civil sphere, what will bring about the innovative changes Transcendentalism associated with individual experience and vision? Conversely, if individuals are what Thoreau called "pretty perfect institutions" in themselves, who will adjudicate between conflicting individual interests? For these philosophies to function as social theory, they needed to be fused to combine the self-perpetuating futurity of institutions and the embodied agency of individuals.

This fusion takes place in the groundbreaking work of the man credited with founding political science in the United States, Francis Lieber (1798–1872), who wrote the codes of conduct for the Civil War (later incorporated into the Hague and Geneva conventions), coordinated the collection and preservation of Confederate government records, and arbitrated disputes between Mexico and the United States.[25] Although his work is all but forgotten by cultural historians today, Lieber's best-known book, *On Civil Liberty and Self-Government* (1859), is the most thorough account of institutional life in nineteenth-century America, as well as the strongest assertion of the power of institutions—and only institutions—to maintain the democratic innovation of the Revolution. A democratic society, according to Lieber, must honor the insight of imaginative citizens, but it must also demand as its first principle that citizens regulate themselves according to the best interests of the public, as determined and publicized by civil institutions. Characterizing institutions in terms of what Steven Samson calls "tenacity, assimilative powers, and transmissible character,"[26] Lieber combined the three constitutive elements of antebellum institutionality: futurity ("tenacity"), surrogated agency ("assimilative power"), and interiorized values ("transmissible character"). Most important, Lieber combined individualism and institutionality in such ways that, in the years since, Americans have rarely recognized tensions between the two or perceived the pervasive presence of institutionality in everyday life.

Setting forth the core of his philosophy in a succinct sentence, Lieber declared: "self-government is the corollary of liberty."[27] His provocative statement raises several important questions about one of antebellum America's most overused yet ill-defined philosophical concepts.[28] If self-government is "corollary to" liberty, what causes the difference that makes the two visible as analogues, not synonyms? More perplexing, perhaps, is whether liberty is best served by government by the self or government of the self, or whether the two are synonymous. Given Lieber's association of self-government with liberty, we might assume that he meant to promote government by the self—and, indeed, Lieber condemned a growing federalism that left citizens only one toothless form of civic agency: "There is no greater error," he warned, "than the idea of making the vote or election the sole basis of liberty" (290–91). Lieber particularly opposed the tendency of centralized governments to deploy bland and homogenizing abstractions that leave citizens only vaguely aware of the stakes in political action or debate. If citizens, for Lieber, are capable of "widely extended and vigorous action," such action is threatened by politicians who use the abstraction " 'the People' " as "a mere term of brevity, and for the impossible enumeration of all individuals, without inherent connection." The substitution of a "term of brevity" for an "inherent connection" is, arguably, another way to describe the shift from association to Association, resulting for Lieber in an "egotism which loses the very power of protecting the individual rights and liberties" (54). Politicians, answering to abstractions ("the People") rather than to the citizens who elect them, Lieber wryly noted, "seem to think that there is a fate written somewhere beyond the nation itself, and independent of its own morality, to which everything, even justice and liberty, must be sacrificed" (42).

As abstractions wander "beyond the nation itself," so for Lieber do political and economic interests. He therefore extended his analysis of the democratic costs of political abstractions to a broader condemnation of those who "seem to believe that the highest destiny of the United States consists in the extension of her territory, a task in which, at best, we can only be imitators, while, on the contrary, our destiny is one of its own and of a substantive character" (43). By establishing a relation between empire and political rhetoric, Lieber revealed whose interests are formulated and served by seemingly "universal" abstractions. Even within national borders, however, political abstractions grant rights on the basis of conformity to codes of character that produce a misleading racial commonality of interest among those (self-)named as "white," a move that not only denies the diverse cultural identifications (of class, gender, region, labor, or ethnicity) of those so named, but artificially generates racial differences destructive to public life, the process Dana Nelson has analyzed as the formation of an imagined fraternity of white manhood.[29] Writing, "It is certain that we conceive of the rights of the citizen more in the abstract and more as attributes of his humanity, so long as this means our own white race" (266–67), Lieber related the granting of "rights" justified by character to the racial violence condoned by the Supreme Court's decision in Dred Scott, "founded exclusively on the power which the white race possesses over the colored, and which elicit little examination because the first basis of all justice, sympathy, is wanting between the two races" (267).

A necessary counter-force to federalizing and imperial abstractions comes for Lieber through three features that, when combined, enable the nation "to act with originality" (297). First, he believed in a proto-libertarian independence of the self-reliant citizenry from interference from the state. Self-government, "consistently carried out and applied to the realities of life, and not remaining a mere general theory," is

> founded on the willingness of the people to take care of their own affairs, and the absence of that disposition which looks to the general government for everything, as well as on the willingness in each to let others take care of their own affairs. It cannot exist where the general principle of interference prevails, that is, the general disposition in the executive and administration, to do all it possibly can do, and to substitute its action for individual or minor activity and for self-reliance. (253)

Recognizing each citizen's "priceless individual worth and value" (50), democracy ensures his or her "untrammeled political action" (36).

Second, Lieber expressed a liberal commitment to diversity and minority representation. Writing Emersonian self-reliance into political theory, he asserted the need for a democracy founded not on homogenous value or "sentiment," but on diverse opinion and informed debate. "The absence of toleration is the stigma of absolutism, the establishment of 'the opposition' is the glory of freedom," Lieber contended. "Freedom allows of variety; the tyrant, whether one or a multitude, calls heretic at every one who thinks or feels differently" (56). Representative democracy can function effectively, he warned, only when there is "a fair representation of the minority" (178). An immigrant who supported the Union and advocated tirelessly against slavery throughout his teaching career in Confederate South Carolina, Lieber understood the value of diversity of experience and opinion.[30] With keen insight into the mediocritizing tendency of discourses that take equality to mean homogeneity, Lieber eloquently declared, "Diversity is the law of life; absolute equality is that of stagnation and death" (30).

Finally, then, Lieber evinced a radical faith in the transformative power of collaborative and creative exchange. Encouraging bonds of affinity across differences, he believed, is the only way to avoid "political apathy and that moral torpidity or social indifference" (255). Indeed, Lieber, like Tocqueville before him, was an advocate for associational life as the founding trait of democracy in America. He acknowledged the connection between people's need to live in voluntary and unhindered relation to others. "No one can imagine himself free," he stated, "if his communion with his fellows is interrupted or submitted to surveillance" (89).

> There is nothing that more forcibly strikes a person arriving for the first time from the European continent, either in the United States or in England, than the thousandfold evidences of an all-pervading associative spirit in all moral and practical spheres, from the almost universal co-partnerships and associations, the exchanges of artisans, and banks, to those unofficial yet national associations which rise to real grandeur. Strike out from England or America this feature and principle, and they are no longer the same self-relying, energetic, indubitably active people. The spirit of self-government would be gone. (129)

Drawing on the vocabulary of phrenology, Lieber asserted that "adhesiveness" —the human instinct to live in harmony with others—balances the self-interest he saw as the necessary outgrowth of liberty.

Despite his advocacy of associational life, however, Lieber was no naïve populist. Like most Americans who recalled accounts of the French "Terrors," Lieber knew that collectivities can quickly become mobs. Power thrown "unchecked into the hands of the people," he counseled, "remains power, and is not liberty, and people still remain men" (303). Having used "self-government" to take democracy from the control of the federal government, Lieber remained skeptical about citizens' capacity to know their own best interests. "The doctrine Vox populi vox Dei is essentially unrepublican," he wrote. "The doctrine that the people may do what they list [is] an open avowal of disbelief in self-government" (414). Ever the classical rationalist ("it is with rights, in our political relations, as with the principles of our physical and mental organization. The more elementary and indispensable they are, the more dangerous they become, if not guided by reason" [128]), Lieber was especially suspicious of the unregulated, irrational, death-driven emotions popularized by the romantics of his age, as well as the milder forms of inner sensation associated with the (political) sublime. ("Enthusiasm is not liberty, nor does the reality of liberty consist in an aesthetical love of freedom" [303].) "All subjective arbitrariness," he warned, "is contrary to freedom" (108).

Lieber's account of "self-government" thus leads to a conundrum. How can self-reliant individualism be fostered in citizens without generating random "subjective arbitrariness" or tyrannical "mobism"? The answer came in the form of an apparent oxymoron of self-limiting liberty: the apparently tense relation between freedom and restraint, for Lieber, is resolved by voluntary self-surrender. Civil liberty, he asserted, can occur only through the "limitation of self-determination" (28). If civility, resisting federalization, becomes "decentralized self-government" (18), it also assures the social order that makes "subjective" disruption unlikely.[31] Through consensual "limitation of self-determination" (28), Lieber wrote, citizens consensually regulate themselves through shared conventions. Government by the people is thereby transformed into government *of* the people, without the unthinkable surrender of consent.[32]

The only sure means to generate consensual self-surrender for Lieber is a system of stable institutions. Self-government, he insisted, is "organic," meaning, "organs of combined self-action, in institutions, and in a systematic connection of these institutions" (254). Lieber redefined "the people" as "the people, combined as the totality of organic institutions, constantly growing in their character, as all organic life is, but not a dictatorial multitude" (254–55). If civil institutions ensure that the voices of diverse citizens reach the ear of an indifferent state, they also guarantee order throughout the (now privatized) lives of citizens. Connecting governmentality and bodily interiority, Lieber argued, "Self-government requires politically, in bodies, that self-rule which moral self-government requires of the individual; the readiness of resigning the use of power which we may possess, quite as often as using it" (256). Embodied politics come to mean, then, the adoption of agency in the paradoxical surrender of agency, the realm of political action removed from the social give-and-take of public life and refocused on the administration of the body itself. At the same time, the move from public agency to individual self-regulation produces an excess, a citizen-supplement, in the form of an amorphous volition—institutionalism—detached from the interference of the state, but removed as well from the creative advocacy (now a tainted "subjectivism") of particular citizens.

Asking himself how "real and essential self-government, in the service of liberty, [is] to be obtained and to be perpetuated," Lieber answered, "There is no other means than a vast system of institutions, whose number supports the whole, as the many pillars support the rotunda of our capitol" (304). Lieber defined an institution as "a system or body of usages, laws, or regulations of extensive and recurring operation, containing within itself an organism by which it effects its own independent action, continuance, and generally its own further development. Its object is to generate, effect, regulate or sanction a succession of acts, transactions or productions of a peculiar kind or class" (304). There are, then, four stages to institutionality, as set forth by Lieber. In the first, citizens' actions generate a repetitive or habitual pattern ("extensive and recurring operation"). At that point, action separates from the embodied agents, attaches instead to "a system," and assumes the power of "independent action." Institutional "action" then assumes the power to "regulate or sanction" its constituent members through the generation of abstract categories ("a peculiar kind or class") disseminated as standards of behavior, or "character," to which citizens believe they must conform. At the finish of this process, individualism distinct from institutional order vanishes, leaving behind the phantom subject Lieber named a "self-institution." "Self-government implies self-institution," Lieber insisted, "not only at the first setting out of government, but as a permanent principle of political life" (253).

If, through institutions, "untrammeled political action" leaves the body to become self-institution, a supplementary agency without agents, the body becomes in turn overly corporealized, the locus of involuntary desires, emotions, and spasms indicative of the need not for more direct action, but for more regulation. "It is panic, fanaticism, revenge, lust of gain, and hatred of races that produce most of the sudden and comprehensive impulses" of the people (412), according to Lieber. Above all, he warned against "the psychological processes by which liberty has been lost," such as "gratitude, hero-worship, impatience, indolence, permitting great personal popularity to overshadow institutions and laws" (277). "The organic life which silently pervades the whole with a creative power," Lieber wrote, "is not readily seen, while convulsions, eruptions and startling phenomena attract the attention, or cause at least the wonder of the least observing" (257). Creating a schism common to much institutional reform, Lieber splits the citizen between the emotional paroxysms of particularity so embodied as to become involuntary and the dissociated self-regulation (invisible and all-pervasive) now expressive of an agency located amorphously above and beyond the body itself.[33]

The question arises: Why do citizens voluntarily transform themselves into institutions? Or, put another way, how do citizens, through the process of performatively generating institutions, come to believe in the external authority of the categorical order their own imaginations have constituted? Perhaps an explanation lies in the affective traces of abstracted sociality carried within the "kinds and classes" generated by the institutional-performative (that is, citizens' affective imaginations are never, as Marx feared, entirely estranged). Institutionalism traffics in human interiority, creating a seemingly organic relationship between institutions and citizens' "adhesive" desires. Through his organic metaphors, Lieber can assert that institutionality supplants neither individualism ("we call a body of laws or usages an institution only when we unite the idea of an independent individuality with it. It must have its own distinct character, its own peculiar action, and it must not owe its continuance to the arbitrary mandate of a will foreign to it" [311]) nor sociality ("every institution ought to stand in connection with others" [310], establishing a surrogate sociality between surrogate individuals). Rather, it unites the best qualities of both.

If his theories of "civil liberty" seemingly preserve both individuality and social relations, however, they also make it hard to distinguish interior (what comes out of the body as "instinct") from exterior (what is imposed on the body as "law") regulation. Assuming "the political embodiment of self-reliance," institutions evacuate the unruly emotions that make citizens democratic free agents ("The institution is the opposite of subjective conception, individual disposition and mere personal bias" [315]) and reconceive the subject as a repository of performative order. The crux of this transformation is "character," which appears as deep selfhood and, simultaneously, as abstract order, making subjection to codes of behavior appear, paradoxically, as self-reliance, "the union of liberty and order" (169). Little wonder that Lieber claimed, "Liberty stands in need of character" (304). For Lieber, an institution "trains the mind and nourishes the character for a dependence upon law and a habit of liberty, as well as of a law-abiding acknowledgment of authority" (329). If institutions generate "the love of the law as our master" (275), they do so not through prescription, but through a performative subordination conceived through "acknowledgement" as the citizen's consent. Arising both from within us and from without, character is a hybrid that renders subjection ("habitual" "dependence") unobjectionable. "We do not obey a person whom as individual we think to be no more than ourselves," Lieber reasoned, "but we obey the institution of which we know ourselves to be as integral a part as the superior, clothed with authority" (332). For Lieber, when "liberty and law have become firmly interlocked" (295) within the institutional public sphere, then we have "the only self-government which is a real government of self, as well as by self" (329).

Like most political ideals, however, Lieber's was easier to imagine than to execute. If suffusing sociality with the order necessary to the state prompts disciplinary restrictions on human interactions, it also permits intimacy to generate epistemological (and juridical) crises within institutions. Lieber acknowledged as much when, anticipating George W. Bush and Sandy Rios, he took up the "institution" of marriage. While for Bush marriage rests on heterosexuality, for Lieber it relied on monogamy. The difference indicates that what emerged in the twentieth century as social institutions based on presumed identity began in the nineteenth century as institutional regulations of modes of affiliation. The interiorized forms of social subjectivity known as "identities" are the fossilization of nineteenth-century struggles over the forms and meanings of sociality.

Claiming that "we call marriage an institution in consideration of its pervading importance, its extensive operation, the innumerable relations it affects, and the security which its continuance enjoys in the conviction of almost all men, against any attempts at its abolition" (305), Lieber could not guarantee that "innumerable relations" might not prove too unwieldy for institutional order. Specifically, he came face to face with the Mormons, who, defining marriage differently, provoked an epistemological instability: "The potent question which will offer great difficulty will be, whether a Mormon state, with its 'theo-democratic' government, as they term it, can be called a republic, in the sense in which our constitution guarantees it to every member of the Union. It will then, probably for the first time in history, become necessary legally to define what a republic is" (102).[34] In particular, the Mormons challenged the right to restrict the number and form of citizens' intimate alliances ("innumerable relations") by questioning the validity of monogamy, which Lieber called the first principle "of our whole western civilization, as contra-distinguished from oriental life" (102). Intimacy and institutionalism, unlike individualism and institutionalism, make messy bed fellows. Or, rather, the mess that intimate relations create in institutional order seems to call for increasing juridical neatness, insisting that national rhetoric—whose looseness leaves citizens unclear of what rights or privileges they are entitled to enjoy or who, precisely, is entitled to enjoy them—declare its constituent and surrogatory relation to affective interiority. "The Constitution of the United States has no definition of liberty," Lieber acknowledged. "The framers thought no more of defining it in that instrument, than people going to be married would stop to define what is love" (36).

In the end, though, the Mormons helped make Lieber's point. If the people of the United States cannot be trusted to regulate their relation to sexual, much less social, reproduction, institutions, taking on individualistic self-reliance without the complication of wills or desire, happily fulfill that function, spreading "the framework of the same system of law over sets of men periodically renewed, prescribing their line of action" (309). In return, citizens purportedly gain an agency that extends beyond the limitations of their bodies. In particular, citizens purchase a supposedly stable future, if not for themselves, then for some endlessly deferred generation to come. While institutions appear to arise from the practices of ancestors such as the Founders (an institution, Lieber wrote, "becomes a consistent continuation of that which their predecessors have done" [309]), their more compelling power is to grant futurity (the institution, Lieber asserted, "insures perpetuity, and renders development possible, while without it there is little more than subjective impulsiveness, which may be good and noble, or ruinous and purely passionate, but always lacks continuity, and consequently development and safe assimilating growth" [310]). As Lieber ambivalently, if succinctly, stated, "Citizens are born and die, but the state is a continuum" (309).

Given the specific examples Lieber offers—"A bank, parliament, the court of justice, the bar, the church, the mail, a state are institutions, as well as the lord's supper, a university, the inquisition, all the laws relating to property, the sabbath, the feudal system" (305–6)—one might wonder how, in practice, institutions guarantee perpetuity or a "safe assimilating growth" (the Inquisition?), much less a stable "continuum" into the future. Lieber most often, however, took his examples of what he famously called "institutional liberty" (304) from the world of antebellum reform. Choosing from a range of what Emerson called the "grand phalanx of the best of the human race, banded for some catholic object,"[35] from the American Colonization Society (128) and societies seeking to improve "the position of woman" (85) to reformers espousing "habits of cleanliness" (85) among the urban poor, Lieber saw the vast network of reform organizations as a realization (even, one might speculate, a cause) of his vision of the institutional civil sphere. His connection of institutionalism and reform helps explain how the latter arose from the crisis of sociality dramatized in Foster's novel and how, proclaiming greater volition to its members, reform generated the schisms (between unruly bodies and abstract reason, desire and will, appetite and self-restraint) that orchestrated populations of Americans into "identities" that would govern social relations for the coming century.

In yoking reform and institutionalism, Lieber helped make "identity" a matter of institutional management, thereby also placing it at the core of a new civil sphere generated through the distribution of interiority. He also, however, cloaked that management in the mantle of benevolent progress. In taking social relations out of the realm of the social and placing them in the individual domain of identity (he would have said "character"), Lieber made the privatizing work of "self-government" appear even more pressingly *social* (tied to progressive improvement) than before. This is the trick of reformist interiority, one that brought about the loss of social participation in public life while giving citizens the impression that they had lost nothing at all, thereby allowing for no protest or resistance. Yet institutionalism was not without its troubling— indeed, its often gothic—alter egos, which filled the space of doubt potentially opened in the consciousness of citizens told that privacy was their only space of operation and that institutions would take on the work of public agency. The most powerful of such alter egos, as the Amory lectures make clear, was the Catholic church. If the pervasive spread of Lieber's theory of civil self-government shows that institutionalism was becoming the prevailing order in antebellum America, the anxious persistence of anti-Catholicism shows that not everyone was falling in line.[36]

The Roman Institution

The connection between the strengthening of social reform and anti-Catholic anxiety was clear in the press coverage of the Amory Hall lectures. The Boston press lampooned Garrison as a would-be priest propounding a rigid orthodoxy to credulous believers over a series of Sundays. Responding in the *Liberator* to those who "say we are just as formal and Sunday-bound as the sectarians against whose outward worship we are registering our testimony," Garrison asserted that the Amory reformers shared "a laudable desire that had long been felt by many who had become weary of the barren theology of the pulpit"—namely, to "vindicate the right and ability of THE PEOPLE to meet on Sunday for intellectual, social and moral improvement, without any artificial or arbitrary religious forms, and *without a priest*."[37] Garrison in turn characterized the Boston press as "bigotry" and "craftiness," "the venomous mendacity of priestcraft."[38]

Throughout this volley of accusations, Garrison and his critics shared "priestcraft" as a term of insult. Neither specify *which* "priestcraft" it loathed, but the invocations of mendacious and manipulative priests reflect the prevalent anti-Catholic rhetoric of the 1830s and 1840s. Jenny Franchot reports the antebellum publication of twenty-five newspapers, thirteen magazines, 210 books, forty fictional pieces, forty-one histories, and scores of annuals, gift books, and pamphlets devoted to anti-Catholic sentiment.[39] Often such rhetoric erupted in physical violence, as when in 1834 two thousand citizens watched a mob of sixty disguised workingmen storm a convent in Charlestown, Massachusetts; drive twelve nuns and forty-seven female pupils into hiding; and rob the convent and burn it to the ground. The attack haunted American political rhetoric for decades. In 1835, Lyman Beecher invoked the Charlestown mob to denounce "lawless force," the dire enemy of "argument and free-inquiry,"[40] while Lieber asserted the sacredness of private property in opposition to laws proposing "that certain offices should have the right to enter nunneries, from eight A.M. to eight o'clock P.M., provided there was strong suspicion that an inmate was retained against her will" (1859, 63–64).

Even more common than condemnations of Protestant mobs, however, were xenophobic representations of an invisible but all-pervasive foreign control robbing citizens of both Emerson's self-determination and Lieber's self-government. Not content to control Europe, Beecher reported, the Pope, "opposed to the principles of our government" (61), was sending "accumulating thousands to the polls to lay their inexperienced hand upon the helm of our power" (54). As a result, "ignorance and prejudice, and passion and irreligion, and crime are wielded by desperate political ambition and a corrupting foreign influence" (75).[41] Beecher's paranoid nationalism divides Protestants, abstracted into "the whole nation" (62), from Catholics, described in terms of unruly interiority ("passions"). Faced with such a threat to democracy, Beecher urged Protestant Americans to maintain "keener vigilance and a more active resistance" (63).[42]

The problem with vigilance, however, is that Catholics, like most rhetorically effective enemies, remain hidden, always only imminent. Calling Catholicism "the most powerful secret organization that ever existed" (163), Lieber represented Catholic priests, particularly Jesuits, as working "in full organization, silent, systematized, unwatched, and unresisted action among us, to try the dexterity of its movements, and the potency of its power upon unsuspecting, charitable, credulous republicans" (148). As opposed to the "open" democracy practiced by Protestant Americans, Jesuits, Lieber warned, "are essentially injurious to all liberty," being, "as all secret societies must inherently be, submissive to secret superior will and decision,—a great danger in politics,—and unjust to the rest of fellow-citizens, by deciding on public measures and men without the trial of public discussion, and by bringing to bear a secretly united body on the decision or election" (138).

The most powerful weapon in the Pope's secret arsenal, as Franchot notes, is the confessional.[43] While Protestant ministers never "dare to attempt to regulate the votes of their people," Beecher asserted, Catholic priests use the confessional to "learn all the private concerns of their people, and have almost unlimited power over the conscience as it respects the performance of every civil or social duty" (60). Despite his claim that priests were telling parishioners how to vote, however, Beecher showed their power as arising from effective *listening*. Hearing "all the private concerns of the people," priests, possessing "deep knowledge of human nature" (147), remain familiar with the "private concerns" of parishioners. As Beecher's invocation of "deep knowledge of human nature" indicates, Catholicism's association with secrecy arises not only from the secluded architectures of the convent and the confessional, but also from the mysterious *human* interiority that is its stock in trade. While Beecher denounced "priest-craft" for "the bad passions gather[ed] about its perverted standard" and for setting "loose the malignant passion of the desperately wicked heart" (140–41), in the end he could not help noting, with some apparent envy, that Catholicism, working in the interior realm of the passions, was "unlimited in its powers of accommodating to the various characters, tastes, and conditions of men" (144). Because of that ability, priests maintained "alliance[s] of affection" (127) that threatened to compete with the "evangelical" institutions Beecher advocated. "Nothing is more easy," Beecher lamented, "than the perversion of associated mind; or difficult, than its recovery to society and a healthful self-government" (131–32).

Lest Catholic "alliance[s] of affection" should begin to sound like a viable alternative to Protestant institutions, Beecher characterized the Roman church as a *hyper*-institution. Distinguishing between Protestant ministers, "chosen by the people who have been educated as freemen," and the "Catholic system" (61), Beecher insisted that Catholics threatened democracy not individually, but through a "system" that "commits its designs and higher movements, like the control of an army, to a few governing minds, while the body of the people may be occupied in their execution, unconscious of their tendency" (188–89). Lieber similarly called the Catholic church a "gigantic institution," which, like trade unions, "becomes an agent of ruin by making the objective prevail more than is desirable, or by making the annihilation of individuality one of its very objects" (315–16). Beecher and Lieber echo the editor of Rebecca Reed's bestselling *Six Months in a Convent* (1835), who characterizes the church as "so extensive an institution" as "to give to Catholics a controlling influence over the minds of our youth, and disseminate their tenets, by an imperceptible, winning way of not seeming to disseminate them at all."[44] Unable "to justify a foreign institution established among us under the control of a hierarchy adverse to a republican form of government" (12), the editor, like Beecher, insists that "the whole interior discipline of both pupils and teachers ought to be known" (9). To ensure his case against the "cold-blooded, Jesuitical system of espionage" (34), the editor refers to Catholicism as an "institution" no fewer than thirty times.

In attempting to cast Catholicism as a threat to democracy insofar as it operates institutionally, nativists like Beecher and Lieber ironically betray the danger to citizens of the institutionalism they themselves advocated. Just as the Pope seeks to fuse diverse Catholic populations into a single voting bloc, so institutions orchestrate various social alliances into "a secretly united body" through the regulation of public opinion reflecting the interests of the Protestant elite. If Rome works surreptitiously to make its dictates appear as the will of individual Catholics, so Protestant institutions, in Beecher's account, exert an invisible influence through the norms of good character and healthy living they generate and publicize. Above all, just as priests draw strength from delving into the secret sins of individual Catholics, so Beecher authorizes Protestants to undertake the prying surveillance he charges to "priestcraft," although the two forms of "prying" appear different because Catholicism operates through individual agents (priests) while Protestantism abstracts those agents into a generalized (institutionalized) "public." Asserting that Protestants "are not annoyed by scrutiny," Beecher advocated turning on Catholicism "the searching inspection of the public eye, and compelling it, like all other religions among us, to pass the ordeal of an enlightened public sentiment" (87). He called for "governmental supervision of the subject of immigration, which shall place before the nation, annually, the number and general character of immigrants, that the whole subject may experience the animadversion of an enlightened public sentiment" (178–79). "When the eye of the nation is fixed on the subject," he concluded, "unless infatuation has fastened upon us, there can be no doubt of the result" (184).

More telling than the similarities between Catholicism and Protestant institutionalism, however, are their perceived differences. While Protestant institutions operate through publicity—especially print forms such as newspapers and pamphlets, increasing the distance between authors and readers—priests, according to Beecher, maintain the intimacy of personal contact. Catholicism's greater localism is matched, furthermore, by its super-national reach. While Protestant institutions are figured as metonyms of the nation-state, securing national identity (even while expanding the nation into Western territories), Catholicism's global influence wreaks havoc with national autonomy. If, as Beecher claimed, Catholicism "perverts" alliances of affection, one of those alliances is potentially citizens' patriotic ties to the nation-state itself. Catholicism functioned, then, both as institutionalism's competition and its troubled conscience, an archive of alternative social arrangements, modes of communication, and cultural allegiances that institutionalism, while presenting itself simply as the outgrowth of the peoples' will, sought to eradicate.

As the press controversy over the Amory lectures demonstrates, however, not everyone accepted the opposition men like Beecher and Lieber drew between Catholic "priestcraft" and Protestant institutions. Even within Amory Hall, some drew the connection between institutional religion and organized

Protestant reform. Claiming that "the Church, or religious party, is falling from the church nominal, and is appearing in temperance and non-resistant societies, in movements of abolitionists and of socialists, and in very singular assemblies, called Sabbath and Bible Conventions" and comparing reform practices "of homeopathy, of hydropathy, of mesmerism, of phrenology" to "wonderful theories of the Christian miracles!" Emerson placed reform on a continuum with "the church nominal."[45]

In making this charge, Emerson echoed the conservative Whig Calvin Colton, whose *Protestant Jesuitism* (1836) contended that reformers not only rivaled but surpassed their Catholic counterparts in the institutional arts of priestcraft. "It is impossible not to observe," Colton wrote,

> in the progress and operations of the Temperance Society, a prominent and leading development of that spirit of Jesuitism which has of late been showing itself in various associations, professedly organized for the purposes of moral and religious reform. The beginning of all these enterprises is good— pure in motive, and commendable in their objects. So was the institution which owed its origin and character to Ignatius Loyola.[46]

"Whatever [reform] is started," Colton charged, "a national society must at once be got up, which is imposing in its very name" (52–53). Such national societies oversee "subsidiary" reform societies "multiplied over the length and breadth of the land" (53), forming a "complicated and vast machinery; with wealth at its disposal, and influence to sustain it; with innumerable pens ready for use, and tongues convulsed with spasms of zeal" (75). This institutional structure, despite being a "system of quackery" (75), generates "unexpected possession of power and influence, on an extended scale, over the public mind" (96–97). Even the best-intentioned reform efforts thus give way, Colton warned, to "arrogance, dictatorial airs, and tyranny" (51). A citizenry "simple, honest, confiding" does not "understand when and how the whole frame of society is getting into a new structure, leaving the great mass in subjection to the will and control of select, and often self-elected, combinations of individuals" (107). If this description sounds uncannily like Beecher's account of the Pope's subversion of credulous Catholics, the resemblance is due to a shared commitment to institutionality ("a new structure"). Organized reform efforts such as the American Temperance Society, according to Colton, betrayed "a revival of the reign of Jesuitism, adapted to our time and circumstance" (110). Four times referring to the Society of Jesus as an institution, Colton leaves little doubt about what Catholics share with their reform-minded critics.

The institutional power of both groups arises for Colton from their ability to manipulate public opinion, a power that undermines "the self-respect of the community" (69) and therefore "desolates society" (58). Reformers "are not satisfied," Colton warned, "till they have got the consciences of the public in their own pocket, and put their judgments under mortgage" (69). Just as the Pope steals the free will of American Catholics, so "the weight of public opinion has been forestalled, gained by stealth, and abused" (101). Confronted by "a declared public voice acting upon them from all directions" (90), the "wide public are to be informed only on points which concern them to know, and as they may be convenient instruments of power" (109), until "policy becomes, at last, the reigning principle" (109). In a world generated by institutionally controlled public opinion, "credit in all statements goes by authority" (53). Meanwhile, Colton observed, "the public are unsuspicious, till finally the whole system of operations is accommodated to the ambitious designs of a few, who have usurped the powers as their own which were only yielded to them in trust" (97). Describing the "system" of public opinion as a panoptical civil sphere, Colton reported that "eyes are everywhere; they see and understand all movements" (111), and anyone who "dissents from their opinions is proscribed as a heretic" (61). "The field of open and fair debate," Colton complained, "has been closed" (100), and what reformers "intended to benefit, they injure; that which they are brought in to save, they destroy" (55).

What proves "so radically subversive of social order" (100) in reform publicity, as in Catholic rituals of confession and contrition, is their traffic in interiority. Both institution builders, Colton argued, rely on testimonials of indulgence and repentance centered on an unruly, demanding, insatiable, and unpredictable interior.[47] Instilling what Colton names "a sense of shame and mortification" in their followers, reformers undermine the ethical deliberation necessary for public action, "till the unhappy subject finds his self-reliance giving way, and the keeping of his conscience, the use of his judgment, and his personal virtue passed over by covenant into the hands of others" (86). As they rob citizens of self-trust, such rituals forestall dissent by granting, by way of apparent compensation, a turbulent interior over which to exert control, thereby substituting self-management as an apparent equivalent to participatory civic action. Reformers generate habitual and "unnatural appetites" that turn the human interior into an apparent microcosm of the social sphere, appetites into an equivalent of social demand (represented as "unnatural"), and self-management into a microcosm of institutional efforts to maintain order in the face of such demands. This chain of equivalences gives citizens the illusion of social participation while focusing their attention on an imaginary interior that, stirred up by objects and people who awaken "unnatural" wants, can be ruled only insofar as it is isolated from the social altogether. Given that the human interior can never be entirely safeguarded from social intrusion, however, it necessarily proves "ungovernable" (58), provoking cycles of always failed repentance that generate an unceasing demand on citizens' vigilance. Never achieving "reform," pulled between invisible danger and impossible control, citizens thus exist in a state of perpetual anxiety. "We have actually seen," Colton reported, "men who, under the influence of these principles, have so utterly lost all confidence in their own virtue, and in the virtue of the species, as to become nervous" (69). The worst effects of institutionalism are not seen on the individual body, however, but on the social body, generating "a false and morbid intimacy and mutual dependence" (85) that creates "artificial relations in society" (105).

Despite his criticism of such "artificial relations," however, not even Colton seemed to believe that citizens could be trusted to manage their social relations by themselves. "Even now," Colton complained, "the public have become so dependent on this factitious system, so enervated by its chains, that, if set at once at liberty, they would hardly know how to govern themselves" (105). The irony, of course, is that for Colton, as for Beecher and Lieber, the only solution to the effects of institutional control is more institutional control, making Catholics and Protestants, reformers and anti-reformers, sound uncannily alike in their advocacy of "general control" as "the only safety of a community of rights and privileges" (111).

As institutionalism became so prevalent as to absorb even such radically opposed social forces, Catholicism remained an obsessive source of cultural ambivalence, both too institutional and not institutional enough, preserving local, inventive models of social affiliation even as it threatened their autonomous operation. Ambivalence marks even those who took up anti-Catholicism for profit, as Maria Monk's scandalous *Awful Disclosures of the Hotel Dieu Nunnery in Montreal* (1836) dramatically demonstrates. Playfully referring to the "department of nunnery discipline,"[48] Monk conflated the "tortures" of the convent and the more banal institutional practices productive of "discipline" in a civil sphere increasingly made of service "departments." More seriously, oscillating between the interior states (shame, anxiety, and desire) of institutional discipline and the social relations that occupy the institution's margins, Monk's narrative dramatizes the debates brought about by institutionality among men such as Emerson, Garrison, Colton, Beecher, and Lieber. Perhaps this ambivalence is what led an estimated three hundred thousand readers to Monk's narrative, making it the bestseller of its day. Feeling institutionalism pervading their lives, perhaps they found in Monk's narrative their own inexpressible ambivalence.

Department of Nunnery Discipline

Claiming to be a factual account of a young girl's seven-year captivity in a Canadian convent, *Awful Disclosures* was by far the bestselling work of anti-Catholic rhetoric in antebellum America.[49] Raised by her mother, a poor widow unable adequately to educate her daughter or provide religious instruction (10), Monk, hungry for maternal affection, turned to a convent school. There, despite finding the nuns "rather rough and unpolished in their manners" (11), Monk resolved to join what she believed to be a life of solitude, devotion, and charity. Soon, however, she discovered her mistake: "All the holiness of their lives, I now saw, was merely pretended. The appearance of sanctity and heavenly-mindedness which they had shown among us novices, I found was only a disguise to conceal such practices as would not be tolerated in any decent society in the world; and as for joy and peace like that of heaven, which I had expected to find among them, I learnt too well that they did not exist there" (126). Among the "practices" that the convent conceals are the imprisonment, torture, and murder of nuns, who, raped by priests, dump their babies in a lime pit in the convent's cellar. Despite her horror at what she has discovered, however, Monk seems strangely attracted to the convent. Although she leaves the convent three times, without apparent opposition, the first two times she returns of her own volition. (The second time she "escapes," Monk marries a man about whom "a report was circulated unfavorable to his character" [28], and whom she leaves after a few weeks, stealing her dead father's military pension from her mother to buy her way back into the convent.) Monk finally leaves for good only when she discovers that she is pregnant. While the moral imperatives of publication required that Monk proclaim outrage at the convent's criminality, these persistent returns, as Carina Pasquesi observes, suggest her more ambivalent identification with the convent as a site, like Catholicism more broadly, both hyper- and inadequately institutional.[50]

The capacity of institutions such as the convent to compel identification begins, as Monk's narrative suggests, with their power to erase experiential memories to reorient members toward identification with the institution. Often this involves a ritual renaming that confers, along with a new identity, an interiority that comprises the institution's sanctioned values. In entering the convent, the young Maria not only transforms from a Monk to a nun, she gains a saint's name that marks her as a full member of the convent. In a ritual of death and rebirth, Monk sleeps in a casket before reawakening as Saint Eustace (37). Monk soon learns, however, that "I had several namesakes among the nuns, for there were two others who had already borne away my new name, Saint Eustace" (63). The dangers of identification with institutional values, even if such identifications purchase a promised futurity, becomes clear to Monk when she hears reports of a formerly wealthy nun, never seen except behind glass. She "had no name" (24), Monk learns, and "did not mingle with the other nuns, either at work, worship, or meals; for she had no need of food, and not only her soul, but her body, was in heaven a great part of her time" (24). This nun, Maria is told, is especially holy, having been guaranteed entrance to heaven. While such assurance—the ultimate institutional futurity—is appealing, Monk also recognizes that, unable to surrender her competing wants (she likes food and company) or her lingering identifications (she keeps leaving the convent), "Futurity . . . appears uncertain" (v).

The convent's power to confer identity on its members is related, in *Awful Disclosures*, to the panoptical apparatus Jeremy Bentham placed at the center of modern institutions. Whenever someone from outside the convent inquires about an inmate gone missing, the nuns, fearing that the Superior may be listening behind a partition "to hear whether all performed their parts aright" (58), strive to outdo one another in telling the most convincing lies on her behalf (57). This scene of internalized surveillance appears more explicitly in Monk's description of the convent's sleeping quarters:

> without curtains or anything else to obstruct the view; and in one corner was a small room partitioned off, in which was the bed of a night-watch, that is, the old nun who was appointed to oversee us for the night. In each side of the partition were two holes, through which she could look out upon us whenever she pleased. Her bed was raised a little above the level of the others. There was a lamp hung in the middle of our chamber, which showed everything to her very distinctly; and as she had no light in her little room, we never could perceive whether she was awake or asleep. As we knew that the slightest deviation from the rules would expose us to her observation as well as to that of our companions, in whom it was a virtue to betray one another's faults. (21–22)

Foucault argues that anyone living under the jurisdiction of institutions, unable to determine when she is being watched (as the nuns are unable to see when or whether the night watch is observing them), begins to act as if continuously observed.[51] As surveillance is internalized, then, it requires the generation of a simultaneous realm of potential discord located not in the external sphere of social relations, but in the internal realm of turbulent feelings and impulses. The "watched," in other words, imagine themselves possessed of interiority, divided between the impulse to defy rules (instinct or desire) and the imperative to restrain such impulses (conscience or soul). Most obviously, interiority takes the form of turbulent emotions, of which the convent is a hothouse. From the outset, Monk recollects her experiences with "painful emotion," which she must overcome to live "shamelessly" (vi). Writing of the priests that "they would glory, not only in sating their brutal passions, but even in torturing, in the most barbarous manner, the feelings of those under their power," leading their victims to "violate our own feelings" (154), Monk transforms physical torment into a contest between passion and shame, shifting the focus from interpersonal struggle (between priest and nun) to the guilty nun's struggle with(in) herself. The institutionality of both the Catholic convent and the Protestant print public, eager to consume Monk's "awful disclosures" and thereby gain "access to the interior" (50), requires that the drama of possession and redemption be enacted not over Monk's body, but over her "feelings," that punishment be transformed into an interior state.

The most efficient discipline, however, operates not on emotions, which are susceptible to conscious control, but on the most interior of states, the unconscious. Monk describes the nuns as "directed to keep a strict and constant watch over our thoughts" and "kept in a constant state of activity, which proved very wearisome" (61). Such activity is the result less of physical coercion than of what she terms "unconscious exercises." "Required to keep our minds continually on the stretch," she reports,

> both in watching our conduct, in remembering the rules and our prayers, under the fear of the consequences of any neglect, when we closed our eyes in sleep, we often went over again the scenes of the day, and it was no uncommon thing for me to hear a nun repeat one or two of her long exercises in the dead of night. Sometimes by the time she had finished, another, in a different part of the room, would happen to take a similar turn, and commence a similar recitation; and I have known cases in which several such unconscious exercises were performed, all within an hour or two. (130–31)

In this state of unconscious activity, the nuns lose the capacity to distinguish between compulsion and consent, troubling the concept of "voluntary" participation in public institutions. (If Monk can walk out the door whenever she pleases, why does she feel she is "captive" in the convent? If one can be the "captive" of apparently open institutions, when and where does one's consent operate?) The nuns, Monk reports, often undergo "voluntary sufferings" to show their devotion to God (154), leading Monk to feel "bound by a regard to truth to confess, that deluded women were found among us, who would comply with [the priests'] requests" (155). Given that all of the nuns suffer from the disciplinary productions of "unconscious exercises," Monk's distinction between delusion and "the free exercise of . . . reason" (179) becomes impossible to maintain.

Even more troubling, Monk's deployment of the language of coercion ("bound") to represent compliance to virtuous truth telling underscores that the freedom associated with civil life outside the convent may appropriate consent in analogous ways to those enacted by the nuns. Monk's description of her return to "freedom" is therefore suffused with the interiorizing language of impulses and feelings, limiting her conscious role in her own actions. She is finally led to leave the convent, for example, by "some extraordinary impulse," while the composition of her narrative comes from an involuntary outpouring of interiority: "I was soon seized with very alarming symptoms; then my desire to disclose my story revived" (178). Given this production of compulsive interiors, the disciplinary processes Foucault attributes to modern institutions appear to render conscious deliberation, and hence consent, inoperable.

In the end, however, institutional interiority impinges most forcefully not on individuals (the possessors of consent), but on alternative sociabilities. The convent increasingly isolates the nuns first from the outside world, then from each other. "It is remarkable," Monk reports, "that in our nunnery, we were almost entirely cut off from the means of knowing anything even of each other" (136), "permitted to speak with each other only in hearing of the old nuns who sat by us" (21). Even after her escape from the convent, Monk finds it difficult to establish social relationships: "to this day, I feel an instinctive aversion to offering my hand, or taking the hand of another person, even as an expression of friendship" (177). As for Eliza Wharton, friendship figures for Monk the relational operations of consent ("offering my hand") in opposition to the coercive and interiorized dictates ("I feel an instinctive aversion") generated by the "unconscious exercises" of institutional discipline.

Sociability persists throughout *Awful Disclosures*, however, in the person of Monk's tormentor, co-conspirator, and occasional friend, Jane Ray. Soon after entering the convent, Monk begins to question her decision, until Jane Ray speaks to her cheerfully, suggesting "that she felt some interest in me. I do not remember what she said, but I remember it gave me pleasure" (22). Producing sociability ("interest") and gratification ("pleasure") in a disciplinary regime intended to eradicate both, Jane Ray is, to say the least, an odd nun. Most notably, in a world striving to produce disembodied spirits, Jane is extraordinarily embodied: "rather old for a nun; that is, probably thirty; her figure large, her face wrinkled, and her dress careless" (22), possessing a "loud and well-known voice, so strongly associated with everything singular and ridiculous, [which] would arrest the attention of us all, and generally induce us to laugh" (77). "It would be very difficult to give an accurate description of this singular woman," Monk writes, "dressed in the plain garments of the nuns, bound by the same vows, and accustomed to the same life, resembling them in nothing else, and frequently interrupting all their employments" (48). Monk recalls that Jane was "under less restraint than the others," even though she "set the rules at defiance. She would speak aloud when silence was required, and sometimes walk about when she ought to have kept her place; she would even say and do things on purpose to make us laugh, and although often blamed for her conduct, had her offences frequently passed over" (22). In one instance, Jane obtains permission to tell the nuns her dreams. "With a serious face," Monk reports, "which sometimes impressed upon all of us, and made us half believe she was in a perfect state of sanctity, she would narrate in French some unaccountable vision which she said she had enjoyed; then turning round, would say, 'There are some who do not understand me; you all ought to be informed.' And then she would say something totally different in English, which put us to the greatest agony for fear of laughing" (25). On another afternoon, Jane assigns names to the figures in Hell depicted in a painting, and then breaks up the other nuns during lessons by shaping her fingers into the first letters of these names, suggesting that the teachers resemble the designated figures of the damned (88).

No matter how egregious her transgression, however, Jane is forgiven, an anomaly that leads Caroline Levander to speculate that the renegade nun serves the convent by preventing her peers from lapsing into despair.[52] "Nothing but the humor of Jane Ray could rouse us for a moment from our languor and melancholy" (90), Monk admits. "I was always inclined to think that [the Superior] was willing to put up with some of her tricks, because they seemed to divert our minds from the painful and depressing circumstances in which we were placed" (97–98). Beyond simply keeping the nuns' spirits up, however, Jane actively serves the convent's interests, as when she explicitly tells Monk that she "had better comply with everything the Superior desired" if she wants to stay alive (41). Jane embodies the panoptical discipline of the convent, as "her habit of roaming about it, and of observing everything," makes her "acquainted with things which would be heard with interest" (105). "She would often go and listen, or look through the cracks in the Superior's room, while any of the priests were closeted with her," Monk reveals, "and sometimes would come and tell us what she witnessed" (105). Despite Jane's claim to disdain nuns "ready to inform of the most trifling faults of others, and especially those who acted without any regard to honour, by disclosing what they had pretended to listen to in confidence" (97), she herself snitches on occasion (91). More threatening, Jane often takes up the burden of punishment, leaving the Superior free to appear relatively tolerant. Beating and torturing her enemies, Jane promises to kill those who threaten her intimacy with the Superior (102). She "would never rest," Monk writes, "until she had brought such a one into some difficulty" (103). Little wonder that Monk confesses of Jane, "We were all convinced that it was generally best to yield to her" (96).

Jane Ray serves the convent (and Monk's efforts to become an author) most effectively, however, by bringing about narrative digression, taking Monk from her moral message into anecdotes and recollections that provide much of the allure of *Awful Disclosures*. In particular, Jane infuses the convent with a gothic mood that suggests depth of meaning. "One of the most shocking stories I heard of events that occurred in the nunnery before my acquaintance with it"— a graphic account of tortured nuns who kill themselves—was "told me by Jane Ray" (143), she writes. After a detailed catalog of torture devices, Monk ends with Jane's report of nuns driven mad by torture (152). As Monk acknowledges, "there seemed to be always something deeper than anybody at first suspected, at the bottom of everything she did" (99). The embodiment of significant interiority, Jane, like the convent's lime pit, is bottomless and unfathomable. Monk adopts Jane's strategy, suggesting that the convent's horrors are always worse than any the reader can imagine ("suspicion cannot do any injustice to the priests," she reports, "because their sins cannot be exaggerated" [89]), inviting the reader to dredge up the worst scenes in her imagination to fill in the gaps left by Monk. In so doing, Monk invites her readers to assume a gothic interiority as well, entering into the "unconscious exercises" that result in institutional identification within the narrative.

At the same time, Jane undermines the institution's disciplinarity by turning interiority into a performance so extreme as to forbid any claim to naturalness. Monk recognizes her friend's "customary artfulness, in keeping up the false impression" (95) of insanity. When the nuns are encouraged to confess their shameful thoughts, for instance, Jane generates a list so extreme as to "throw ridicule on confessions" (100). Even as Jane shows that one must perform interiority in order to be protected by institutions, her "customary artfulness" turns interiority into a performance that reveals and subverts the disciplinary apparatus.

The key to exteriorizing interiority is, for Jane, sociability. While the convent seeks to isolate nuns from each other, forbidding them to tell their histories or to share their thoughts, Jane is continuously "roving about, and almost perpetually talking to somebody or other" (48). Jane's "roving," however, proves metaphysical as well, establishing a connection between independence from institutional knowledge and the maintenance of friendships. "Jane Ray appeared to be troubled still more than myself," Monk observes, "with wandering thoughts; and when blamed for them, would reply, 'I begin very well, but directly I begin to think of some old friend of mine, and my thoughts go a wandering from one country to another'" (106–7). While the convent's disciplinary virtues are oriented toward the future (the perpetually deferred rewards of heaven), Jane's intimate longings are nostalgic. While the convent's disciplines draw borders between interiority and exteriority, between the convent and the "outside world," Jane's intimacies cross borders ("wandering from one country to another"). Refusing to relinquish historical experiences (past-ness) that challenge institutional futurity or to surrender the social expression of those histories that generate alliances counter to the interests of institutional discipline, Jane from the start gives Monk "pleasure," not because of the content of her talk ("I do not remember what she said"), but through the very act of talking, of establishing a social relationship. For Monk, repeatedly hurt by always already institutionalized relationships—her mother, her husband, the convent—Jane's sociability proves institutionalism's welcome anomaly.

Jane Ray, in other words, embodies ambivalence, resisting and serving the convent's disciplinary order. As such, she is an extension of Monk herself, fleeing from the convent and then returning, drawn and repulsed by its power over her identifications, her volition, and even her unconscious. Despite its dungeon prison cells, torture devices, and corpse-filled lime pits, which are evocative of pre-modern punishment, the convent is a fully modern institution, Monk shows, making self-management rather than sociability the principal duty of the well-disciplined citizen. If such institutions promise the "freedom" from social entanglements and a blissful horizon of futurity, they do so only at a cost. "I would most gladly have escaped from the nunnery, and never returned. But that was a thing not to be thought of," Monk writes. "I was in their power, and this I deeply felt, while I thought there was not one among the whole number of nuns, to whom I could look for kindness" (40). Left without social relations ("to whom I could look for kindness"), Monk so completely loses her sense of agency ("I was in their power") that even her imagination becomes passive ("that was a thing not be thought of"). Placing the panoptical mechanisms of modern institutionality at the core of the convent's apparatuses of control, Monk demonstrates that, Beecher and Lieber notwithstanding, discipline and punishment, Catholic and Protestant institutions, are never entirely separate or sequential. (If discipline fails to work, that is, physical punishment is always waiting in the wings.) Putting institutionality and its nominal other, Catholicism, in explosive proximity, Monk makes clear the coercive force at work throughout the civil sphere, leaving citizens with increasingly less power of social invention. Readers of *Awful Disclosures* may have found in its ambivalence (its dis/closures) a way to comprehend the paradoxical institutional sensations of restriction and stimulation in their own lives.

The alternative to ambivalent institutionalism in *Awful Disclosures* is sociality as a means to inventive freedom. The relationship between Maria Monk and Jane Ray might not at first seem an ideal model for sociality. The two women have almost nothing in common, apart from living in the convent. Sharing no character traits, few interests, and no permanent commitment, the two women are the opposite of institutional sociability, which, for men such as Beecher and Lieber, involved shared (good) character, common interest, and contractual commitments that presumably ensure permanence (futurity). Jane Ray and Maria Monk are friends, however, not because they are the same and hence believe they share a future, not even because they always like each other. Rather, they become friends at the moment they perceive in one another a potential accomplice in and audience for a critical reading of and alternative to the interiorizing logic of the institution that attempts to leave them powerless and alone. As they seem to recognize, sociality, like freedom, is often contingent and ephemeral, characterized as much by conflict as by unity. While such moments of association might appear insignificant and even comically local, their operations nevertheless remain public and inventive and, in an institutional civil sphere that generates obsessive self-management as the simulacrum of participation, perhaps the most powerful site of democratic sociality.

3

ABOLITION'S RACIAL INTERIORS

AND WHITE CIVIC DEPTH

How social order became understood in relation to the description and reform of specific types of citizens' interiority (their "natures" or "characters," emanations of the "deep" self) is central to how social reform affected public opinion in the nineteenth-century United States and how it continues to shape American understanding of "race" and of social identities more broadly to this day. The "inward turn" of disciplinary control at/as the advent of modernity, made famous by Michel Foucault, enhanced the possibilities for human freedom while simultaneously restricting those options by regulating subjectivity through the statistical knowledges ("norms") of human character that made accusations of "bad" interiority, of delinquency or perversion, more dangerous than the loss of freedom. In the United States, the antebellum movements for social reform played an instrumental role in the shifts Foucault describes, providing a range of discourses through which human "depth" was scrutinized for signs of social unrest. Through reform rhetoric, Americans came to see such unrest as caused less by economic or political inequality than by defects of the human will, personality, or character. In locating the vectors of social inequality and dissent in proximity to normative character, and by seeking to remedy social ills through the re-disposition of delinquent interiority, nineteenth-century reformers, while making significant social gains for America's underclasses, facilitated the individualization and affect saturation—the interiorization—of political life.

Nineteenth-century reform has remained resistant to this analysis, however, in part because of trends in American historiography that have tended toward either–or choices: freedom or oppression, containment or liberation, revolutionaries or reactionaries. These trends have meant that Foucault's central insight—that the generation of citizens' interiority is particularly restrictive precisely because it is rooted in discourses of freedom (including, as this chapter shows, the freedoms nominally gained by normative civic virtues), increasing the possibilities of human agency while prescribing the terms through which that agency can be understood—-has been largely ignored.[1] Yet the frustrations often expressed by those reformers who achieved greater personal liberty for abject citizens without accomplishing their revolutionary (that is, structural) visions invites a reading of antebellum interiority that conceives of individual liberty and collective restriction as simultaneous phenomena. In part this reading requires that we recognize the institutions of the civil sphere not simply as sites of popular debate, as Habermas has suggested, but as locations where subjectivity and state interest blend into affective hybrids that create both the possibilities for independent critique and forms of self-management that limit those possibilities.

The nineteenth-century reform that most acutely experienced this bind of expansive liberty and restrictive subjectivity is the movement to abolish slavery, culminating in the American Anti-Slavery Society. Historians have long critiqued nineteenth-century theories of innate racial inferiority that supported slavery, recognizing their seemingly objective eugenicist rhetorics as instruments of social power. At the same time, more progressive theories of innate virtues arising from racialized conceptions of interiority have remained relatively unexplored, even though these theories, in many ways complementary to their more racist counterparts, have had a longer shelf life in American racial thought. To hasten that analysis, I want to examine the rhetorical interiorization in the writings of two prominent antebellum abolitionists: the founder of the American Colonization Society, Robert Finley, and of the American Anti-Slavery Society, William Lloyd Garrison. I choose these figures not because they invented the interiorizing tendency of nineteenth-century reform or even because they were its most determined progenitors. Rather, I choose Finley and Garrison because the discrepancy between structural and interiorized reform— and the consequences of that discrepancy—is so pronounced in their work: their ambitions being genuinely revolutionary, the tensions generated within those ambitions by interiorization were more acutely felt and responded to with striking rhetorical creativity. Only by understanding abolitionist reform at the tense crossroads of its day—mediating, as most antebellum social reform did, between structural and interior analyses of power and inequality—can we understand apparent contradictions within figures such as Garrison, who was at once anti-institutional and the center of a national network of abolition institutions; anti-nationalist and the primary advocate for considering African Americans national subjects; anti-imperialist and yet capable of imagining a de-nationalized republicanism free to extend beyond the national borders. These apparent contradictions were not weaknesses of abolitionists' courage or powers of conception, but symptoms of a shift in nineteenth-century social thought, as the workings of power moved out of the structural life of American society and into the interior lives of its citizens.

The least-noted tension within nineteenth-century reform arises between the identifications of sympathy and the attribution of differentiated interiors to the abject and the privileged. Several critics have demonstrated the importance granted affective states—especially sympathy—in antebellum America. Equally disturbing, however, is the distinction between *two* interior states: affect, which characterizes white Americans as fully feeling subjects, and civic abstraction, which becomes the possession of black Americans. If slavery, as critics have argued, forced black Americans to bear the burden of embodiment spared white Americans who, in contrast, could identify with national abstractions such as virtue and liberty (abstractions that, as Toni Morrison argues, take on meaning only in visible contrast to enslaved black bodies), reformist abolition invested blacks with the burden of abstract civility, now viewed as defining their interior "characters."[2] While Garrison began his career by criticizing and condemning the practices of the American Colonization Society, he shares with its founder a persistent inscription of racial difference not on the physical body as an index of inferior character (as pro-slavery advocates claimed), but as differentiated interior states requiring different relationships to address, to social agency, and to the entitlements of citizenship. Imagining African American interiority as constituted by (the desire for) civic abstraction, white abolitionists saw black Americans first as pupils needing lessons in, and then as stable embodiments of, civic "character" that sympathetic affect entitled white abolitionists to teach, challenge, and change. At the same time, sympathy as an affective state that is particular to liberal whites allowed a mobility of identification only for the already enfranchised white subject. White reformers took on blackness not on the surface of the skin, but as a suffering interior, a civic depth. With an inner experience of black suffering, white reformers claimed a public authority that differentiated them from other whites even while it maintained an affective difference from persecuted blacks.

Pedagogical Discipline and the Lessons of White Citizenship

In December 1816, Robert Finley, a New Jersey schoolteacher and Presbyterian minister, traveled to Washington, D.C., with a plan for the first national organization to address the status of free blacks in the United States. Finley quickly gathered the support of many of Washington's Federalist leaders, including Henry Clay, Elias Caldwell, Francis Scott Key, Charles Mercer, and Bushrod Washington. Early in 1817, these prominent men voted into existence the American Colonization Society, dedicated to transporting free blacks to the African colony of Liberia. In its century of operations, the society oversaw the removal of 15, 385 people to Liberia.[3]

Although the American Colonization Society had lost most of its popular appeal by the late 1830s, largely due to its ambivalent stand on slavery, it nevertheless played an important role in defining early nationalism by articulating the racial exterior—and, by implication, the racial *interior*—of the United States.[4] If "the process of organizing American coherence through a distancing Africanism became the operative mode of a new cultural hegemony," as Morrison has argued, the first organized movement to distance blacks (literally as well as metaphorically) from the new nation provides a vital example of what she calls "American Africanism": the defining of white citizens by imagining their black "others" who must take on as their "character," in the realm of representation if not in lived experience, those contradictory traits that white Americans did not wish to acknowledge in themselves.[5] By advocating the expulsion of blacks characterized as lazy, docile, primitive, and violent, the American Colonization Society helped make ambition, civilization, and sensibility seem the natural and exclusive, if interior and hence intangible, property of whites. By asserting that whites alone belonged in America, then, the American Colonization Society helped establish citizenship in the image of whiteness, which it also shaped and defined. That the society came into existence soon after the ratification of the Constitution, amid the struggle to define a uniquely American character, suggests the central role racial differentiation played in the framing of national belonging. The "knowledge" of white and black character produced through debates about slavery and the "knowledge" of viable citizenship became mutually supporting structures of social order in the new republic.[6]

The expulsion of blacks projects the stability of the white subject as the grounds for exclusion and suggests that whiteness must be articulated before it can be used as a yardstick for acceptable citizenship. The coherence of the white subject begins in cultural discourses—religious, educational, and patriotic— that predate the founding of the American Colonization Society. Those interiorizing discourses locate the ontology of whiteness in those ineffable locations —spirit, character, disposition—that are beyond the reach of empirical evaluation and offer modes of address that arranged identities in hierarchical relationships. While expulsion confirms the apparent coherence of white national hegemony, then, the white subject is already constituted at the moment she or he addresses the condition of blacks from a position both apart from and superior to those marked as permanently "other."

The history of disciplinary address and its relation to national racial ideology takes exemplary form in the man who conceived the plan for colonization. Robert Finley's career as a teacher and minister presents a series of self-defining moments of address, or pedagogies, that generated an apparently coherent and stable character by disciplining auditors who were portrayed as wayward, ignorant, and dependent. Through these moments of address, Finley formed regional, class, and gendered subject positions that led him finally to engage a racial pedagogy that in turn generated a character at once national and universal, bounded and unmarked. Finley's career thus demonstrates the discursive processes through which citizens of a young nation came to think of themselves as white and American (American *because* white).

The trajectory of Finley's career—from schoolroom to church, from revival meeting to national organization—also sheds light on the emergence of a public sphere that was growing in terms of its purview and authority while narrowing in terms of its access. That Finley achieved a public stage by means of a racial pedagogy that gave shape to white citizenship is not, I argue, coincidental. Race, as Finley's biography demonstrates, is crucial to the genesis of a national public sphere. Even as Finley solidified his authority through the creation of demographic divisions, each involving increasingly larger groups of people based on region, class, and gender, his racial pedagogy swallowed up these preliminary divisions and created the illusion of a large collective that could believe itself linked by a common character (whiteness) and a common interest (eliminating the threat of blackness). In so doing, Finley and the American Colonization Society generated a *race* of Americans in the sense of both a common public constituency and a naturalized group character linked to the body. If the public sphere was the site of dialogic contestation in early America, then, such a contest occurred within the limited discourse of white self-definition.

The emergence of a white national public from educational and religious discourse had the effect, furthermore, of presenting white self-interest as liberal benevolence in ways that have made whiteness not only unmarked but, in its position on the moral high ground, unassailable. Each stage of Finley's career was enabled by his claim to self-sacrificing action. The connections in Finley's career between benevolence and increased public power are illuminated by a useful distinction Foucault draws between a "centralized and centralizing" state power that arose with the emergence of nation-states, and another "oriented towards individuals and intended to rule them in a continuous and permanent way," which he calls a "pastoral or individualizing power."[7] While state power defines the borders of the nation, pastoral power allows citizens to believe both that they are individuals possessed of free will and that this will coincides with the interests of the nation. The state relies on pastoral supervision to convince citizens that they choose, as individuals, to labor in the collective interest of the state, even while those state interests are reimagined as the interior states (the "will") of each citizen. Organized movements to end slavery and to decide the status of free blacks generated a central pastoral discourse in the United States, most obviously in their efforts to convince African Americans that their interests lay with those of the "general" (white) population of America. What those interests were, however, was anything but certain at the end of the eighteenth century; defining the interests of white America (in fact, defining "whiteness" as the grounds of American interest) became a subtle but significant duty of benevolent organizations.[8] Race became a knowledge of character—white character as well as black—central to the regulation of citizenship and of labor not only through the explicitly racist discourses generated by pro-slavery forces, but through pastoral discourses of benevolence generated by abolitionists as well.

Finley's pedagogical strategies began with the lessons of his own teacher, John Witherspoon, who was instrumental in transforming education from a system of corporal correction into what Richard Brodhead calls "disciplinary intimacy," operations of benevolent care "less visible but more pervasive, less 'cruel,' but more deeply controlling" than applications of the rod.[9] Witherspoon's pedagogy of disciplinary intimacy, which established an instructional philosophy centered on the panoptical control made more famous by his British contemporary, Jeremy Bentham, formed an important backdrop to the self-defining strategies of his pupil, Finley. In his 1772 "Letters on Education," Witherspoon first blurred any potential distinction between social control (including the training of servants as well as the instruction of children) and domestic affection. "In the former age," Witherspoon wrote, "both public and private, learned and religious education was carried on by mere dint of authority," a "savage and barbarous method" that proved "in many instances terrible and disgusting to the youth."[10] In place of severe authority, which may "irritate instead of reforming" (137) and thus provoke counterproductive rebellion, Witherspoon encouraged the use of "every soft and gentle method . . . on such terms as plainly lead to a relaxation" (133). Although Witherspoon had not entirely given up on corporal direction—"the rod itself is an evidence of love" (141), he assured his readers—parents could obtain more effective obedience through benevolence than through severity.

Benevolence is not to be confused, however, with liberty, for Witherspoon urged the adoption of pedagogical discipline as a more effective form of restraint than bodily force. "Children, habituated to indulgence for a few of their first years," he advised, "are exceedingly impatient of restraint, and if they happen to be of stiff or obstinate tempers, can hardly be brought to an entire, at least to a quiet and placid submissiveness; whereas, if they are taken in time, there is hardly any temper but what may be made to yield, and by early habit the subjection becomes quite easy to themselves" (134). Key to the productive operation of pedagogical discipline is that order and "subjection" become "quite easy" to the governed, become in fact part of their very consciousness. "If then, you can accustom your children to perceive that your will must always prevail over theirs," Witherspoon assured parents, "when they are opposed, the thing is done, and they will submit to it without difficulty or regret" (135). The connection between an ideological formation (the "content" of instruction) and regulated habit (learned content internalized as self-directed behavior) is the cornerstone of Witherspoon's pedagogical discipline. As he told readers, "An association of ideas is, as it were, the parent of habit" (135).

The habits born of parental ideas produce not only good education, but dutiful service and profitable labor as well. Witherspoon offered examples of how masters could discipline servants to produce more effective service, building on such discussions to argue that children could be disciplined to yield property itself to the demands of authority. When children eight or nine months old like to hold things in their hands, Witherspoon instructed, the parent should take the objects away repeatedly (136). "I can assure you from experience," he boasted, "having literally practiced this method myself, that I never had a child of twelve months old, but who would suffer me to take any thing from him or her, without the least mark of anger or dissatisfaction; while they would not suffer any other to do so without the bitterest complaints. You will easily perceive how this is to be extended, gradually and universally, from one thing to another, from contradicting to commanding them" (136). Witherspoon's pedagogy joins the ability to command to the ability to demand willing transfer of property and of service, both of which come to seem like the habitual desire of the disciplined rather than the authoritative demand of the parent/master. Witherspoon's discipline does not mention, but clearly requires, what Bentham termed "panopticism": constant surveillance by an inspector of the governed, who may not always be watched but always believe themselves potentially to be so. To know when a child has taken up a cherished object, the parent must be ever watchful, until the child behaves under an imagined scrutiny that may not in fact be operative.

If Bentham's inspectors shape the subjectivities of inmates, however, the needs of effective discipline shape the subjectivities of guards as well. The latter effect of discipline becomes evident in Witherspoon's reliance on pedagogical exemplarity. While discipline assumes a direct line of influence between examples and imitations—"What we see every day has a constant and powerful influence on our temper and carriage" (143)—the efficacy of mimetic discipline requires that pupils recognize a consistency in their teachers. Witherspoon warned that "husbands and wives ought to conspire and co-operate in every thing relating to the education of their children: and if their opinion happen, in any particular, to be different, they ought to examine and settle the matter privately by themselves, that not the least opposition may appear either to children or servants. When this is the case, every thing is enforced by a double example: but when it is otherwise, the pains taken are commonly more than lost, not being able to do any good, and certainly producing very much evil" (126). Failing to achieve absolute stability as the exemplary object of the mimetic gaze, one risks the very right to rule, bringing about the "evil" that children may learn, instead of habitual discipline, "the art of overcoming their parents, which they will not fail to manifest on a future opportunity" (137). "There are some families, not contemptible either in station or character," Witherspoon cautioned readers, "in which the parents are literally and properly obedient to their children, are forced to do things against their will" (138). In achieving effective rule, however, the parent must internalize the gaze of the child, just as the child must internalize that of the parent. "He who would preserve his authority over his children," Witherspoon asserted, "should be particularly watchful of his own conduct" (139). Parents must regulate themselves through the imagined monitory gaze of their children, then, imposing discipline on themselves as well as on their charges.

Parents are self-disciplined, in Witherspoon's pedagogy, not simply into consistency, but also into idealized Enlightenment citizenship. Witherspoon is quite specific about what constitutes "decency of conduct" and "dignity of deportment" (139), urging parents to show themselves "always cool and reasonable in their own conduct; prudent and cautious in their conversation with regard to the rest of mankind; not fretful or impatient, or passionately fond of their own peculiarities; and though gentle or affectionate to their children, yet avoiding levity in their presence" (139). Serious but gentle, dispassionate and prudent, purged of "peculiarities" into the abstract qualities that can be shared through mimetic imitation, the effective teacher, for Witherspoon, is also the exemplary citizen. Such a citizen comes into being, however, in the pedagogical moment: only when one sets out to teach subordinates how to model themselves on an exemplary subject does that subject—that *citizen*—come into being. Giving rise to "national characters, and national manners, and every characteristic distinction of age and place" (143), education thus becomes for Witherspoon a patriotic act, as "there is no part of your duty, as a Christian, or a citizen, which will be of greater service to the public, or a source of greater comfort to yourself" (125). Patriotism makes order "easy" ("of greater comfort") to parents as well as to children, to teachers as well as to students. Yet even as citizenship comes into being as "national character," it does not take on ontology, although it does take on distinctive characteristics. Rather, citizenship, arising in the moment of pedagogical address, is always relational, locking citizens (teachers and students, parents and children, masters and servants) into hierarchical and regulated positions, none of which is "free," although some are more powerful than others.

The power imbalances of Enlightenment citizenship become clear in the gender, class, and racial specificity of Witherspoon's exemplary teacher. Brodhead argues that disciplinary intimacy arose in part from an effort to distinguish the coercive operations of education from those of slavery. Witherspoon demonstrates, however, that the excessive indulgences of "intimacy" itself could also be characterized as slavery, making the rigors of pedagogical discipline, by contrast, a means to emancipation. "Many a free born subject is kept a slave for the first ten years of his life," he observed, "and is so much handled and carried about by women in his infancy, that the limbs and other parts of his body are frequently misshapen, and the whole very much weakened; besides, the spirits, which under confinement, are generally in a dull and languishing state" (129). Witherspoon here deploys the very language his contemporaries used to condemn slavery, which produced dull and languishing spirits and malnourished, misshapen bodies, to argue for disciplinary rigor. At the same time, the intimacy of domestic education is spared effeminacy by placing women—and particularly mothers—in the position of slaveholders. Women for Witherspoon are notoriously poor teachers. Having "fewer opportunities of being abroad in the world," they lack proper social character, a "failing" they share with members of the working class. Children of that class who want to become full citizens must forever separate themselves from the "vulgarity of sentiment" and "provincial dialect" of their upbringing and must "construct an intimacy with persons of liberal sentiment and higher breeding, and be as little among their relations as possible" (147). Disciplinary education, through these intersecting discourses, is thus presented not only as liberating and determinate, but as middle class, masculine, and white.

Witherspoon's pedagogy depends on a voluntary regulation of all citizens in the social orders that, originating at the scene of instruction, radiate in both directions, giving shape to family life and to the state, which are in turn idealized as divine conditions. Witherspoon refers to the "lawful" demonstration of affection toward one's children, provided the latter are "quiet, gentle, and submissive in their carriage" (139); citizens "under the law" are entitled to benevolence from the state, by implication, only under similar conditions. Order, once established at home, can be transferred from parents to increasingly larger social units. He likens authority over children to that of "a magistrate over other citizens" (138) and compares the orderly family to "the greater bodies of men, the army and navy," in which "those who keep the strictest discipline, give the fewest strokes" (134). Ultimately, Witherspoon universalized educational discipline to divine order, claiming, "I will tell you here, with all the simplicity necessary in such a situation, what I have often said in my course of pastoral visitation in families, where there is in many cases, through want of judgment, as well as want of principle, a great neglect of authority. 'Use your authority for God, and he will support it' " (141). Having transferred exemplary power up the secular chain of command (fathers, magistrates, armed forces), Witherspoon finally invests it with a sacred and omnipotent (and, most to the point, unassailable) authority, thereby erasing the social investments in hierarchical structures of order and making acquiescence to those structures a moral duty—indeed, the only option one has.

The efficacy of pedagogical discipline in forming such ordered and orderly citizens requires permeable borders between morals and customs, public and private realms, sociality and interiority. Witherspoon condemns as a "dangerous snare" (146), for instance, the notion that politeness and piety are opposed; politeness, given a moral weight, then becomes both "a habit of sentiment and conversation" (147), a seamless merging of the affective and the customary, the individual and the collective. "The form without the spirit is good for nothing," he concluded, bringing disciplinary habit to the height of ethical principle, "but on the other hand, the spirit without the form, never yet existed" (154). Having denied the separation of the affective and the social, Witherspoon can better assert that the values of (the top tiers of) society should govern the habits and emotions of each citizen. The very ease with which Witherspoon moves between child, student, servant, and citizen as the proper object of pedagogical discipline makes clear the permeability of the borders of home, school, workplace, and nation.

But if Witherspoon's pedagogy linked these sites in ways that made the operations of social hierarchy palatable as affectively satisfying relationality, it also had to present the disciplining of those relations as the outcome of liberal concern and (at least potential) "advancement." Here Witherspoon parallels Bentham's presentation of the labor of prisoners and guards as willingly yielded, the end result of disciplinary utopia: prisoners are spared meaningless and unprofitable labor, receive better health care and nutrition, and suffer less bodily constraint, while guards become more considerate of the well-being of their charges, constrained from cruelty and neglect by the desire for profit. Coercive discipline thus gives way to liberal concern, enabling Witherspoon's pedagogy to appear as both a program for producing regulated obedience and an evidence of love.

For Bentham, the origin and most useful site of panopticism was not the prison or the madhouse but the school, a use that did not escape the notice of one of Witherspoon's earliest students, Robert Finley, who translated his teacher's model of domestic instruction into a self-constituting program of classroom discipline. So effective was Finley's deployment of Witherspoon's lessons that the principal surviving account of Finley's thoughts and actions is a "memoir" composed not by the subject himself, but by Isaac Brown, who conceived the plan of writing the biography while "under the influence" of Finley's powerful address.[11] The representation of Finley's life through the lens of Brown's interpretation might suggest that the object, not the subject, of address has ultimate narrative control. That Brown, an educator, minister, and colonization advocate, spent most of his life fulfilling Finley's missions suggests, however, that the former set the terms of the latter's desires, a pedagogical relay from which Brown apparently profited. It is not that Brown *became* Finley. Mimesis in the form of imitative identification is always a failed endeavor, necessarily producing deviation even as it seeks to enact complete merger. Thus, one finds in Brown's own writings on slavery philosophical suppositions —Brown builds on Locke and Blackstone to argue against slavery on the basis that it inhibits free will, reason, and "freedom of choice or action" (11)—that neither Witherspoon nor Finley entertained in his formulations of national discipline.[12] Despite these differences, however, Brown enables the fantasy of mimetic merger in his text, in which memory, shaped and suffused by scenes of instruction that form the bulk of his account, allows two lives to (e)merge as one. Even though it is tempting to take Brown's account as transparent "evidence" of Finley's life, the text reproduces even as it recounts the genesis and relay of identity—and hence, of power—from teacher to pupil and, in turn, on to readers, making "memory" an integral part of the powerfully interiorizing technology that is pedagogical discipline.

Expelled Pupils, Racial Incorporation, and the Whiteness of National Address

Born in 1772, Finley was the son of a Scottish yarn merchant who emigrated to New Jersey in 1769 with Witherspoon and clothed soldiers throughout the Revolutionary War. As a boy Finley proved "very interested in the elements of the English language" (14), according to Brown, and entered the College of New Jersey (later Princeton) at eleven. Following his graduation in 1788, Finley began his career as a grammar-school teacher, where his first challenge was how "to introduce order, and establish discipline" among students, many of whom were Southerners, who proved "irregular and insubordinate in their temper and manners" (17). Although Finley "proceeded with energy," the students "manifested a refractory temper, resisted his regulations, and, on being urged to comply, broke out into open rebellion, in hopes of intimidating the youthful instructor and constraining him to connive at their idle and disorderly habits" (17).

Three features stand out in Brown's account of this pedagogical crisis. First, far from today's more common narrative of youthful rebellion against established authority, this crisis stages an intra-generational battle among the young, Finley's students being roughly the same age as their instructor. Given the occurrence of this battle on or around 1788, the year of the Constitution's ratification and just prior to George Washington's inauguration as the first U.S. president, it is tempting to see Finley's pedagogical struggle as reflecting national unease, in which young citizens chafe under rules that, without a recognizable older authority or tradition to back them up, may appear arbitrary or uncertain. Such a reading is strengthened by two additional details in this account. First, this battle is ultimately about influence and imitation; the fear is not that the students will fail to learn grammar or even character, but that the teacher will be taught, that Finley might be made to "connive" in the behavior of his pupils. The struggle, in short, is over who has the authority to shape and define the behavior of others. The struggle to maintain order as a means to shape character is as necessary for the subject position of the teacher as it is for his students, for the "example" is as malleable as the protean personalities of the intended acolytes. The national character of this ontological struggle is underscored by the fact that, more than bad boys challenging a good teacher, these are Southerners challenging a Northern authority. Generational difference is thus translated into regional difference, the effort to transmit knowledge represented in terms of control over the definition of national culture and character.

Finley responded to the challenge to his pedagogical control with a two-part strategy that became characteristic of his career. First, he opted for expulsion, suspending the "refractory" from his school. Once the expulsion was complete, however, Finley had to establish an order that would allow for the reincorporation of the wayward and a reshaping of the pupils into a functional whole. To this end, Finley not surprisingly appealed to Witherspoon, who "visited the school; investigated the whole matter; pronounced his full and decided approbation of the measures and conduct of Mr. Finley; established the influence of his young friend, by the whole weight of his own dignity and authority; compelled the disorderly to make suitable acknowledgments, and to return submissively to their studies, under the very system against which they had revolted" (17). This event implies a triangulation of authority that in turn establishes a relay between three mutually informing structures of patriarchal rule: the family, the church, and the school. Witherspoon is connected to the young schoolteacher through his father, John Finley, who has by this point disappeared from the story. The familial structure, of which John Finley is head, yields to the church structure, of which Witherspoon is head; he in turn passes along his "dignity and authority" to the schoolteacher. That Witherspoon figures in Brown's account·primarily as a minister, even though he holds the presidency of Princeton, and Finley is presented primarily as a teacher, even though he will shortly become a Presbyterian minister, points to the generational transformation of institutional authority that Brown apparently wished to foreground—the school has taken on the authority of the church, just as the church has taken on the authority of the family—and foregrounds the school as a crucial site for the forming of proper citizenship.[13] The authority of all three institutions, as Finley's crisis suggests, rests on apparently stable subject positions arranged in dutiful and affective hierarchies (father/child, minister/congregant, teacher/student) that in turn create the national and even universal "belongings" they purport merely to mirror and transmit.

Most important, however, is the establishment of pedagogical stability. No longer threatened by his pupils' bad behavior, Finley, under Witherspoon's sanction, quickly becomes the stable example that brings order to those "below" him. "Being himself accomplished as a scholar, energetic in all his movements, possessing a peculiar talent to forward boys rapidly in their course of improvement, and his assistants being generally selected with great care, and promptly and assiduously taught to enter into his views and to follow his example," Brown reports, "the plan of education pursued was calculated to make sound classical scholars, and to implant in the pupils' minds, principles and habits of subordination and good morals." Witherspoon brings order in these anecdotes by the sheer presence of his authoritative self, but Brown seems to use him as shorthand for the pedagogical philosophy that Witherspoon espoused, designed to bring subordination first and good morals only in its wake. As a site of exemplarity and imitation, of surveillance and submission, Finley's classroom became almost indistinguishable from Bentham's workhouse or Witherspoon's household. "On account of the acknowledged pre-eminence of his capacity for government," Brown observed, "very intractable and turbulent youths were at times committed to his care, for the purpose of reformation as well as instruction. This frequently afforded an opportunity and created the necessity for the exertion of all his masterly powers. The insidious and artful could not escape his deep, persevering and irresistible scrutinies. The most hidden disorders and crimes he would, by some means, detect and bring to light, often to the astonishment of the perpetrators" (34–35). Though the consequences of his discipline were potentially dire—Brown reports that, following "a considerable exercise of discipline," Finley told a friend, "They *will* find out after all that I will quite *kill* them" (36)—the social payoffs in productive labor and patriotic duty proved worth the risk: "On the whole, this institution was highly respectable, and very extensively used. A considerable number of men, from several states in the union, who received the elements of their education in its bosom, are pursuing professional occupations, and filling distinguished stations in society, promising increasing honour to this seminary, and to the name of its founder, reputation to themselves, and usefulness to their country" (38).[14]

As befits the pedagogy of disciplined imitation, Finley's power to adjudicate questions of moral worth must not simply be asserted and accepted; it must be written on the body. Most striking, however, is that moral order is inscribed not only on the bodies of the pupils but on that of the teacher as well. Brown's description moves from the moral code as a scene of instruction (the assistants are taught Finley's views) to the body of the teacher, whose "aspect was naturally stern and commanding" and who "could assume a countenance, voice and manner truly terrific" (36). The panoptical pedagogy of imitation produces the apparent ontological stability of the exemplary teacher, who comes to look, in Finley's classroom no less than in Witherspoon's home, like the ideal moral citizen.

If addressing a "wayward" audience helps generate the stable subjectivity of the exemplary teacher, Finley's efforts to find increasingly larger groups of "refractory" pupils suggests a need for more powerful technologies of address to define an expanding conception of authority in an emergent public sphere. It also suggests, however, the nagging insecurity of that authority. Finley first extended his sphere of address through his career as a Presbyterian minister. As in the classroom, Finley's nominal mission was to conjoin "gospel knowledge and discipline" (38). And, as in the classroom, the effect of that disciplined knowledge was the (presumed) erasure of difference in favor of an abstract unity: "Old divisions and animosities disappeared, and the people became of one heart and one mind" (38). Yet the effects of Finley's ministrations were limited: "notwithstanding the external attention and order which had been exhibited, and the salutary influence of the stated administration of the divine ordination," Brown writes, "it was manifest that the life and power of true piety were but little felt, and that religion, in its essence and spirit, were at a low ebb" (39). In fact, outside his own parish, Finley's "zeal" appeared "immoderate and his manner extravagant" (51). Only those trained from the very beginning of their educations to perceive Finley's style as natural and universal seemed to feel its effects: of the fifty-five people reportedly converted by Finley, most were pupils at his academy.

Finley was an ambitious man, however, not content to preach to the converted. Faced with the indifference of his suburban neighbors, he "endeavored to hunt out the poor and ignorant in their retired dwelling places, to rouse them to a sense of sin and danger, and to convey to their houses and hearts, the glad tidings of pardon and salvation, through the blood of Christ" (71).[15] Finley's sense of "sin" is at once personal and social, inscribed in both "heart and house" and enacted in particular relation to those "in dependent circumstances" (53). These descriptions of Finley's pastoral labors assert absolute distinctions between the dependent and the independent, the seer and the seen, invested in both the affective responses of individuals and the structured relations of differentiated social groups. Such distinctions enable Finley's faith in the stable authority of his benevolent (and thus relatively empowered) subject position.

Finley's use of evangelical oratory to shape the affective responses of his "dependent" auditors places him firmly within prevalent modes of coercive oratory that shaped early American citizenship. In the mid-eighteenth century, as Jay Fliegelman has shown, oratory, which previously existed as "a decorous, rule-governed, and class specific behavior that articulated the public virtues of civic humanism," transformed into the revelation of a speaker conceived in terms of "private rather than public virtues: prudence, temperance, self-control, honesty, and, most problematically, sincerity."[16] Oratory, insofar as it expressed the true inner self of the speaker, made the fixing of elocutionary norms a vehicle for regulating through the body of the orator the "vagaries" of post-Revolutionary citizenship. But to authorize the orator, oratory had to regulate audiences, requiring affective responses that were consistent with the ideological formations of the state, or what Fliegelman characterizes as "soft compulsion": "No longer conceived of as the stigmatized power to coerce, political authority became redefined in a republican setting as the ability to secure consent, 'to command,' in Jefferson's phrase describing the Declaration, not individuals as subordinates, but 'their assent.' "[17] The post-Revolutionary era, at once "republican and evangelical," devoted both to autonomous equality and submissive conversion, privileged "the harmonizing power of an eloquence that draws forth the indwelling moral and social nature of its auditors, compelling them to submit to law in charmed silence," thereby creating "the new affective version of the consent of the governed."[18] Finley's oratory was clearly designed to bring forth this kind of harmony, in which the social order found direct expression in the "indwelling nature" of individual citizens. What is surprising about Finley's "soft compulsion," however, is that it apparently elicited no such response. Although Finley believed that his "*labours of love*" among the lowly "were productive of extensive benefit to many individuals and families" (72), Brown offers no evidence for this conviction. Where Finley's inability to produce discernable responses in his suburban neighbors was interpreted as a sign of failure, however, among the "dependent" it became evidence of success. Finley's "work of grace" proceeded "in a silent and hidden manner," Brown reports. "The impressions, which were most powerful and alarming seemed to produce, in general, no audible out-cry, nor any very striking and visible emotion; but multitudes of careless sinners were filled with solemn concern, and the people of God were deeply affected and moved by the quickening influences sent down from on high" (81). This passage asserts a conversion not from sin to faith, but from carelessness to obedient acquiescence, a rhetorical transformation that is in turn taken as a sign of exemplary success.

A distinctive difference emerges, then, between the lack of affective response in those Finley considered his social equals and in those he considered his inferiors. Among the latter, he was able to project his own desires onto their emotional and spiritual interiors, fashioning them in his own image *because of their imagined difference* in a way he did not with his neighbors. In so doing, Finley made individuality a prerogative specifically of the middle-class subject. While Finley was separated from his neighbors, thus becoming more truly exemplary, the "dependent" members of his congregation became a *class*, differentiated from the minister en masse and given an individual identity only as a collective (as a group they took on the virtues of the exemplary individual). The difference that this fashioning nominally grants the congregants exists only at the whim of the minister, who has asserted his power to appropriate their difference through a projected unity made, finally, in his own image.

If the responses of the lowly congregants were not essential to Finley's mission, what was at stake was what the minister felt in the moment of instructing, for it was in shaping the sensations of his audience that Finley shaped himself, becoming an omniscient judge, an embodiment of the panopticism of moral law. "He was an acute discerner of the ends and springs of action, in every character," Brown notes, adding, "he possessed an uncommon share of judgment and prudence:—he was calm and dispassionate, in a very high degree: he was firm and unmovable in his adherence to justice and fairness on every subject; he was meek and submissive, patient and persevering:—and he was a peculiar lover of peace and harmony" (58). Like Witherspoon's ideal parent, Finley becomes abstracted ("calm and dispassionate"), but only in relation to dependent auditors, whom he imagines (without apparent evidence) as the embodied bearers of aroused sensation. While Finley "performed these duties with an importunity and solemnity of mind, fully convincing every beholder that he felt his awful responsibility," he also "appeared verily to lose sight of himself, of his academic engagements, of his domestic concerns, of his personal ease" (82). To the degree that abstraction made Finley invisible—in his own "discerning" eyes, at least—his earthly responsibilities presumably fell to those who were fully in sight: his wife, his children, his servants, his students. They, like the dependent congregants to whom he preached, bore the burden of Finley's self-definition, which allowed the minister to be master both of sensations ("he felt his awful responsibility") and of abstraction, the total Enlightenment man. Finley's status as a benevolent, caring pastor, bringing needed relief and inspiration to the downtrodden, thus relied on a hierarchical social scale that granted him alone the qualities of citizenship.

The minister pays a price, however, in basing his own sensational transformation (into teacher) on the imagined responses of his congregants, for Finley's revivalism risked an incorporation as well as a projection. At the same time that he imagined a unity arising from his instruction, Finley's "nervous system presented evidences of great debility and disorder" (75). If his ontological order is an effect of the rhetoric of harmony, his body registers a discord, displaced from the body of the congregation onto that of its minister. While there is a certain Christological martyrdom to Finley's taking on the sins of his congregation so they can achieve harmony, his unruly body brings to pass precisely the pedagogical crisis his revivalist discipline was meant to forestall: he has been made to connive in the sins of the disorderly.

Having still not achieved stability, Finley needed a bigger pulpit, a more dependent congregation. Following his pastoral "success," therefore, he entered the national stage with his campaign to found the American Colonization Society.[19] Not surprisingly, Finley saw slavery as a problem of pedagogy. Slavery excited "indolence" not among slaves, but among whites, he wrote. "It can scarcely be doubted that slavery has an injurious effect on the morals and habits of a country where it exists. It insensibly induces a habit of indolence."[20] The operations of slavery, like those of disciplinary education, insensibly induce habits of production through surveillance and imitation. As a pedagogical

discipline, however, slavery is dangerous because it shatters the illusions necessary for *voluntary* servitude, especially the illusion that labor produces teleological growth, futurity, and that a homeland, a community, or a race to which one
naturally belongs will benefit from one's labor.[21]

In response to such dangerous teachings, the American Colonization Society, under Finley's lead, took up abolition as a national pedagogy. The "free
blacks must be instructed," Finley wrote, "that it would be to their interest to
remove to the land which gave them origin, and instruction provided to raise
their minds to the degree of knowledge which would in turn fit them for self
government" (2). Finley's pedagogical intent was to discipline free blacks to
know their "interest" in a land to which they "belong" as "origin" and to give
them a "degree of knowledge" for government of the self. All of this reveals a
good deal, however, about national pedagogy as a federal apparatus at home as
well as abroad. For new (white, male) citizens of the United States no less than
for potential (black) citizens of Liberia, myths of national origin are linked to
collectivizing technologies of production in ways that make obedient labor on
behalf of the state the self-willed "interest" of each patriotic citizen. In other
words, citizens come to "belong" to a land in ways that reinforce, rather than
remedy, the base conditions of slavery in relation to the possibilities of dissenting agency. Yet by becoming supporters of colonization, the wayward students
(white Americans) become benevolent teachers, erasing their own submission
in a moment of "self"-constituting pedagogical address. Colonization will in
turn reproduce the pedagogical mission of benevolent white Christians, enabling "a seat of liberal learning in Africa, from which the rays of knowledge
might dart across those benighted regions" (7).

Of greater concern than turning African Americans into obedient pupils,
however, was turning whites into creditable teachers. And as in Finley's earlier
pedagogical crisis, becoming an exemplary teacher involved asserting one's
fixed subjectivity in relation to changeable pupils. Whereas Finley's exemplary
address to his dependent congregants involved a fixity based on class, however,
his address to free blacks involved the establishment of a stable subject position
based on race—or, rather, it established "race" *as* the grounds of identities, the
borders of (and between) which, like those of dependence and independence,
could be clearly distinguished. William Lloyd Garrison accused the American
Colonization Society of hypocrisy, charging Finley with making the irreconcilable claims that slaves were naturally degraded and therefore could never become proper citizens and that free blacks must be sent to Liberia as missionaries
to teach benighted Africans the lessons of American virtue. In fact, Finley did
not base his colonization plan on claims that slaves were naturally degraded or

that free blacks were incapable of "improvement." On the contrary, he suggested that African Americans, like all wayward pupils, were extremely changeable. Rather than a liberal concession that blacks were "just like" whites, however, his acknowledgment that African Americans could change became the grounds for establishing stability for whites. Proponents of colonization therefore argued that *whites* could not change; their prejudices were "too deeply rooted to be eradicated" (5). Elias Caldwell, Finley's brother-in-law and secretary of the U.S. Supreme Court, expressed the opinion of many involved in the American Colonization Society: "Some people may call it prejudice. No matter! Prejudice is as powerful a motive, and will as certainly exclude them, as the soundest reason" (107). Even if whites are characterized as prejudiced and ruthless, even undemocratic, the important thing is that, in relation to their prejudices (if not in any positive qualities), whiteness is rescued from flux (the flux of identification, since freed slaves, according to Finley, might teach whites to imitate their slothful habits) and given the illusion of fixity. The leaders of the colonization societies, moreover, are granted individuality even within the stable class of whites, since they are aware of and nominally condemn white prejudice, which they nonetheless render inevitable.

If the leaders of the American Colonizaton Society emerge as individuated whites, that ultimate paradox of full citizenship, Finley above all becomes the exemplary citizen. In founding the society, Brown reports, Finley's

> supreme object was to bring forward some great and benevolent scheme, of an elevated and extensive nature, that would make a deep impression—set a noble example—assume a national character—contribute largely to mitigate the sufferings of some aggrieved portion of the human family, and augment the general mass of individual and public happiness. For this purpose he fixed his eye early upon the condition of the colored people in these United States, as presenting a suitable sphere for the exercise of his profound and ruling passion. All his observation and knowledge of the colored race, gave stability and power to his convictions and desires on this subject. (93–94).

In this account, Finley's self-fashioning takes on the full force of the federal imaginary, at once abstract and national, invested equally (and simultaneously) in pedagogical discipline, surveillant judgment, and liberal benevolence. In his most ambitious moment of exemplary pedagogy, Finley has defined, in the image of whiteness, the "national character" and in so doing has achieved "stability and power" (power *through* stability). That Finley established national whiteness in relation to people *not* doomed to fixed character or opinion (indeed, one of the key events in Finley's life was his ability to change the minds of the African American leaders in Philadelphia to support the colonization scheme) may account for the increasing belief, even among Northerners, in theories of biological difference espoused in the nineteenth century by men such as Josiah Nott and George Fitzhugh.[22]

The risks of white ontology lie not only in the instability of relational self-definition, however, but also in the unpredictable uses to which its strategies may be put, as we can see in Brown's description of Finley's final pedagogical crisis. In January 1817, after twelve years as a trustee of Princeton, Finley became president of the University of Georgia. As had happened in his preaching, however, the success of his projection opened up the possibility for a disruptive incorporation. Having founded a society to deport blacks, Finley was in turn exiled to Georgia. Like deported blacks, Finley went to Georgia with "a missionary spirit," Brown writes, but in the face of the cultural differences he encountered, he was soon beset by "considerable depression" (181), and in September 1818, he died.[23] The death scene, as rendered by Brown, proves an ironic illustration of the dangers of teaching too well. On his deathbed, Finley received a letter from the secretary of the American Colonization Society attesting to the group's growing popularity, which "greatly refreshed his languid spirits, and forced from him expressions and manifestations of peculiar satisfaction" (201). "It is much to be regretted," Brown concludes, "that Dr. Finley's observations in this trying hour on the subject of colonizing the people of color, which, next to the plan of salvation for sinners, had occupied his mind for years, more than any other subjects, could not be distinctly heard and recollected" (201). Finley momentarily becomes a "dark" enigma: "The removal of Dr. Finley to Georgia and his sudden death, present an instance of darkness and mystery in the government of God, awful and impenetrable to the view of mortals" (204). Yet like the dark enigma of the black body, Finley's opacity proves no obstacle for the colonizing appropriation of Christian gloss:

> In an hour after he awoke, almost suffocated—called for air—said he was going. His lips moved for some few seconds, as we supposed in prayer. He then sunk into a state of total insensibility, in which he lay nearly two hours, and then with a gentle sigh breathed out his soul into the bosom of his Savior. The joy of his soul illuminated his countenance, and rendered it the most interesting object I ever beheld. The very place appeared to be sanctified by the presence of the Savior and the spirits of the dear departed saints who had been given to him as seals of his ministry, appeared to be waiting to be the crowns of his rejoicing. (203)

Just as the "insensible" responses of Finley's congregants had served as invitations for pedagogical imposition, so now did Finley's allow Brown to read his own suppositions on the teacher's unresponsive and dependent body. Brown and Finley have become one, as students, in the model of exemplary pedagogy, must ultimately become their teacher. If their unity—a unity that has already been suggested by the genre of the biographical memoir—gave Brown access to the divine harmony for which Finley had always hungered, it did so by rendering Finley a blank object. The merging of these two ministers into a sanctifying unity ultimately served the interests of both, deifying Finley while giving Brown ultimate interpretive power, both of which strengthen the various technologies —pedagogical, pastoral, and philanthropic—through which they operate. The consequences for the black "pupils" of Finley's national pedagogy, whose desires he imagined to be simultaneous to his own, were more dubious.

Finley's pedagogical career moved from an unruly classroom to an unruly class, from a degraded class to a degraded race, and finally to a benighted continent. With each change in venue, his pedagogy became more apparently national, his self-constitution more powerfully exemplary. In the end, there are several lessons we can learn from Finley, apart from those he set out to teach: that pedagogy is at least as much about forming the subjectivity of the teacher as it is about forming that of students; that those moments of pedagogical self-constitution also establish hierarchical relations of power; that such hierarchical relations can be translated between the only apparently separate realms of family, education, labor, and citizenship; that power is enacted in federal America as liberal benevolence; that power is most effectively enacted as a racial pedagogy, constituting whiteness as benevolent empowerment so that whiteness is yoked to exemplary citizenship in ways that perpetually exclude blacks; and finally, that white efforts to "improve" blacks mark a permanent difference (as between teacher and pupil) that the promise of eventual inclusion renders "soft." Finley's career demonstrates how racial thinking in federal America, as it emerged as a pedagogy of national address, generated a mode of white self-constitution and social control consistent with the benevolent rhetoric of the Constitution, giving rise to the reformist problematic of sympathy that governed abolition in the next decades. In those moments of national address, whiteness emerged as the grounds of republican citizenship, neither as a flat assertion of ontology nor as an obviously chauvinistic assertion of racial superiority, but as an anxious consolidation of exemplary interiorized traits composed in response to anticipated social disorder. In this brief examination of Finley's pedagogical career, I have suggested that the character of the exemplary American citizen—the affective subjectivity that makes the concord of national belonging possible—came into being as it was taught to subordinates. Benevolent education, surveillant discipline, and national citizenship arose simultaneously in post-Revolutionary America to form what would become in the nineteenth century America's predominant pedagogy of racial difference.

The Surprising Affects of Sympathy

In 1834, James Birney, a prominent agent of the American Colonization Society, announced that his opinions of the organization had "undergone a change so great, as to make it imperative on me no longer to give to that enterprise that support and favor which are justly expected from all connected with it."[24] Chief among the society's activities that Birney found "cruel, unmanly, and meriting the just indignation of every American" were its efforts to convince free blacks to emigrate to Africa by manipulating their "civil disabilities, disenfranchisement, exclusion from sympathy" (7). Birney's letter registers a shift in political influence away from the colonization societies, which governed national debates about race and citizenship in the 1820s, and toward the organization to which Birney defected: the American Anti-Slavery Society, which beginning in the mid-1830s argued for the incorporation into full citizenship of black Americans. Whereas the colonization societies strove to define citizenship by placing blacks outside the borders of the nation and therefore to define the national interior as white, the antislavery societies defined citizenship in relation to the individual characters of citizens. With this shift came a move to define racial injustice and to argue for national citizenship on the basis of interiorizing logics—the correct affective states for sympathetic whites and the deserving civic characters of black Americans—that corresponded to, and in many cases supplanted, more explicitly social arguments about economic opportunity, education, and class structure.

This shift is symptomatic of abolition's broader transformation from a relatively anomalous social movement in the 1820s to one in a spectrum of reformist projects in the 1830s and 1840s. Antebellum reform often conceived social problems as arising from deformed or disabled interior states (bad morality, wounded character, perverted feelings) and increasingly envisioned the proper object of reform not as the poor, degraded, or disenfranchised, but as the middle-class subject engaged in the act of reform. As abolition organizations experienced this shift, its leaders, as Birney indicated, became occupied with whites' feelings toward blacks. As Birney's rhetorical order makes clear, "civil disabilities" were measured increasingly in relation not only to economic and political "disenfranchisement," but also to "exclusion from sympathy," an affective state. Birney's distinction reflects broad trends in abolition rhetoric, suggesting not only the "inward turn" of reformist abolition, but also the ways in which interior differentiation came to substitute for morally intolerable social differences asserted on the basis of bodies.

Sympathy is never simply an outpouring of individual sentiment, however. It is an emotional register of more obviously collective social arrangements.[25] Some contemporary critics have celebrated sympathy for creating a fellow feeling that prompts the privileged to imagine themselves in the place of the less fortunate.[26] This account of affective sociability builds on the first step in Adam Smith's *Theory of Moral Sentiments* (1761), which argues that sympathizers create mental tableaux in which they see themselves in the place of the sufferer, thereby creating an imaginative bridge between socially separated peoples. Others have complicated such formulations of democratic sociality, noting how sympathy generates theatrical distance by creating suffering as a spectacle watched from afar.[27] The second model makes more careful use of Smith, who, denying the merger of sympathizer and sufferer, claimed, "Mankind, though naturally sympathetic, never conceive, for what has befallen another, that degree of passion which naturally animates the person principally concerned."[28] Sympathetic identification, for Smith, is "but momentary," kept in check by the sympathizers' self-concern: "the thought that they themselves are not the real sufferers, continually intrudes itself upon them, and though it does not hinder them from conceiving a passion somewhat analogous to what is felt by the sufferer, hinders them from conceiving anything that approaches to the same degree of violence" (26–27).

In both models, self-transformation lies with the person who extends sympathy. For Smith, however, sympathy also transforms the sufferer, who, sensing the spectatorial distance maintained by the cautious sympathizer, "longs for that relief which nothing can afford him but the entire concord of the affections of the spectators with his own" (26–27). The sufferer may achieve this "entire concord," Smith wrote, only "by lowering his passion to that pitch, in which the spectators are capable of going along with him. He must flatten, if I may be allowed to say so, the sharpness of its natural tone, in order to reduce it to harmony and concord with the emotions of those who are about him" (27).[29] If one expresses an emotion too extreme or a suffering too unusual, the audience will be unable to identify and will experience no sympathy. The burden therefore falls on the sufferer to conceal extremes or anomalies or to translate them into scenarios with which the audience will be familiar. Sufferers must transform themselves, in a model of panopticism: just as the spectators place themselves in the sufferer's situation, Smith wrote, so the sufferer must "imagine in what manner he would be affected if he was only one of the spectators of his own situation" (28).[30] In sympathetic abolition, for instance, the suffering of slaves might be shaped to correlate with texts white audiences had previously encountered: other slave narratives, white reports of slavery such as Theodore Weld's *Slavery as It Is*, or popular works of fiction such as *Uncle Tom's Cabin*. Even while serving as the keynote of benevolence, then, sympathy was a form of surveillant discipline—what we might call sympathetic discipline—in which the black sufferer had to imagine himself or herself always in the eyes of whites, becoming a body shaped by an idea of a body.

At the same time that sympathy asks the sufferer to model his or her suffering on the expectations of the sympathizer, it also separates the two parties into distinctive "classes," characterized by different interior capabilities (what Smith called "virtues"). The extension of sympathy gives rise to the "soft, the gentle, the amiable virtues, the virtues of candid condescension and indulgent humanity," while the self-modifications that invite sympathy generate "the great, the awful and respectable, the virtues of self-denial, of self-government, of that command of the passions which subjects all the movements of our nature to what our own dignity and honour, and the propriety of our own conduct requires" (3). In the end, sympathy generates affective knowledge of human "virtues" that become the basis of differential power. The sympathizer extends agency over the sufferer, while the latter controls only himself or herself. Sympathy affectively naturalizes social hierarchy without necessitating government involvement, order being maintained as the result of a newly privatized civility, what "our own dignity and honour, and the propriety of our own conduct requires" (3).

Unlike other racializing logics in antebellum America, what is striking about sympathetic discipline is that it is not predicated on marked bodies. In fact, Smith's formulation of sympathetic difference requires the *absence* of bodies. Sympathy, according to Smith, is aroused by assaults on the sufferer's imagination—"the loss of his dignity, neglect from his friends, contempt from his enemies" (42), along with romantic disappointment—rather than by sensations of the body (hunger, sexual desire, pain), "because our imaginations can more readily mould themselves upon his imagination, than our bodies can mould themselves upon his body" (42). Translated to the racial context of antebellum America, Smith's observation has conflicting implications. On the one hand, it suggests a way for whites and blacks to merge through the imagination, suggesting an affective "sameness" once the burden of marked bodies is removed; in this sense, sympathy is consistent with other universalizing ("we're all the same under the skin") forms of liberal humanism. On the other hand, racial difference moves inward, naturalized as the product and sign of individual affect. By making the knowledge of civil behavior implicitly a racialized knowledge, sympathetic whites closed the borders between sympathizer and sufferer, ensuring that whites might flirt with imaginative racial merger while maintaining autonomy through the distance of white observation (what Eric Lott has called "the pale gaze").[31]

Despite its powerful role in generating a democratically feasible system of racialized difference and social hierarchy, sympathy has remained relatively invisible as a political force largely due to its status as a "private" or "personal" emotion in an age when privacy was distinguished from the realms of capital and state regulation. Smith suggests, however, that affect was imagined in the interest of economic and social order, even as it generated the authority to criticize the nation-state. While sympathetic white abolitionists made differences between blacks and whites predicated on bodies appear prejudicial and even ridiculous, then, they also helped establish an affective economy that allowed the regulation that might otherwise have been carried out on the basis of bodies to appear as individual (that is, consensual) emotional response. Sympathetic discipline, in short, was part of a watershed in American sociopolitical discourse. While eighteenth-century social critics issued declarations of independence that called for more equitable economic and political systems, their nineteenth-century counterparts generated "declarations of sentiment" that increasingly tied social dysfunctions such as racism and poverty not only to economic inequality, but also to disabled emotions (as indicated by Garrison's use of psychosocial terms such as "negrophobia" and "colorphobia" to account for American racism).[32] Perhaps progressive politics are never possible without some appeal to the compassionate, imaginative identity crossings that we call sympathy, and certainly the politics of sympathy practiced by white abolitionists in antebellum America helped produce seismic social transformations, especially the end of slavery. Yet sympathy became the predominant political discourse in the course of the nineteenth century, obscuring the social construction and structural distribution of power in a rhetoric of individual interiority. Sympathy, in short, is central to the double bind of nineteenth-century reform.

"A Stupendous Republican Imposture": Anti-Nationalism and the Citizen Form

"Sympathy" generated particular contradictions in the construction of *citizenship* in abolitionist discourse. Citizenship is rooted in the institutions of the state, to which citizens are subject. To gain public authority, however, white abolitionists had to conceive citizenship in opposition to the state, as a form of free moral will.[33] At the same time, abolitionists sought the enfranchisement of black Americans, arguing for their right to enter the very state institutions from which white abolitionists distanced themselves. In response to these contradictions, sympathetic abolition generated two kinds of citizenship based on differences of virtue, desire, and agency: one for the empowered (white) sympathizer and another for the self-regulating (black) sufferer.

Through the American Anti-Slavery Society, which he directed from 1833 to 1865, and the abolitionist newspaper the *Liberator*, which he edited from 1831 to 1865, William Lloyd Garrison was the strongest voice to insist, contra the popular colonization societies, that black Americans must be made full U.S. citizens.[34] Garrison was also, however, an avid critic of patriotic nationalism. Believing that the U.S. government was colluding with slavery, Garrison refused to vote, honor American law, or hold public office, and he once tore up a copy of the Constitution in public protest against federally sanctioned slavery. While Garrison rejected citizenship for himself, however, he enshrined it as the highest goal black Americans could attain. These apparently inconsistent positions become compatible, however, if we recognize Garrison's conception of citizenship freed from its institutional (and hence ideological) origin in the nation-state, making it a purely personal (hence "consensual") phenomenon consistent both with the affective register of sympathy and his conscientious anti-institutionalism.

Garrison's citizenship without nations might usefully be called, building on Etienne Balibar, the citizen form.[35] Garrison's construction of the citizen form provided the illusions Balibar attributes to the nation, universalizing the state by making citizenship the result of divine wisdom, while individualizing the state by asserting the reflection of divine will in personal affect. Garrison's divorce of citizenship from the nation began with his public stand against institutional and political organizations (a somewhat paradoxical stand given the vast national and nationalizing network of antislavery societies within which Garrison operated). As Garrison declared on December 6, 1833, to the American Anti-Slavery Committee in Philadelphia, slavery "is a base overthrow of the foundations of the social contract," and therefore abolitionists were not bound by social institutions.[36] Placing the individual (and interiorized) "character" in ascendance over both collective social formations and faddish commodification, Garrison declared, "There never yet was a divine human organization. Associations are not of heaven, but of man. They are no positive test of character. Men shape them as they do their coats, their hats, or their dwellings, according to their own taste and convenience" ("Claims and Positions of the Clergy," 236).

While Garrison publicized his disdain for all conventional organizations, he reserved his particular animosity for the nation. Declaring America "a stupendous republican imposture" ("The American Union," 119), he made his position on secession unmistakable. "If the Republic must be blotted out from the roll of nations, by proclaiming liberty to the captives, then let the Republic sink beneath the waves of oblivion, and a shout of joy, louder than the voice of many waters, fill the universe at its extinction" ("No Compromise with Slavery," 139). The "Republic that depends for its stability on making war against the government of God and the rights of man," he declared, "though it exalt itself as the eagle, and set its nest among the stars, shall be cast into the bottomless deep, and the loss of it shall be a gain to the world" ("No Compromise with Slavery," 140). And, he insisted, an abolitionist "cannot love his country, for he declares it to be 'laden with inequity,' and liable to the retributive judgments of Heaven"; nor can an abolitionist "be a good citizen; for he refuses to be law-abiding, and treads public opinion, legislative enactment, and governmental edict alike under his feet" ("The 'Infidelity' of Abolition," 4).

In place of patriotism, Garrison argued for global universalism. "Our country is the world, our countrymen are all mankind," he told a Boston Peace Convention in September 1838. "We love the land of our nativity, only as we love all other lands. The interests, rights, and liberties of American citizens are no more dear to us, than are those of the whole human race. Hence, we can allow no appeal to patriotism, to revenge any national insult or injury" ("Declaration of Sentiments," 74). His appeal to universal citizenship relied on "moral power alone for success. The ground upon which we stand belongs to no sect or party—it is holy ground" ("A Fourth of July Oration," 199). Appeals to divine ground not only assured Garrison's moral authority; they also placed his word above the give-and-take of public debate, since God's truths "are absolute and immutable" ("War Essentially Wrong," 89) and may "be denied, only as the existence of a God, or the immortality of the soul, is denied. Unlike human theories, they can never lead astray; unlike human devices, they can never be made subservient to ambition or selfishness" ("The Anti-Slavery Platform," 317).[37] Speaking God's truth, Garrison universalized his positions through appeals to "human nature" without needing to sway public opinion. "The nature of man has been the same in all ages," he asserted, "and it has ever rebelled against oppression" ("The Great Apostate," 210). The abolitionist, in Garrison's metaleptic construction, derived his opinions about "the rights of man [not] from any book, but from his own nature" ("Infidelity," 10–11) and might therefore assume a position both within and against national ideology.

In these proclamations, Garrison detached citizenship from the nation-state and attached it instead to God. Yet like Emerson's divinity, Garrison's manifested itself in the virtuous composition of individual souls, which was evident in the cluster of civic virtues commonly known as "republicanism." For Garrison, republicanism would outlive the nation because its virtues, encapsulated as "the rights of man," were "inherent and inalienable, and therefore not to be forfeited by the failure of any form of government, however democratic." He declared, "Let the American Union perish, [yet] these rights would remain undiminished in strength, unsullied in purity, unaffected in value, and sacred as their Divine Author" ("The American Union," 116). Abolition's "principles are self-evident, its measures rational, its purposes merciful and just," he asserted. "It cannot be diverted from the path of duty, though all earth and hell oppose; for it is lifted far above all earth-born fear" ("Fourth of July Oration," 200). Thus, Garrison constructed his moral exemplar from the stuff of Enlightenment republicanism, including the language of the Declaration of Independence, rationality, benign duty, and responsibility. Locating virtuous rights in the universality of divine edict and the autonomy of the individual soul, Garrison advanced a citizenship that was affect-dense and universalized and, by virtue of these attributes, separate from the interests of the state.

Garrison was by no means unique in dividing citizenship from the state. As Habermas has shown, citizens throughout the late eighteenth century and early nineteenth century increasingly came to see their position in the civil sphere as distinct from, even opposed to, the state—a position that was fortified, as Garrison's was, by a moral rectitude drawn from both private affect and institutional affiliation. One can speculate that this conception of citizenship within the civil sphere aided the abolitionists' efforts to move public opinion against slavery and toward readiness for civil war. Not only did it provide critics of the nation with an aura of personal passion and divine sanction that made them seem more patriotic than more obviously invested defenders of slavery, but it also placed the values most Americans cherished in regard to the nation beyond the reach of federal dissolution, assuring Americans that they could be patriots without remaining loyal to the nation. At the same time, however, the divorce of citizenship from the nation-state placed the stuff of civic virtue everywhere but where one might suspect the operations of power. Whether universalized through God or individualized through affect, that is, citizenship came to function outside the reaches of ideology. The ways in which republicanism and the interests of the nation-state might be mutually reinforcing were obscured by the emphatic separation of citizens and nation that became an emblematic gesture of nineteenth-century reform.

Yet the divergent positions Garrison advocated in his writings suggest that the sites of potential overlap between radical reform and state interest were at times significant. A republicanism freed from the state, for instance, potentially works in tandem with (indeed, provides a liberal veneer to) the spread of nationalism beyond the nation's borders espoused by growing enthusiasm for the entrance of the United States into the global economy. At times, Garrison strenuously opposed imperial expansion, writing passionately against imperialist ventures in Mexico and Africa, especially in his diatribes against the American Colonization Society. At other moments, however, he indicated his support of consensual colonization. "If our free colored population were brought into our schools, and raised from their present low estate," Garrison declared, "I am confident that an army of Christian volunteers would go out from their ranks, by a divine impulse and under the guidance of the Holy Spirit, to redeem their African brethren from the bondage of idolatry and the dominion of spiritual death."[38] Ironically, the very forces that would "enlighten" Africa, according to Garrison, would "darken" America. Those institutions that Garrison entrusted with securing the consent of African Americans—education, religion, filiopietism—he named, in regard to white Americans, as sources of pro-slavery deception. The overlap of coercion and consent, which was central to his conception of the citizen form, makes his notion of voluntary emigration seem consistent with his condemnation of the American Colonization Society and other imperial ventures, even though his anti-institutional writings made that overlap seem, at best, questionable.[39]

While the displacement of citizenship onto divine will shares a logic of irresistibly expansive republicanism with nineteenth-century imperialism, the "privatizing" of citizenship into individual affect had equally conflicting results. Since privileged Americans, in entering the public, risked evacuating privacy, other Americans had to bear the burden of representing interiority in its threefold nature: morality, virtue, and emotion. An extensive body of criticism has demonstrated that the association of white womanhood with a supposedly natural relationship to domestic privacy allowed white men to develop a commercial sphere unimpeded by emotional or moral qualms, while limiting the legal, social, and economic potential of antebellum women. Black Americans bore a similar burden, representing traits of piety, nurturance, and conjugal fidelity threatened by the outrages of slavery: mothers could not raise their children; husbands could not provide homes for wives or even ensure their wedding bond; women could not control their sexuality; slaves were not permitted a spiritual life. Constructed as desiring purity, piety, and domesticity, black Americans came to represent an already feminized privacy. The division of abolition authority into (black) privacy and (white) publicity meant, on the one hand, that black Americans themselves could not be represented as properly "public" figures (hence Garrison's objections to Frederick Douglass's decision to edit a newspaper and honor national institutions—that is, to enter the discourses of national publicity—without Garrison's mediation).[40] On the other hand, it meant that white abolitionists needed to pass through a black interior (experiencing, through sympathy, black pain so as to speak with a public authority), allowing themselves a racially bivalent persona that blacks themselves were denied. While whites such as Garrison could move in and out of racial subjectivities, criticizing the nation so as paradoxically to gain ground in its public discourse, blacks, who had no privileged place in that public, were positioned as the unwavering bearers of (privatized, interiorized) virtue.

"In Your Sufferings I Participate": Black Virtue and White Civic Depth

The pure virtues that black Americans developed through their degrading exposure to the outrages of slavery did not remain simply "private," however. Their very purity made them potentially synonymous with the idealized republican traits of the citizen form. This translation of "private" into "civic" virtues was necessary to enable the cross-identifications central to white abolitionists' disciplinary sympathy. For Garrison, pain and disgrace became outward signs of a civic righteousness in his own life and for persecuted blacks. Indeed, with Southern gentlemen offering rewards on his head, legislatures throughout the country banning his writings, and a lynch mob in Boston dragging him through the streets with a noose around his neck, Garrison understandably considered himself a persecuted American. At times, however, he seemed to take satisfaction in his exclusion, emphasizing in his writings and public speeches that the "whole nation is against me."[41] Garrison's status as "outsider" not only granted him public authority; it also rationalized his identification with black Americans. Wounded and despised, he appeared to share their condition.

Garrison's identification with black Americans—and the limitations of that identification—gave rise to a complex pedagogical discourse. Garrison imagined black citizens as abstract markers of civic virtues (making blacks more worthy of American citizenship than prejudicial, and hence unvirtuous, whites). Through sympathy with blacks, then, white abolitionists absorbed the virtues born of private purity and public pain. The yoking of sympathy and the citizen form, in short, permitted radical reformers such as Garrison to imagine "blackness" as white interiority, as a shared, yet unmarked, bond that rendered certain whites more virtuous and ultimately more "deep" than their opponents. While white sympathy potentially locked black Americans into "characters" that were distinct from those of whites, it also allowed whites an identificational mobility that is a hallmark of privilege.

While abolitionists could maintain black Americans as abstract markers of civic virtue in writings aimed to shame or convince (and hence distance themselves from) other whites, this became an awkward position to hold in relation to blacks as actual social agents. Not only might black Americans have a different notion of what constituted virtuous citizenship; they might define themselves in ways that challenged white abolitionists' sympathetic identifications. When Garrison addressed black audiences, therefore, he paradoxically represented his black auditors both as markers of abstract virtues and, echoing Finley, as pupils needing instruction in those very civic virtues. In their construction as pupils, black Americans rhetorically marked a civility that they, by definition, did not possess, an always alienated civility available for possession both by white abolitionists (as civic depth) and by civil institutions (as the abstract virtues of the citizen form). The rhetorical position of black Americans as both indexical of and lacking (needing instruction in) civic virtue allowed Garrison to incorporate black interior virtue as the basis for his public, institutional authority while maintaining a pedagogical distance from his black "pupils."

In 1833, just prior to his departure for England, Garrison delivered an address to audiences of free blacks in Boston, New York, and Philadelphia that provides a striking example of abolition's disciplinary pedagogy. In his absence, Garrison warned, the free people of color would have to deport themselves civilly if they were to earn the sympathy of white Northerners—civility defined initially as New Testament forbearance: "Conquer their aversion by moral excellence; their proud spirit by love; their evil acts by acts of goodness; their animosity by forgiveness. Keep in your hearts the fear of God, and rejoice even in tribulation; for the promise is sure, that all things shall work together for good to those who love His name" ("Words of Encouragement," 172). Love of the name of the Father—the law of civil order and self-regulating obedience that rests on the affective relay of family, church, and state—here becomes the precondition first of white sympathy and then of its definitional corollary, civil entitlement.

In the address, Garrison sutured the universalizing and irresistible imperatives of divine law to the social work of nineteenth-century citizenship and labor: "I beseech you fail not, on your part, to lead quiet and orderly lives. Let all quarreling, all dram-drinking, all profanity, and violence, all division, be confined to the white people. Imitate them in nothing but what is clearly good, and carefully shun even the appearance of evil."[42] Urging black auditors to be resigned, sober, hardworking, and polite, Garrison echoed his characterization of freed West Indian slaves as "industrious, economical, orderly, docile almost to a fault, filled with grateful emotions, aspiring after intellectual and moral cultivation, and rejoicing continually over the boon of liberty" ("West India Emancipation," 345). Throughout his writings, and particularly in his addresses to black audiences, Garrison inscribed the citizen form as the character of those who, as emulators of republican virtue (good workers and loyal citizens, at once docile and free), would be even more representative (but not innately "possessed") of civility than already enfranchised white citizens.

Garrison encouraged black "emulation" by promising not only white acceptance (probably not a very creditable incentive), but also those "rights and privileges" provided by the very institutions from which he had freed white abolitionists through his critique of nationalism. The question of whether blacks would enjoy the same rights and opportunities as whites under the national contract is moot, however, since Garrison's imagining of black civility rhetorically separates black Americans from the body politic. Asking his audience, "Do you not congratulate yourselves that you are so united?"[43] and relegating "division" to licentious whites, Garrison defined "civility" as group cohesion. Even while Garrison asked blacks to become model citizens in ways that seemed to promise incorporation within the national public, then, he also asked them to remain coherent as a group that was presumably distinct and distinguishable from the national body as a whole.

The dynamic of always already failed emulation is prefigured in the pedagogical structure of the address itself. Praising his audience for the "spirit of virtuous emulation so great among you, as to pervade all classes, from the grey head to the youth,"[44] Garrison asserted a common trait—the desire to imitate—that united internal factions while also putting a permanent difference between this new united "class" and the exemplary teacher whom they were to emulate. Above all, in contrast to the courageous figure of the enraged abolitionist who actively fights the prejudices of his country, Garrison praised his auditors for "bearing all your trials and difficulties in the spirit of Christian resignation."[45] In other writings, Garrison revealed the disciplinary intent of the "resignation" that he attributed in his address to free blacks. In "West India Emancipation" (336), for instance, Garrison, imagining the charge that freed slaves would seek revenge, replied, "On the contrary, is it not to be taken for granted, as a matter of course, that they will manifest the liveliest gratitude, be docile as lambs, perform their enumerated labor with alacrity, and make each field and hill vocal with melody? 'Instinct is a great master.'" As Garrison suggested in the address, "instincts" are not innate but are the products of his rhetorical inter-pellation: "it is said that I am exciting your race against the whites, and filling your minds with revengeful feelings. Is this true? Have not all my addresses and appeals to you had a contrary effect upon your minds?"[46]

While Garrison's portrait of freed blacks instructed by white abolitionists in the lessons of republican self-regulation is on one level strategic, pacifying white anxiety about black retribution following emancipation, it is also a condi-tion and a justification for the authoritative pedagogy of the address itself. The costs to his audience of such a pedagogy are indicated when Garrison grounds the authority by which he instructs those more intimately acquainted with the horrors of slavery and racism: "not that I am qualified in all things to instruct you," he acknowledged; "yet you have shown, in a thousand ways, that the course I have pursued has secured your cordial approbation—that the language I have spoken has been the language of your own hearts—that the advice I have given has been treasured up in your memories, like good seeds sown in good ground, and is now producing fruit, ten, thirty, sixty, and even a hundred fold."[47] Having gained his public authority from their experience (their ap-probation has secured his right to speak and instruct), Garrison used words that first reflect but then improve ("producing fruit") that experience. His agricultural metaphor naturalizes his pedagogical power over the memory of black Americans, while echoing, albeit in a liberalized and sympathetic form, the plantation structure he was working to abolish. Black citizens become the conduit between profit (what is produced through them without credit to their labor) and the identity of the master (who accumulates his authority as the surplus value of their uncredited labor) in ways that repeat, rather than subvert, the labor hierarchies of the Southern plantations. Because of this echo, perhaps, Garrison was able to characterize his address as both a reflection of and a substitution for the interiors of black citizens: his words become interchange-able with their hearts and memories. Their experiences have circulated through his public address and return to them in the twinned form of improved affect and white public authority, a sympathetic circuit that leaves the emulative pupils devoid of a language to critique that authority or to express a dissenting counter-memory.

If the lack of civil virtue signified by their emulative desire threatens to deny black Americans access to public authority, their very exclusion opens a space of authenticating identification for the sympathetic abolitionist. In the course of the address, Garrison increasingly names himself among the persecuted. Dis-cussing the widespread change in public opinion regarding slavery, Garrison told his audience, "Scarcely any credit belongs to myself. To you, much of the applause belongs. Had it not been for your co-operation, your generous confidence, your liberal support, as a people, I might have been borne down by my enemies."[48] Expressing his humble gratitude to his black supporters, Garrison, asserting that prejudiced whites were his enemies, not theirs, could imagine that his audience supported him, and not the other way around. An outcast in the nation-state, he—in his own mind, at least—was no longer fully white. "I never rise to address a colored audience," Garrison began the address, "without feeling ashamed of my own color; ashamed of being identified with a race of men, who have done you so much injustice, and who yet retain so large a portion of your brethren in servile chains. To make atonement, in part, for their conduct, I have solemnly dedicated my health, and strength, and life, to your service. I love to plan and to work for your social, intellectual, and spiritual advancement. My happiness is augmented with yours; in your sufferings I participate."[49]

If blacks represent outcast purity in Garrison's address, other white people represent the corruption caused by over-identification with the state, signified by a fear and hatred of suffering blacks. Yet corrupt whites, by virtue of their control over national rhetoric, also represent extraordinary public authority. If Garrison took on a persecuted but pure interiority associated with blacks, through his pedagogical acumen—he was the object of admiring applause—he assumed a public authority that distinguished him from his emulative auditors. Sharing a "complexion" with whites but a suffering interiority with blacks, Garrison could assume a place in national politics without surrendering his incorruptible purity. From this position, Garrison could appear as either an idealized white or an abject black (but never a prejudiced white or a dutiful black) citizen.

Although he gained an ideal authority through his cross-identifications, Garrison also risked a good deal, as the Boston mob made clear when it threatened to blacken his face and hands before lynching him. The mob apparently understood better than Garrison himself that freed blacks were a potential threat to the racist underpinnings of the industrial North, not just the docile emulators of its civil principles. Less physical but perhaps no less threatening, Garrison's cross-identifications suggest a lack at the heart of public authority. Garrison's address suggests, as had Finley's racial pedagogy, that public authority exists only in the circulation between blacks and whites, nation and citizens, teacher and student, but belongs finally to no one. If white civil virtue circulates in a purely discursive space, so Garrison, who wished to possess those virtues as the grounds of his public authority, must also circulate between the "whiteness" and "blackness" he created. In gaining his authority, then, he risked his claim to authenticity (the in-dwelling "truth" of one's "character") on which that authority depended.

Neither the appropriation of another's suffering nor the consequent inauthenticity is particular to the remarkably earnest Garrison. Rather, both were central to the allure and the anxiety caused by antebellum reform in the United States. Appeals to the sufferings of a "group" to which one did not belong—the poor, alcoholics, criminals, sex workers—increasingly supplied the intimate pain that entitled more privileged citizens to engage in public debate with an authorized moral authority. Taking one's authenticating interiority from a group by definition alienated from one's social identity both generated and forestalled claims to civic depth. To be sure, these reformers brought about significant changes in America, relieving suffering and remedying social policies through their moral activism. Despite their label as "reformers," however, some, such as Garrison himself, wanted a social *revolution* and blamed the absence of that radical change on outside forces: Southern racism, government cynicism, weakness of white Northern resolve. But part of the failure surely resulted from reform's own program, for liberal sympathy worked not only on behalf of the suffering subaltern, but also in the interest of national pride, aggressive global expansion, and white civility. Such politics follow an affective circuit from compassion to empathy to inclusion, whose trajectory is to pull the suffering "other" into a state of normative plentitude—the state of civil health—from which "proper" feelings (gratitude, docility, and ambition but never rage or resentment) emanate. Once social relations became the domain of interior states—sympathy and character, phobia and human nature—reform came to be limited to initiatives (medical, moral, and domestic) aimed at standardizing "human nature" toward a set of fixed social virtues, foreclosing social analyses of structural ills and diminishing the value of cultural difference. In suggesting the normative work of civil inclusion, then, I am not attempting a cynical argument in which power is all-pervasive and irresistible. Rather, I am suggesting that part of what makes power unassailable is precisely its equation with "natural" or "universal" (the two become the same) civic sentiment and that, if power were denuded of its discursive associations with "inner life," we might ultimately create more liberating modes of civil organization that are better suited for public justice.

4

ARDENT SPIRITS: INTEMPERATE SOCIALITY

AND THE INNER LIFE OF CAPITAL

In the most famous episode of Timothy Shay Arthur's bestselling temperance novel *Ten Nights in a Bar-Room and What I Saw There* (1854), a heated conflict erupts between Simon Slade and Joe Morgan, lifelong friends now opposed by Morgan's addiction to the alcohol sold in Slade's tavern. Each night, Morgan's young daughter Mary, afraid that her besotted father will stumble off a bridge on his ramble home, ventures into the tavern to retrieve him. On the fatal night of her father's argument with his former chum, Mary enters just as Slade, provoked by Morgan's accusation that the bar is responsible for bankrupting the Morgan family, hurls a tumbler at the drunkard's head. Missing its target, the glass strikes the innocent child, inflicting a gash that in turn produces a fatal fever. Before she dies, however, the angelic Mary exhorts a promise from her father that, until she recovers her health, he will never leave the house except to go to work. Thanks to the promise he makes to his dying child, Joe Morgan sobers up, returns to his former employment as a miller, and establishes himself as a responsible husband and solid citizen.

While Mary is apparently yet another victim of antebellum America's obsession with the redemptive morality of childhood innocence, I want to suggest, rather, that Mary functions in this episode as a highly ambivalent *agent* of the emerging contractual economy and of its presumed stable location in—or, more properly, *as*—the interior workings of the middle-class unconscious.[1] Mary's reformation of her father relies on her ability to engage him in a contract made on unfair terms: while Joe naively trusts that contracts can and will pay off for both parties—his daughter will regain her health, enabling him to resume his visits to the barroom—Mary knows that she never will recover, and therefore she negotiates with her father in bad faith. Mary's intuitive understanding of contractual operations binds her father for life to the options of limited social interaction—home and work—that are characteristic of middle-class masculinity. Contracts, then, unfairly (even fatally) limit, with the consent of those so bound, the public sociality now characterized as a violent threat to the sanctity of the home. In return for denying his thirst not just for alcohol, but for sociality itself, Joe Morgan gains the respectability (he goes from being called "Joe" to being hailed as "Mr. Morgan") appropriate to the self-restraint and trim order manifest in the "neat" cottage purchased on his modest income. Mary's contract, in other words, turns his thirst into taste.

If *Ten Nights* uses Mary to transform the unruly and unpredictable sociality of the barroom into the well-ordered and tasteful affections of the family, however, the child's unconscious registers ambivalence over its own agency in effecting this change. Or, rather, the transformation of sociality *into* the interior state reflected by the unconscious generates ambivalences that Arthur registers in the bizarre dream work of the feverish child. Descending into death, Mary projects her broken promise (to recover) onto her father, dreaming that Joe Morgan, forgetting his pledge to his daughter, has set off again toward certain ruin. Realizing that her father has broken his promise (thereby releasing Mary from the guilt of breaking *hers*), the girl reports, "I felt as strong as when I was well, and I got up and dressed myself, and started out after you."[2] Arriving at the tavern expecting to discover her father drowning in drink, Mary instead finds him "dressed so nice." "You had on a new hat and a new coat," she tells her father, "and your boots were new, and polished just like Judge Hammond's."

> I said—"O father! is this you?" And then you took me up in your arms and kissed me, and said—"Yes, Mary, I am your real father. Not old Joe Morgan— but Mr. Morgan now." It seemed all so strange, that I looked into the bar- room to see who was there. But it wasn't a bar-room any longer; but a store full of goods. The sign of the Sickle and Sheaf was taken down; and over the door I now read your name, father. Oh! I was so glad, that I awoke—and then I cried all to myself, for it was only a dream." (93)

Without moving Mary from the deathbed to the couch, we can analyze this dream for tensions within what were emerging in antebellum America as the ambivalent desires of the middle-class unconscious. To begin with, Mary's dream suggests a profound ambivalence about the purported goals of temper- ance as a reform movement. In the dream, Mary draws strength ("I felt as strong as when I was well") not from her father's reform (which she never lives to see), but from his betrayed promise and threatened ruin. The strength of reform, in Mary's dream, relies on its perpetual failure: Mary's agency as re- former would vanish if its ends were accomplished (hence, Joe Morgan's reform coincides with the death of his reforming daughter, the two unable to exist simultaneously).

Even the anticipated postmortem reform of her father provokes ambivalence, however, since it procures not the enhanced domestic intimacy that Mary seeks, but the commodification of that intimacy, generating consumer desires that perpetually destabilize the tranquillity she expects. In the dream, Mary's enthusiastic encounter with her newly reformed papa arises not from his tamed appetites, but from his transformation into a showcase for fashionable novelty. Commenting obsessively on the "newness" of her father's respectable attire, Mary renders questionable the claim to authenticity ("I am your real father") on which domestic relations, and hence private intimacies, rely. Returning her father to his "old" and more "real" self, Mary discovers only the accumulation of fashions predicated on an unappeasable hunger for the ever changing "new." (Naming the inception of consumer desire in a new commodity market, some-one later exclaims in the novel, " 'The possession of a coveted object so soon brings satiety' " [136]). Far from eliminating ungovernable appetite, then, Mary has made her father the subject of consumer desire, which, like all desires in the novel, deprives one of conscious agency. As Mary says to her father of his need to drink, "It seems almost as if you couldn't help it" (92). Joe Morgan's transfor-mation into a "real" father does not transform Mary into a "real" daughter, moreover, but makes her a stand-in for an appraising community that perceives Joe not as "father" but as "Mr. Morgan." Making her father a respectable if aloof emblem of middle-class manhood and herself an ideal consumer of new (and hence, like all commodity satisfaction, always precarious) respectability, Mary's dream makes consumption and domesticity synonymous, thereby destabilizing the divisions between private and public, home and market, on which the reform logic of the novel relies.

If her contract restricts her father to the home and the workplace (which the dream reveals to be one and the same), however, Mary's dream registers doubts about the elimination of other, competing social environments. One of the oddest features of Mary's dream is that, encountering her newly respectable father, she does not return home with him, but instead pushes farther into the barroom. Mary thus searches for fulfillment not in the redemption of her "real" father (already, at this point in the dream, saved), but in something else that might be found in the tavern. Perhaps Mary desires more disreputable men whose weakness will allow her to continue to feel "strong." Or perhaps Mary desires what drove her father to the barroom in the first place: the social desire "to see who was there." In either case, Mary's contractual logic has already turned potential social companions into buyers and sellers, so her search for people produces only more commodities ("a store full of goods"). Perhaps for this reason, although Mary purports to feel "gladness" at the transformation of good into goods, of temperance's virtuous self-control into the uncontrolled

consumption of the marketplace, in fact she awakens to cry "all to myself."
While Mary's identification with her father's waywardness momentarily replaces anxiety over the barroom's dangers with desire for its social interactions,
sociality is already foreclosed by the commodification that locates consumer
desire in the privatized home that substitutes family for community and makes
that family, which will consume the goods sold in Mr. Morgan's store, a locus
of consumer desire. More disturbing, Mary's dream relocates sociality in the
unconscious realm of the dream itself. The transformation of sociality into
middle-class interiority, in other words, produces a melancholy unconscious:
the ambivalent incorporation of presumably lost social relations, producing the
divided impulses—to weep and to wander—characteristic of the anxiety-ridden
unconscious of the middle-class citizen. If Mary's dream maintains the residual
trace of sociality, it registers as well her sadness at the sacrifice of sociality
brought about by her own faith in contractual self-control.

In presenting the "reform" of her father as a contest between social relations and interiorization, Mary's dream uncovers one of temperance fiction's
most dangerous misrepresentations: the claim that alcoholism was spreading in
American culture due to the social spaces—bars and taverns—where alcohol was
consumed. Throughout the antebellum period, alcoholism did rise at an alarming rate, but primarily among solitary drinkers. As the price of alcohol fell and
the shameful experience of failed upward mobility spread, Americans began to
drink secretly at work and, more typically, at home.[3] Despite the prevalence of
solitary drinking, however, temperance novels insistently depict the *public* setting of alcohol consumption as the problem, not the alcohol itself. By presenting
the tavern as the site of intemperance and the family or the workplace as the sites
of reform, the novels rationalize the move from public sociality to private
domesticity, resulting in the isolation that leaves Mary crying by herself. What
this apparent "choice" between public and private conceals, however, is the
ubiquitous presence of capital, which is structuring both the social relations of
the barroom (where customers have gathered to buy alcohol) and the domestic
relations of the home. The fact that Mary makes an unfair bargain with her
father—paralleling the swindles carried out in the barroom by the sinister
Harvey Green—undermines the opposition of public and private, tavern and
home, in ways that trouble the structuring logic of temperance narratives.

The ambivalences represented by Mary's dream saturate Arthur's novel,
plaguing even the unnamed narrator, an advocate of prohibition legislation
who, over a period of years, visits Simon Slade's barroom while traveling "on
business." While the narrator presents himself as a cool-headed and detached
observer of the events unfolding before him, he reveals his own desires, which

motivate his investments of time and capital in a bar he nominally abhors. That motivation takes the form of passionate and obsessive fascination with young men whose "innocence" he alternatively celebrates and laments. That the temperate narrator, in his cycles of desire and disavowal in relation to the innocence of charming young men, shares with the barroom's drinkers the struggle between hunger and self-control suggests that the cycle named in these novels has less to do with increased inebriation than with changing conceptions of middle-class masculinity and the social opportunities it endorsed and prohibited. In particular, as Mary's dream suggests, temperance novels typically transform the free-and-easy sociality of the barroom (a sociality, however, necessarily—although not exclusively—invested in consumer culture) into exclusively economic relationships structured through hierarchies of middle-class masculinity. Tense same-sex eroticism arises in temperance fiction not from drunken orgies but from moments when sober men circulate their stories among other men, generating economic networks that substitute for other social alliances *and* that translate eroticized want into desire for profit, respectability, and approbation that appear as gratifying substitutes for other social pleasures. In telling the story of how rich men and poor men became *middle-class* men, temperance novels are as much about the interiorizing of economic relations between men—triangulated not through women but through the feminized erotic hungers of the men themselves[4]—as they are about alcohol. In either case, however, temperance fiction presents the struggle of middle-class masculinity as one of contested interiority. The broad sociality of the barroom was recast as troubled male *desire*, while the professional networks of speculative capital became interiorized as reformed men's proper *ambition*. Both are necessary for producing modern capital. The trick, as temperance fiction shows, is walking the line between desires—whether erotic or economic—and self-restraint, between hunger and taste.

Erotic and economic sociality existed simultaneously, however, in a state of perpetual contest. Temperance novels such as *Ten Nights* attempted to settle this contest by arranging sequentially events that were in fact occurring simultaneously in antebellum America. More precisely, the novel seeks to give the impression that a yet undecided conflict *has* been decided not by human agency, but by temporal inevitability, the outmoded practices of the past "naturally" giving way to the irresistible forces of the future. The "past" was a time of mutual responsibility, social collectivity, friendship. The "future" is invested in the habits of competitive individualism required by the marketplace. The irony, of course, is not only that the novels show us that both exist in the *present* in a tense contest for the meaning of social life, but, as the "future" of competitive profit seeking becomes the present of ruthless self-interest, reckless profiteering, and the intemperate consumption that compensates for failed social mobility, the values of the past reorient themselves *as* a new future, in which the reformed collectivity of temperance *societies* modify the unregulated desires of the competitive market. Responsible sociality can shift vertiginously from the past to the future but can never rest in the same temporal frame as the speculative market, which in these novels is America's only present.

This chapter analyzes the ambivalences and crossed identifications, visible in Mary's dream, in *Ten Nights in a Bar-Room* and *Franklin Evans*, two of antebellum America's best-known temperance novels. The novels share important plot elements: the imbrications of alcoholism and capital, the emergence of same-sex eroticism at that nexus, and the ambivalent "reform" of promiscuous sociality in the name of marriage, privatized domesticity, and good taste. Both novels, with greater or lesser conviction, establish consumer desire, competitive ambition, and a (chronically shamed) same-sex eroticism as the interior substitutes for an inventive and demanding sociality represented as the cause of crime, perversion, and disease. Tasteful self-management thus emerges as the "healthy" interiority that promises to (never successfully) restore order to a social world of ungovernable hungers. These fictional depictions of redemptive interiorization naturalize an emergent middle class whose interior self-management becomes visible as "sobriety": institutional rather than popular governance, taste rather than demand, empiricism rather than imagination, self-management rather than sociality. This is the primary inversion necessary to the novels' reform agenda: to make interiority seem the cause, not the effect, of interpersonal ("social") arrangements, and hence to make self-management the solution to structural unrest. What kept the newly interior state of middle-class taste so intensely habituated that it began to appear as human nature, these novels show, was the unseemly threat—or revolutionary promise—of ardent spirits, an unpredictable sociality whose inventive demands might prove the most dangerous intemperance of all.

"It Is Worse than the Mere Abstraction of Money": The Inner Life of Capital in Ten Nights in a Bar-Room

While the self-made man became the characteristic figure of nineteenth-century U.S. mythology, his counterpart, equally mythologized, was the washed-up drunkard, alienated from the honors of patriarchal manhood by ill-regulated habits and ungovernable thirsts, the fatal outgrowths of his shameful nature. These two figures are, in fact, one and the same, as can be surmised from

Tocqueville's observation that the myth of self-making ultimately serves to cast each man "back upon himself alone, and threatens in the end to confine him entirely within the solitude of his own heart."[5] Tocqueville rightly attributes the alienated isolation of an imprisoning interiority ("confine him entirely within the solitude of his own heart") to new market models of competitive manhood, but the consequences of those changes were more affectively dire than Tocqueville predicted. The promise of self-making proved, to say the least, a cruel swindle. In 1860, 73 percent of the national wealth was owned by the richest 10 percent of Americans, while of the two thousand wealthiest citizens of the three largest Northeastern cities, only 2 percent began life poor; the staggering majority (98 percent in New York, 94 percent in Boston, and 92 percent in Philadelphia) came from already wealthy families.[6] As the historian Charles Sellers speculates, in a culture where economic mobility was nearly impossible but that nevertheless publicized entrepreneurial successes through narratives that, while largely fictional, were so widely distributed as to seem real, acute shame at perceived self-inflicted failure must have been nearly ubiquitous.[7]

The shame generated by economic stagnation was particularly paralyzing for men, as geographic mobility eroded conventional social status and masculine prestige. As family members, including wives and children of both genders, moved from small communities to cities to seek labor, men were forced to establish an ill-defined masculinity within the shifting terms of the marketplace rather than by replicating the patriarchal models established by their fathers (the notion that sons should surpass their fathers rather them *become* them is typical of this ideological shift).[8] In the new marketplace, "manhood" relied on increasing consumption visible to and judged by an abstract "community." Given the illusory location of that "community," however, its values were ill defined and ever shifting, making the equation of consumption and respectability highly precarious. In an effort to stabilize respectability, workers were encouraged to reach ever greater levels of production and consumption, generating what Sellers calls "a morality of effort" (those who work hard demonstrate good character) that could be measured through commodified display (the more one has, the harder one must have worked).[9] Consequently, interiority ("character") became linked to commodities, and just as the latter are fated to obsolescence in repeated cycles of fashion, so "character" became subject to patterns of exhaustion and renovation on which reform societies—particularly those in which shameful habits are exchanged for productive ones—relied.

No wonder people drank, and at escalating rates. As whiskey distilled in the United States from domestically grown grains replaced rum produced from West Indian sugar, the price of alcohol dropped to twenty-five cents per gallon, cheaper than tea or coffee, and average annual consumption by Americans over fourteen soared to 9.5 gallons in 1830.[10] In response, national temperance organizations publicized the dangers of alcohol consumption and called for greater self-discipline, lowering the annual per capita consumption to 1.8 gallons by 1845.[11] In particular, stories of young men who had achieved economic success and social status through newfound sobriety circulated widely, particularly among working-class readers, through temperance fictions that enjoyed a vogue in the late 1830s and early 1840s.[12] Yoking self-discipline to self-making, and thereby turning the *labor* of self-monitoring and self-restraint into the necessary down payment on upward mobility, temperance appealed first to aspiring mechanics and manufacturers, and membership in the societies soared after the depression of 1837.[13] While self-making and self-discipline often proved mutually defeating, both ideologies institutionalized the subject each took for granted, the "self." Whether in relation to the competitive ambition of the market entrepreneur and his animating hungers (for profit, respectability, and authority) or the ungovernable appetite of the unruly drunkard, both the marketplace and the temperance society generated an equally individual subject who was locked not in the comforts of the middle-class home, but in the tumultuous interior of what Sellers calls the "middle class of consciousness."[14]

Before the middle class could occupy a consciousness, however, it first had to leave the barroom. To privilege the isolated and self-possessed individual, in other words, temperance societies needed to demonize the social spaces where a diverse urban population formed often unpredictable and powerful alliances. As social historians have noted, temperance societies targeted places where gossip, economic opportunity, political strategies, and oppositional anger circulated along with alcohol. While barrooms prove the downfall of many in temperance novels, historically they served as important community centers, particularly for immigrants seeking comfort and connections in an otherwise hostile environment. Taverns provided public toilets; cashed checks; lent money; provided a mailing address for patrons who moved frequently; and offered space for labor and political meetings, recreation (cards, pool, darts), sex (prostitutes were sometimes allowed to rent back rooms in which to entertain customers), and even sleep.[15] As industrialization organized workers' days in relation to time clocks and dull, repetitive, and isolating labor, taverns offered a space without time limits, one that encouraged self-expression and fellowship.[16] Patrons treated tavern-goers to drinks, making bars particularly important settings for working-class politics, where information could be shared, strategies debated, and voting blocs consolidated.[17] In a more philosophical vein, Timothy Gilfoyle contends that the group intoxication common in antebellum bars "endowed the participants with feelings of liberty and independence while inducing a sense of equality. The group drinking binge was an ideological inebriation; to be drunk was to be free."[18] Generating both the psychological predisposition toward freedom *and* the institutional means to direct that impulse toward specific political ends, barrooms understandably made nativists and other traditional politicians uneasy, contributing to the impetus for temperance reform in the 1840s and 1850s. In New York, for instance, upstate Whigs pushed for laws prohibiting the sale of alcohol in order to impede the political power growing in urban taverns.[19] More subtly, temperance societies appropriated the buoyant sociality of the tavern, re-creating songs, poems, and activities that, as Sean Wilentz observes, were "almost obsessive in their exuberance."[20]

Temperance fiction certainly participated in this vilification, depicting bars as sites of counter-entrepreneurial sloth, greed, and rudeness as much as of drunken violence and debauchery. More insidious, however, temperance fiction used the barroom setting, itself a site of spending, to disavow the *social* nature of production and consumption by assigning the latter to an "idle rich" and the former to a "degraded poor." Demonizing the material sociality of both groups' designated activities allowed a new intermediate position—the middle class—to emerge as *unsocial*. Unaffiliated by identification with social practices or locations, the middle-class subject is self-identical, isolated and contained by his very self-ownership ("his own heart"), but also able to move anywhere or do anything without, presumably, surrendering status. As I have suggested, however, the interiority that allowed the middle class this positional mobility was constituted by the trace conflicts—of production and consumption, effort and idleness, status and shame—that characterized the *social* divisions of the rich and the poor in antebellum America. The refuge from sociality provided by middle-class interiority proved unstable, then, precisely because it internalized economic divisions even while isolating citizens from the social realm within which such divisions might have been rectified. While interiority in temperance fiction might seem to be a suitable surrogate for what Sellers calls "the kind-and-neighbor cooperation of use-value production," moreover, it does so only at the expense of what makes interiority seem so attractive in the first place: the creativity of what Tocqueville called "most intimate and personal to each man, his own inclinations," or what Sellers identifies as "the human need for love and trust formerly met in a wider net of communal/kin relationships."[21] In the end, it is this abstraction of human interaction and social cooperation into the turbulent but (because) morally conformed and effortful human interior that appears, paradoxically, as a particularizing *personalization* in the novel.

In the end, however, temperance fiction could not eliminate sociality, even within its own pages. In *Ten Nights in a Bar-Room*, the unnamed narrator keeps coming back to the Sickle and Sheaf to eavesdrop, observe, and converse, even as he claims to be horrified by what he sees and hears. On a broader scale, although the townspeople gather at the end of that novel to vote a "Maine law" into place, they do so in the only social space available to them: the barroom itself. In such moments, temperance fiction reveals the residual social nature of antebellum interiority. Even this formulation, however, betrays the powerful narrative logic of temperance fiction, which substitutes a sequential order (the passing of one social "moment" into another interiorized "moment") for a struggle between modes of social organization in the *same* historical moment. *Ten Nights* establishes this sequential logic by placing narratives of generational transformation—of wayward sons' rebellions against well-meaning fathers—at the center of the novel's dramas. Fathers are always trying, unsuccessfully, to save the sons who self-destructively flout the opportunities their fathers have laid before them. The implication, then, is that opportunity, figured as America's legacy, is threatened by the sociability that substitutes instant gratification for measured self-restraint and steady progress.

The novel's plot shows, however, that this temporal logic is at best questionable, as the "opportunities" provided to sons are both the enablers of their intemperance and themselves the outcome of intemperate economic speculations. Far from narrating the falling away of wayward sons, then, *Ten Nights* troublingly demonstrates the uncomfortable resemblance of patriarchs and progeny. Just as the town's elder statesman, Judge Hammond, is driven to the poorhouse by ill-advised land speculations, so his son Willy, "a warm admirer of new ideas and the quicker adaptation of means to ends" (12), is bankrupted by intemperate card playing with unscrupulous men whose characters he wrongly believes himself capable of reading. The "free market," for father and son, turns out to be a con whose operation they believe, wrongly, they can outwit.

For the men in the novel, the solution to the anxieties brought about by this resemblance—and by the fatal generational transmission of intemperance—is heightened entrepreneurial effort. Judge Hammond installs his son Willy at the head of his new whiskey distillery, hoping, counter-intuitively, that the position will cure the errant lad of his thirst for both profit and alcohol. Joe Morgan appears to take a different tack: he returns to his job at the mill with a new dedication to diligent labor. With Joe's apparent triumph, the narrative logic of *Ten Nights* seemingly reinstates a prior, community-based economy as the necessary antidote to the new speculative economy, yet the two are, in the end, mutually dependent. As I suggested, the speculating entrepreneur and the continually reforming drunkard are both driven by cycles of appetite and restraint, obsolescence and revival, that generate the perpetual effort on which the market relies. Instilling in readers the virtues of effortful production *and* the dangers of excessive ambition, the joys of leisure *and* the dangers of pleasure, *Ten Nights* reveals the contradictions of antebellum America's myths of self-making. Faced with those contradictions, the novel proposes a compromise— taste—an interior state that, balancing commodified pleasure and disciplined refinement, becomes the characteristic trait of middle-class consciousness in the novel and beyond.

Arthur's temperance loyalties might have led him to blame Cedarville's downfall on Demon Drink, but *Ten Nights* is far more critical of the intemperate desires for profit, leisure, and status unleashed by a new speculative economy. *Ten Nights*, like many temperance novels, begins with a nostalgic idealization of a pre-urban, pre-industrial economy in which honest craftspeople exchange healthy goods to earn an adequate, but not excessive, income from which they ensure the general well-being of the community. Exemplary of Cedarville's idyllic past is Simon Slade, formerly the town's miller, "industrious, active, and attractive to customers" at work and "companionable, quick-witted, and very kind-hearted" (29) among his neighbors. In Cedarville's past, laborers engaged in "useful work, occupying many hours through each day, and leaving them with wearied bodies at night, for their safe passage from yielding youth to firm, resisting manhood" (42). The town's troubles began when its exemplary miller "got tired of hard work, and determined to lead an easier life" (13) by opening a public house, the Sickle and Sheaf, an ironic tribute to the miller's hardworking past. While the novel attributes Slade's decision to his flawed character, it also shows his desires to be part of a larger economic shift, in which land and commodity speculation, producing unprecedented levels of wealth, generated "leisure and freedom to go in and out when you pleased" (42). Even as it provides a space of often unpredictable sociality, the Sickle and Sheaf attaches social relations to patterns of consumption that make the barroom a place both of community formation and of business, demonstrating how a new "service economy" commodified friendship in ways that made the novel's apparent choice between profit and pleasure, entrepreneurship and sociality, moot. One customer, who faults Slade for not adding "'to the general wealth,'" suggestively misreads the changing economy represented by the barroom, claiming that Slade "'produces nothing. He takes money from his customers, but gives them no article of value in return—nothing that can be called property, personal or real. He is just so much richer and they just so much poorer for the exchange'" (119). The customer misunderstands what Slade sells, which is the status signified by newfound leisure. Rather than exchanging *things*, in other words, the Sickle and Sheaf traffics in *sensations*: pride, desire, innocence, affection, even what the narrator repeatedly refers to as "the thrill of horror." These interiorizations of value—the inner life of capital—are the placeholders of "property, personal or real," necessarily deferred in a speculative market whose payoffs are always necessarily cast in the future tense. Interiority, in other words, becomes the (seemingly) compensatory supplement for a fortune never made, a wager never paid.

Such interiorizations are necessary to sustain effort in an economy whose tangible benefits, as the novel repeatedly demonstrates, are few and far between. For the poor, the losses resulting from the new economy are painfully apparent. Although in his own version of trickle-down economics Slade believes that gain from the barroom will produce benefit to the entire community, one of his prescient customers warns, "'If he gets richer, somebody will be poorer!'" (20). The prediction proves painfully true. Although he initially does "all in his power to save his early friend from the curse of intemperance," Slade, having "grown selfish, grasping, unscrupulous, and passionate" (124) through his pursuit of profit and ease, abandons Joe Morgan, who, fired by the mill's new owner, falls quickly into inebriated poverty. Joe's impoverishment, the novel suggests, is due to his drinking, yet the irony of *Ten Nights* is that *no one* profits from economic speculation. All of the novel's speculating men end up ruined, mad, or dead, including Simon Slade. Whereas at the start of his speculative ventures he had "always been on hand, with the cash, when desirable property went off, under forced sale, at a bargain," Slade soon allows deals to slip through his fingers, selling properties at a loss, because he no longer has any sense of a commodity's "true value" (124). In Cedarville, both the grasping rich and the degraded poor are doomed by their social excesses, leaving, on the one hand, an ephemeral inner sensation, and on the other, an abstract and hence respectable economic agency without agents, the hidden hand that Adam Smith celebrated as the governing force of modern capital. This unmarked labor is represented in the novel by the temperate and aloof narrator, who visits Cedarville on "business" (7), the nature of which is never disclosed and at which he never seems engaged. His status as temperate observer relies on his business remaining, unlike that of the laboring poor and the speculating rich, abstract, immaterial, and unsocial. The problem for the narrator is that the line between abstraction and interiorization, supervision and sensation, proves permeable, passages between the two unpredictable and perilous.

Although the consequences of economic speculation on individual characters are dire, the more significant affect is on sociality generally, as the degenerating relationship of Slade and his "very particular friend" (60) suggests. On the one hand, the novel aligns sociality with an irretrievably lost, if lamented, past (Slade's benevolent care of the Morgan family). On the other, it presents sociality as the very *heart* of the economic operations on which the town's future is presumably based. Slade is able to make a success as a barkeeper because he is "cheerful, social, chatty" (118), while Willy "had a dangerous gift—rare conversational powers, united with great urbanity of manner" (155)—that made him vulnerable to "social allurements." The novel's delegation of sociality to the past and the future denies its central position *in the present*. It is the sacrifice of sociality in the here and now, its translation into the interior realm of desire and the abstracted temporality of past and future that, as one of the characters claims, " 'is worse than the mere abstraction of money' " (122).

Sociality does not vanish from Cedarville's present, however, but transforms into managed relationships oriented toward status and profit rather than mutual responsibility and social demand. Throughout the novel, *networks* replace friendships and other more improvised and unpredictable social alliances. Having made his fortune with the tavern, Slade brags that people " 'treat me in every way more as if I were an equal than ever they did before' " (15). Perceiving himself no longer as a member of a community but, instead, as a member of a class of wealthy men who join in economic speculation (Slade includes not his poor customers or his wife but the judges and politicians with whom he invests among the "people" whose respect he enjoys), Slade can misconceive a hierarchy of status as democratic egalitarianism. Having done so, he can also substitute networks that seemingly solidify class identity for friendships that diminish the economic discrepancies on which those identities rely. Slade forms such a network with the wealthy Judge Hammond, who bankrolls the miller hoping that "the building and opening of a good tavern" will increase "the value of his property at least five thousand dollars" (16). Having bought Slade's mill and fired Joe Morgan, Hammond opens in its place a distillery to supply Slade's tavern with alcohol (41). Just as Slade draws on a receding social value (egalitarianism) to justify an emerging competitive market that will make equity impossible, so Judge Hammond relies on an ethical language drawn from interpersonal obligation—he puts his son Willy in charge of the distillery to teach the young man "responsibility" (111)—to create a commodity, alcohol, that will make obligation obsolete. Yet networks, like the status they seemingly guarantee, prove brittle in *Ten Nights*. Because of the money he makes at the distillery, Willy Hammond begins to drink and gamble and is ultimately murdered. His murderer, the villainous Harvey Green, epitomizes the antagonism of profit and sociality, seeking "to secure the largest possible share of property yet in his power to pledge or transfer" (162), refusing to "spare even his friend in evil" (125).

While the individual men who form economic networks end badly (Harvey Green is literally "abstracted" when an angry mob beats the features from his face), networks survive the death of their embodied members through their ultimate transformation into institutions. *Ten Nights* ends in an orgy of institutionalization, with characters whisked off to prisons, insane asylums, and poorhouses. The fate of Judge Hammond is both typical and, in its details, revealing. Having returned to Cedarville after a long absence, the narrator, shocked to find the judge wasting "in pain or grief" within his dilapidated mansion, sets off "in search of some friends to take charge of him" (228). Unable to find anyone who " 'seemed to have any sympathy for the broken-down old man' " (229), the narrator shifts from bonds of affection to economic relations, declaring, " 'I must find somebody whose business it was to attend to him' " (229). Finding that everyone to whom he turns on the judge's behalf shuns him " 'as they would a criminal' " (230), the narrator ultimately turns to institutional authority, going to the county officer, who arranges to have the judge sent to the poorhouse (229). While the narrator blames the judge's downfall on Simon Slade, " 'too lazy to work at an honest calling' " (230), Hammond's ruin is a necessary byproduct of his success, which relies on the very substitutions mapped by the narrator's search for aid: networks replace friendships and are in turn replaced by institutions, each abstracting responsible sociality and over-embodying (as drunkards, lazy schemers, or criminal madmen) the embodied agents of the relational mode it supplants.

Although networks apparently supplant friendships, embodied and pleasurable sociality persists in Cedarville, troubling the leisure of the town's status-seekers. The Sickle and Sheaf is a site of raucous and dissent-ridden debate, of which "politics was the most prominent" topic. Despite the narrator's efforts to turn such conversations into meaningless babble—he claims to have "heard nothing in the least interesting but only abuse of individuals and dogmatism on public measures. They were all exceedingly confident in assertion; but I listened in vain for exposition or even for demonstrative facts" (46)—such unmannerly talk disturbs "the self-satisfied harmony of the company" (21) and "interrupt[s] good feeling among gentleman" (22). In this regard, too, the relationship of Morgan and Slade stands in for community relations more generally. Just as the political debate in the barroom disturbs the narrator's sense of propriety, so Morgan produces "ruffled feelings" (20) in Slade by insisting, " 'We're old friends, and friends are privileged to speak plainly' " (22). The plain truth

Morgan speaks to Slade has to do with the commodification of friendship into economic relations, a shift he makes literal when, putting his last coin in the barroom till, he remarks that the other coins " 'will be lonesome without their little friend' " (21).

More striking than the direct challenges offered by the barroom's sociality are its alluring charms, which none in the town seems able to resist. The novel insistently relates good characters with social talents, and business networks are formed, ironically, on the basis of social skills that those networks will ultimately render abstract and, hence, prone to fakery. Of Simon Slade, the narrator reports, "the grasp of his hand was like that of a true friend" (7), while everyone loves Willy Hammond because he is "such good company" (11). Even the temperate narrator cannot resist the barroom's allure, acknowledging "interest enough in the characters I had met there a year before" to "choose this way of spending the time, instead of visiting at the house of a gentleman who had kindly invited me to pass an evening with his family" (45–46). Sociality is thus associated less with drinking than with an urban intimacy that the novel opposes to family life. In the end, the anonymous and mobile intimacies provided by the barroom, not the domestic rituals of self-disclosure and mutual recognition, prove too alluring for even the starchy narrator to resist.

The most disturbing pleasure generated by the barroom's sociality, however, is the same-sex desire it reveals at the heart of speculative capital. The narrator notes "the girl-like beauty" (9) of young Frank Slade and finds the "personal qualities" of Willy Hammond "strongly attractive" (12). "The little that I had heard and seen of him greatly interested me in his favour" (33), admits the narrator, who seems incapable of entering the barroom without thinking, obsessively, of Willy: "Where was he now? This question reoccurred over and over again" (34). Perhaps the narrator's instantaneous dislike of the gambler Harvey Green reveals a shameful self-knowledge. "At a glance," he reports, "I saw that this man could only associate himself with Willy Hammond as a tempter. Unscrupulous selfishness was written all over his sinister countenance; and I wondered that it did not strike every one as it did me, with instant repulsion. There could not be, I felt certain, any common ground of association, for two such persons, but the dead level of a village bar-room" (17–18). Despite the narrator's attempts to distinguish the gambler's selfish desires from his own "ground of association" with the young men of the barroom, what he says of Green—"there is something about Cedarville that always attracts him" (18)—is equally true of himself. Not surprisingly, the narrator is pulled from his objective position and implicated in a strangely erotic twist of events involving his nominal nemesis. Fleeing the mob seeking to capture Green after his murder of

Willy, the narrator retires to his hotel room, only to find the murderous gambler under the bed. The skeleton in the narrator's closet turns out to be the swindler under the bed, the eroticized desire for selfish possession that, despite their apparent opposition, binds both men in a network of implication that makes innocent "association" appear a naïve dream of the past.

In recasting the barroom as the bedroom, political exchanges as eroticized desire, however, the novel quite literally does sociality in. From its beginning, *Ten Nights* works to interiorize sociality, recasting the public conflict between demand and discipline as an inner struggle of passion and shame. The shift from social relations to inner drives is necessary to the logic of temperance, which seeks to mitigate alcoholism not by responding to the political, economic, and social demands of those who use the barroom as a space of organization, recuperation, and redress, but by urging the individual management of desires, appetites, and passions, the unruly and destructive imperatives of nature. Willy Hammond, readers are told, is driven by a "terrible necessity . . . impelling him outward" (158), whereas proper self-management would take him *inward* to the self-scrutiny and self-discipline demanded by temperate citizenship. " 'Poverty and crime have their origin in the corrupt heart' " (130), the narrator claims, urging readers to locate social unrest not in economic relations generated by widening divisions of capital, but in the interiorized and particularized passions of the "heart."

At the same time as the novel forces social relations into the confines of the heart, however, it represents passion—more than drink—as the source of the town's troubles. Rather than producing heartfelt harmony, then, the interiorization of sociality as passion produces only anxiety and anguish in need of ever greater (yet never fully available) reform. Frank Slade, made frantic by "evil passions" (233), kills his father, himself "nearly blind with passion" (219). Although Harvey Green "looked as if he had slept soundly on a quiet conscience, and now hailed the new day with a tranquil spirit" (134), his interior, the narrator assures us, is a realm of "evil passions" (25), as is that of Judge Hammond, illuminating his "dark, quick eyes with the brightness of unquenched loves, the fires of which were kindled at the altar of selfishness and sensuality" (34). Nor are the seemingly temperate free of ungovernable passion. On the contrary, the zeal of reform produces the same effects as alcohol, as when one patron proclaims his temperance beliefs to the barroom, "warming with his theme" until he becomes "overmastered by his feelings" (30).

The interiorized counter-force of "passions" is shame, or what the narrator calls "self-humiliation" (57), a phrase that isolates the management of such passionate demands within the self-contained realm of the individual conscience (thereby transforming shame into guilt), dividing the "self" between unconscious and conscience. At certain moments, Arthur reveals how social relations produce precisely this division in the self, as when Mary's shaming appeals to her drunken father generate " a struggle within him" (63) that, after her death, takes on the interiorized form of "self-humiliation." Given their responsibility for instilling, as Mary does, the inner restraints of shame, women in the novel are doubly bound by the isolating interiorization propounded by *Ten Nights*. Dependent on men who abandon them, make ruinous investments without consulting them, and ignore their sound advice, the women in *Ten Nights* have particular grounds for social demand, which find an even more bitter expression in the inner realm of mourning and madness. Joe Morgan's abandoned wife "thinks, and questions, and grieves inwardly" (65). As Mrs. Slade watched her beloved son sink into drunkenness, "a shadow fell upon her heart," driving her to the isolating silence of despair. Her daughter, Flora, accompanies her "unconscious mother" (210) into that silence, gathering "the mantle of oblivion about her heart" (210). While women occasionally find ways to turn grief into grievance—the mad wailings of Mrs. Slade, the shrieks of Mrs. Hammond, or what Fanny Morgan makes audible in "the excitement of her feelings" (65)—women, unlike men who "reform" themselves back into public life, remain locked in the turbulent interior, a "kind of living death" (211).

As the body's interior becomes disconnected from collective life, social groups detach from the powers of rational control, giving rise to the ungovernable mob. A violent mob forms in *Ten Nights* after Harvey Green kills Willy Hammond, setting off "a hundred different and exaggerated stories" (170–71) that the empirical narrator characterizes as a destructive conflagration: "Like fire among dry stubble ran the news of this fearful event through Cedarville, [until the] whole town was wild with excitement" (170). Thus excited, the mob turns first on Simon Slade "with a restlessness and want of evidence that illustrated that reckless and unjust spirit by which a mob is ever governed" (179). As usual, the narrator cannot discern a rational outrage on the part of the townspeople against the speculative grasping that has destroyed their community (they turn not only on Harvey Green, but on Simon Slade and Judge Hammond), but also against the legal and institutional structures that have allowed that speculation to flourish. When the town's sheriff tries to convince the mob to relinquish Green, saying, " 'The law must have its course; and no good citizen will oppose the law. It is made for your protection—for mine—and for that of the prisoner' " (183), the crowd scornfully rejects the sheriff's justice as the self-serving tricks of " 'blackleg judges, and blackleg lawyers' " (184). Once again, the narrator renders the voice of the crowd inarticulate, its leadership irrational, and its motivations instinctual. Despite the narrator's claim that the mob, like individual drunkards in the barroom, is propelled by a "great moving impulse" (171), an irrational "current of passion" (176), however, the economic message of the crowd—" 'Let no man in Cedarville do a stroke of work until the murderer is found' " (172)—is unmistakable, as is its unwillingness to surrender the social space of the barroom. Throughout the mob's activities, the narrator reports, "the drinking at the bar was not suspended for a moment" (185–86).

This episode is particularly revealing, as the mob's refusal to become irrationally instinctual prevents the narrator from constructing himself as detached, disinterested, and rational by contrast. If his objectivity can be measured by his ability to name in the townspeople an implicating passion that bars them from his own temperate authority, the mob reverses the positions of interiority and objectivity, of implication and adjudication, on which narrative authority depends. Setting itself up to judge the activities of the town's authorities, the mob appropriates the narrator's position, leaving him no option but to occupy the space of shameful and inarticulate passion. Watching the mob, the narrator begins to feel "anxious and excited" (180); "my quickened pulses were now audible to my own senses," he reports, "and obscured what was external" (180). Forced by his " 'over excited' " (181) imagination into the realm of the turbulent interior, the narrator's rationality gives way to "mere fancy" (180). Suddenly, the narrator gains a new respect for the voice of impulse, as "a strong internal conviction" (191) warns him that he, too, may be accused by the mob. Retreating to his room, where he finds Green hidden beneath his bed, the once detached narrator is now fully implicated in the actions of the barroom and, like the other bar patrons who have come under his moralistic observation, he finds himself paralyzed by his own ardent spirits. The narrator earlier allows his passions to bypass social decorum and legal rights. The murder of Willy Hammond—and hence, the violent actions of the mob—comes to pass when the narrator allows his excited feelings to overstep social decorum. When one of Willy's friends invites the narrator to join him in intruding on Green's hotel room, claiming to have reasons to suspect foul play, the narrator eagerly complies: "I did not object, for, although I had no delegated right of intrusion, my feelings were so much excited in the case, that I went forward, scarcely reflecting on the propriety of so doing" (165). Interiority ("feelings") suspend social responsibility not only for gamblers who prey on innocent dupes, speculators who defer value and unsettle community ethics, or impulsive mobs who generate social mayhem, but for temperate reformers who use passions to suspend "delegated right" and common "propriety" as well.

With the narrator's fall into shameful passions, no character in *Ten Nights* is left unscathed. The town has lost its barroom; speculators have lost their investments; fathers and mothers have lost children; and even the narrator has lost his right to narrate. If ardent spirits have overtaken one and all, however, one unlikely man is left to lead the town in taking the vote that will close the Sickle and Sheaf once and for all. Reformed and respectable, as his daughter Mary dreamed he would someday be, Joe Morgan is neither ambitious nor lazy, rich nor poor, passionate nor shameful. Rather, he is the novel's ideal, "sober and industrious" (232), self-monitoring without shame, effortful without greed. Above all, Morgan exemplifies the narrative's interior compromise between passion and shame. He is, the narrator reports, "tasteful" (225). Tastefulness has been the novel's yardstick all along. From the start, the narrator claims to be drawn to the barroom's lads because their "language was not marred by obscenity, profanity, and vulgarity" (46). Tasteful speech is the public equivalent of what Fanny Morgan displays in the domestic realm, an air of "neatness and taste" (55). The narrator measures Cedarville's decline against his "familiarity with other and more elegantly arranged suburban homes" (107), compared with which establishments such as the Sickle and Sheaf have "grown coarser in growing larger" (108), while Judge Lyman's gardens, which once "charmed me with their order, neatness, and cultivation" (226), now seem shabby. Among such vulgar disrepair, one cottage displays "the hand of taste" (225): Joe Morgan's "small, but very neat cottage" (230), exhibiting "taste and comfort" (231). Like his home, Morgan himself "was well-dressed, stood erect, and though there were many deep lines in his thoughtful countenance, all traces of his former habits were gone" (235). While *Ten Nights* figures this respectable taste as a thing of the past—Joe Morgan, the reader is told, " 'set himself to the restoration of the old order of things' " (231)—in fact the middle class is a new phenomenon, produced from the nexus of self-restraint and productive effort that are the palatable shadows—not the respectable opposites—of the drunkard and the entrepreneur, of unquenchable appetite and unlimited self-making. Having turned thirst into taste, Morgan is exemplary of Cedarville's middle-class future: possessed of enough interiority to make self-regulation necessary, but without the embodied imperatives of desire or appetite, he is content to live the life he pledged to his daughter, prescribed by the narrow limits of home and work.

Despite Morgan's reformation, however, *Ten Nights* has a hard time reaching a satisfactory conclusion, in large measure due to its difficulty in naming the source of Cedarville's troubles. (Is it laziness or ambition, too much fathering or too little, domestic isolation or public licentiousness, passion or shame?) The novel ends with the passage, despite "some little chafing" (240), of a "Maine law" prohibiting the sale of liquor. "There were, in Cedarville, regularly constituted authorities," through whom the townspeople "must act in an orderly way" (240). Having expressed themselves through proper channels, "the people dispersed to their homes, each with a lighter heart, and better hopes for the future of their village" (240). This rather vague ending leaves some unsettling questions, however. For one, the novel never adequately addresses the fears some dissenting characters express about the advisability of permitting laws to encroach on civil rights. " 'Touch the liberties of the people in the smallest particular,' " one character opines, " 'and all guarantees are gone' " (127), for the Maine laws open " 'too wide a door for fanatical oppression' " (139). The benevolent care of "regularly constituted authorities" (200) has already been cast in doubt, furthermore, by the novel's depiction of how easily such men are corrupted by lobbyists and parties. The town's decision to pass the law comes, after all, as a result not of following proper electoral channels, but of forming a violent mob precisely to circumvent those authorities. The town now pledges to respect "the right of property which the law secures to every man" (239), even though that "right" led to the opening of a distillery and a barroom in the first place.

In the end, the happy return of the townspeople to the privacy of their individual homes to await the "future" raises the most disturbing questions of all. The town has reached this resolution by gathering collectively to pass a law in a barroom that their law will close forever. Will any space of social deliberation, demand, or pleasure remain in Cedarville, or are isolated, private homes the only sphere of action in the future? Will the town ever again gather as a social body, or, as Joe Morgan pledges, will they live "dispersed" in the circuit of domesticity and labor to which Mary has bound her father? Without such sociality, can happiness ever exist in the here and now, or must it be perpetually deferred, as it is at the novel's end, to the future?

These questions are rendered moot by the end of *Ten Nights*, as the novel's preferred program—reform—allows the ineffectual semblance of sociality in the interiorizing regime of what one character calls " 'habit' " (217). " 'We must teach our children the evils of intemperance, and send them out into the world as practical teachers of order, virtue, and sobriety. If we do this, the reform becomes radical' " (139). But without addressing the inner life of capital— of renewable value, of frustrated effort, of tasteful privacy and its turbulent unconscious—how "radical" can any reform be? When the narrator says that he sees why a former drinker is anxious for his son's welfare, given the boy's predilection for ardent spirits, his interlocutor says of the anxious father, " 'I don't see that they have done him much harm. He sowed his wild oats—then got married, and settled down into a good, substantial citizen' " (49). Drunkenness and citizenship, appetite and entrepreneurship, desire and normalcy turn out to be shockingly compatible in *Ten Nights*, each enabling and enabled by the interiorizations on which the dialectic of control lost and regained, pride exhausted and renewed, depends. That there " 'may be something beyond the money to take into the account' " (14) in these dynamics—that something being social life itself—is a problem *Ten Nights in a Bar-Room* can no more "radically" resolve than could the speculative market in which it became a bestseller.

Ambivalent Identification in Walt Whitman's Franklin Evans

Unlike *Ten Nights*, Walt Whitman's one and only published novel, *Franklin Evans*, never finds a tasteful resolution to the disruptive instabilities generated by the inner life of capital. Even more haunted than *Ten Nights* by the same-sex eroticism at the heart of speculative capital, *Franklin Evans* nearly loses its temperance theme to the various desires—economic, sexual, and nationalist— that overtake the narrator. In particular, Whitman's temperance message is repeatedly undermined by the interiorizations that, for Arthur, make sobriety a question of self-managed habit. *Franklin Evans* demonstrates how identifications across seemingly naturalized boundaries of gender, race, and nation arise from the interiorization of capital that makes the tasteful assumption of "identity"—rather than of "character"—the mark of a successfully, if ambivalently, self-disciplined subject. In so doing, *Franklin Evans* reveals how reformist codifications of identity sought to naturalize the class boundaries that Arthur's novel naturalizes through "taste," a project repeatedly undone by the ardent spirits that drive Whitman's protagonist to identify in unsettling ways.

Throughout 1842, the year he wrote and published *Franklin Evans*, Whitman experienced the contrast between self-management and erotic self-abandonment required by the interiorization of capital and popularized by revivalist reform. Whitman was fascinated and troubled by the Washingtonians, a temperance association begun in Baltimore in 1840 with a mere six members, which claimed half a million members only two years later. Unlike the earlier American Temperance Society, the Washingtonians were led not by clergy and abstemious gentry, but by working men and women who were themselves drinkers. While earlier temperance literature focused on how the pure could avoid temptation, Washingtonian literature, directed at the already "fallen," encouraged drinkers to reform themselves and each other.[22] In 1842, sixteen thousand New Yorkers claimed to be members of the city's twenty-three Washingtonian Societies.[23] While partly resulting from the broad circulation of print materials (*Franklin*

Evans, for instance, explicitly endorses the Washingtonians), the movement's popularity is primarily attributed to the public gatherings known as "experience meetings," where people were brought to tears by repentant drinkers' dramatic stories. Advocating inward-directed scrutiny while maintaining the pleasures of social engagement, requiring both self-restraint and ardent spirits, the Washingtonians embodied the contradictory inner life of capital, producing fissures in the self-making, self-managing entrepreneurial citizen.

The text of *Franklin Evans* is riddled with the same tensions, especially concerning the role of reform in creating and circulating interiority (advance publicity promised that the novel would "create a sensation") as a substitute for social interaction.[24] Moments of reform coincide in *Franklin Evans* with economic investment, in which speculators put a down payment on a profitable future made possible by vigilant self-management. Franklin must give up momentary pleasures to purchase an upwardly mobile future made possible not by his "nature" (his inclinations always lead Franklin astray), but by "habit" (a word that appears obsessively in *Franklin Evans*). "*Once thoroughly regenerated*," Whitman writes, "the remembrance of his old deformation will stand before his eyes like a pillar of fire, and warn him back from any farther indulgence in his vicious courses" (107).

One can never become regenerated, however, at least not in *Franklin Evans*, which is as much a tale of recidivism as of reform. Despite his innocent regret ("Perhaps if I had filled up my time with active employment, I might have kept to my resolution, and even in the end totally reformed" [105])—Franklin, substituting resolution for revolution, must be serially reformed, his craving for alcohol repeatedly rekindled by other forms of addiction generated by modern capital (not by "active employment" but by speculation and leisure). When Franklin tries to leave New York and its temptations, for instance, he quickly tires of the countryside's "monotony" (102), having become addicted to the variety of the city. Even the repeated ritual of confessing and redemption becomes addictive for Franklin. Whitman seems to have understood that, despite the novel's conventional moral ("I would advise every young man to marry as soon as possible, and have a home of his own" [183]), normalcy has no narrative, being antithetical to capital and its repeated generations of novelty. If Franklin were ever to become "thoroughly regenerated," the desire of readers for more narrative—parallel to the desire of interlocutors in the novel for more confession, and of inebriates for more drink—would be unprofitably frustrated.

Whether engaged in economic speculations, homosocial bonding, or barroom binges, everyone in *Franklin Evans*, drinkers and reformers alike, is prone to ardent spirits, none capable of desiring moderately. Throughout its plot, *Franklin Evans* equates economic speculation and addiction, as in the subplot involving the crooked speculator, Andrews, who "died of grief at the failure of some stock-jobbing operations, wherein a cunning fellow-broker overreached him" (128). Economic appetites rarely stay within the limits of legitimate profit, but fail from "overreaching" excesses of greed. Whitman again links drinking and investment in the interpolated story of a schoolteacher who falls into ruin both because he "invested in stocks" (108) and, at the same moment, began drinking excessively. Just as alcoholics in *Franklin Evans* conceal their binges, the economically intemperate are skilled deceivers. After Andrews's death, his properties "were found to be as fallacious as the basis on which they had been reared" (182). The greedy Demaine cheats while "keeping up appearances"; hence, Whitman compares him to a stage illusion, "as far removed from true gentlemen, as the gilded sun, in stage melo-dramas, from the genuine source of light himself" (182). The problem, for readers of *Franklin Evans* as for characters in the text, is how to discern real from feigned virtue, given that interior "nature" rather than public actions has become the guarantor of trust. When Whitman describes the Marchions as "among the most respectable and respected families in the city" (182), the proximity to Demaine's story casts doubt on how Marchion acquired *his* wealth or how well deserved his respectability is. Little wonder that when, at the novel's finish, Franklin inherits a benefactor's enormous fortune, he admits that, despite rejoicing in the windfall, "I could not help wondering at the method of it" (178).

In a world of deceptive appearances, where the economy relies on greater and less controllable desires and therefore no reform is final, trust is a complicated affair, continually lapsing into skepticism ("wondering"). The future behavior of people, like that of stocks and markets, is highly unpredictable, yet social and economic contracts, even "moral" ones like the temperance pledge, require just such predictability. When Stephen Lee decides to leave his estate to the young and virtually unknown Franklin, he claims he is convinced that Franklin's wild oats have all been sown, although such a conviction, as he acknowledges, can be based not on empirical fact, but on "whim" and "fancy." "Whim," however, is close kin to impulse, as is "fancy" to desire. *Franklin Evans* never gets over a certain speculative wildness, then, and in the end the hero has to acknowledge that he is, despite his habitual reform, a bad return on the investment (125).

Surrounded by such shifting appearances, Franklin is understandably plagued by ambivalent identifications—with the suffering drunkard *and* the moralistic reformer, the degraded poor *and* the enterprising rich, the socially disenfranchised *and* those in positions of institutional authority—that render the plot of Whitman's novel haltingly episodic. Whitman's seeming inability to maintain a consistent story line in *Franklin Evans* has been interpreted as proof of the author's lukewarm commitment to the novel's temperance agenda.[25] I contend, on the contrary, that the halting narrative of *Franklin Evans* suggests how well its author understood the dynamics of temperance reform, which produced a never-ending series of "new starts," producing, in Washingtonian meetings no less than in the novel, perpetually backsliding characters who career inescapably between social appetites and self-managing discipline.[26] Despite a plot that Alexander Cowie called "wobbly at best,"[27] then, *Franklin Evans* has a structural logic that reveals much about the unsteady relations between reform and capital, same-sex eroticism and homosociality, and urban heterogeneity and racial identification in antebellum America.

The novel begins when the young Franklin leaves his rural Long Island home for New York City, seeking economic opportunity. Franklin shares the carriage with another young man, Colby, who quickly befriends the young Franklin, and the older, respectable antiquarian, Stephen Lee, who amuses the young men with tales of the nation's past, including the story of the Indian chief Unrelenting, one of the plot's notorious interruptions. Once in New York, Franklin begins an apprenticeship with the unscrupulous speculators Andrews and Demaine. At the same time, Colby introduces Franklin to the dissipated world of the theaters and taverns, from which Franklin flees by marrying an innocent young woman who soon dies as a result of his drunken neglect. Despondent, Franklin drinks more, loses his job, and inadvertently falls in with a gang involved in a robbery, for which he is arrested. While in jail, he is sought by a benefactor, Marchion, whose drowning daughter Franklin had saved in an earlier episode, and who now secures the young man's freedom and persuades him to take the Old Pledge, forbidding the drinking of hard liquor. In the hope of starting a new life away from the city, Franklin travels to Virginia, moves in with a bachelor planter, Bourne, and, during a drunken spree, marries a passionate "creole" slave, Margaret. Once sober, Franklin regrets his marriage, leading him to ignore his loving wife and take a white mistress, Mrs. Conway, which drives Margaret to kill the mistress and herself. Franklin returns to New York, where the dying Stephen Lee tells his young friend the sad tale of his children's death as a result of their mother's drunkenness, prompting Evans to sign the total abstinence pledge, in return for which Lee leaves the young hero his enormous fortune.

In each episode, Franklin takes a moralistic stance in relation to the city (a cesspool of sin), women (full of corrupting excess), and above all liquor. Over time, however, he attaches himself to increasingly rich men, causing panic manifested as a drinking spree. The panic is resolved when Franklin displaces his desire for men (always also a desire for capital) onto women, who become embodiments of whatever excess aroused Franklin's desire in the first place.[28] As Franklin's desires become more ambitious, his female surrogates become more unruly and are punished in increasingly violent ways. As the women suffer, Franklin styles himself, in contrast, as rational and judicious in the manner of his male mentors. Only by displacing his desires onto women, in other words, can Franklin achieve the homosocial identifications that seemingly displace the erotic desire that capital both requires and shames.

The most striking instance of this pattern occurs in the story of an impoverished and besotted mother whose death Franklin witnesses after he accompanies home a bedraggled child who begs money to buy his mother liquor. The chapter immediately follows Franklin's first alcoholic crisis, in which he leaves undone an important errand assigned to him by his employer, Stephen Lee, while he carouses in theaters and saloons with his drinking mates. In the scene of the mother's death, Franklin projects *his* shame at having proved a bad son onto a "bad" mother. The poor woman has her own interpretation of her situation, however: "It was as if around the room, and peering down from the upper corners of the wall, the death-stricken outcast fancied she saw faces, bodiless, and working with strange grins of mockery" (92). Recognizing that she is mocked by "bodiless" figures that are—and the verb is telling—"working," the delirious woman brings to the surface the economic shame at the heart of Franklin's projection. Franklin's appetites have led him away from Lee's paternal ideal of abstract—and hence bodiless—virtue, which Franklin experiences, as does the mother, as panoptical judgment. In her vision, the mother turns this bodiless ideal into a gothic horror, simultaneously making a cruel mockery of Franklin's voyeuristic benevolence. The mother's interpretive power in turn transforms Franklin from an objective witness into the abjected object of scrutiny he attempts to make *her*: "I was half petrified as her look was directed toward me, and the child at my feet. I stood as still as a statue" (92). When she takes her foul and tattered rags and throws them at Franklin, he "half shrieked with fear" (93). Even as Franklin attempts to generate his own wholeness as a benevolent and relatively self-managing male in opposition to a neglectful mother who is ruled by her ungovernable appetites, he is only partially successful (the odd phrase "half shrieked" is one of several instances in this chapter in which Franklin describes himself as divided or "halved").[29] However identified with abstract virtue he may be, the appetite-ridden Franklin is never as distinct from the degraded woman as he wishes to believe.

An earlier episode in the novel similarly shows Franklin's identifications divided in ways that challenge his status as objective narrator. As Franklin describes his disgust at finding his co-worker Denis drunk, *Franklin Evans* departs for the first time from its first-person narration. Whitman contrasts Denis's downfall and arrest with the elaborate swindles perpetrated by Demaine and Andrews, which Franklin could not have witnessed firsthand. Omniscience, in this juxtaposition, struggles with shameful experience for control of the narrative. Both scenes of intemperance and secrecy, however, represent aspects of Franklin's desire: he is given over both to the dissipation of pleasure and the lure of upward mobility. (This episode occurs as Franklin is about to leave Andrews's employ to work for Lee, thereby doubling his salary.) The juxtaposition of the two stories makes visible the relation *between* the two desires, both of which Franklin must disavow in order to reform himself *and* inherit the "honest" wealth associated with Lee (the source of whose money, like the "business" of the narrator of *Ten Nights*, is never named). Only by disavowing his own implicating experiences of desire and pleasure can Franklin achieve the disinterestedness required by virtue. Yet the novel's Washingtonian faith in first-person testimony pulls in the opposite direction. This episode contains both forms of narration—first-person and omniscient, experience and virtue—in a tense proximity that continues to trouble the divided protagonist.

While Franklin cannot resolve this conflict in relation to Denis and Demaine, gender difference allows him apparent resolution. Franklin concludes the story of the drunken mother's death by asserting, "There is a sacredness in some of our sorrows, which prevents them from being fit subjects for the rude and common gaze" (95). The very fact that Franklin goes on narrating suggests his separation from the "sorrows" that consign the mother to invisibility and silence. Yet Franklin cannot quite leave this poor woman alone. Immediately after differentiating himself from her silence, Franklin relates the story of his first wife, Mary (95), also the name of the dead woman's daughter. The doubling of Mary transforms the victimizing mother, whose intemperance has destroyed a household, into a victimized wife whose household has been destroyed by economic intemperance. "We never purchased until we saw the means of payment," Franklin begins his tale of ideal marriage. "But about a year after our marriage, the serpent came into our little Eden. Ambition—the poison that rankles in the hearts of men, and scorches all peace, and blights the bloom of content—ambition entered there" (97). Engaging in speculative investments to earn money to build a house, Franklin goes bankrupt and begins drinking

(98). Realizing "she has bound her fortunes to a *drunkard*" (98), Mary, forsaken and forlorn, soon sickens and dies. While Franklin cannot escape blame in both stories, he does escape punishment, which falls solely to women.

Despite his ability to project his shame onto women who are punished for the betrayals and passions he himself experiences, Franklin is fatally linked to the women he punishes by his persistent desires for men of means. That these transactions take place over exchanges of cash suggests that capital, in *Franklin Evans*, is a queer business. Franklin's life of urban dissipation begins with Colby's invitation to "'go out and cruise a little'" (67).[30] The intoxication that will give him so much trouble comes to Franklin, then, in the form of the urban *flâneur*, whom Walter Benjamin describes as "someone abandoned in the crowd" who "is not aware of the special situation, but this does not diminish its effect on him and it permeates him, blissfully like a narcotic that can compensate him for many humiliations."[31] The intoxication "to which the *flâneur* surrenders," Benjamin observes, "is the intoxication of the commodity around which surges the stream of customers."[32] The connection Benjamin draws between urban anonymity, intoxication, and commodification establishes Whitman's protagonist as one of U.S. literature's first *flâneurs*, moving through crowded city streets, taverns, and theaters in ways that fill him with intoxicating sensation while also enabling the transfer of desires cleansed of the taint of embodiment. As Mark Turner observes, the flâneur is also the prototype of the modern homosexual, moving unseen through the cityscape as both the embodiment of desire and the commodified object of exchange (between, for instance, the lawyers and policemen who populate the pages of *Franklin Evans*).[33]

Such a development can only occur, however, when economic relations are understood as interior sensations, in the form of Franklin's shameful identifications with punished women and the panics occasioned by his eroticized relationships with men. Caught between these forces, Franklin cashes in on the other social relationships that sustain him when he first arrives in New York. Despite his claim, "I was never the person to forget a friend" (181), he forgets many friends, among them the man with whom he first cruises New York, Colby, whom Franklin leaves drunk on the street, and Denis, whom he leaves to die. To honor one's past with other men is to acknowledge one's ardent spirits, which leave "a stigma for the future" (88). A "few hours' casual gratification," after all, can render youth "useless" (88), and Franklin, whose investments in futurity promise great things, cannot risk such a taint. Cruising with other men, partaking in ardent spirits rather than denying one's pleasures in favor of abstract identifications with patriarchal virtues, risks one's future, counter-intuitively, not by leaving one in bad company but by alienating one from the heteronormativity from which that company continually draws Franklin. If the company of his drinking buddies offers Franklin "sensations" all too embodied, the company of men of wealth promises a network that offers participants abstraction from their bodies. If ardent spirits only leave one in the street, in other words, abstract networks place one in a normativity figured as national-ism, as Franklin makes clear in his description of the French expatriate and Southern plantation owner Bourne. "I rather thought, from his accent and manner," Franklin reports, "that he was not an American. In the course of our talk, I learned that he was a bachelor" (137–38). To be a bachelor is to be un-American, a double alienation from "normality" Franklin risks in his extended sojourn as Bourne's guest and drinking buddy.

If ardent spirits risk national alienation, race reintegrates Franklin into the comforts of what Dana Nelson terms national manhood.[34] Showing national-ism to be deeply tied to land speculation and exploited labor, which required the often violent "vanishing" of Native Americans and the enslavement of African Americans, *Franklin Evans* narrates the formation of national identity in opposition to discredited and victimized bodies. In so doing, the novel transforms the struggle between self-management and intemperate greed from a class dynamic, where it remained for Arthur, into a matter of racial identifica-tion. Masculinity has fled America in *Franklin Evans*, driven out not by the unstable patterns of status and subjection instituted by modern capital, but by drink and desire. Whitman turns the loss of masculinity into a national phe-nomenon by equating it with the "vanishing" of Native Americans, the last inhabitants of a purely homosocial world. Establishing Native American cul-ture as (white) America's "past," as a primitive stage in a natural progression toward mature nationalism, Whitman helps bring about the very disappear-ance he seeks to commemorate.

Franklin Evans begins with the "vanishing" of Indians. As a wagonload of passengers travels from the countryside to New York, Stephen Lee, the self-proclaimed antiquarian, tells the story of the Indian chief Unrelenting. As a young warrior, Unrelenting kills a Kansi warrior but spares a young boy to tell the story of the victory. Years later, that boy, now a grown warrior, comes to the dwelling of Unrelenting and his only son, Wind-Foot, who offer the stranger lodging. When Unrelenting sets off "on some public business for his tribe" (51), the Kansi warrior kidnaps Wind-Foot. The fleeing men are pursued by the enraged father, who kills his enemy just moments after the warrior kills Wind-

Foot. With these deaths, Lee's story implies, two native tribes tragically "vanish," without a white person entering the tale. As survivors and inheritors, whites like Lee serve only to memorialize inevitable loss.

Lee transforms the aggressive appropriation of Indian lands by white settlers into a tale of a "race" vanquished by its own natural intemperance. While Lee promises a story about the impact on Indian life of "the greatest curse ever introduced among them"—namely, "the curse of *rum!*" (45)—no one in the story ever drinks, for the presence of alcohol would implicate white settlers in these "vanishings." Indian intemperance is not as simple as one swig too many of rum, an act that, Washingtonian rhetoric contended, Indians could be led to forswear. Rather, theirs is intemperance of *affect*, so deeply a part of their natures as to be ineradicable. Indians, in Lee's tale, are victims of their own intemperate aggression, rage, and desire for vengeance. Sounding very much like the drunkard of temperance literature, Unrelenting "trembled with agitation" in telling his story, during which he "wrought himself up to a pitch of loudness and rage" (49), while the Kansi warrior's violent emotions are displayed through "two fiery orbs, rolling about incessantly, like the eyes of a wild beast" (50). The struggle between whites and Native Americans, Lee suggests, is properly understood as the latter's battle with ardent spirits, their unlucky fate sealed in and by their own turbulent nature.

Despite Lee's assertion of racial difference, however, his tale is haunted by moments of cross-racial identification, just as Franklin's would be by identifications across genders. Lee "survives" to tell Unrelenting's tale, just as the Kansi boy in that tale does, and like Unrelenting, who narrates his story to his young son, Lee tells the same tale to his surrogate son, Franklin. Franklin and Colby have grown bored listening to a female passenger describing her daughter's wedding, which the boys find "totally uninteresting" (43). Just as the speech act of Lee's narration creates an all-male alternative to the mother's domestic sentimentality, so the tale itself conjures an almost exclusively male world in danger of extinction. The tale, like the novel generally, is animated by fears of effeminacy. Unrelenting claims that the Kansi warrior has a "'coward arm [that] warrest with women and children'" (54), while the warrior in turn torments Wind-Foot by calling him a girl (53). If male homosociality disappears in America's past due to intemperance, the same force, arising in taverns and boardinghouses, resurrects it as Franklin's future. Even as Lee warns Franklin against such sites of temptation, his tale disavows his own "unrelenting" paternalism and family duty. Just as intemperance dissolves family ties (and hence obligations) in the tale of Unrelenting, so alcohol gives Franklin a way to resist *his* obligations to the persistent Lee.

If race "vanishes" at the outset of *Franklin Evans*, it returns, midway through Whitman's text, in Franklin's account of the slave woman, Margaret, which displaces hostility and desire between men onto the "savage" appetites of women. Having received a sum of money from Marchion, Franklin leaves New York for Virginia on a journey "partly of business, and partly of pleasure" (137). He soon meets the plantation owner Bourne, with whom, after many shared bottles of wine, Franklin takes up residence. If Franklin is potentially effeminized by the liquor and the same-sex desires that seemingly keep him in Virginia (the "pleasure" part of his trip), he is elevated, through the most violent displacement in the novel, to a position of adjudication and hence of cultural superiority. Threatened with becoming less than a man, in other words, Franklin is saved by becoming more than a slave.[35] Threatened by a licentious overseer, Margaret "lifted the instrument of labor she had been using, and felled him to the earth with a single blow" (142). When the slave is brought before her master and Franklin, the latter becomes infatuated, intercedes with Bourne on Margaret's behalf, and marries her. In becoming her advocate, Franklin reverses his own disempowerment in the previous episode, in which, having been arrested for robbery, a humiliated Franklin has stood before a judge as an accused criminal. Displacing his guilt onto Margaret, he accomplishes his desired identification with the lawyer Marchion, who serves as Franklin's advocate just as Franklin now does for Margaret. In marrying Margaret, moreover, Franklin distinguishes his own lustful interest in Margaret from that of the distasteful overseer. Yet the violence inflicted on Margaret by Franklin turns out to be even more devastating and less open to resistance. When Franklin abandons Margaret for a white woman, Mrs. Conway, the abandoned woman kills her rival and herself. Before she dies, however, Margaret makes the overseer and Franklin hear her confession together. Putting the two men in parallel positions, Margaret reveals the kinship of benevolence and violence, unmasking the innocence on which Franklin's (racial) self-representations depend.

Seemingly in response to Margaret's insistence on his implication in patterns of racial violence, Franklin rewrites Margaret's story as an interior drama in which reform de-racializes imperial profit. Midway through his narration of Margaret's downfall, Franklin interrupts himself to relate an "imaginative mania" that again implicates white men's investments in imperial capital and reform, both of which publicize the "savage" desires that Margaret is forced to embody. Franklin imagines a city in a "mighty and populous empire" that is "almost without boundary," a seaport "filled with rich navies, and with the products of every part of the earth, and with merchants, whose wealth was greater than the wealth of princes" (166). His is an imperial fantasy in which the "products" brought into port might have included slaves. In the fantasy, however, business "seemed to be suspended" (167), transformed into the civic spectacle of reform: on this day, the last inebriate will sign the pledge, making literal the nation's symbolic emblem, a flag depicting a white woman crushing the snake of temptation beneath her heel. If imperialism generates slavery and the racialized appetites that result in Margaret's death, abstract whiteness, in Franklin's "mania," is the solution to the nation's internal flaws. If Margaret cannot be saved by temperance, the dutiful subjects of the triumphant white woman will be. As a banner in Franklin's imagined city declares, "The Last Slave of Appetite is Free" (170).

Margaret haunts this fantasy, however, as the reformed inebriate declares to the assembled crowd, " 'I throw off the chains, and take upon myself the pleasant bondage of good" (170). The chains of the slave fail to turn "freedom" into an unbounded state, for imperial ambitions require intemperate appetite. The persistence of enslavement, even in proclamations of liberty, highlights the inconsistency between the idealized political rhetoric and the legal protection of chattel slavery in the United States. Franklin's host, Bourne, lives in the United States rather than in his native France because he loves "liberty" (138), yet he participates in what Whitman characterizes as "that most abominable of all man's schemes of making money."[36] Above all, Franklin, having projected his passion and shame onto Margaret, continually reveals his similarity to the poor slave woman and her turbulent interior. In an earlier episode, Franklin, discovering that a business partner has swindled him, goes "mad with resentment and agitation" and strikes the man "to the earth" (114), just as Margaret does to the overseer. At the center of *Franklin Evans*, its eponymous protagonist is not only, as Emory Holloway observes, "fatally fascinated by the exotic sensuality of a Creole slave,"[37] he is inescapably tied to her by a pattern of projection and incorporation, the turbulent inner life of capital.

In the end, however, Franklin is different from Margaret in two important ways. Unlike the self-annihilating slave woman, Franklin not only survives but profits from the unpredictable interiorizations that are the gaming fee in modern speculative capital. But that survival comes at a cost. While the vengeful Margaret and the enraged Unrelenting may misname their enemy, turning their anger against other disenfranchised women and Indians, they nevertheless refuse an enforced choice between resignation and rage, domesticity and adventure, virtue and pleasure, coded as a difference between disembodied whiteness and a hyper-embodied "race." For white characters in *Franklin Evans*, however, transgressing these borders necessitates the self-monitoring and habitual self-regulations that temperance requires of all ardent spirits. If *Franklin Evans* as a reform tale insists that improvement, like identity, comes through diligent effort, the tale's passionate characters contradict that moral, showing that whims, accidents, and ill-defined attractions leave Franklin, as Holloway observes, "rewarded with a fortune he in no way deserves."[38] Despite this fortune, however, Franklin is also left without a community, having abandoned all the friends, lovers, and mentors who, as living people, are prone to the ardent spirits he believes must be sacrificed in the name of success. Without a social world in which to experience pleasures, value responsibilities, and invent new narratives, Franklin is consigned to the unconscious realm, where ardent spirits cause manias, not revolutions.

5

ANXIETY, DESIRE, AND THE NERVOUS STATE

Fraught nerves—more than sentiment and sympathy—dominate the pages of antebellum literature, giving the clearest picture of the relation between citizens and the state in the period. Despite the axiomatic assumption that "psychology" became popularized in the United States only in the late nineteenth century, it is nearly impossible to crack open an antebellum novel without finding characters proclaiming themselves "nervous" or "anxious."[1] *Uncle Tom's Cabin* alone produces a seemingly inexhaustible variety of nervous states: Eliza's panicked scurry across the ice, Augustine St. Clare's aesthetic excitability, Simon Legree's traumatized relation to his own oedipality, Marie St. Clare's narcissism, Topsy's hysterical sobbing, Mammy's exhausted headaches, and the list could go on. I invoke these instances of troubled nerves not to invite more psychoanalytic readings of early American texts, but to suggest that productions of states of interiorized (un)consciousness in antebellum America popularized and naturalized changing models of volition, subjection, and sociality that were central to relational framings of citizenship and the state. Nervousness, in other words, was both symptomatic and descriptive in antebellum literature, charting the isolation of citizens from various and variable social relations. In discourses of nervous citizenship, predictable patterns of social order became imagined as "systems" immune to conscious control and yet perpetually "symptomatic" and hence in need of vigilant self-management. The ubiquity of nervous states—which included new conceptions of desire as well as of anxiety—suggests the widespread dissemination throughout the popular imagination of psychological discourses that radically short-circuited social agency, even while the disruptions caused by jangled nerves attested to a trace dissent against the interiorization of social relations into self-managed—yet ultimately uncontrollable—states of (un)consciousness.

By the early nineteenth century, European science had developed a complex theory of the human nerves.[2] George Cheyne's *The English Malady* (1733) connected a range of bodily disorders, from asthma and dyspepsia to consumption and cholera, to nerves that had been overly stimulated by excessively luxurious living, spicy foods, tea, coffee, and alcohol, all of which would become targets of reform movements in the 1840s.[3] In people with nervous disorders, Cheyne asserted, stimuli might enter the body from without, but reactions were blocked at the body's limits, manifesting themselves as symptoms. The nervous body thus became a check on its own volition, turning stimuli inward but allowing no means to consciously affect exterior sources of excitation. This seemingly simple innovation prompted nineteenth-century neurologists to sever all communication between the inside and the outside of bodies, conceiving nerves not as mediators, but as a fully interiorized and self-contained network. Philippe Pinel, writing after the French Revolution, argued that nervous disorders stemmed from lesions on the nerves themselves, thereby eliminating the need for external stimuli in accounts of nervous disorder.[4] By the mid-nineteenth century, the Scottish neurologists William Cullen and Robert Whytt had conceived the "nervous system," involving the transfer of stimuli from one part of the body to another through what Whytt called "sympathy of the nerves" (a phrase repeated in the United States by both Catharine Beecher and Lydia Fowler).[5] By mid-century, then, external stimuli produced by social relations ("sympathy") had been interiorized within a self-contained network, the agitation of which—what Cullen named "neuroses"—caused shutdowns of stimulus intake and, more frequently and debilitating, various forms of bodily paralysis.[6] Giving this newly conceived "system" even more autonomy, scientists cut the nerves off from direction by the brain, thereby placing the nervous "system" beyond the reach of conscious will. Even as the body was conceived as a space of interiorized social relations ("sympathy"), then, it became the check on its own volition to affect those relations. This is precisely what makes the nerves a valuable and naturalizing figure for the modern state that, like nerves, suffused the body politic, inscrutably but irresistibly, leaving its citizens in a constant state of agitation without a clear sense of the sources of or solutions to their excitement or of what volition they had to affect the state even if they could identify its movements.

The effects of neurology on U.S. reform are evident in Catharine Beecher's *The American Woman's Home*, which establishes a private nexus of affect and governmentality that Beecher called "the family state," a nerve system organized around what she, echoing Whytt, called "the great sympathetic."[7] Containing a constitution and laws, the family state, like the nerves, seems at first to be an autonomous "system." Unlike the neurologists she echoed, however, Beecher could not close the porous borders of the home, which were repeatedly permeated by commodities and immigrant laborers. In the face of the home's permeability, families maintain order (Beecher would have said "health") by habits of affective self-regulation that are at once hyper-vigilant and volitionless. "For it is not 'by works of righteousness' that we are to be considered and treated as righteous persons," Beecher instructed, "but through a 'faith that *works by love*;' that *faith* or *belief* which is not a mere intellectual conviction, but a *controlling purpose* or spiritual principle which *habitually controls* the feelings and conduct" (459). What at first appears to be Calvinist skepticism about works moves quickly to a distinction between intellectualization and involuntary action: whether the involuntary power over the righteous body came from within ("faith") or without ("habitual exercise') Beecher tellingly left unclear.

The controlling "faith or belief," invisible but irresistible, compelling but involuntary, that dictates the terms of health or paralysis allows Beecher to justify domestic order through a corporeal constitution derived from continental neurology. Beecher divides the nerves into two functions: the first, located in the gray matter of the brain, controls feelings and actions and is therefore volitional. The second, located in the white matter of the nerves, creates *involuntary* motion. While the volitional nerves are directed by the brain, the involuntary nerves govern the structural workings of the body, over which the brain has no sustained control. In fact, mental stimulation for Beecher runs the risk of illness and paralysis. "Whenever that part of the brain which is employed in thinking, feeling, and willing is greatly exercised by hard study, or by excessive care or emotion," she warned, "the blood tends to the brain to supply it with increased nourishment, just as it flows to the muscles when they are exercised" (90). "It is necessary for the perfect health of the brain and nerves," Beecher prescribed, "that the several portions be exercised sufficiently, and that no portion be exhausted by over-action" (89–90). What constitutes "sufficient" exercise is precisely the self-regulated middle-class life that Beecher extols in *The American Woman's Home* against the degraded labor of the Irish and the luxurious decadence of the urban rich.[8] Yet Beecher repeatedly renders the middle class, like the nerve system governing its health, invisible. While she describes the lives of the wretched poor and the frivolous rich, she leaves the middle-class home unoccupied, the stage setting for actors who, having a script but no power to act, never appear.

Just as neurologists were concerned about closing off the epidermal surface where the nerves and external stimuli communicate, so Beecher worried about all sites where inside and outside—the "laws of health" and leisure and labor— come into contact. The body and its porous borders are safeguarded, in *The American Woman's Home*, not simply by a regulated home interior that, as Amy Kaplan notes, made domesticity the rationale for and stabilizing counterbalance to imperial expansion, but by the nervous system itself. Better than the conscious mind, prone to the temptations of pleasure, the nerves control movement, regulating ingress and egress in ways that make volition unnecessary. At the same time, invited to surrender investments in the law to police their obedience to the laws of their own bodies, those living in the nervous state are necessarily anxious (and none more anxious than Beecher herself, who frets away, chapter after chapter, about the ignorance of her countrywomen, the state of the nation, and, in the end, the sales of her book). One function of the nervous state is precisely to produce anxious citizens not to lead them to reform—thus making the reform apparatus obsolete—but to perpetuate institutionality as the satisfactory transfer between a now inscrutable and inalterable state, imagined as a nerve system in the body politic, and the trace volition maintained as/in the troubled unconsciousness of its citizens.

The substitution of institutional authority for self-imposed reform allows the citizen to fail in her or his efforts at self-management, a failure necessary for the production of anxiety and hence of heightened attention to interior states (with a corresponding lessening attention to exterior ones). In his anti-masturbation tract *Amativeness* (1854), Orson Fowler inscribed a habitually self-governing citizen but one who was ultimately *unsuccessful* in that self-governance. Self-abuse, for Fowler, was the naturalized but ungovernable force that had to be continually surveyed without ever being finally controlled or overcome. Subject to the dialectic (without synthesis) of desire and anxiety, of identification and disavowal, the citizen for Fowler was also the subject without volition. Fowler asserted that nine out of ten boys older than eleven, and half of those between seven and eleven, masturbated. At the same time, Fowler also contended that, once started, the masturbator is never fully redeemable. The masturbating citizen is thus irretrievably prone to a desire that he must strive unsuccessfully to master. A masturbator, Fowler proclaimed, is "addicted" (5) to his desire. The desiring citizen (and Fowler inscribed the majority of citizens as infused with desire) is therefore also the subject of anxiety.

While Fowler's theory of masturbation makes reform impossible, then, it inscribes a nervous system into his readers. Inflammation is more likely from masturbation than from any other activity, Fowler argued, because "a large amount of *nervous tissue* is found ramified upon that part of the apparatus more immediately brought into action, than upon almost any other portion of the body" (9). Given that "inflammation breeds desire" (16), those who mess with nerves will necessarily become nervous: one masturbator, diagnosed because his "mind was flighty" (3), exemplifies the "wild, excited, preternatural, irregular, abnormal, painful action" (9) typical of the nervous. Precursors to postbellum neurotics, masturbators suffer "horrid dreams, and idiotic manners" (13), melancholy and excessive remorse (14), "an irritated, craving state of the nervous system, which aggravates desire from the first" (26–27). This last diagnosis is telling, as the nervous system, which at first appears as the victim of self-pollution, turns out to be its incentive. While Fowler seems to present the possibility of reform, then, agency is invoked only to be absorbed by the *involuntary* promptings of desire, the exclusive property now of the nervous state.

Throughout these texts, nervousness becomes an orientation, enhancing citizens' sense of their own vigilance—a predisposition to action—while removing the need for action itself. Governed by rather than governing their nerves, citizens were left only the obligation to "*investigate the laws*" of their nature, as Fowler wrote, "and then obey them" (32). Fowler realized, however, that laws were made to be broken and that, therefore, only institutionalized science would prevail, providing the parameters of the new nervous state, leaving the fate of volition—especially *imaginative* volition, the power to conceive what Judith Butler calls the not-yet-real—uncertain.[9] Fowler, whose own institutional authority rested on the perpetuation of anxiety, made imagination his principal target, warning that masturbation was likely to addict "especially those that cultivate (vitiate) the imagination" (4).[10]

Despite Fowler's best efforts, however, imagination and its inventive reconstructions of social affiliation survived in/as the melancholy unconscious of nervous citizens, necessitating new interior vocabularies—the romantic language of dreams, reveries, and manias—through which to stage protest, make demands, and, most powerfully, assert forms of sociality seemingly "reformed" into obsolescence within the institutional civil sphere. Ungoverned desires, Fowler warned, might "rush in unbidden, and renew former associations and habits" (28). In attempting to contain the disruptive demands of unconscious desire, nineteenth-century bio-reformers—most notably, the Fowler siblings, who popularized phrenology in the United States—developed a science of desire that made sexuality the interior site of self-managing volition for the modern citizen. Turning desire into palatable anxiety, Orson, Lorenzo, and Lydia Fowler, I will argue, made jangled nerves into the political unconscious of antebellum America.[11]

While its role in medicalizing sexuality as an inner disposition is noteworthy, phrenology's transformation of a relational sensation (pleasure) into an individual and interiorized phenomenon (desire) is its most significant contribution to modern sexual discourse. Rather than being centered on relational acts —fornication, for instance—desire, like other phrenological predispositions, is a self-contained *propensity*. Shifting from pleasure to desire, then, phrenology makes possible the judgment not of acts, but of inclinations, which can be evaluated only through the self-monitoring and confession of interiority. Privileged, in fact, as the *fundamental* propensity of human nature (phrenology gives more attention to desire than to any other proclivity), desire comes to appear identical to—indeed, necessary for—personality and as such subsumes the social agency previously attributed to the conscious (moral, rational) will. Not only are the particular forms of antebellum desire interiorized, however, they are also ontologically frustrated (if desire is gratified, it ceases—at least, in that moment—to be desire). Desire becomes, then, not an itch demanding a scratch, but the pleasure of the itch itself. Reconceived in this way, desire, as the second section of this chapter argues, naturalized and interiorized the necessary dissatisfactions of a new speculative market, which, unlike earlier modes of exchange, required investors to wait, sometimes indefinitely, for returns on their investments. Analogously, antebellum Americans learned to see desire as an investment in pleasure; if the payoff never comes, then desire, demonstrating the predispositions that shape personality, becomes a never quite satisfactory end in itself.

At the same time, desire produced the *imbalance* that made perversion, not heterosexuality, the prevailing, if anxious, state of antebellum literature. (Fowler's discussions of masturbation in *Amativeness* are a case in point.) Without breaking with scientific reform's mandate that all citizen demand be articulated in a vocabulary of interiority, perverse desire became, as the third section of this chapter shows, a call for alternative conceptions of association and justice. Through its eruptions, the unconscious produced not the "truth" that grounded one's sexual identity, but a series of counterfeits and forgeries that challenged the status of normative identities and the deferred desires necessary to an emergent economy. In setting loose the unconscious, in other words, reform not only popularized a range of perversions, it queered the economy as well.

A state run on the basis of a centralized "system" of power, Francis Lieber argued, will inevitably become totalitarian. Such states, for Lieber, tend to conceive of themselves "on the centrally directed nervous . . . system of the animal." To foster democracy, Lieber suggested that the state instead model itself "upon the vital generative power of the disparate systems [that] act and produce independently."[12] Setting the state free from nerves opens it to a free play of democratic vitality that Gilles Deleuze and Félix Guatari describe as rhizoid: a plurality of interrelated "systems," each operating independently, yet in relation to one another. Freed from the nervous state, in other words, citizens might return to an imaginative and productive sociality that permits cooperative relationship without requiring the surrender of independent action. To privilege such a state over one based on the nerve system requires that we conceive "independence" apart from individuality, however. It also requires that, unlike Deleuze and Guatari, we see agency as more than the unsatisfied yearning of desire. We might, in short, inaugurate a state of cooperative and deliberative sociality without the presumption of "desire" that constitutes interiority and hence humanness; in so doing, we might produce queer lives in defiance of the nervous state. If such a de-interiorized state was beyond the articulated political imaginary of antebellum writers—wrestling as they were with the combined forces of neurology and aesthetics, anxiety and desire—their dreams and queer manias are nevertheless a retrievable archive of a social imaginary that continued to haunt the public spaces of a newly nervous state.

A Ball in a Deserted House

On August 27, 1834, Orson Squires Fowler presented the Amherst College commencement address on the theme "Temptation—Its Influence on Guilt."[13] In the address, Fowler disputed the proposition that guilt diminishes in proportion to temptation. If such were the case, he argued, angels, who were above temptation, would have no right to abjure guilt, while Satan, powerfully tempted, should experience no guilt whatsoever. "Such a doctrine," Fowler contended, "would demolish a *main pillar* in the moral government of God." Guilt rightly exists, he argued, in relation not to temptation, but to "*corrupt propensity*": to have a "propensity" toward sin was to fall prey to temptation and hence to be always already guilty by virtue of predisposition.[14] Although Fowler's address assumed a juridical context (in which one evaluates the claims to guilt or innocence put forth by another), his theory diverged significantly from traditional jurisprudence. While the law adjudicates based on social acts, Fowler's model did so on the basis of *impulse* toward action. For Fowler, then, one could rightly feel guilt without having transgressed. Locating all three adjudicative parties—lawmaker, criminal, and judge—in a single body (divided internally into conscience, impulse, and guilt), Fowler effectively transformed criminality from a social to an interior state.

Central to this shift is a transformation from legality as a principle of abstract unity—one statute legislates all acts of theft, for instance—to the infinite *particularity* of transgression, a change that permits the distribution of guilt across an infinite range of "propensities." "The fact is," Fowler asserted, "that no two moral agents can possibly share the guilt and punishment of a single criminal act. For though *millions* of beings may do *similar* acts, yet no two of them can do the *very same identical* act—any more than similar things can do the *very same identical* thing. And since no two moral agents can possibly commit the very same criminal act, they cannot surely share the guilt and punishment of that act." Just as each distinct act for Fowler should produce its customized punishment, so each *propensity* to act requires a particular self-inflicted guilt. For Fowler, an abstract legal structure premised on types of criminality is replaced by the assemblage of particular predispositions that serves as both the source and adjudication of guilt. While particularity in contemporary cultural criticism is often made the antidote to abstract legality, what Fowler's commencement address makes clear is that the diffusion of particularity—not as social phenomena (the wide distribution of individual civil liberties) but as a dispersal of "natures" (which would, in time, become "identities")—had the counter-liberatory effect of making consciousness the exclusive site of crime and punishment.[15] Gaining the infinite variety of inner propensity, moreover, citizens lost the grounds of social relatedness: moving inward, they surrendered the public realm of deliberation; gaining self-management, they lost an external authority with whom to register claims of injustice.

By removing guilt from the domain of law, Fowler implicitly privileged sites of individualization—the family, medicine, and education—to which he gave his subsequent professional attention. Those sites became responsible, under the guidance of men like Fowler, for rendering visible, nurturing, and regulating inner "propensities." Through his advice manuals addressed to these privatizing institutions, Fowler encouraged the de-socialization of the subject through a double inwardness: a turn from public spaces to a privacy where personality could manifest itself, and a self-regulating inner scrutiny that encouraged subjects to monitor and evaluate their "propensities" and hence their worthiness of guilt. In this system, one inward turn produces the other. The more one is encouraged to demonstrate personality, the more one will display the instincts and affects that indicate the "propensities" that lead to rightful self-condemnation ("guilt"). In turn, the more guilt one feels, the more likely one is to withdraw into the hidden spaces—the bed, the closet, the doctor's office—that will (never quite) conceal one's guilt. The more one withdraws from public scrutiny, in fact, the more one may self-indulge. This self-perpetuating cycle of interiorization produces the anxiety characteristic of modern citizenship in the United States.

The promise and problems with leaving crime and punishment in the interior realm of the body become clear in the work of Fowler's brother-in-law and publishing partner, Samuel Wells. In his *A Manual of Etiquette; or, How to Behave* (1857), subtitled, *A Pocket Manual of Republican Etiquette*, Wells echoed Fowler's dissatisfaction with a properly *social* legality. The Constitution, Wells asserted, opened up a Pandora's box of social liberties. As public culture became more privatized in the early decades of the nineteenth century, legal rights were translated into personal "freedom," making the private authority of parents tantamount to public tyranny. The social entitlements promised by the Revolution, Wells argued, spoiled the republic's children, who transformed anti-monarchic revolution into disrespect for parental authority.[16] In the face of this transformation, public legislation similarly had to be privatized, becoming, in Wells's manual, nationalized etiquette, "a truly American and republican school of politeness" (viii).

A more pressing social problem arises, according to Wells, from the overlay of national autonomy and modern capital. Even while asserting a static and self-evident republican character, Wells acknowledged a civil sphere saturated by continually changing "fashions," the mutability of which made "taste" an unreliable yardstick for acceptable behavior. At the same time, he insisted on the individual's duty to avoid offending the "customs" of others, thereby making "taste" into a moral imperative. "One cannot commit a greater mistake," Wells asserted, "than to make politeness a mere matter of arbitrary forms. It has as real and permanent a foundation in the nature and relations of men and women, as have government and the common law" (ix). Yet, as Wells conceded, "government and the common law" are themselves rooted in fashion, making "mere dead letters on the statute-books" transmutable in relation to "the conditions on which they were founded ceasing to exist" (ix). If "government and the common law" are mutable products of changing fashion, but simultaneously serve as the standards for national character, the danger is that citizenship will become just another form of commodification. This is precisely the destabilizing insight of revolution, which demands that citizens become "something better than mere imitators of foreign manners, often based on social conditions radically different from our own" (vii). In making this demand, however, Wells tacitly acknowledged that "manners" are matters of imitation, eminently social, leaving citizens hopelessly bound to the restless domain of variable fashion. National character, in other words, becomes defined not by the stable borders of the nation-state, but within the shifting transnational productions of commodified taste. Insisting that citizenship is not a juridical construct—located in the dead statute books governing national law—but the gestural production of the well-mannered body, Wells, even while trying to save citizenship from the variable domain of fashion, showed it to be one of the most unstable commodities of the world economy.

Responding to this dilemma, Wells removed taste from the vicissitudes of time and place, relocating it in a Kantian realm of "general principles over which time and place have no influence" and which, removed from "special observances," are "always and everywhere binding" (ix). In that realm, he asserted with inescapable irony, "good taste" is "never out of fashion" (ix). Once Kantian principles are located in the corporeal realm of etiquette, however, universal taste tends to become particularized appetite, which, "like all other instincts or feelings of our nature, is likely to become perverted, and to lead us astray" (21). "Attend to the demands of appetite," Wells warned, "but use all your judgment to determine whether it is a natural, undepraved craving of the system which speaks, or an acquired and vicious taste, and give or withhold accordingly" (21). The "system" that becomes the adjudicative standard of healthy appetite appears, in Wells's text, as the internalized form of his "general principles," which stand in contrast to both "nature" and convention ("acquired and vicious taste"). This system, not changing "fashions," becomes the standard against which individual appetites must be calibrated, a process of interior regulation in relation to a timeless ideal that Wells, like many of his contemporaries, called "self-culture." To be polite, one needed only to act "always and everywhere in accordance with the laws of our being, as revealed in our own physical and mental organization," which "harmonize with universal principles and consequently with our primary duty in reference to ourselves" (49). By regulating one's action according to these principles, at once universal and interiorized, one will develop "an easy and complete control of all your words and actions, and feel *at home* wherever you are" (46). But just how easy or complete could such self-control be? Even as Wells assured readers that they possessed infallible inner edicts, he also warned them that they were "constantly liable to do something amiss" (46). Wells never fully "universalizes" the social etiquettes by which the republican citizen is to act. "You are placed in a particular community," he wrote, "or you are invited or wish to gain admittance into a certain circle. Different communities and circles require, to some extent, different qualifications. Ascertain what you lack, and acquire it as speedily as possible; but remember that good sense and good nature are out of place in no company" (43). Wells's manual, after all, was a pocket book, located in the fashionable garments of a mobile citizen who would need to consult its advice away from the leisure of inner contemplation or the domestic stability of the home library. While Wells told his readers that they were right to "become imbued with the spirit of the society (if good) in which you move, rather than to copy particulars in the manners of any one" (46), he offered little guidance on how to discriminate between (good) "spirit" and (perverse) "particulars" in a society at once universal (governed by timeless "spirit") and historically and geographically specific (governed by "different qualifications").

While interiorizing laws might appear to give citizens more self-determination, then, Wells binds the citizen to an irresolvable contradiction. On the one hand, one's "nature" is purportedly the inscription of universal codes of behavior. On the other, inner "nature" is the home of potentially perverse desires and appetites that make those codes necessary in the first place. Listening to one's nature, in other words, one can never be sure whether one is hearing the command of abstract principle or the seduction of perverse appetite. The tension animates the authority of Wells's program of etiquette and of "self-culture" more broadly. If one could simply consult and regulate oneself along the lines of "general principles," there would be little need for continual self-evaluation or for etiquette as an evolving apparatus of self-culture. While manners must be removed from fashion and relegated to an unchanging universality, then, etiquette as a regulatory practice relies precisely on the social flux that makes the achievement of "good manners" an uneven and unattainable goal. Caught between these incompatible imperatives, the polite citizen of the American republic necessarily became perniciously anxious.

Despite the interior state inscribed by Wells's dialectic of universal law and individual appetite, however, the anxious citizen continues to inhabit a social world. Rather than allowing sociality to constitute an alternative behavioral ethos, however, Wells transformed relationality into a system of offense and shame that insured the interior self-regulation of the anxious citizen. "The proper care and adornment of the person is a social as well as an individual duty," Wells acknowledged, adding that while one may have a *legal* "right to go about with unwashed hands and face, and to wear soiled and untidy garments," one had no right "to offend the senses of others by displaying such hands, face, and garments in society" (15). "Other people have rights as well as yourself," Wells asserted, "and no right of yourself can extend so far as to infringe theirs" (15). Rights, like smells, should not extend beyond one's own body. If one cannot contain one's "rights" within those narrow limits, but continues to engage in nasty habits that violate universal taste (spitting, using tobacco, drinking ardent spirits, eating onions, ignoring one's grooming, picking one's nose, and scratching one's head are particularly egregious infractions), it is the "office of friendship, though not always a pleasant one, to point them out" (28). "Friendship" thus becomes an apparatus of shameful interiorization, making "conformity . . . an implied condition of the social contract" (52). "If by means of our non-conformity," Wells declared, "we cause ourselves to be cut off, like an offending hand, or plucked out, like an offending eye, our usefulness is at once destroyed" (53). Sociality returns, then, as the limit on individual self-determination, forced to conform not to timeless principles, but to popular taste. "Rights," in other words, are only inalienable if they are fully alienated. The troubling persistence of the "social" in Wells's manual required a more complete interiorization away from relational influences and historical redactions. What Wells lacked, in short, was a *biological* account of character, located in the physiology of the brain. Such would be the contribution of Wells's in-laws, the Fowlers, who popularized phrenology to the American public.

A year before delivering his commencement speech, Orson Fowler accompanied his Amherst classmate Henry Ward Beecher to hear the noted German phrenologist Johann Spurzheim lecture in Boston.[17] Inspired by what they heard, Beecher and Fowler determined to debate phrenology for the benefit of their classmates, Beecher arguing in favor of the new science, and Fowler against. Fowler won the debate but in the process convinced himself of phrenology's merits. He began producing "character readings" for his classmates, charging two cents a reading, and thus began a career that would bring him fame in New York, where he and his brother, Lorenzo, generated phrenological charts for Walt Whitman, Margaret Fuller, Sarah Josepha Hale, and Horace Mann, among others. In addition, the Fowlers lectured widely on phrenology (Orson received upward of forty dollars per lecture) and produced advice manuals through the publishing house of Fowler and Wells.[18]

Phrenology asserts that social traits—the ability to marry for life, to nurture children, to labor manually, to conceive abstractions, to provoke arguments, to speak eloquently—are determined by greater and lesser muscular development in thirty-seven sections of the brain. These sections (or "organs") are located in two cranial regions. The "animal" propensities are at the base, "close to the body which they serve, and whose wants they supply, so that the intercommunication between the two is greatly facilitated by their juxtaposition, the condition of each exerting a reciprocal influence upon the status of the other." The "moral" organs, "the higher, religious and God-like sentiments," are located in the upper brain, "as far removed as possible from those influences which disturb the body, (a wise provision this,) whilst intellect is located in the forehead."[19] Combined, these regions house six subdivisions: the "social organs" (amativeness, inhabitativeness, philogenativeness, union for life, adhesiveness, concentrativeness), the "selfish propensities" (combativeness, destructiveness, alimentiveness, acquisitiveness, secretiveness), the "selfish sentiments" (cautiousness, approbation, self-esteem, firmness), the "moral and religious sentiments" (conscientiousness, hope, marvelousness, veneration, benevolence), the "semi-intellectual sentiments" (constructiveness, ideality, sublimity, imitation, mirthfulness), and the "perceptive faculties" (individuality, form, size, weight, color, order, calculation, locality, eventuality, time, tune, language). When the section of the brain that generates each of these traits is large, it produces strong propensities for the corresponding trait; when the section of the brain is weak, the trait is diminished. By reading bumps and recesses in the skull of a patient, then, the phrenologist produces a reliable chart of the patient's character. If the client is weak in desirable traits, he or she can, in turn, practice those traits to increase the size of the mental organ or, correspondingly, can refrain from certain bad habits until an undesirably large organ shrinks.

Although phrenology seemingly grants individuals greater control over the dictates of the brain, the anatomical disposition of "temperament" remains so strong, in the Fowlers' account, as to assume the status of law.[29] By replacing Wells's "general principles" with anatomical imperative, the Fowlers achieved a more successful interiorization of social behavior. Promising to aid readers in "expounding the laws of their physical and mental being" and "in obeying these laws,"[21] phrenology conflated statute and anatomy succinctly in positing "the constitution of the human mind," governing "common sense, correct judgment, and enlarged views of subjects."[22] Pushing the limit of this analogy, Noyes Wheeler produced phrenological charts of the nation's most eminent statesmen, including Henry Clay, Andrew Jackson, Daniel Webster, and John Quincy Adams. Not surprisingly, he found these men "strong" in the traits necessary to Enlightenment leadership, including benevolence, conscientiousness, adhesiveness, self-esteem, and ideality, and "weak" in marvelousness (marking their evolution beyond credulous superstition and intolerant religiosity) and acquisitiveness (protecting them from charges of self-interest in private and national affairs, such as Jackson's policies of Indian removal).[23] Most significant, however, is that in producing these readings Wheeler affirmed the Fowlers' basic assumption: legislators (and, implicitly, their legislation) are determined by anatomy, and not the other way around. Elections, public opinion, and lawmaking or law breaking are subsumed by the anatomical imperatives of the individual body.

Beyond reading the particular patient's character, however, phrenology organized cranial traits into hierarchical clusters (animal and spiritual, base and superior, intellectual and appetitive) that turned each body into an index of— and helped naturalize the divisions of—the *social* body. The Fowlers thereby provided a scientific rationale for the social organization of group identities based on those traits and similarly segregated into geo-stratifications (of slum and posh, home and business, city and country, native and alien).[24] Phrenology divided mental organs, for instance, according to age (children were strong in conscientiousness, eventuality, veneration, benevolence, ideality, and order), religion (Jews had strong "eventuality," being "required to tell the Lord's doings, to their children and grand-children"[25]), race (Native Americans were strong in "animal and knowing" propensities, which made them unusually eloquent[26]), and nationality. Hindus were low in amativeness, while the Irish had it to spare.[27] Canadians had strong firmness, self-esteem, amativeness, alimentiveness, combativeness, destructiveness, hope, and perception, while they lacked causality, conscientiousness and acquisitiveness.[28] The English and Germans had large concentrativeness, but Americans did not, "which corresponds with their national habits. The former usually devote themselves exclusively to one study or occupation, and can make a living at no other, while the versatile talents of the latter enable them to turn their hands to almost any and every thing with success."[29] Within the United States, regional differences corresponded to different mental development: New York women had unusually large organs of acquisitiveness, while Yankee ladies had stronger industry.[30] Above all, phrenology used mental propensities to naturalize gender difference. "Women are universally noted for fondness for children," Lorenzo Fowler observed, "strength of attachment to friends—for disinterestedness—for kindness, deep religious and devotional feeling, strong curiosity—for taste and susceptibility of impressions, together with quickness and readiness of resource, occasioned by their narrower brain and consequent greater mental activity: while man is acknowledged to have naturally more dignity, pride, resolution, independence, force and energy, together with greater mental power, growing out of the greater width of his head—it being a phrenological rule, that length of fibre is an index of activity, while width denotes power."[31]

Underlying its division of the social landscape into anatomically distinct cranial regions was a pervasive concern with codifying and naturalizing the racialized class distinction between "native" populations (Anglo-Saxon Protestants identified with elite culture) and immigrants, who challenged stable geopolitical borders and yet who, being predisposed to manual labor, were economically necessary.[32] These two classes corresponded to two temperamental types: the "bodily-muscular" and the "mental-nervous." Those possessing a "muscular" temperament had "dark skin and hair" and were "not fond of hard work, or great mental labor; but like action and exercise, and are generally good-natured, kind, affectionate, and sympathizing."[33] They possess "hardiness and endurance, a love of exercise and hard work," according to Lydia Fowler, and "generally accomplish what they undertake."[34] Those who possessed the "mental-nervous temperament," by contrast, had "light, fine hair, a thin, clear, and delicate skin, a small frame, a small chest, sparkling eyes, and quickness of motion" and were predisposed to "think, read, study, and acquire knowledge."[35] Although these people, who were "very smart, bright, and precocious, and mature[d] early," might seem to have a natural advantage over their muscular counterparts, they were particularly prone to nervous prostration (often due to their propensity to masturbate) and tended to "die young, because all their vitality is expended through their brain and nervous system."[36] Distinguishing class positions in relation to anatomical development, the Fowlers enabled the regulation of social and economic production in terms of "health." If the bodily-muscular organs became too strong, producing rowdy and unmanageable public behavior, then social restraint and even national expulsion might be necessary to produce anatomical balance. However, if that nature became too weak, increased labor would be necessary to restore the brain to a healthy state of balance.

In marking the rich and poor in terms of their excessive anatomical developments, the Fowlers left unmarked their only ever immanent standard of health: the balanced middle, which restrains from excessive exertions of either mind or body. What phrenology forecloses is the possibility that a single person or group *outside* that ideal middle could possess both temperaments simultaneously: to engage in mental effort is to surrender the pleasures of the body; to engage in social pleasures is to sacrifice contemplation. Workers, in other words, cannot think, and thinkers cannot work. Only those in the middle, doing both activities to a limited degree, can achieve the perfect balance, coded now as "health," that releases them from the marked embodiment that determines one's place in economic or cultural production.

As with Wells, however, one might well wonder why, if balance were easily or permanently achievable, one needed the perpetual self-regulation administered by the Fowlers. Not surprisingly, the brain, in the Fowlers' account, becomes a site of perpetual conflict, the animal and spiritual propensities locked in an irresolvable struggle. In becoming the interior simulacrum of a social realm increasingly riven by the divisions of wealth and opportunity naturalized by phrenology, the brain, too, incorporated violent antagonism—what the Fowlers call "perversions"—between the high and the low. "If the propensities become perverted," Orson Fowler cautioned, they will "*conflict* or *quarrel* with each other," and "civil war" will ensue. To prevent such inner contestation, one must "array the moral sentiments and intellect against them in mortal combat," striving to ensure the (only ever unstable) sovereignty of the brain's upper region over its base. Setting the higher faculties against the lower, Fowler promises, will "reform them if they can be reformed." Internal reform ("self-culture"), however, requires perpetual effort, and without any achievable goal. Constantly seeking "to govern and subdue his easily besetting sins," even as the brain goes on generating those perverse appetites beyond the reach of restraint, the phrenological subject must carry out the work of self-regulation, "not 'here a little and there a little,'" but "HABITUALLY."[37] Only through habitual self-examination can one practice necessary "self-control and self-denial" in a perpetual effort to ensure "the ascendancy of the higher facilities over the propensities, or at least, that the latter be *governed, guided, directed, and restrained*, by the combined action of the moral sentiments and intellect."[38] Humans "are not *fated* to act *only* as these [propensities] dictate," Lydia Fowler assured readers, "but they *can* be so trained, cultivated, or restrained, that their influence is often greatly modified or entirely counterbalanced."[39] Yet given that the outcome of interiorized reform, as the Fowlers acknowledged ("if they can be reformed"), is uncertain at best, the effort of self-culture is endless, its practices, as the Fowlers insist, habitual. If readers worried abut the apparent narrowness —if not to say vanity—of this self-regard, the Fowlers insisted on the social benefits of its habitual disciplines, repeatedly equating self-culture and social reform. "Moralists and religionists have yet to learn," Orson Fowler insisted, "that reform must begin and be continued, by throwing the *body* into a healthy condition."[40] "The first step toward making mankind wiser or better—toward disciplining their vices, promoting virtue and happiness, &c.," Fowler declared, is "to *rectify their physiology*."[41]

In making self-culture the equivalent of social reform, phrenology reduced the social realm to the size of the cranium, apparently without sacrificing agency on the part of civically minded citizen reformers. In assuring readers that biology was not destiny, furthermore, the Fowlers rationalized the interiorization of agency without short-circuiting individual *effort*. The reassurance provided by the Fowlers' insistent analogies notwithstanding, however, self-culture reduced agency to the work of *self*-modifying, extending no farther than the limits of the body. This not only eliminates the possibility of *social* change, it places a significant burden on individuals, whose health—but, more urgently, the health of society as a whole—relies on their ability to frustrate perverse communication within the brain. While the effort exerted in self-culture might seem to compensate citizens for the loss of social engagement, moreover, it also produces a tension between identification (insofar as one was to restrain unruly impulses, one needed to identify with abstract virtues) and disavowals (one needed to disown one's own perverse propensities). This internal division could hardly avoid producing anxious insecurity and instability. In responding to the nervous propensities its own self-divisions perpetuate, then, self-culture both results from and perpetually produces anxious effort. If such anxiety became the interior state of self-cultivating citizenship, its reward was the dark twin of anxiety, which passed as its remedy and release: desire.

Insight into the relationship of anxiety and desire is provided by one of Freud's most significant revisions of his theory of neurosis.[42] Initially, Freud claimed that anxiety arises from libidinal frustration: a person engaging in sexual activity interrupted before orgasm, he believed, will show symptoms of anxiety. Revisiting this theory years later, Freud suggested that the fear of castration, rather than repressed libido, produced anxiety, generating a dread without an identifiable cause. In both theories, Freud put desire at the center of anxiety (and vice versa), although he shifted, importantly, from attributing anxiety to the drive toward relational pleasure (sex) to making anxiety the effect of anticipated loss caused *by* libidinous relations (the erotic cathexis on the mother and the oedipal castration it threatens). Freud's two theories of anxiety are perhaps not as different as they at first appear, however. If by "castration" Freud signified, more than physical loss, the psychic loss that is its traumatic aftereffect—the loss, that is, of the sense of power and other orientation ("cathexis") in the face of a traumatic (if only ever illusory) danger that leaves the subject fretfully isolated—then relationality is itself the loss symbolized by castration, individual subjectivity its "castrated" effect. Frustrated relational pleasure and fearful loss (of relationality) occur simultaneously, and Freud's two theories of anxiety and desire are consistent.[43]

Freud's theory of pleasurable relationality and anxious individualization thus provides a valuable *social*, rather than ontological, account not of changes in the unconscious but, rather, of the rise in the nineteenth century of the unconscious as the self-perpetuating consequence and apparent compensation for lost relationality. If in the 1830s and 1840s the Fowlers generated an anatomy whose interior divisions between base and upper regions determined the vicissitudes of predisposition and temperament, Freud filled that brain with drives (predispositions) and personality (temperaments) without mitigating—indeed, while accelerating—the anxious experience of loss and isolation. And just as Freud compensated the anxious and mournful individual with the promise of pleasurable relationality interiorized as "sexuality," so the Fowlers, in the course of their careers, turned increasingly to romantic and reproductive affect—which they also codified as "sexuality"—as the most potent site of self-restraint and compensatory (if perennially deferred) promise.

Initially, that promise appears as a utopian fantasy of interiorized social harmony, cleansed of the fragmented particularity—essential, as I suggested earlier, to the Fowlers' conception of the brain's segregated "temperaments"— that fractured the social realm. Imagining the "organ[s] capable of speech," the phrenologist could "personify them—that is, invest them with life," and hence could present the individual brain as internally sociable. "One organ scarcely ever acts, or is exercised, alone," Lydia Fowler claimed, and, like any social body, the organs are affectively joined by sympathy, "a connecting link between all the other parts of the body; so that when one part suffers, the others sympathize or suffer with it."[44] While Lydia Fowler's anatomical account of organic relationality—what she, like Catharine Beecher, called the "great sympathetic"—seems to maintain sociality across the differences codified by the same anatomy, it also locates both the subject and object of sympathy in the same body, thereby ensuring that sympathy circulates within a logic of sameness—of identity—that makes difference a cause of disharmony and even illness. The fantasy of an interiorized social harmony can only be a reformer's fantasy (as Fowler acknowledged by imagining the phrenologist "personifying" the brain, the closest the siblings ever got to acknowledging the projective sources of articulate anatomy). But the utopian pleasures of reform *require* a prior disparity of capability and opportunity that makes reformation possible in the first place, which the Fowlers' account of conflicted cranial organs also ensures. Difference, then, both enables and frustrates fantasy. Or, to reverse this formulation, where there is the fantasy of harmonious sympathy, there will also be the production of ever more anxious difference.

This paradox, which animates the Fowlers' theories of desire, increasingly functions as the anxiety-producing instability that makes "private" relationships of romance and family the microcosm of broader social schisms, even as it presents those relationships as the utopian *response* to civil disruption. Sexuality, in other words, becomes for the Fowlers the place where the internal harmony of self-identical affect meets the social relations made anatomically *distinct* by phrenology. Producing texts with titles such as *Love and Parentage, Applied to the Improvement of Offspring* and *Familiar Lessons on Phrenology, Devised for the Use of Children and Youth in Schools and Families*, the Fowlers sought, quixotically, to apply the abstract and unappeasable principles of anatomy to the fluctuating affects of romantic and filial relationships. "Love," Orson Fowler asserted, is "the fulfilling of the law."[45]

Of all of the brain's organs, the one requiring the most scrutiny and habitual discipline—the cause of the most potentially hazardous disruption ("perversion") but also the most blissful harmony—according to the Fowlers, is "adhesiveness," the organ of relationality. Adhesiveness, Lorenzo Fowler explained, "is not confined . . . to mere friendship, but extends to sympathy, sociability, attachments not formed upon the generative instinct, and the disposition of adhering to, remaining with and embracing the object of attachment without regard to sex, animate or inanimate, human or mere brute." Adhesiveness is not only "the bond of society," it also, as Fowler informed readers, secures all forms of private and public belonging, providing "the mental chain which is infinitely more efficacious in uniting families and nations than the naked law or force of interest."[46] Quickly, however, this range of social intimacies narrows to the private realm of domesticity. "Man's enjoyment in his life," Fowler claimed, "depends more upon the proper exercise of the social feelings and their gratification in the domestic relations, than upon any other condition in life."[47] Having located sociality within the brain's anatomy, phrenology can shrink its sphere of operation without acknowledging the surrender of broader civic interaction.

If the domestic propensities exert a greater "influence upon character . . . than any other given number of faculties," however, they are also especially liable to become "perverted."[48] In the Fowlers' accounts, perversion perpetually threatens domestic balance, which is no more easily achieved than mental balance generally. Perversion begins with desire, which can produce the heaven of normative domesticity or the hell of promiscuous appetites. When one follows the straight and narrow, unprecedented bliss follows, as Orson Fowler enthusiastically proclaimed: "Connubial love! Thou 'holy of holies' of human emotions! Thou queen of earth! Thou glorious sun of our nature! Thou garland of terrestrial loveliness! Thou solace and sanctifier of man. Thou life and soul of woman! Thou precious relict of Paradise! Thou Paradise itself!"[49] His typographical extravagance suggests, however, that "connubial love" may produce its own supplemental excesses, ensuring that the self-regulating family member and the hungering pervert are always potentially one and the same.

For this reason, phrenology removed "private" relations of love from the domain of adhesiveness, granting it an autonomous "organ"—amativeness— that gives protective anatomical borders to the purity of "connubial love" and counterbalances the excessive sociality initiated by adhesiveness. Once again, however, what makes phrenology useful as a generator of self-disciplining *effort*—the malleability of cranial proportion—is also what unsettles its utopian balance. The organ of amativeness may grow too large, leading to perverse tastes and insatiable appetites. The organ could be unnaturally swelled, according to the Fowlers, by a host of common stimulants, including overeating, enticing dress, reading romances written "by persons of morbid feelings, sickly sentiments and extravagant hopes," all of which constituted "highly wrought scenes of amatory happiness and earthly felicity—thus exciting the feelings and weakening the judgment, creating a distaste for commonplace transactions, and giving false and imperfect ideas of human nature."[50] If too much amativeness is a danger, however, so is too little, for "if the organ is small," Lorenzo Fowler cautioned, "the person is less susceptible to emotions of love; is cold-hearted and distant—disposed to avoid the company of the opposite sex, and manifests a want of refinement, tenderness, warmth and delicacy of feeling, which should exist between the sexes."[51] While such feelings may be legitimized as "purity of feeling and platonic attachment,"[52] these challenges to hetero-normative reproduction represent "perversions" that are as hazardous as excessive sexual appetites. Without properly developed organs of adhesiveness, Lydia Fowler warned, "we should not have as many handsome, thickly-settled villages as we now have," but "would live alone in the wilderness or in the thick forest."[53] Amativeness cannot be eradicated, as only "the open exercise of this organ" can bring "to our social relations new life and a rich coloring, refinement, courtesy, gallantry and all which sheds lustre upon human nature in a state of companionship."[54] One must exercise the organ, the Fowlers prescribed, "to enlist, cement, perpetuate, or re-kindle, as occasion may require, those tender feelings of conjugal affection, so incalculably productive of both parental happiness, and human endowment."[55] Domestic balance is fraught, then, by the brain's own composition, making "love" a particularly potent site for perpetual and anxious self-regulation, even while "private" relations, the sanctioned supplement to social relationality, become the exclusive site of individualized effort. On one side of domestic balance is perversion, on the other is the utopian promise of permanent tranquility. Between these equally uninhabitable positions (the former because unsanctioned, the latter because utopian), the sexualized subject swings anxiously, pulled between the unrealizable imperatives of want and wait.

The Fowlers' descriptions of desire as ephemeral, contingent, nostalgic, and self-gratifying—the psychic crystallization of social impulses running counter to the developments of private, middle-class domesticity—make desire the corollary of those social groups to which reform granted similar traits: women, immigrants, African Americans, the poor, addicts, all of whom were also demonized due to excessive desire. Not only does desire produce perversion, then, it also apparently generates a strong expectation of "earthly felicity" and of relationality *in excess* of the normatively domestic ("commonplace transactions"). Social demand (the call for "earthly felicity" in the present, rather than at some deferred time and place) and inventive relationality thus combine under the rubric of "perversion," ensuring that those committed to expanding the possibilities for social and pleasurable association—those who want to redefine the patterns of livable sociality—are placed under the disciplinary regime of "sexuality," love's other.

For the Fowlers, the problem with desire, in other words, is that it exists too much in the *present*, whereas the institutional structures to which they lent their efforts require a future orientation coded as the opposite—indeed, the remedy—of desire. Where amativeness seeks only immediate gratification, adhesiveness, being "the *principle* of all *association* not formed upon *selfish motives*," becomes the impulse toward futurity, "causing man to remain united after the season of his love is passed," the "future" institutionalized as "the couple continuing together in the most affectionate union, the heart of one uniting in that of the other."[56] "When, but *only* when, mankind properly LOVE and MARRY, and then rightly GENERATE, CARRY, NURSE and Educate their children," Orson Fowler insisted, "will they be in deed and in truth the holy and happy sons and daughters of the 'Lord Almighty' compared with those miserable and depraved scape-goats of humanity whom infest our earth."[57]

If "social relations" shrink to family ties, and adhesiveness is in turn constituted by its management of amativeness, then all human happiness, for the Fowlers, amounts to the regulation of desire. Little wonder, then, that Orson Fowler named his most baldly disciplinary tract, simply, *Amativeness*. Against the serpentine wiles of desire, only constant self-analysis can "out" the perverse workings of desire. "Satan never keeps secrets," Fowler promised. " 'Murder will out.' And so will sexuality." Fowler drew on novelistic language to turn perverse dispositions into embodied libertines, the very external "tempters" he argued against in his Amherst address. Perverts, Fowler explained, "are dangerous, and ought to be exposed—at least, allowed to tell their own carnal story. Let every sensualist, especially *private* libertine, remember, that he is marked and known, and read, by all men who have eyes and know how to use them. This exposition is made, in part, to *shame* them out of degrading vice, into moral purity and virtue." Perversion's cure, Fowler told his readers, comes from "*effort, perseverance, and temporary self-denial*." To become self-regulated and hardworking is to bring one's wayward interior into line with a public sphere imagined in relation to the production of national belonging. Those who refuse to undertake the scrutiny and discipline of others are "BAD CITIZENS, and deserve the curses of their progeny." Transforming Patrick Henry's call for revolutionary independence into a demand for self-regulatory inhibition, Fowler declares, "ABSTINENCE OR DEATH is your only alternative."[58]

And yet, as my analysis of the Fowlers' system demonstrates, desire cannot be fully eradicated, but must remain an imminent threat, a source of potential disruption, that requires the continuous *effort* of self-management. As such, phrenology naturalized not puritanical reform, but the vacillations of desire and anxiety necessary to modern capital. Requiring effort *and* desire, production *and* consumption, capital belies the conflicted relationship between discipline and pervasion anatomized by phrenology and turned into social policy by antebellum reform. As enterprising businesspeople, the Fowlers had a vested interest in perpetuating and naturalizing the dynamics of capital, as Lydia Fowler suggested in a telling anecdote about a Parisian beggar "who lost a part of his skull by an accident; the brain was slightly covered by its membrane, and he was accustomed to allow any one who would give him a small sum of money to press on this exposed part."[59] The Fowlers, too, would "uncover" the brain (although not their own) for any paying customer, making them equivalent—in Lydia Fowler's unconscious, in any case—to a common beggar. Yet capital proved as fickle in providing its promised rewards for the Fowlers as it did for most nineteenth-century Americans. Having established a profitable practice, Orson Fowler began to build a mansion, nicknamed "Fowler's Folly," in rural Fishkill, New York. The Panic of 1857 dried up his funds, however, and the unfinished house became a plaything for locals. During a particularly raucous party, which the local paper described as "A Ball in a Deserted House," teenagers set fire to the house and burned it to the ground.

The paradox of this description—if one is having a "ball" in it, can the house really be "deserted"?—succinctly captures the conundrum of phrenological "consciousness." As an individuated and isolated space that nevertheless bore the supplemental traces of sociality in the form of the communication, harmonious or conflicted, between the "speaking" organs, consciousness became, indeed, a ball in a deserted house. While the Fowlers may be credited—or faulted—with reducing sociality to the space of individualized anatomy, at least they left open the possibility of conscious volition (even if that volition was yoked to anxious and irresolvable effort). Even with a deserted house, to draw out the metaphor, one could choose whether to dance or light a match. The danger comes when consciousness gives rise to its alter ego, unconsciousness, which separates the workings of temperament from the conscious direction of will. Lydia Fowler's Parisian beggar, for instance, produced *unconsciousness* for his paying customers, during which time he did not know "what was going on around him, or where he was; but as soon as the pressure was removed, his consciousness was restored."[60] If, as I have argued, consciousness in phrenology becomes an internal simulacrum of social relations, then *unconsciousness* becomes a state of social helplessness, removing the subject from the locality and historical conditions ("what was going on around him, or where he was") necessary for effective social agency. It was in that realm, not in the conscious propensities of the brain, that desire came to dwell in antebellum America.

Emerging economic systems, Raymond Williams contended, require new structures of feeling, affective logics that enable citizens to believe that changes are natural and hence inevitable; that the market rises not due to external forces, but in response to deep human need.[61] One of the structures of feeling that emerged in the early nineteenth century to interiorize (individualize and naturalize) the deferred satisfactions of a speculative market was a notion of desire—speculative desire—that encouraged citizens to *invest* in pleasures deferred to some unspecified future. In turn, speculative desire made the *dis*satisfactions that might arise from deferred satisfaction the sign of a psychologically rich interiority and hence of proper personhood. Desire, in other words, became an end it itself, surrendering its claim to an achievable *object*. As desire cut agency off from its capacity to achieve satisfaction in the here and now, it subsumed agency into itself, becoming by midcentury the force that propelled people toward ends that, in order to experience desire, they could not achieve. Subsuming human agency while deferring its identifiable outcome, desire produced necessary effort (the *pursuit* of happiness) while forestalling the demand for a payoff. To say that speculative desire arises with changes in nineteenth-century economics is not to contend that no one *wanted* anything before the emergence of a speculative market.[62] It is to suggest, however, that the conception of that want changed, layering *wait* onto *want* and therefore pulling the desiring subject in two equally strong, if mutually exclusive, directions.

In addition to deferring individual satisfaction, speculative desire foreclosed the possibility of pleasurable sociality, as becomes clear in Marx's account of commodification. For commodities to be exchanged, Marx argued, they must be granted value, which requires the abstraction of labor (a coat is worth the hours put into its making). Placing commodities in a relationship of relative value (one coat equals three shirts) renders relations between laborers also relative and abstract (five hours of labor in one trade equals ten in another), despite differences of skill or practice within a given trade. But because value is always relational (a coat takes on value only in relation to a number of shirts), the relationship between workers, too, becomes abstract. And just as value is deferred along an endless chain of potential commodities, so human relations become deferred, through commodities, to an unreachable satisfaction that relative abstraction itself forecloses. The creation of an exchange economy based on the relative value of commodities, then, creates a social practice that occurs on an abstract plane, producing not just alienation but deferral, and not just of labor, but of social interaction itself.

Sociality's satisfactions do not simply evaporate into abstraction, however, but create a corollary space of human interiority, wherein they linger in the shadowy forms of desire. Faced with the deferred gratification of commodified exchange, Marx wrote, the consumer "desires to realise the value of his commodity, to convert it into any other suitable commodity of equal value, regardless of whether his own commodity has or has not any use-value for the owner of the other."[63] The deferred gratification of commodified value exchange—and the labor relations it abstracts—thus produces desire, both as a faith that a residual satisfaction can be regained and as the speculative force that allows commodity exchange to function. The interpellative force of commodification, what kept consumers buying, was for Marx speculative desire. "A commodity," Marx wrote, "is, in the first place, an object outside us, a thing that, by its properties, satisfies human wants of some sort or another. The nature of such wants, whether, for instance, they spring from the stomach or from fancy, makes no difference" (13). Although Marx declined to undertake a taxonomy of desire, he nevertheless located a plurality of "human wants" in the interior (as opposed to commodities, which are "outside us") and at the (dis)juncture of satisfaction and economic speculation. What we are trying to regain through speculation, however, is not wealth or material comfort, but the gratifications of human connectedness itself: "some social relation," Marx said of commodification, "lies at the bottom of it" (31).

The satisfaction promised by the commodity ("in its properties") is necessarily illusory, however, for, as Marx showed, the commodity never exists "in its properties" but only in relation to other, also deferred commodities. The residual memory of the pleasures of proximate interaction persists, however, in a lurking suspicion that the commodity is always, in essence, its own counterfeit, a substitute for satisfaction. Little wonder, then, that Marx proclaimed that, although a "commodity appears, at first sight, a very trivial thing, and easily understood," it is, "in reality, a very queer thing, abounding in metaphysical subtleties and theological niceties" (42). Desire is not simply the accumulation of innate "wants" that call the commodity into being. It is also the phantasmagorical space of not quite evacuated satisfaction, the relative burden that, along with abstract labor, the commodity is forced to bear from its traffic with human satisfaction. The commodity's queerness comes from the slippage, then, between surface significations and the elusive signified, between promised satisfaction and present want. Although Marx put it before the rise of commodification, then, desire perhaps is the commodity's promised compensation as well as its shadowy past.

As desire splits sociality into the particularized materiality of the commodity and the deferred abstractions of value, it establishes a secondary division between space (the realm of the particular) and time (deferral's orientation toward the horizon of futurity). In antebellum America, this division structures the tense characterizations of *types* of people according to their differing relations to desire. In gothic fiction and reform tracts alike, those who refuse desire, insisting on satisfactions in the present, are demonized for their lack of a contractual frame of mind, unable to see beyond immediate gratification. Such figures—the insane, children, alcoholics, criminals, prostitutes—are characterized, paradoxically, as embodied *and* ephemeral, addicted *and* scheming. So committed to pleasure as to produce deformity in themselves, uninterested in and often antagonistic to the well-being of permanent institutions, locked in repeated patterns and melancholy nostalgia rather than teleological progress, and insistent on the use of their agency to accomplish identifiable goals, these figures became the dark others of the deferred and reproductive futurity of speculative desire. Although these traits would ultimately cohere in the modern homosexual (superficial, illusive, narcissistic, addicted to gratification), the same traits, still imbricated in the economic conditions that made them socially legible (indeed, highly charged), circulated first through a diffused interiority, the shadow resentment of deferred satisfaction, that attached to social status—mainly in relation to economic entitlement—rather than to sexual identities.

If these monstrous figures became the denizens of the past (figured as the bodily space of addiction and the geopolitical space of taverns, brothels, and other dens of iniquity), futurity gave rise to fictions of temporal generation, of sexual and social reproduction (hence the focus, in much reform literature, on the transmission of "virtue" from parents to children). Those who consent to the economic and sexual futurity of speculative desire are granted the superior domain of temporality, while those who oppose it are characterized by the (often confining and claustrophobic) particularity of space. In gothic and reform literature, the un(re)productive, denied the integrity of the fully human, are associated with the particularities of their bodies, their speech, or their individual (and almost always traumatic) histories. The monstrous, the criminal, and the addicted are also associated with clearly identifiable neighborhoods, living quarters, and sites of pleasure, which are invariably characterized as "dark" and "mysterious" sites of unpredictable sociality increasingly characterized as "perverse sexuality." The effect of their spatialization is to place the un(re)productive outside the movements of history, making their "monstrosity," for instance, the result not of socioeconomic victimization or demand, but of an almost mythic "evil" that threatens to thwart the progress of time. In contrast, the fully human, associated with futurity, are temporally organized, associated with narrative (the temporal sequencing of events), reproduction (the biopolitical orientation toward the future), and desire. The heroes and heroines of popular fiction are not those who seek gratification in the present (these are the villainous libertines of eighteenth-century melodramas), nor are they moralistic prudes. Rather, the figures of identification become those capable (mirrored in their readers' ability) of investing in a gratification deferred to the ending, if at all. While most reform literature relies on this binary between the spatial and the temporal, the irony is that the *atemporal* locality associated with the reformable also characterizes speculative desire itself. Operating in a circuit of unmarked cause and unnamed consequence, speculative desire—like the "monsters" it supposedly counters—operates in a human interiority that is both localized in the body and placed beyond the vicissitudes of historical change.[64]

Such orientations are, of course, only ever idealizations, unachievable as either social positions or psychic identifications. If the future is never fully achievable, except as a theoretical potential, the post–Enlightenment subject is never fully reducible to the particularities of embodied history. Stuck between an idealized future promised by the state (and presumably achievable through the habitual effort animated by desire) and the restless wants localized by the particular arrangements of bodies in space, the citizen occupies an anxious middle ground. This jerky choreography leaves most citizens neither transcendent nor embodied but in a state of continual anxiety, generating the affect-saturated rupture between what is and what might be.[65]

Exemplifying the dynamics of speculative desire, George Lippard's bestselling thriller *The Quaker City; or, the Monks of Monk Hall* (1845) tells a number of intertwined stories of deceit, deception, rape, and murder set in an ancient gothic mansion on the outskirts of respectable Philadelphia.[66] The novel's ostensible purpose is to reveal and reform the hypocrisies of the city's economic and social elite, who, sanctimonious in the daylight, show their greed, lust, and murderousness during their nighttime exploits within the secrecy of Monk Hall. Against early critics who faulted Lippard for compromising his reformist agenda with titillating "pornography," producing in readers the very licentiousness he sought to reform, recent critics have defended him as interested not in sex but in fostering class solidarity among workers. "Although an emphasis on the body can work at times to naturalize distinctions of class, race, sexuality and gender, or to provide footholds for normalizing projects," Shelley Streeby argues, "an in-your-face body politics can also unsettle such distinctions and provide perverse sensations which stimulate different constructions of collective identity," particularly those conducive to Lippard's faith in a coming "world revolution, not the gradual refinement and perfection of U.S. democracy."[67]

While critics are certainly right to foreground Lippard's critique of capitalism and its class structures, they have, in their efforts to counter charges of his prurience, obscured his insights into the simultaneous production of sexual and economic desires in the society he chronicled and condemned. It is not that sexual desire for Lippard had an anterior status, naturally above or before economic exploitation. To make that argument is to accept a theoretical formulation of the alterity of desire itself. On the contrary, what Lippard depicted is a world in which desire arises as a naturalizing supplement to the projective dissatisfactions resulting from economic speculations that cohered a new contractual economy and, with it, a normalized middle-class citizen.

Holding to the divisions of spatiality and temporality endemic to speculative desire, The Quaker City provides an allegorical cartography of social interiority. Lippard tenanted the central space of the novel, Monk Hall, with monstrous caretakers and service providers: Mother Nancy, the aged alcoholic who supervises the seduction of innocent girls; Bess, the ruined, strong-willed prostitute; Mosquito and Glow-worm, black house servants and strongmen; and, above all, Devil-Bug, doorkeeper, man-of-all-trades, and mastermind of Monk Hall's nefarious intrigues. Although its inhabitants may occasionally leave Monk Hall, they live almost entirely within its confines. Monk Hall therefore renders simultaneous interiority and depravity: to be in Monk Hall is to be depraved; to be depraved keeps one within Monk Hall. If the mansion provides a sheltering privacy for interiority, it also gives way to a bodily confession, for the depravity of Monk Hall's inhabitants manifests itself in the exaggerated deformities of their bodies. So connected are the monstrous and their spatial locations that Lippard writes that Devil-Bug is the soul encased within the body of Monk Hall. And just as Devil-Bug's "soul was like his body, a mass of hideous and distorted energy" (105), so Monk Hall, a forbidding and decayed edifice, is full of seething and eruptive desires that respectable Philadelphia cannot acknowledge. Through Monk Hall, Lippard mirrors the logic of antebellum reform, which also located the problems of society (its de-formations) within the interior, while reading human interiority through bodily "signs" so as to classify the reformable into populations that, like the inhabitants of Monk Hall, assume spatial and social boundaries that define the normative "freedom" of Philadelphia at large.

If The Quaker City seems to accept the reformist imperative that social ills be first inscribed in the human interior and then confessed through a "natural" bodily exteriorization, however, Lippard insists on the ultimate inscrutability of Monk Hall, the receptacle of "the *secret life* of the great Quaker City" (23). In introducing Monk Hall, Lippard tells of the many theories about its past and present existence, but ultimately, he writes, "the most remarkable ignorance prevailed in regard to the structure, its origin and history" (49). The unknowability of Monk Hall's secrets is made literal by its architecture, in which it "'is easy enough for a stranger . . . to find his way *in*,'" one character warns another early in the novel, "' but it would puzzle him like the devil to find his way *out*'" (63). Monk Hall's impermeable secrecy is particularly striking given that many of its regular visitors, including the editor of a notorious scandal sheet, traffic in rumor and gossip. In this regard, Lippard's location of Monk Hall within a "municipal geography" (48) seems significant: "a printing office on one side and a stereotype foundry on the other, while on the opposite side of the way, a mass of miserable frame houses seemed about to commit suicide and fling themselves madly into the gutter, and in the distance a long line of dwellings, offices, and factories, looming in broken perspective, looked as if they wanted to shake hands across the narrow street" (48). A lacuna within the public knowledge created and circulated by nineteenth-century print, Monk Hall is crowded by its technologies, print relying on the stereotypes, in the sense both of the print mechanism and the predictable human "types," which make visible and easily consumable a deeper layer (either of embossed print or of human complexity). If Monk Hall is squeezed by print's public sphere, however, that sphere, rather than being abstracted, shares with the infamous den an architectural—and economic—particularity: the professionalism of offices, the industrialism of factories, and their corollary "miserable" suburban frame houses that Lippard describes as more suicidal than the secretive grandeur of the depraved Monk Hall. That the sites of capital and of private, reproductive normalcy reach out to shake hands like contractual partners suggests the mutual dependence of economics and the institutions of privacy, as well as the speculative desire—the projection of satisfaction into the futures of commodity or biological reproduction—that drives both. Between these forces there is little wiggle room, only a "narrow street," except for that provided by the depraved secrecy that lies at the neighborhood's heart and defines its public virtues.

Monk Hall's corollary, its architectural "other," is neither the factory nor the frame house, however, but the State House, which is referred to repeatedly in the novel, usually in reference to its clock tower, at which characters continually gaze to orient themselves temporally. If Monk Hall is pure interiority, the State House has no interiority at all. Rather than depicting "sanctioned" interiority (a tedious if, indeed, producible narrative), the State House temporally orients the events of the novel, offering a workplace regularity to even its most depraved plots and a sequential logic to the novel itself. Referring to the State House clock sixteen times in the course of the novel, Lippard conflates narrative sequence, order of action, and the state, all set in opposition to the unruly, timeless, and lawless interiority of Monk Hall.

The architectural opposition of the State House and Monk Hall might suggest that the urban society Lippard chronicles is indeed structured by the hierarchical divisions between exteriority, abstraction, and temporality on the one hand and, on the other, interiority, particularity, and spatiality. Such divisions, however, prove illusory. The majority of the Quaker City's citizens live at neither site but circulate continually between them: F. A. T. Pynce, an ersatz minister with incestuous designs on his supposed daughter, Mabel; Gus Lorimer, who seduces and rapes the innocent Mary Arlington; Byrnewood Arlington, Lorimer's unknowing accomplice in the seduction of his own sister; Algernon Fitz-Cowles, the forger who has seduced Dora Livingstone from her merchant husband by promising her a life of British aristocracy; Von Gelt, Fitz-Cowle's Jewish co-conspirator in his forgeries; Albert Livingstone, who enters Monk Hall to witness his wife's infidelity and seek his murderous revenge; Dora Livingstone, who engages her lust for status with Fitz-Cowles and then, discovered by her former lover, comes to Monk Hall seeking his murder; and Luke Harvey, who moves in and out of these plots without any clear motive of his own. While most of these characters end up dead or jailed, the survivors—and hence, the characters most open for identification—are those who experience an anxiety produced by the perpetual movements between the abstractions of outward character (the exclusive exteriority of the State House) and the stirrings of inner want.

As this catalogue of Philadelphia's mobile schemers suggests, *The Quaker City* shows desire and anxiety to be mutually generative interior states propelling the (almost always shady) speculations of Philadelphia's economy. The novel makes the connection between interiority and economics, speculative desire and contractual investment, explicit through the continually imbricated narratives of economic deceit (forgery, counterfeit, swindle) and sexual deceit (seduction, incest, rape), a parallel that gives the novel's seemingly unwieldy plot its underlying logic. The novel begins with a sexualized and speculative wager: Lorimer and Byrnewood bet on Lorimer's ability to seduce the respectable maiden who turns out to be the other man's sister. One of the odd features of the novel is that Lorimer defers his seduction of Mary long enough to make a wager with Byrnewood, suggesting that the "pleasures" taken here are not principally those of immediate gratification (which might result in the rape, rather than seduction, of Mary), but rather of speculation, of deferred satisfaction, produced as much by the economic wager as by the sexual seduction. Both forms of satisfaction are projected into the future, despite the fact that, in addition to the frustrations of delayed satisfaction, only one party can possibly profit to the degree he desires. Lorimer suggests the necessary conflation of sexual and economic speculation, bragging, "Woman—the means of securing her affection, of compassing her ruin, of enjoying her beauty, has been my book, my study, my science, nay my *profession* from boyhood" (101). When he acknowledges to Byrnewood that he has been engaged in "the business itself of enjoyment" (24), he makes explicit what underlies every sexual plot in the novel, whether it be Dora Livingstone's attempts to sleep her way into status, Byrnewood's seduction and abandonment of a serving girl in his father's house, or Bess's abandonment by Paul Western, a man "convulsed with the fever of speculation" (61). That these plots all produce not the anticipated satisfactions but pain, ruin, and death suggests Lippard's critique of the sexual or economic payoffs of speculative desire.

Nor does the fault for speculative desire lie entirely with libertines and greedy merchants. Even the supposedly innocent victim of this wager, Mary Arlington, turns out to have rather bizarre desires of her own. Raised in "the abode of luxury and affluence," Mary embodies economic profit, not like the women Thorstein Veblen describes through conspicuous consumption but, rather, internally, through what Lippard calls "unspeakable affection" and "a warm glow of feeling" (17). Her heightened affect leaves Mary paradoxically more empty, "a woman formed to lean, to cling, to love" (18)—that is, never satisfied in herself. For all that, Mary's inner state—the state of her speculative desire—is capable of the same projective fantasies in which her father engages through his mercantile trade (with the same possible ruin through forgery or seduction). Mary, Lippard writes, "loved Lorimer for something he did not possess," but which "the weird fascination" of "*her own soul* had flung around his very existence" (84). Mary acknowledges the constitutive powers of her "weird fascination," telling Lorimer, " 'Is there not a strange mystery in this affection, which makes the heart long for the love which it will one day experience, even before the eye has seen the beloved one?' " (129). What Lippard makes clear in his characterization of Mary is that desire is first and foremost a product of economic relations, which create not only the superfluous affections that allow Mary to venture into "weird fascination," but also its deferred satisfactions. Longing for what can be seen only in the mind's eye, Mary naturalizes the logic of contracts through the "strange mystery" of her affection, making the deferred gratifications of speculative investment engaged in by the men in her life comprehensible to readers as the "natural" longings of sexual desire. Given the economic production of supposedly irresistible and natural inner "drives," and not the other way around, it is hardly surprising that, as Mary's speculations materialize in her seduction by Lorimer, "she felt a strange unconsciousness stealing over her senses" (131). The "unconscious" becomes the internal space of individualized dissatisfaction, site of the speculative economy of desire.

Both forms of speculative desire are disseminated through novel reading itself, which encourages readers to project a likely outcome for events based on their interpretation of external clues to character(s). Reading gets layered onto the intertwined structure of economic and sexual speculation in *The Quaker City* when Lorimer seduces Mary by narrating a romantic tale of domestic tranquility in a pastoral landscape. As Mary listens to Lorimer's tale, her desires become aestheticized, causing her to exclaim, " 'It is all beauty and feeling' " (126). Mary connects the emergence of her desire with past experiences of reading, declaring of Lorimer's seductive narrative, " 'How like the stories we read in a book!' " (86). At stake in all three forms of speculation—economic, sexual, and aesthetic—is the ability to purchase consent. Expounding on his philosophy of seduction, Lorimer boasts of the superiority of interiorized control (" 'deeper means' ") over physical coercion (" 'Force—Violence!' "). " 'I employ neither force, nor threat, nor fraud, nor violence!' " he says. "My victim is the instrument of her own ruin—without one rude grasp from my hand, without one threatening word, she swims willingly to my arms!" (127). Lorimer's plot relies on an interpellative strategy—he names her repeatedly "Mary," then "*my wife*"—always backed by potential phallic violence. (When Mary fails to consent, Lorimer rapes her [132–33].) His imagined satisfaction comes in procuring Mary's consent—first as consumer, then as reader, and finally as sexual partner—through fictions that have little to offer her.

Yet Lorimer's bravado is undercut by the fact that, while he interpellates Mary in his tale of domestic conquest, she has already interpellated *him* in her "weird fascination" with desire itself. While Lorimer insists on the oneness of his interests, of business and pleasure (101), Mary's power to project her own "fascinations" onto their object radically divides Lorimer into subject and object of desire, inner and outer life. "The truth is," Lippard reports, "there were *two* Lorimer in *one*" (89).[68] No one involved in speculative desire avoids this division. Of the wealthy Livingstone, for instance, Lippard writes, "He was a fine man, a noble merchant, a good citizen—we but repeat the stereotyped phrases of the town—and yet, quiet and close, near the heart of this cheerful-faced man, lay a sleeping devil" (37). The split is not simply an indictment of the merchant's hypocrisy; it is also an indictment of the schizophrenic identi-fications offered *all* citizens, torn between their inner desire to achieve satis-faction and the speculative delay that makes outward achievement nearly im-possible. Even Devil-Bug, who prides himself on never disguising himself (222), is plagued by the terrible two-ness brought about by desire: "Deep in the heart of this monster, like a withered flower blooming from the very corruption of the grave, the memory of that fair young girl, who, eighteen years ago, had sought the shelter of Monk Hall, lay hidden, fast entwined about the life-cords of his deformed soul" (223). While sexual desire divides women's inner and outer lives, splitting their unruly "animal natures" from abstract conceptions of purity and innocence, so it splits men between their gallant exteriors and their lusty, violent inner desires (or, in Devil-Bug's case, the inverse). Desire produces an endless disunity within the citizen subject, a dissatisfaction that manifests itself throughout the novel in the ambitions that, arising in economic longing, materialize themselves in the individual narratives of sexual want. Even after all her tribulations, Mary Arlington, encountering her rapist's portrait at the con-clusion of the novel, utters Lorimer's name "in a whisper, like the sigh of a broken heart" (575). The "weird fascinations" of speculative desire, having divided the subject between want and wait, are never subject to the wisdom of experience. Made interior, desire has, in the end, an irresistible life of its own.

Against the dangerous divisions of desire, characteristic of both the rich and the poor, the novel presents the integrated virtues of the middle class, repre-sented by Luke Harvey, who appears to have no ambitions of his own. Although he begins humbly yet ends the richest character in the novel, he neither schemes for his advancement nor expresses any desire for it. Without speculative desire, Luke is spared the extremes of the elite and the abject, becoming the ideal-ized middle-class consumer. "You would not have called this gentleman well-proportioned," Lippard writes, "and yet his figure was long and slender, you could not have styled his dress eminently fashionable, and yet his frock coat was shaped of the finest black cloth, you would not have looked upon his face as the most handsome in the world, and yet it was a finely-marked countenance, with a decided, if not highly intellectual, expression" (33). Neither seductively hand-some nor monstrously ugly, fastidiously fashionable nor slovenly, Luke is the ideal middle between the extremes of his speculative peers.

As the paradoxical consumer without ambition, Luke is the ideal reformer of wayward desire in others, as becomes clear in his "rescue" of Dora Livingstone.

After Luke saves Dora from the ravages of Devil-Bug and promises to keep her scandalous affair private, Lippard writes, "All her dreams of ambition passed away, and a terrible memory agitated her soul" (358).

> "Dora, there is yet a glorious hope for you!" cried Luke, as his ghastly features warmed with an expression of enthusiasm that might almost have been called holy. "Promise me that you will renounce all unhallowed love, promise me that you will from this time forth, dissolve all connection with the poor creature who has dishonored you by a foul crime, promise me that you will ever be to Livingstone a true and faithful wife; and I swear before God, to sustain you in your course, to defend you from all harm!" (364)

Dora promises, and immediately her "ambition, her recklessness of soul alike were gone; she felt the modesty of a wife once more" and "wondered to herself that idle toys like the world's ambition and the love which is born of guilt, should ever have lured her from the duty of a wife, and purity of a woman" (365).

If Luke imagines himself a savior–reformer, however, Lippard has other notions, describing him as having "snake-like eyes" (258) and speaking with a voice "like the hissing of a snake" (255). The deception offered by this snake in the garden is the promise of fulfilling middle-class life.[69] Desire, produced in a speculative market reliant on its dissatisfactions, is never fully reducible to the tranquil evacuations of normative privacy, as Devil-Bug suggests when he comments of Dora, " 'The han'some woman is bought and sold' " (354). Far from "rescuing" Dora from the speculative market of desire, Luke transforms her from a consumer into a commodity. Robbed of her competitive edge, Dora's fate is sealed, and she is soon poisoned by her jealous husband. Luke has been trafficking in Dora all along, as his status as "middle" relies on the production of extremes that mark him as a center that is, in and of itself, without distinctive properties. Put differently, "normalcy" itself becomes a speculative commodity in a desire market whose necessary deferrals spark greater want at every turn, even while promising its utter extinguishment.

Evacuated normalcy—the pure exteriority of the State (House)—is never a real possibility, then, where speculative desire marks the truly human. Dora is never entirely redeemed, pulled instead between Luke's promise of normalcy and her own "weird fascinations," a tension that leaves her neither satisfied nor complacent but marked by anxiety: "She was very beautiful, and yet along each cheek of her queenly countenance there flashed a spot of vivid and burning red, which betokened the feverish anxiety which absorbed the soul of the proud woman" (355). Anxiety is the only possible state for citizens cruising the "narrow street" between Monk Hall and the State House, desire and/as deferral. If, at the end of the novel, the surviving characters arrange themselves into couples, they can do so only through radical displacement. Luke and his wife, Mabel, return to Europe, while Byrnewood and Alice retire to a cottage eerily resembling the fictional home in Lorimer's seduction of Mary. Indeed, their simple domesticity has at its center a secret room reminiscent of the gothic interiority of Monk Hall, to which Byrnewood retires daily to gaze upon a portrait of Lorimer. This bizarre ritual—Byrnewood's own "weird fascination" —suggests the inability to relinquish desire, even (especially) if one wishes to reside in the fictive, speculative locations of middle-class normalcy. Desire produces the heart of that vision and, turning to the heart, one can only gaze upon desire.

Queering Desire

The "fascinations" produced by speculative desire, stuck in repetitive and addictive patterns that work counter to the forward movements of progressive time, are more than "weird." They are *queer*. Queerness appears frequently in antebellum fiction, connected not to sexuality, but to economic instability, signifying a counterfeit ("queer as a three dollar bill") or a swindle (to "queer" a deal). As Marx's description of the commodity as a "very queer thing" suggests, queerness arises as an insuppressible doubt about the promised satisfactions of economic speculation. Queering speculative desire, novels such as *The Quaker City* register a residual demand for present satisfaction and a recognition that the restraints on such satisfactions arise from inner forces only as a scripted corollary to external economic structures. From the unstable interiors produced by speculative desire thus arises an unsettling social demand in the form of "queer" dreams, reveries, and manias, a counter-normative trace history cast as the uncanny queerness of a turbulent unconscious. To use the term "queer" to describe the economic conditions of 1840s America is not to appropriate anachronistically a contemporary sexual label, but to suggest that the codification of sexuality in the late nineteenth century around a series of denigrated interior states (narcissism, polymorphous perversity, melancholia) was a second-effect development of an earlier reformist endeavor to stabilize economic disruptions caused by the advent of investment capital. What by Freud's day had become understood as the constituent traits of (homo)sexual *desire* already circulated, that is, as the interiorizing logics of speculative desire, which sciences of sexuality segregated from their economic sources by making them the effects of unconscious mandates ("drives"), a development that obscured the role of economic interiorization in generating the unconscious as a space of abjected sociality. Queerness is not a late development in the history of sexuality, then. It *precedes* that history, arising from the demanding and noncompliant responses to the growth of speculative capital.

Lippard's characters describe many things, peoples, and practices as "queer" (the term appears thirty times in the first half of the novel before dwindling, for reasons discussed later, to a mere three mentions in the second half). In the novel's first episode, while Byrnewood and Lorimer wager over the seduction of Mary, a lamplighter, oyster cellars, one of the character's eyesight, and gaslights are all called "queer." The wager at the center of this scene *produces* its attendant queerness: the sureties governing the agreement being counterfeit (sham appearances, faked representations, withheld information), the wager rests on false premises that pervade its entire setting. This sense of queer(ed) contractual speculation is reinforced when the two men visit the astronomer whom they expect to corroborate their predictions about the future. Instead, the astronomer queers futurity itself, telling them that their wager will result not in satisfaction, but in death, consequent on their contractual arrangement (one will die by the other's hand). In a speculative economy based on the reliability of future actions based on apparent character, yet involving participants who are changeable, scheming, and unpredictable, the outcome of wagers can become fatally queer.

This early scene establishes a pattern for the first half of the novel, in which "queer" most frequently describes figures engaged in speculative trade. Luke Harvey claims that Philadelphia's economy bears "queer fruit" (35); Becky Smolby, who becomes wealthy by fencing stolen goods, is "queer and whimsical" (200); Paul Western, the speculative explorer, has "queer old bachelor ways" (69); and Southern planters are three times labeled queer (218). Most strikingly, Luke Harvey, narrating his own rags-to-riches ascent, describes himself six times as queer (34). If even the exemplar of middle-class normalcy can be a "D——d queer fellow" (34), queerness becomes not a sexual alienation from reproductive normalcy, but a constitutive instability within the economic relations and Franklinian narratives that undergird its regulatory structures. The only "character" called queer in the novel as often as Luke Harvey is Monk Hall itself, five times described as that "queer old house," as are its permanent inhabitants, Mosquito and Glow-worm (52) and Bess (335). Once again, the "normalcy" promised by reformers like Luke does not exist in opposition to the degraded interiority represented by Monk Hall. Rather, Lippard shows that Monk Hall's depravity shares the queerness that produces—and destabilizes— the speculative economy necessary to Philadelphia's rising middle class.

The queerness of Monk Hall suggests two constitutive features that resonate with late-nineteenth-century constructions of homosexuality. First, although Luke Harvey suggests to Dora that middle-class identification is simply a matter of consenting to a stable set of social values, the novel shows how unstable identifications and narratives become in an economy that rests not only on the deferral of gratification, but on geographic movements occasioned by a national and increasingly global economy. The novel's many characters circulate in and out of plots, motivated by the economy rather than by any defining narrative of their own. Representing what Dana Nelson calls "a riot of sexual excess, violent pleasures, disorderly mixing and uncontrolled hybridity," Lippard's characters bring about a "forfeited pure group ideal."[70] These figures— the "Jew" Von Gelt, Becky Smolby's Irish servant Peggy Gurd, Fitz-Cowles's Creole servant Dim, to name a few—are all mobile figures of liminality in the novel, having no social identity, no economic position, and no narrative of their own. Entering and leaving Monk Hall, serving the pious as well as the infamous, these characters destabilize reform's insistent binaries of inner and outer, vicious and virtuous, respectability and reprehension.

Because they challenge the binaries that make intrinsic character traits seem stable and inherent, these characters also destabilize the borders of the identities such traits helped define and naturalize. As Nelson notes, these are figures of racial undecidability in the novel, representing anxieties about national borders triggered by the incorporation of Texas, slavery, immigration, and urban race riots, all of which figure in the novel's action.[71] Through *The Quaker City*, the not-quite-not-white, as Nelson astutely observes, challenge the racial purity of national whiteness and, consequently, permit a counter-fraternity among creolized Others (Devil-Bug, for instance, imagines himself a twin of the Jew, Von Gelt [227]). What is queered here, then, is interpellation itself, which turns (reveals) subject positions into counterfeits and forgeries. The anxiety produced by these figures is never only—or indeed primarily—*racial*, however, but economic (Von Gelt is described as "a forgery, a complete swindle" [34], Fitz-Cowles as "a mere counterfeit of a drunkard's manner" [58]). The swindle lies in contractual speculation itself, as the novel makes clear by involving these racially hybridized characters in narratives of economic fraud and forgery all too easily carried out within the normal operating logic of investment capital. Those relations, by the end of the novel, are sexualized, economic mobility, forgery, and counterfeiting supplanted by the bed-hopping promiscuity and seductions that characterize queer deviations from the ownership of bodies (monogamy) organized on contractual predictability (marriage) within private property.

The second aspect of Monk Hall's economic queerness that would become associated with sexuality is its radical *privacy*. When Mary's father warns her about the "queer" old maids who will try to discover her "secrets" (19), or when Devil-Bug muses on the "queer old chaps as used to keep house here, all alone to themselves" (115), both suggest a fierce privacy (indeed, both parties extract "confessions" without having to make their affairs public) that permits social configurations that diverge from the conventional family. While the latter would become the principal occupant of juridical "privacy," turning it into a form of social regulation that was extraordinarily *public*, Lippard appears to have imagined privacy as a space of radical refusal, both to the normative arrangements of social interaction and to the public confession of its queer deviations. Privacy in *The Quaker City* becomes a space of imaginative sociality that is the most radical form of queerness. Early on, reporting that he has heard rumors about Monk Hall's existence, Byrnewood exclaims that he "always deemed them fabulous" (23). If fabulousness means the ability to imagine what is not empirically existent—to see something rendered un-seeable by hegemonic social arrangements—then the queerness of Monk Hall is fabulous indeed. Its fabulous imaginings, moreover, differ in kind from the economic speculations of the surrounding culture, for these privately queer folk—the old maids, the monks, or the inhabitants of Monk Hall—are not productive investors, nor do they engage in the romantic speculations that presumably invest satisfaction in biological and social reproduction. Theirs is not the co-opted privacy of "private property" or the "private family," then, meant to segregate social units from each other. Rather, as the old maids open their doors to Mary, as the Monks increase membership in their orders, as Devil-Bug makes Monk Hall a flophouse for the degraded, their queer privacy becomes expansive, inclusive, generous.

While establishing a radical privacy becomes necessary to preserving the resistant demands of queer sociality, the segregation of the queer from everyday life also produces an explosive and exhortative rage that lays claim to public sociality. Midway through *The Quaker City*, Devil-Bug dreams of the ruin of Philadelphia, a vengeful fantasy with striking social implications. The dream is brought about by a transition within Devil-Bug himself, who, in the preceding chapters, has experienced speculative desire for the first time. Asked by Dora to murder Luke, Devil-Bug contracts to do so in return for sex with Dora. In the end, both parties renege, Devil-Bug failing to kill Luke and Dora refusing Devil-Bug her body, instead calling on Luke, who knocks out the doorkeeper and helps Dora escape. As with Mary Arlington, Devil-Bug's participation in speculative desire ends in an "unconscious" state in which he falls even more deeply into desire's thrall. Recovering and taking Luke hostage, Devil-Bug, at the verge of killing his prisoner, impulsively rushes off to check on Mabel, the daughter of his old flame, Ellen, and, he has reason to believe, his own daughter. As the forces of speculative desire—first economic, then romantic—crowd Devil-Bug's unconscious, his queer rage erupts in a vision of economic and civic retribution —" 'My heart's full of all sorts o' queer tantrums' " (337), he exclaims—aimed at desire's cherished institutions and laying bare, literally, the bones of the " 'liberal mob' " that " 'encourages manufacture' " (389).

The first part of Devil-Bug's dream queers population, fulfilling a growing need for fabulous sociability on the part of the often isolated "monster." Haunted throughout the early sections of the novel by the mangled specter of an early victim, Devil-Bug, rather than shrinking in terror from this phantom, develops "a longing desire . . . to lay another corpse beside his solitary victim" (106). No simple adherent to coupledom, Devil-Bug soon expands his desires in ways that parody the numerical logics of demography: Devil-Bug "longed to surround himself with the Phantoms of new victims. In the *number* of his crimes, he even anticipated pleasure" (107). While Lippard's language attributes to Devil-Bug his own deferred satisfaction—an "anticipated pleasure"—based on speculative desire ("longing"), the important difference is that Devil-Bug takes the outcome of his speculation into his own hands, making literal the phantom projections of speculative desire by ghoulishly populating his self-made world. If population becomes a tool in the isolating marginalization that keeps Devil-Bug and his associates segregated from the rest of civil society, his fantasy queers population with beings who, without bodies or souls, escape the disciplinary knowledge that separates the depraved and the normal. Devil-Bug's "phantoms" are not quite bodies (lacking the particularities grouped by disciplinary demography into hierarchized identities) and not quite souls (lacking the transcendence or abstraction that characterizes the pure legal subject). These figures, instead, deconstruct the body–spirit or particularity–abstraction binary altogether, generating a post-disciplinary imaginary beyond the individual control of desire. At the same time, these corpses, weirdly fretful and impatient, encapsulate the anxious state of citizens caught between transcendence and embodiment, driven on by the uneasy, dissatisfied promptings of desire. As such, they indicate that anxious citizenship has at its heart the undead yearnings that, in Devil-Bug's vision, continue to animate an increasingly mortified democracy.

The "phantoms" with which Devil-Bug populates Philadelphia are the civically dead: the poor, children, the disenfranchised, and, later, an army of skeletons representing slaves and wage laborers who bang their chains as they march through the city. Astonished that the living do not notice the phantoms he sets roaming among them, Devil-Bug cries out, " 'Good folks don't you see that the dead's among you?' " (376), but his cry is ignored. The "invisibility" of this population is its defining feature, the principal cause of its demise. The novel has repeatedly foreshadowed this scene, as when Devil-Bug exclaims of the recovered Byrnewood Arlington, " 'Dead—Dead and come to life!' " (135), or when Becky Smolby cries out, " 'The dead have come to life!' " (208). Monk Hall becomes a haven for the civically (un)dead, a place where they recover their sociality and civil entitlement. Lippard describes its banquet hall as the repository of what Russ Castronovo has called the nation's necro-citizens.[72] The "spiritual fraternity," Lippard writes, "determined upon a National Convention of all the ghosts in the union; a sort of death's head festival, with the Skeleton-God himself in the chair" (199). Given Monk Hall's status as not a counter-public but as a *counter-privacy*, a space in which the debased citizenry finds camaraderie and refuge, it is fitting that Devil-Bug should be the hall's door keeper, for he alone among the city's living has empathy with and therefore can still see the dead. "Derided and scorned by that fellow man," Lippard writes, "whom he never yet called, brother, the offcast of the world from his very birth, a walking curse and a breathing execration upon all mankind, why should old Devil-Bug fear the Phantom-World, which dawns upon his solitary eye?" (304). Although empathy keeps Devil-Bug from fearing the phantom world, his less open-minded neighbors are driven to insanity and death as they slowly become aware of the hosts of dead among whom they move. Such a rude eye opening is, Devil-Bug declares, "the vengeance of the People" (347).

Devil-Bug's "queer tantrums" echo Franklin Evans's "mania" in Whitman's temperance novel, which similarly places a nationalist celebration at its center. If Franklin's mania announces the advent of liberty with reform's conquest of appetite, however, Devil-Bug's dream commemorates "the anniversary of the death of Freedom" (386). " 'Liberty long since fled from the Quaker City,' " an antiquarian tells Devil-Bug in the dream. " 'The spirit of the old Republic is dethroned, and they build a royal mansion over the ruins of Independence Hall' " (373). Because the spatiality of Monk Hall has outlived the temporality of the State House, its inhabitants are again free to walk the streets of Philadelphia, in a vision of counter-democracy.

Ultimately, however, Devil-Bug imagines not a revolution of the ballot, an increase in enfranchisement, or Marx's class revolution brought about by the working class who in *The Communist Manifesto* appear as the specter haunting Europe, just as Devil-Bug's phantoms haunt Philadelphia. Rather, Devil-Bug's revolution occurs within the everyday practices that organize "normal" middle-class life in an economy whose desires make the promised stability of normalcy untenable. Devil-Bug's dream ends with him, suspended atop a column of fire, watching while the members of a nuclear family capping another pillar angrily throw one another to their deaths to save their own lives. The "private family" thus becomes the last bastion—the fiery pillar—of public corruption, the final institution in Devil-Bug's systematic destruction of the mechanisms of social marginality. As the last members of the family fall into flames, to Devil-Bug's delight, letters of flame spell out on the blackened sky, "WO UNTO SODOM," associating sodomy with conventional intimacy, not with the deviant sexualities that Devil-Bug and his associates might be said to embody.

Devil-Bug's "tantrum" is quite literally the return of the (socially) repressed in the novel, as it follows Luke Harvey's attempt to kill Devil-Bug by burying him alive in the dank cellar of Monk Hall (311). Unfortunately for the middle-class ideal Luke would represent, Devil-Bug will not stay down (313) but rises with a queer vengeance to witness (envision) "the Massacre of judgment" (391), which he describes as "a sight of glory" (387). Devil-Bug watches the destruction of Philadelphia's civic institutions "and [is] not harmed" (391). His ludic queerness—as he tells the cynical reformer F. A. T. Pyne, "'Parson, you save souls; I tickle 'em!'" (328)—survives as the counterfeit at the heart of deferred desire and hence of institutional futurity. Its status as dream suggests that Devil-Bug's vision of resistant queerness is already contained within the dominant logics of speculative desire, however, interiorized into the unconscious life of the psyche and expressive of an unfulfilled wish—a desire for justice—projected into a future outside history and, hence, beyond the very struggles that, the dream suggests, would make possible its satisfying achievement. While Devil-Bug's dream heats up the queer swindle at the heart of speculative capital, the disciplines of modern sexuality were already (apparently) stabilizing desire's "tantrums" through discourses of normative—and, more importantly, *aestheti-cized*—intimacy that would themselves counterfeit the economic roots of desire. Luke Harvey, not Devil-Bug, has the last laugh. At the end of the novel, Devil-Bug commits suicide to enable Mabel to inherit the fortune that, through marriage, passes to Luke Harvey, the contractual arrangements of normative sexuality apparently stabilizing the unpredictable movements of capital and desire in the first half of the novel. While Devil-Bug dreams, the world around him continues to speculate in an economy that, increasingly naturalized through emergent public understandings of sexuality, makes deferred satisfaction a delightful, if only illusorily profitable, end in itself.

* * * * *

Following Devil-Bug's dream, *The Quaker City* introduces a new character whose plot dominates the rest of the novel and represents the sexual-aesthetic logics that rendered cultural the economic speculations depicted in the novel's first half. The new plot takes place primarily within a space that integrates the public order of the State House and the secret interiority of Monk Hall. A combination madhouse, dissecting hall, and sorcerer's den, this "Temple" conflates the nineteenth-century disciplinary institutions regulating sanity, health, and spiritualism. The master of this establishment, Ravoni, self-described as "'a soul, an Intellect, a deathless Power'" (422), embodies the disparate objects produced by what Foucault calls power knowledge.[73] "'I gathered knowledge,'" Ravoni claims. "'I won science from the earth'" (423). From this science, Ravoni produces a disciplinary utopia that counters the post-disciplinarity of Devil-Bug's dream. In Ravoni's vision, the streets are filled with "'free and happy people. There are no rich; there are no poor; I see neither church nor gaol, priest nor gaoler, yet—yet—all are happy'" (529). "'All men from the slave to the prince, from the dull boor to the man of genius, are connected with each other by an universal sympathy,'" Ravoni proclaims. "'This influence or sympathy, call it what you will, is the atmosphere of souls, the life of intellects'" (447). Ravoni's radical equality, consistent with the stated goals of much antebellum reform, is conceivable, however, only when he displaces the *inequality* of citizens living in cruelly disparate material conditions to an aesthetic realm outside the contestations of history.

To interiorize and disseminate this displacement, Ravoni assembles a group of young white men, his enthusiastic disciples, anticipating "'a dread and awful experiment, not with machinery or wood or iron, or with the air of the lightning in its bosom, or with the earth or the secrets of its depths, but with something more terrible than all, the Soul of Man'" (445). Ravoni advertises that he will raise from the dead the corpse that Devil-Bug has robbed from one of the city's cemeteries. Showing once again the limitation of anticipated pleasure, however, Lippard reveals Ravoni's spiritualized science as a fatal hoax. The first body Devil-Bug retrieves from the cemetery turns out to be a mass of festering sores, exposing the audience to smallpox and representing Ravoni's spiritualized sympathy as the contagion arising from the material conditions in which bodies become sites of depravity and corruption. The second experiment is more successful. Ravoni administers a potion to the despondent Annie (the serving girl seduced and abandoned by Byrnewood Arlington), causing a deathlike state. At a certain time, Ravoni knows, the potion will wear off, and he chooses that moment to "revive" Annie before his credulous audience. Here Lippard returns the reader to the themes of economic swindle that dominate the first half of the novel. Annie falls under Ravoni's "protection" when her mechanic father, having invested his life's savings in a bank that has defaulted, visits the wealthy bank owner, an ardent philanthropist and member of several tract societies, to ask for a personal loan to support Annie and her newborn baby. When the banker proves immune to the pitiful story, the destitute mechanic commits suicide, leaving the gravely ill Annie prone to Ravoni's "protection." Lippard represents the shift from economic to scientific exploitation as a chain of swindles promising immediate satisfaction—the "resurrection" of the alienated body—that covers for the deferrals that can end only in painful death.

The relay of swindles is rendered palatable, however, by the aestheticized pleasures that provide, affectively, the satisfaction that sexual and economic speculations have removed. Ravoni not only naturalizes power relations through a supposedly outward-directed science, he interiorizes social relations by aestheticizing them, appealing to the instinctual promptings of the senses:[74]

> I will teach men that in the Refined cultivation of the Senses is Happiness. Not a pore on the body, but may be made the Minister of some new Joy; not a throb in the veins, but may become a living Pleasure. Every outrage committed against the refinement of the Senses brings its own punishment. When Mirth sinks into Drunken Revelry man is a brute. When Love sinks into coarse Lust man is a brute and devil. In order to acquire an influence over the minds of men, which shall be irresistible and eternal, I shall appeal to a principle rooted deep in every human heart. I will evoke the love of Mystery! I will awe and terrify by Miracles and Pageants and Shadows! (425)

Ravoni moves pleasure from the realm of material satisfaction sought by the mechanic—making a living wage to feed and house his family—to that of aesthetic "refinement," depicting pleasures that are principally achieved through the denial of gratification. Refining the stimulating "throb in the vein" into the pleasure of self-control, thereby deferring the satisfaction of that "throb," Ravoni aestheticizes dissatisfaction, making mystery—the absence in the here and now that leaves one oriented toward revelation in the undisclosed "future"—the incentive of desires no longer tied to the body through either sex or economics. At the same time, the irresistible and eternal "influence" Ravoni hopes to exercise depends on an aestheticized self-control carried out precisely through the body's senses. The body thus becomes a repository of orders originating from outside, requiring the disciplined denial of competing demands for gratification and offering by way of compensation the pleasures of aesthetic sensations that give each citizen the impression of a self-generated connection to the external world.[75]

The effect of aestheticized order on the material fate of bodies becomes evident in Ravoni's relationship to Mabel, Devil-Bug's daughter, whom F. A. T. Pyne intends to rape. Continually exchanged in economic relations between men that result in economic and physical violence, Mabel—like Dora, Bess, Annie, and Mary—epitomizes the fatal effects of speculative desire on women. Ravoni purports to clean up this history, however, by transforming Mabel into Izole, the "goddess" of his new faith, " 'not like a living thing, but like a carved statue of some pure and holy Enthusiasm' " (432). Mabel/Izole becomes the relay between aesthetic interiorization—"Already the words of the Sorcerer were bursting into fulfillment" as "a strange panorama of beauty glided on her Soul" (462)—and the heterosexual "adoration" that her idealization as the iconic embodiment of womanly purity awakens in Ravoni's homosocial acolytes. Lust, transformed into the deferred pleasure of aesthetic appreciation, is translated back into the body through the idealized heterosexualization of aesthetic sensuality.

Ravoni's circuit of power—interiorized into the body through self-denying disciplines of deferred gratification, exteriorized through aesthetic sensations that make a pleasure of that denial—thus reverses the end of Devil-Bug's dream, apparently ending queer challenges to the primary institutions of normative privacy. Ravoni's counterfeit miracles depend on his power over Devil-Bug, to whom he boasts, " 'I will take from you the power to think, or act without my consent. My will shall be yours' " (400). Just as he appropriates Devil-Bug's consent, thereby quelling the challenge of his "queer tantrums," so Ravoni's experiments appropriate queer fakery in order to stabilize the heterosexual "normalcy" threatened by speculative desire in the first half of the novel. Ravoni performs the "miracle" that allows Byrnewood, who has become one of his disciples, to reconcile with his abandoned Annie. More important, Ravoni detaches Mabel/Izole from both Devil-Bug and Pyne, allowing her to be "rescued" by Luke Harvey, who ultimately marries her. The marriages that apparently make good on the deferred promises of speculation and provide satisfactory closure to a frenetic plot therefore rely on a series of "inevitabilities" that Lippard shows to be the result not of fate, but of hoaxes, trickery, and swindles. Those counterfeits are "revealed" and denounced in the novel by Luke Harvey, who brings Ravoni to his bloody end. Declaring Ravoni an " 'Imposter!' " (532), Luke makes his own middle-class position appear, by contrast, innocent and transparent, although it rests on the same speculative economy and its promise of satisfaction through (not *of*) desire. In the market of speculative desire, then, conventional romance remains, despite Luke's posturing, its own queer counterfeit. In the end, the incommensurability of promise and satisfaction, of contract and fulfillment, maintains the opportunity for queer fraud, which turns out, paradoxically, to be the very condition of the "normal" world of romance and commerce. Ravoni's temple remains haunted by the corrupted bodies of the monstrous, the ruined, and the diseased, as does nineteenth-century Philadelphia, despite the police raid on Monk Hall that supposedly ends its history of depravity and, insofar as it aestheticizes the social conditions that erupt in Devil-Bug's queer dream, to the depravity of history.

More Fantastic than Desire

If, by the end of *The Quaker City*, the "queer tantrums" of abjected citizens seem contained by the aesthetic manipulations of fraudulent normativity, the powers of inner dissent did not entirely vanish. Writers throughout the 1850s deployed fantasy, daydreams, and reveries as a crucial archive of critique and imaginative reconstruction—of democratic possibility—in the only register seemingly available to a rapidly interiorizing citizenry. Within the space of the imagination, the socially sanctioned "real" and the abjected fantastic inter-mingled, robbing heteronomative marriage and its attendant institutions of domestic reproduction and private property of their inevitability while opening the possibility that other social imaginings—foreclosed through their dismissive characterization as whimsy or utopian fantasy—might occupy the position of the possible.

Donald Grant Mitchell's *Reveries of a Bachelor: A Book of the Heart* (1850) is a transitional text between the visible antagonism to speculative desire, middle-class respectability, and aesthetic disciplinarity characteristic of city thrillers of the mid-1840s and the melancholy archiving of an increasingly phantasmatic sociality central to the romances of Hawthorne and Melville. Resisting the imperative that citizens be "reduced to the dull standard of the actual" in a world that leaves no "more room for intrepid forays of the imagination—no more gorgeous realm-making" (478), Mitchell's "book of the heart" credits inventive interiority—the "reverie"—with the power to accomplish what Lauren Berlant and Michael Warner term "queer world-making," the counterpart to "gorgeous realm-making."[76]

Before reveries can become the blueprints for alternative socialities, however, "normal" intimacies must be revealed as speculative investments with highly dubious payoffs.[77] Mitchell's text begins by drawing a parallel between speculative capital and desire. "Does a man buy a ticket in a lottery—a poor man, whose whole earnings go in to secure the ticket," Mitchell's narrator inquires, "without trembling, hesitancy, and doubting?" The analogous question, for the narrator, is whether a man can "stake his bachelor respectability, his independence, and comfort, upon the die of absorbing, unchanging, relentless marriage, without trembling at the venture?" (478). The answer, for Mitchell's narrator, is no, for although the eroticization of speculation adds an enticing frisson to the mundane deliberations of deal making, once engaged— "our bargain was struck" (509)—the betrothed must turn "to such dull task-work, as thinking out a livelihood" (478) for a wife who "will annoy you by looking over the stock-list at breakfast time; and mention quite carelessly to your clients, that she is interested in *such* or such a speculation" (479). What begins, then, as a "little heart-redundancy" (484) soon turns into a bad bargain with purely anxious returns, "making you pay in righteous retribution of annoyance, grief, vexation, shame, and sickness of heart" (479). Over time, Mitchell's narrator asserts, anxiety about "the boundless Future" fatally generates "the death chamber of life" (507). In a less dramatic register, the narrator, echoing Hannah Foster's Eliza Wharton, suggests that the most dangerous feature of normative intimacy is that "sympathies are narrowed down" (537) until a single "heart-bond . . . absorbs all others" (488). "You do not now look men in the face as if a heart-bond were linking you—as if a community of feeling lay between" (488), he warns, suggesting the most damning fatality of normative intimacy is sociality itself. Not only does institutionalized intimacy limit the options for public interaction ("a community of feeling"). It turns intimacy into a stultifying set of contractual obligations.

If narrowing relationality to a single "respectable institution" (521) becomes a fatal restriction, imagination animates the unquiet unconscious of dissenting reverie. "I wonder,—thought I, as I dropped asleep,—if a married man with his sentiment made actual," the narrator ponders, "is, after all, as happy as we poor fellows, in our dreams?" (508).[78] The bachelor's "floating vision" (474) becomes for the narrator not an escape from social realities but an "honester way" of using the supposed spontaneity of the interior to circumvent the conventional pieties that censor public articulation and to suggest how mutually contradictory such conventions often are. Presented as "dreams," in other words, the narrator's observations "come seething from my thoughts, with all their crudities and contrasts, uncovered" (474). If his melancholic refusal to relinquish his conception of a "community of feeling" strikes readers as demonstrating "a little much of sentiment," the narrator need only remind them "that I am dreaming" (474), using the diminutive posture of a "reverie" to disguise the unsettling critique that is the content of his daydreams. The narrator, in fact, claims much for the fantastic, warning, "Let those who will then, sneer at what in their wisdom they call untruth—at what is false, because it has no material presence." But, he also claims, "unreality" does not necessarily "create falsity" (491). On the contrary, asserting that "the heart that has no sympathy with thoughts and feelings that scorch the soul, is dead" (491), the narrator establishes dreaming as a necessary and revitalizing retreat in a world scandalously shrunk by normative privacy.

Dreams, furthermore, are not substitutes for action but staging grounds for social arrangements de-scripted by the conventions of sanctioned intimacy. "He is a weak man," the narrator contends, "who cannot twist and weave the threads of his feelings—however fine, however tangled, however trained, or however strong—into the great cable of Purpose, by which he lies moored to his life of Action" (496). "I know not justly, if it be a weakness or a sin to create these phantoms that we love," he asserts, "and to group them into a paradise— soul-created. But if it is a sin, it is a sweet and enchanting sin, and if it is a weakness, it is a strong and stirring weakness" (502). "Much as hope may lean toward the intoxicating joy of distinction," the narrator poignantly concludes, "there is another leaning in the soul, deeper, and stronger, toward the pleasures which the heart pants for, and in whose atmosphere, the affections bloom and ripen" (568). That other "leaning" is, for the narrator, the broader sociality Foster's heroine called friendship, which populates the imagination in ways that refuse the deferrals of speculative futurity. Insisting instead on the past and, more important, the present, the narrator claims that his "queer fancy" (550) "brings up the old companions, and stations them in the domain of NOW" (555). Mitchell makes fantasy an alternative social history that "brings up not only its actualities, not only its events, and memories, but—stranger still,—what might have been" (527).

Mitchell's depiction of the imagination as an archive of what might have been becomes, for Judith Butler, a promise of what might yet be. Butler shares Mitchell's resentment of normalizing forces that designate anti-institutional socialities as "fantasy." The "real," for Butler, is "a set of exclusionary and constitutive principles which confer on a given indication the force of an ontological indicator." For Butler, fantasy need not be "equated with what is not real, but rather with what is not *yet* real," or "what belongs to a different version of the real." Just as reveries allow Devil-Bug to produce "queer tantrums" and Mitchell's narrator to cease the "dull task-work" of everyday life in order to imagine "gorgeous" alternatives, so fantasy, for Butler, "is the very scene that *suspends* action and which, in its suspension, provides for a critical investigation of what it is that constitutes action."[79] And just as Mitchell's narrator dreams in order to relive the past and inscribe alternative life trajectories, so fantasy deploys what Butler, in *The Psychic Life of Power*, calls "a mourning for unlived possibilities."[80]

The "possibilities" imagined by Butler, like those dreamed of by Mitchell's narrator, are insistently social. Although citizens in the nervous state find their agency rendered as the unconscious, that psychic realm need not be, Butler contends, pre-, ante-, or antisocial, but may constitute "*a certain mode in which the unspeakably social endures*" as "non-state-centered forms of alliance." If "the ideals of personhood that govern self-definition on preconscious and unconscious levels are themselves produced through foreclosures of various kinds," the interior vocabulary of resistant dissent—what Butler names as "the panic, terror, trauma, anger, passion, and desire that emerge in relation to such ideals" (265–66)—should not be dismissed because of their inner staging, or individualized into the "private" domain of the personal history and psychic dysfunction.[81] Rather, such affective expressions are disruptions within the nervous state, the last complaint of a radically de-socialized and anxious—but not docile—citizenry.

Although Butler makes a compelling case for the power of fantasy, however, it is in the end somewhat disappointing, as she leaves social action in the realm of potential. Redefining democracy as "the ideal of a possibility that exceeds every attempt at a final realization, one which gains its vitality precisely from its non-coincidence with any present reality," she deftly positions the not yet real as a life-affirming production.[82] At the same time, however, she follows the speculative logics of capital in making democracy a continually deferred horizon that, drawing the citizen toward a potential that will never be realized, generates effort without reward (or, rather, generates effort *as* reward). Mitchell's insistence that his reveries may materialize his past relationships in the NOW thus remains, in Butler's formulation, a necessary, if dissatisfying, delusion. Butler's notion that fantasy "exceeds every attempt at a final realization" is an effort to avoid the prescriptive pedagogy (this is what *your* idealizations should look like) that characterizes institutional futurity. In so doing, however, she installs speculative desire not as one in a catalogue of inner promptings ("panic, terror, trauma, anger, passion, and desire"), but as *the* organizing principle of democratic imagining.[83] Just as desire always exceeds its own satisfaction, so democracy, now given the shape of desire, exceeds its "realization." Yet one might well ask: Is democracy as unachievable as desire? Can one materialize the not yet real without turning it into the exclusionary apparatus of the normative? Is desire the only or an adequate figuration of agency? Will we ever again imagine social alternatives unmediated by the psychic force of the unconscious? Will we ever do more than speculate for—or about—democracy?

Those questions, as the next chapters will show, animate the romances of Martin Delany, Hannah Crafts, Herman Melville, and Nathaniel Hawthorne. The critical reception of the American romance has assumed that one must either set aside the political undercurrents of the genre to enjoy its aesthetic inventiveness or, conversely, set aside the creative imagination of the romance to properly "politicize" the genre. That the imaginative work of the romance is *itself* political, in the ways Butler's discussion of fantasy suggests, is rarely credited, although it may be on the imaginative level that the romance serves most powerfully as an archive of social possibility in a world organized as a rapidly rigidifying institutional "real." But the imagination of the romance, I will argue, is not invested in the deferrals of desire. After all, the genre's most notorious dreamer, Hawthorne's Clifford Pyncheon, insistently proclaims, "I want my happiness! . . . Many, many years have I waited for it! It is late! It is late! I want my happiness!"[84] Wanting happiness that badly (not *desiring* it) may wake one from one's reveries. That awakening may be, as it so often was for Melville, horrifying, yet it releases, if only momentarily, the speculative power of fantasy into the framework of the real, producing in that release the only sign of a vital democracy. Without such awakenings, we may be fated not to gorgeous realm making, but to the cravings of desire, the nightmare of the nervous state.

6

BETWEEN CONSCIOUSNESS AND REVOLUTION:

ROMANTICISM AND RACIAL INTERIORITY

Few people living in the antebellum United States were as vulnerable to the installation of interiority as were black Americans. Not only did they bear the representational responsibility for civic interiority, as chapter 3 shows, but they were forced to monitor, continually and vigilantly, the borders between what they thought or felt and what they said or showed to a world structured by and serving the interests of whites. The "color line" proclaimed by W. E. B. Du Bois separated not only whites from blacks, but also interiority from exteriority, the inner life of race from the sanctioned expressions or deathlike silence required by the (white) public sphere. When dissenting interiority did find its way into external circulation, it became a volatile incentive to (justification for) white anxiety about slave "disloyalty" or "ingratitude," a "failure" to love the master appropriately. As a vexing "disorder" in the nerve system of the state, black interiority (always a projection of whites' desire and anxiety) legitimated surveillance and domination (the vigilante "patrols" that surfaced throughout the South in response to revolts such as Nat Turner's, for instance) while simultaneously removing the taint of domination. Blacks, the logic goes, brought domination on themselves through the expression of bad *feelings*.

At the same time that they were prohibited from—indeed, brutally punished for—expressing unsanctioned affect, however, black Americans were forced to experience dissent and demand as the trembling agitation of their nerves. Amid scenes of rape, torture, and material prejudice, it is easy to overlook or even dismiss what might be called the inner life of race in antebellum America, but the representation of such scenes—suffused with desire, rage, and anxiety, the interior lexicon of a radically de-publicized citizenry—has much to teach about the *disciplinary* operations of racism. Organized as the nervous border between feelings and expression, systems of power could operate within the self-contained limits of the black body, segregating without physical force (although such force was never far away) and beyond the reach of legal emancipation or enfranchisement.

A particularly chilling example of the violent production and manipulation of black interiority occurs in Martin Delany's *Blake; or, The Huts of America*.[1] A white Northern judge, who boasts of his sympathies with the slave system during a visit to Mississippi, is treated to a performance that brings him too close to its bodily affects. One of his Southern hosts calls for a slave boy, Rube, who is unusually talented at the mimicries often attributed to the enslaved. What his master prizes in Rube's performance, however, is not its verisimilitude or even its comic inadequacies but, rather, the rigid division it seemingly produces between inside and outside, affect and show. The young boy, his master brags, will " 'whistle, sing songs, hymns, pray, swear like a trooper, laugh, and cry, all under the same state of feelings' " (67). In claiming that Rube's highly expressive performance hides a uniform "state of feelings," his master simultaneously produces the black body *as* the location of "states of feeling," forecloses Rube's ability to express those feelings through his performance, and denies (the responsibility for white spectators to know about) those feelings altogether. For it becomes appallingly clear that, far from experiencing "the same state of feelings," Rube passes through a gothic progression of anxiety, terror, and despair. The rupture between what he feels and what he shows—or is credited with showing—is so violent that the exhausted and terrorized boy begins to hemorrhage to death, blood pouring from his mouth in place of the pleading that has gone unheard (" 'O massa, I's sick! Please stop little!' ") and the demands he never gets to make. Interiorization, for Rube, is a coerced rupture and a violent prohibition that ends only with the outpouring of blood, the galling proof that the boy's "inside" contains not a "state of feelings," but the shockingly real gore of his body.

In an astute analysis of this scene, Robert Reid-Pharr argues that black servility dies off in the person of the abused yet docile Rube, while brutal demand is disavowed in the figures of the over-privileged whites. This double disavowal—of black servility and white aristocracy—permits the black male hero of the novel, Henry Blake, to emerge cleansed of the taints of both blackness (servility) and maleness (domination). By making Blake a representative of a new Pan-Africanism, Reid-Pharr argues, Delany similarly cleanses nationalism of the taint of sadomasochistic power relations, in which a dominant state demands the docile acquiescence of a radically disempowered citizenry.[2] In the discussion of *Blake* that follows, I will expand Reid-Pharr's analysis to show how the sadomasochistic relations in the book are not enacted simply between masculinity and effeminacy, domination and servility, but, more important, between institutionality and insurrection, a pairing Delany never "cleanses" of eroticized force.

For now, however, I will focus on Reid-Pharr's claim that Rube's demands are entirely silenced or disavowed.[3] When first summoned to his master's presence, Rube speculates about the master's wants but answers himself, " 'He gwine make me see sights!' " When Rube claims that his "massa" will make him see sights, he might well be indicating the dissociative insertion of fantasy in the place of a painful reality that characterizes the response of many people subjected to persistent trauma. As a *literary* moment, however, this statement enacts a perplexing reversal: at the very moment that the white master proposes making Rube a visual spectacle for the scopophilic pleasures of his companions, Rube insists that the master intends to make him into a spectator, the seer rather than the seen. By imagining that reversal, Rube is able to disavow his own identification with the specularized body, enabling him to wander promiscuously through a range of performative positions while also denying the degrading imposition of specularity implied by his blackness. In deploying vision as a response to imposed specularity, the boy employs a tactic that, as I argue later, similarly structures the dis/identifications animating the plot of Hannah Crafts's *The Bondwoman's Narrative*.

In "seeing sights," however, Rube does not exactly enact a reversal, for if he appropriates the position of seer, he does not relegate the white gentlemen to the position of spectacle. What, then, are the "sights" that Rube anticipates seeing? Perhaps this moment signals Rube's movement not from seen to seer, but into double sight, or what Du Bois famously termed double consciousness.[4] While Du Bois's focus was on the doubling of (a properly unified) consciousness, my focus in this chapter is on the production *of* "consciousness" as intrinsically "doubling," particularly in a racializing context. Intending to install interiority as a means of fixing racial identifications, such disciplinary moments also produced discrepancies between what should be felt (the illocutionary intention of racial naming) and the experiential divergences from such names (discipline's perlocutionary reception).[5] Far from producing a psychic unity ("a single state of feeling"), in other words, interiorization generated a psychic bivalence (*double* consciousness) that effected the psychic disorganization of sanctioned identifications that naturalize "race" as fundamentally and naturally deterministic. The "visions" Rube will see are, importantly, left opaque, inviting readers into inventive guesswork that both aligns us with the tortured boy (we, too, will "see sights") and makes clear that this very act of identification is a projection rather than a discernment (thereby frustrating that identification). Combining identification and invention, Rube's "visions" are an important intervention into conventional dynamics of both specularity and sympathy, which typically—and similarly—assume that to see is to know, the act of knowing creating either too much or too little distance, asserting either that the visual object is distinct from the imaginative projection of the viewer (in the case of specularity) or that there is no distinction at all between the suffering of the object and the comprehension of the sympathizer. Insisting on the distance of uncertainty while still inviting a collaborative act of interpretation, then, Delany transforms possessive specularity into imaginative relationality.

In so doing, Delany takes Rube from the didactic realm of realism (a mode that *Blake*, relentlessly read for parallels with the history of slavery, has rarely been permitted to leave) into that of romanticism in ways typical of novels by black authors of the antebellum period. While the African American novel is frequently credited with forming gothic conventions, or offering historical insight, juridical innovation, even transnational models of global citizenship, the connection between romanticism and racial interiority remains unexplored.[6] There are valid reasons for this oversight. As Joan Dayan has shown, the imaginations of white romantic writers were invested in troubling figurations of the black body, making romanticism a problematic genre for authors struggling with the burdens of racialization.[7] Less explicitly, to credit black authors with the fantastic musings of romanticism might seem to belittle the significant insights the African American novel offers into the historical *realities* of slavery and racial prejudice. Nevertheless, if Dayan is correct that "mystification is always a matter of power" in which "a decreeing subject ordains the terms for a silenced object to obtain the status, or stasis, of myth,"[8] then the deployment by black authors of the "mystifications" endemic to romanticism to rewrite myth, to destabilize stasis, to trouble and refuse the distinction between "subject" and "object," and in all these ways to struggle with racial interiority and hence with the power relations invested in identification, deserves closer critical attention.

At the same time, romanticism was a fraught genre for black writers for whom, as Dayan rightly notes, "there had to be limits on invention—imagination had to be accountable to a reality often invented by someone else."[9] Most important, romanticism often centered on forms of affective civility that thwarted black novelists' advocacy of dissent and rebellion. In *Blake*, for example, Delany's efforts to tell the story of transatlantic insurrection against the tyrannies of slavery are thwarted by plots of romantic intimacy—particularly marriage—that render affective without significantly changing systems of property and ownership. In substituting marriage for revolution, *Blake* simultaneously replaces the give and take of collective insurgency with the hierarchical civility of *organization*, an institutionalization that necessarily defers revolution beyond the horizon of narrativity, satisfying the black characters in the novel with affective sentiment in place of economic and political justice.

If romanticism introduced its own generic obstacles to the black author's ability to imagine collective self-determination, however, it also provided the means to dismantle the narratives—and subject relations—of normative intimacy. The second section of this chapter shows how Hannah Crafts's imaginative agency arises through a persistent play with the process of identification, focused on visual dynamics of incorporation and interpretation. Noting that "to sentimentalize is to colonize the image," since the "master makes the myth through which the other must seek his or her identity,"[10] Dayan implicitly suggests that the *de*colonization of images might open an alternative model for seeking—or a rejection of the imperative to seek—identity. Less ambitious than *Blake* in its historical representations, *The Bondwoman's Narrative* arguably achieves more substantial freedom by tackling the interiorizing dynamics of the romance as a genre. In particular, rather than reining in the extravagances of invention, Crafts heightens the gothic and sentimental registers of the novel to challenge the coincidence of racial representation and affective loyalty, identification, and identity. In so doing, she demonstrates the limitations of the romance due precisely to its idealizing mystifications even as she opens new possibilities for racial reconfiguration through the strategic *disidentifications* permitted by the play of reality and fantasy.

The ambivalence toward romance evident in *The Bondwoman's Narrative* is characteristic of racialized figures throughout the history of the genre, as becomes clear in two important accounts of the romance's formal elements. Northrop Frye describes the romance as a "wish-fulfillment dream" representing an "extraordinarily persistent nostalgia" that sets in motion a quest for "some kind of imaginative golden age in time or space."[11] The "epiphany" of romance, according to Frye, represents a desire to integrate the divine and the everyday—or, to use terms Judith Butler suggests, fantasy and reality—in ways that produce, not ultimate transcendence, but imaginative cross-currents within the logics of reality.[12] As Frye explains, romance represents "the search of the libido or desiring self for a fulfillment that will deliver it from the anxieties of reality but will still contain that reality."[13] It is hardly surprising that antebellum novels written by African Americans would yearn for an alternative social "reality" or even for a previous state of childhood innocence. Frye draws attention to the constitutive relation between race and romance when he describes a central set of characters, exemplified by the "tricky slave," who "elude the moral antitheses of heroism and villainy" and therefore "represent partly the moral neutrality of the intermediate world of nature and partly a world of mystery which is glimpsed but never seen, and which retreats when approached." These intermediary characters, who "retain the inscrutability of their origin," serve to "intensify and provide a focus for the romantic mood" largely by "call[ing] attention to realistic aspects of life, like fear in the presence of danger, which threaten the unity of the romantic mood."[14] Frye's discussion of the intermediate figures, "glimpsed but never seen," who intensify romance by keeping mysterious their origins serves as a description of Delany's Rube, who increases romantic intensity in the midst of a painfully realistic event.

While these intermediate characters, for Frye, are necessary to romance, they are essentially *anti-romantic*, serving to forestall the libidinal "unity" that is the goal of the hero's quest. For these intermediate characters, the hero's vision of social or subjective integrity is intolerable fantasy, for they live in a world not of comic resolution, but of brutal and purportedly irresolvable division ("good" versus "evil"). At the same time, their strategic "inscrutability" produces fantasies of its own, generating a psychic space removed from the norms of civic reality and ultimately inassimilable to its standards of feasibility or rectitude. Forbidding the fantastical construction of an unequal world *as* utopian, while maintaining the mystery of origin and intent, the "tricky slave" resists the moral antitheses of good and evil. She cannot become the architect of counter-realities built on such binaries; instead, she serves as a deconstructive suspension of moral positivism within already existing ethical systems. As such, the "tricky slave" invites, as Rube does, imaginative participation on the part of the reader: the act of such participation, rather than its ethical conclusions (which the "tricky slave" perpetually stalls), is the goal of romantic (inter)mediation. In particular, the "tricky slave" intervenes in normative moral antitheses by challenging the legibility of interiority itself. In portraying the romance in terms of interior states—as the struggle between anxiety and desire, which, as chapter 5 demonstrated, became the ubiquitous inner modes of social dissent and demand in a newly emergent market—Frye suggests that the modern romance emerged as a response not so much to libidinal desires frustrated in everyday life as to the relegation of social demand to the realm of libidinal desire. The romance is not a quest for delivery from "the anxieties of reality" but from conceiving reality *as* anxiety.

The importance of the modern romance in troubling (racialized) interior states such as desire and anxiety becomes clear in Fredric Jameson's suggestive revision of Frye's theory. Jameson notes that the modern romance centers on "a sequence of events that are closer to states of being than to acts, or better still, in which even human acts and deeds are apprehended in relatively static, pictorial, contemplative fashion, as being themselves results and attributes, rather than causes in their own right." The heroic quest to generate a social reality that enables a more complete enactment of communal invention and human aspiration thus becomes reconceived, through the modern romance, as a struggle for what Jameson calls "*character-enaction*," carried out "in the realm of what henceforth must be called *psychology*."[15] As chapter 7 will show, this is certainly the case in the classic romances of the 1850s, such as Melville's *Pierre* or Hawthorne's *The House of the Seven Gables*, in which quests to establish economic equality between a wealthy family and its patriarch's abandoned and impoverished offspring, or to settle a conflict over rightful possession of stolen lands, transform into almost catatonic meditation of the "pictorial" questions of familial resemblance, "proper" identity, and intimate attachment.

Delany's Rube suggests, however, that "character enaction" was particularly fraught for black Americans, for whom the burden of "character" imposed the rigid boundaries *between* action and affect, between the enactment of character and the execution of rebellion. The interiorizing demands of antebellum racial disciplines, in other words, parallel—and, arguably, inform—those of the romance as a literary genre: just as the latter transformed the social realm of heroic action into the psychological realm of *character* (whether Frye's libido or Garrison's civility, the twin—but irreconcilable—forms of black interiority), so logics of race insisted on the relocation of black dissent and demand to the terrain of nervous interiority, separated from white civil space by the barrier of black consciousness itself.[16] Little wonder that, in taking up romanticism, African American authors waged battles on both sides of that barrier, attacking the limitations of romantic civility on the one hand and of psychological identification on the other.

Central to those attacks, for both authors, was what Butler has called "the force of fantasy" in challenging the naturalized status of (racial) "reality."[17] That rethinking race as a category of identification structuring the "realities" of the civil sphere should bring authors to the fantasy structures of romanticism is understandable, especially given the centrality of magic in both Frye's and Jameson's accounts of the genre. Since early modern cultures perceived problems in everyday life as a curse cast by "black magic," Jameson observes, it enabled the remedying visions of the romance to take the form of a counter- or *white* magic.[18] For Jameson, the battle between "white" and "black" magic disguises the structural conflict between economic forces, both the Marxist struggle between class interests and between antagonistic worldviews generated by the competition between pre-market and nascent capitalist orderings of sociality (and, as Jameson insists, of *psychology*). The romance, for Jameson, "expresses a nostalgia for a social order in the process of being undermined and destroyed by nascent capitalism, yet still for the moment existing side by side with the latter." As such, the romance is "an aesthetic counterpart to the problem of ideology."[19] Jameson's location of economic struggle at the core of changing conceptions of magic certainly holds true, as chapter 7 will show, for works such as *The House of the Seven Gables*, in which the "black magic" of the mesmerist Maules, robbed of their land, their social status, and the pre-market economy in which they flourished, opposes the capitalist speculations of the Pyncheons, who make the unsteady transformation from early modern aristocracy to capitalist bourgeoisie.

In *The House of the Seven Gables*, however, economic struggles are intrinsically, if subtly, tied to questions of race. The century-long battle between the Maules and the Pyncheons over the rightful ownership of the land in Maine disguises the important fact that the possession of the land by *either* family constitutes a prior theft from its first inhabitants. Symbolizing the establishment of *both* pre-capitalist and capitalist economic models on racialized acts of theft (whether of land or labor), the first commodity sold in the cent-shop, the opening of which marks Hepzibah Pyncheon's transition from reclusive aristocrat to would-be entrepreneur, is a gingerbread cookie in the shape of Jim Crow. While the "old" order of the Maules relied on the theft of Indian land, the "new" order of the Pyncheons relies on the theft of slave labor as represented by Jim Crow. The economic struggle Jameson sees at the heart of romanticism therefore relies on a *prior* racialization: the "black" and "white" magic of romanticism is not simply a metaphoric displacement of economic struggle, but its precondition.

While romanticism provided black authors with the literary means to enact the economic, social, and psychological tensions produced by racial interiority in antebellum America, however, it did not show how to move beyond those tensions. If the conclusions to these novels bring not the enactment of a post-Revolutionary ethos, but the deconstruction of race itself, that end is a valuable start, but it leaves broader social change unimagined. The generic paradox Frye creates for the "tricky slave" becomes a life-threatening conundrum for those forced to live the plots of racial interiorization. Romanticism seemingly prevents plots from achieving the world-rectifying possibilities they promise (as in *Blake*) or imposes a happy ending in defiance of credibility (as in *The Bondwoman's Narrative*). What can the romance offer beyond the imperatives of interiorization and its attendant racial logics? Is our best hope only the perpetual deconstruction of imposed interiorities, without any risky articulation of an alternative sociality, a more revolutionary "reality"?

The black romance gives little by way of answers to these questions, although novels such as Crafts's and Delany's dramatically thematize the struggles of romantic narrative with its own textual limitations. Both Delany's serialized and possibly incomplete *Blake* and Crafts's until recently unpublished *The Bondwoman's Narrative* take up, analyze, and contest—with greater or lesser success—the problems of fictionalization. That Delany and Crafts did not publish complete versions of their novels in their own lifetimes demonstrates that the difficulty of narrating *narrativity* itself became as daunting as the struggles to achieve personhood, to imagine liberty, and to make post-traumatic use of rage, guilt, and ambivalence. What both novels poignantly demonstrate is how interrelated the two struggles—historical and historiographical, neurological and narratological—are. Just as important, however, the aesthetic innovations of these novels suggest the powerful potential—if, ultimately, the limited conclusions—of imagination, enabling the *dis*identifications and releases of fantasy that remain the interiorized subject's archive of (never quite heard) demand.

The Revolution Will Not Be Novelized

A poster currently appearing throughout Chicago to recruit students to a local university proclaims, "Know yourself first. Change the world second." Simple enough on the surface, the poster presents an epistemological conundrum central to interiority. Until one has, in Hawthorne's words, gnashed one's teeth on human laws, discovering in the process the discrepancies between institutional conventions and the needs and pleasures produced by one's lived relations, where do the motivations, strategies, or comparative ethics necessary for self-knowledge come from? If one seeks self-knowledge as an answer, in other words, where does one get one's *questions* prior to the frustrating challenges that world changing presents? Exemplifying Foucault's critique of "self-knowledge" (what are the differences between the "self" who does the knowing and the "self" who is the object of knowledge, and where is the mysterious and autonomous space of "selfhood" that apparently exists apart from "the world"?), the temporal sequencing of the poster, postulating a "self" *prior to* the relational structures that become clear only *through* efforts at world changing, poses an epistemological impossibility.

The sequencing is not simply naïve, however. Rather, it establishes a hierarchy of value, prioritizing self-knowledge *over* world change. Although the poster posits a seamless continuity between the two activities, the history of interiority suggests that the relationship is more antagonistic precisely because of this hierarchy. If the "self" one "knows" is removed from the vicissitudes of history ("change") and relational give and take ("the world"), then that "self" is perpetually static, its "truths" not simply removed from but *opposed to* the progressive adaptability—the imaginative ethics—necessary to transformative interactions with "the world."

The vexed relation between "self-knowledge" and "world changing," between consciousness and revolution, is the dilemma posed by interiorization, which accelerated dramatically in the United States within reform discourses of the 1830s and 1840s. In the wake of social reform, those with revolutionary aspirations were confronted not only by the military and juridical force of a newly cohered state, but by the more amorphous (and therefore more insidious) imperatives of a newly liberalized (inward-directed, affect-saturated, and self-regulatory) civil sphere. Rather than challenging the institutional or juridical operations of the state, modern citizens became engaged in rituals of codified consciousness ("identity") and patterned sociality ("civility") until those phenomena began to seem satisfactory substitutes for revolution.

At midcentury, however, the struggle between consciousness and revolution was ongoing, and romanticism was the outgrowth of that conflict. Romanticism produces its surreal effects precisely by inverting consciousness and revolution. In the romance, "self-knowledge" produces consent to the intimate conventions governing the "outward" world, while revolutionary aspirations take the quintessentially interior form of fantasy. This seeming paradox situates romanticism at the uncertain moment when inside and outside change places, when sociality becomes individualized (and discredited) as dream work while intimacy becomes institutionalized as the hallmark of conventional civility. At this tense exchange, the romantic novel often gives way to suggestive incoherence, marking the as yet unnarrativized conventions of intimacy as they (never entirely) shake loose from the revolutionary aspirations relegated to the anxious recesses of deep dreaming.

The aesthetic incoherence symptomatic of the struggle between consciousness and revolution is dramatically enacted by Martin Delany's *Blake; or, The Huts of America* (1859–62).[20] Not only does the novel seemingly lack a conclusion (the editor of the *Anglo African Magazine*, announcing the 1859 serialization of *Blake*, promised eighty chapters, only seventy-four of which currently exist), but the text's historical conflations, stylistic extravagances, and at times implausible plot give it the fantastic texture of romance.[21] The aesthetic infelicities of Delany's novel perhaps register the author's frustration at how few "realistic" narratives allow for the revolutionary outcomes he proposes. Delany's free black hero, Henry Blake, vows to foment slave revolution in the United States and Cuba after his wife is sold to Cuban slaveholders, and he spends the majority of the novel organizing that culminating event. Repeatedly, however, Delany takes readers to the brink of insurrection, only to leave us hanging. While it is possible that *Blake*'s revolutionary conclusion comes in missing chapters, I agree with Robert S. Levine's shrewd conjecture that Delany would more likely have ended the novel "with a series of relatively nonviolent scenes that enabled Blake to emerge at the helm of a regenerated society in which blackness is seen not as an exclusive or essential good but as equally worthy (or unworthy) as whiteness."[22] Delany's novel is thus an accurate reflection of the United States itself, begun in a moment of revolutionary indignation, the democratic implications of which could be contained only by translating collaborative agency into hierarchical leadership and by transforming efforts to change institutions so as to better meet the needs of citizens into a program of "uplift" that changes the needs of citizens in order to better serve institutions. Reflecting these transformations, the goals of the novel, as Levine acknowledges, "seem relatively limited."[23]

The most frustrating aspect of *Blake*, however, is how much effort goes into limiting its outcomes. The novel's hero works tirelessly to replace revolution with institutionalism, a transformation signaled by the changing meaning of "organization" over the course of the novel. The center of Blake's revolutionary plans, what he defines as the "good, general secret understanding" (64) among slaves, "organization" appears at first as merely a vehicle toward larger revolutionary goals. Over the course of the novel, however, "organization"—what Levine calls Delany's "black Freemasonry"[24]—becomes an end in itself. The institutional drive of Delany's "organization" directs revolutionary impulses away from material equality and toward internalized "readiness." But "readiness" within Blake's organization, as within institutionality more generally, is a never-ending business (as Blake tells one of his followers, "you must now go on and organize continually" for a de-historicized and delocalized scheme "adapted to all times and places" [40]), orienting citizens always toward institutional abstraction and its horizon of futurity where, like the "lost chapters" of *Blake* itself, revolution hovers as the (never recovered) fulfillment of a labor that in and of itself proves unsatisfying.

Institutionalism's payoffs are unequally distributed, however, establishing certain people as leaders in hierarchical relations to others.[25] Blake's status as leader relies on a possessive logic that allows him alone to know the revolutionary plan in its entirety. " 'The plans are mine,' " he tells his followers, " 'and you must allow me to know more about them than you' " (38). More subtly, however, Blake himself becomes the embodiment of institutionality, which relies on an abstraction beyond historical locality. Blake moves across the United Stats, in the course of the novel's first volume, with a speed that defies plausibility, participating in historically distinct events.[26] In putting together his "organization," in short, Blake *becomes* an institution, abstracted beyond the superstitious and regional practices of place and the physical finitude of time. As Blake tells his adherents, " 'The scheme is adapted to all times and places' " (41), and so, apparently, is its leader. Leadership and institutionality become one and the same, whereas the majority of "followers" become bound by their partial knowledge, their historical and regional specificity, to a locality and an embodiment that Blake himself transcends.

By forming his own institutional transcendence in opposition to his compatriots, however, Blake threatens to short-circuit their motivations for participation and hence for revolution. The African Americans Blake meets in the novel's first volume do not seem to want to be lifted out of their time and place (as demonstrated by the difficulty Blake has convincing his first potential recruits, Mammy Judy and Daddy Joe, to flee with him to Canada). On the contrary, they seem content to work out structures—gossip networks, diversionary festivals, religious meetings—*within* the local conditions that shape their lives. To say this is not to argue that the novel's African Americans are content to be slaves but, rather, that if people are taken out of the social conditions within which they have framed agency (however limited), they must be permitted to generate alternative forms of participation or else they have no choice but to follow. Once revolution is misconceived *as* institutionality, however, citizens find themselves needing to disavow the very locality that marks them as *counter-institutional*. The irony is that Blake undertakes his "organization" largely to remedy the passivity generated among slaves by Christian preachers who encourage them to "stand still" and wait for the Lord's deliverance. By substituting organized revolution with himself as the messiah, Blake has provided his followers with a more self-satisfying mode of identification (if Blake could become a messianic leader, why not them?) without changing the structures that made slaves passive in the first place.

While Blake and his followers find themselves sacrificing their participatory agency, however, they are seemingly compensated by the promise of coherent personhood. By offering himself as an insurrectory imago, with which his followers can identify as a means of uplift, Blake seeks to restore to his black followers, as Levine contends, "a sense of their glorious potential as a unified people."[27] What makes the members of the "organization" function as "a people," the novel suggests, is not their shared commitments and strategies for revolution, but their race, which removes the differences of experience (of location or history) in favor of an abstract signifier derived from none but applied to all. Race, in short, becomes institutionality interiorized, as Delany makes clear toward the conclusion of the novel's second volume. No sooner is the hierarchical structure of the "organization" codified with Blake's appointment as commander-in-chief than dissent arises. A number of the women present on this occasion "instantly commenced whispering," thereby interrupting the "official" proceedings. Speaking for her "female colleagues," Madame Cordora announces that she " 'should like to be relieved of a difficulty' " (257). The women, being Catholic, are troubled by the ecumenical rituals solemnizing Blake's appointment. In response, Blake asserts that any true revolutionaries " 'would discard a religion, tear down a church, overthrow a government, or desert a country, which did not enhance their freedom' " (258). To achieve revolution, Blake tells Madame Cordora, black revolutionaries must follow " 'no existing organization, secret, secular, nor religious; but originated by ourselves, adopted to our own condition, circumstances, and wants, founded upon the eternal word of God, and impressed upon the tablet of each of our hearts' " (258). Madame Cordora is satisfied, until, that is, the Cuban poet Placido proclaims that slaves must be set free by " 'Ethiopia's sons' " (260). Madame Cordora again demands, " 'Are not some of us left out in the supplication, as I am sure, although indented together, we are not all Ethiopians' " (260). The poet responds that those gathered are " 'necessarily implied in the term, and cannot exist without it' " (260).

Throughout the scene, Madame Cordora clings tenaciously to the locality of dissent. Where one lives, one's national origin, gender, or religion: these, for Madame Cordora, are not counter-revolutionary obstacles to the supposed unity of "blackness," but competing forms of identification that disrupt and challenge the applicability of institutionalized identity. Despite Blake's rhetoric of collective agency (" 'organized by ourselves, adopted to our own condition, circumstances, and wants' "), the "blackness" he espouses leaves Madame Cordora no public role (she can speak only in interruption, not as an "official" party in the ritual of leadership).[28] The fact that the women's dissent rises "instantly" with Blake's ascendancy suggests, furthermore, that any attempt to enforce an abstract identity that subsumes all other forms of life narrative ("naturally implied in the term, and cannot exist without it") produces a constitutive excess that challenges Blake's claims to institutional unity.

It is questionable, then, whether Delany's use of "blackness" as an institutional identification "makes pragmatic sense," as Levine contends, "as a way of mobilizing blacks for united oppositional action,"[29] for those participants must either remain coded as "local" in ways that, Blake admits, prevent them from revolutionary action or else identify with a totalizing name that denies the experiential histories that make participation desirable in the first place. As

Danielle S. Allen writes, "The effort to make the people 'one' cultivates in the citizenry a desire for homogeneity, for that is the aspiration taught to citizens by the meaning of the word 'one' itself." Allen counters the desire for oneness with "an effort to make the people 'whole,'" which "might cultivate an aspiration to the coherence and integrity of a consolidated but complex, intricate, and differentiated body."[30]

Levine's claim that Madame Cordora's "embrace of her 'blackness' should . . . be viewed in not only mystical but also political terms as a sign of her solidarity with the oppressed" (192) misses the important fact that—as a Cuban facing colonization, a woman in a patriarchal hierarchy, and a Catholic in an anti-religious "organization," Madame Cordora is *already* among the "oppressed," solidarity with whom she expresses when she raises her objections to Blake's appropriative rituals. To be oppressed, and to *identify* with the oppressed, are, however, different things. The former offers Madame Cordora and the other women a communicative network, a position of public challenge, and an experiential alternative to Blake's "organization." Identification *with* oppression —insofar as that is coded as institutionalized "blackness"—leaves Madame Cordora silent, marked as the superstitious bearer of locality who must be "educated" in the abstractions of organizational uplift. If, however, Madame Cordora is what Frye calls a "tricky slave," the embodiment of romantic interruption who stalls the comic resolutions of institutional hierarchy, then Delany's ambivalence toward his own nationalism and its interpellative interiorizations ("impressed upon the tablets of each of our hearts") suggests that the radical incompleteness of *Blake*—turning Madame Cordora's repeated interruptions into a formal principle—may be the surest sign of the author's imaginative romanticism.

The "tricky slaves" in *Blake* must oppose not only identification, but a more debased form of romanticism itself, what the author often presents in his novel as "civility." While Delany uses "romance" as a synonym for "civility" in *Blake*, the latter functions very differently from the dissenting interruptions written of by Frye and embodied by Madame Cordora. Civility functions throughout *Blake* as a force of self-regulation, imposing politeness where rationality fails and generating a seeming "successful harmony of sentiment" (197). The two versions of romance come into sharp contrast toward the conclusion of the first volume, when an intoxicated and heavily armed man interrupts one of Blake's organizational meetings, insisting that the revolution must occur that night or never. Denouncing the man as an "infuriated" drunkard (105), the "organization" expels him into the street, where he cries, "'Insurrection! Insurrection! Death to every white!'" (106), thereby alarming the already anxious authorities, who declare martial law. Even before this overreaction, however, the expulsion of the "drunkard" signifies how little the whites have to fear, for Blake seeks to imitate the nationalist structures put in place by white Americans (including the disenfranchisement of those seen as "intemperate" by nature of their demands) rather than to overthrow it.[31] The equivalence established by the novel between demands for revolution *in the here and now* and other forms of intemperance suggests that self-regulating "civility"—the imperative, as Placido says, to " 'make ourselves respected' " (263)—forestalls *both* "oneness" and "wholeness" in the novel. Revolutionary demand must be expelled to establish institutional stability in the form of self-regulatory uplift modeled as identifications with sanctioned modes of embodying "blackness." Inviting potentially revolutionary citizens to identify with a structure derived from white nationalism, romance as civility thus forecloses romance as interruption, substituting decorum for demand and self-management for collective action.

In its most extreme form in the novel, civility becomes the romantic sublime, suffusing an urban rather than a more traditional natural vista, but filling the viewer with a similar combination of awe and dread. That urban sociality should become sublime, in *Blake*, suggests the deeply ambivalent sensations brought about within the insistently sociable revolutionary as he gradually withdraws behind the structure of institutional—and literary—civility. When Blake enters New Orleans, for instance, he describes the city in terms both romantic and distancing:

> The season is the holidays, it is evening, and the night is beautiful. The moon, which in Louisiana is always an object of impressive interest, even to the slave as well as those of enlightened and scientific intelligence, the influence of whose soft and mellow light seems ever like the enhancing effect of some invisible being, to impart inspiration—now being shed from the crescent of the first day of the last quarter, appeared more interesting and charming than ever. (98)

The attribution of human initiative ("some invisible being, to impart inspiration") to the romantic sublime leads Blake to an obsessive observation of civility: he overhears "civil banter," in which citizens "of delicate civility" are "all fondly exchanging civilities" (99). While for Blake romantic civility becomes proof of enhanced liberty—"Freedom seems as though for once enshrined by her sacred robes and crowned with cap and wand in hand, to go forth untrammeled through the highways of the town" (99)—the increasingly metaphorical constructions of agency (who embodies the "freedom" that goes "untrammeled" through New Orleans's streets?) suggest how civility replaces the often unruly participation characteristic of "revolution" even while supplementing it with the promise of uplift. "Light, of necessity, had to be imparted to the darkened regions of the obscure intellects of the slaves," Delany writes, "to arouse them from their benighted condition to one of moral responsibility, to make them see that liberty was legitimately and essentially theirs, without which there was no distinction between them and the brutes. Following as necessary consequence would be the destruction of oppression and ignorance" (101). The image of light streaming into benighted ignorance echoes the highly stylized description of the moon illuminating New Orleans, suggesting that the instruments of "uplift" that create civil "readiness" are as much the product of romantic convention as is the trope of lunar inspiration.

Although *Blake* must disavow certain intemperate demands and superstitions in favor of an image of social harmony represented by the civil sublime, however, the novel cannot entirely abandon alternative forms of sociality. Rather, it must maintain them as a critical source of authenticity, cleansed of their dissent and represented as "culture."[32] While such cultural traces might seem important opportunities for public counter-knowledge, they more often serve in the novel as spaces of private retreat, not public—and hence, not revolutionary—participation.[33] As such, "culture" functions vis-à-vis the civil sublime in much the way privacy functions in Habermas's account of public civility: as a staging ground, a place of emotional expurgation and of informed *readiness* to enter the public sphere. This becomes most evident when Blake enters the Dismal Swamp, where he encounters African conjurers who teach him their magic and name him as one of their leaders.[34] Even as Blake uses the "mystical, antiquated, and almost fabulous" (112) powers of the conjurers, they remain *too* local, too rooted in superstition and memory, to permit them to be assimilated into the romantic civility that leads Blake not to revolution, but to rejuvenated federalism. From the Dismal Swamp, Blake moves to Washington, D.C., where the past represented by the conjurers mixes with the equally fabulous futures of nationalism to produce the all-too-real institutional authority of Congress. "Some of the proudest American statesmen in either House of the Capital," Delany reports, "receive their poetic vigor of imagination from the current of Negro blood flowing in their veins" (116). Although he also realizes that the nation's flag displays "stars as the pride of the white man, and stripes as the emblem of power over the blacks" (117), Blake is willing to use the "magic" of the conjurers to render Congress imaginatively flexible enough to abolish slavery, without bringing the conjurers themselves to the state of what Levine calls "representative identity," a place only Blake can occupy. For like Congress (the ultimate House of Representatives), Blake embodies a "mixing," authenticated by his (always already renounced) knowledge of black "culture" and uplifted by his (never quite achieved) identifications with white institutionality. If Blake is a sympathetic character, it is because this position—caught alone between the past of locality and the future of institutionalism—is the ubiquitous state of modern citizenship.

Even before entering the Capitol, however, Blake understands that to reproduce the "representativeness" of identity, he must subordinate other classes of persons, reproducing, as Reid-Pharr notes, the slave–master dynamic he nominally escapes.[35] After Blake's discussion with several slave women, for instance, Delany describes them as a "squad of young maiden slaves" in relation to whom Blake becomes "the singular black man" (79). Singularity requires some undifferentiated "squad," as mobility requires stasis, and civility replaces "fabulousness." Blake's rise to leadership not only leaves his followers behind, then, it requires the "culture" that marks them with "foolishness and stupidity" (136). In the end, though, Delany acknowledges that those who are "more civil" are also "more easily governed as a race than Anglo-Americans" (186). Governed *as a race* is the crucial phrase here, for it is Blake's marking of "blackness" as simultaneously more docile, more identified with the ignorant past, *and* more cultural that makes would-be revolutionaries into civil citizens.

Locking citizens into prescribed identifications while discrediting most others, race's inner life forestalls the ability to bring alternative visions of social relations to the public sphere. It is hardly surprising, then, that *Blake* concludes, as Eric J. Sundquist observes, "in a state of paralysis."[36] Paralysis, however, is also a nervous state, characteristic of those whose participatory volition is curtailed by the isolating forms of interiority, "consciousness" being one of the strongest. Throughout *Blake*, slaves are described as living in a nervous state. Slave owners, of course, make slaves nervous—as when, early in the novel, Mammy Judy and Daddy Joe are "anxious spectators" (14) of events on the Franks plantation—but just as often it is Blake who produces "anxiety." Slaves in Louisiana await Blake's arrival "anxiously" (69), while later slaves are "anxious listeners" (109). Wives and mothers, in particular, watch Blake's movements with "anxiety" (84), directly affected by actions they are not permitted to shape. Slaves are anxious not only because of the monumental nature of Blake's proposal and the risks involved, but also because they understand better than most the nearly impossible border between affect and action, which Rube can cross only through literal hemorrhage. Telling his wife of the tortures he intends to inflict on Blake should the latter protest the sale of his wife, Stephen Franks says, " 'I'll soon settle the matter with him, should he dare show any feelings about it!' " (9). To "show feelings" is to risk physical brutality, yet to keep those feelings hidden—preferable, but far from ideal—is to produce the inner trembling of anxiety and, ultimately, paralysis.

Anxiety often gives way, however, to its palatable twin, desire, and this is certainly the case in *Blake*, in which desire is incited only to be contained by the novel's third form of "romance": the interlocking of interiority and institutionalism that commonly codes national belonging as heteronomative convention.[37] Finding his lost wife, Maggie, Blake listens rapturously to "the sacred and impressively novel words, 'I join you together in the bonds of matrimony!'" (156). "Novel" functions here in the paradoxical senses of new and predictable, the combined effects of novels, which end, at least in America, not in revolution but in the satisfactory establishment of a romantic privacy coded as social justice: "The long-desired end being attained—the object of his desires, his wife found, her freedom obtained, and having secured this simple Magna Charta of her liberty, Henry [Blake] was among the happiest of men" (187). The novel form allows Delany to conflate political and personal, Maggie and the Magna Charta, until the first comes to seem a suitable substitute for the second. The same pattern concludes the second volume. On the brink of revolution in Cuba, Blake's followers go sentimental—"The greatest emotions were frequently demonstrated, with weeping and other evidence of deep impressions made" (259)—and the revolutionary plot gives way to what Reid-Pharr calls "a fit of marriages."[38] "In the midst of revolutionary movement," Delany writes, "there are sometimes the solutions worked out to other problems than that of the political destiny of a people." True enough, but the question remains: does the "political destiny of a people" ever get worked out, or is it replaced by the happily ever after of romance? "The consummation of conjugal union is the best security for political relations," Delany answers, "and he who is incapable of negotiating to promote his own personal requirements might not be trustworthy as the agent of another's interest; and the fitness for individuals for positions of public import, may not be misjudged by their doings in their private affairs of life" (275).

Whether or not one thinks, as most of *Blake*'s critics do, that Delany wrote a more effective novel by holding off on revolution, the fact remains that, having made heteronormative romance seem "the best security for political relations," Delany forestalls not only insurrection, but citizenship itself.[39] Citizen participation—which requires the ability to make unprecedented, "fabulous" (113) conjurations of the not yet real—gives way in *Blake* to interiorizing sentiment, as conventional intimacy is the only space for "the human heart" to manifest "its most delicate sympathies," to pour "forth from its hidden recesses those gifts of God to man; the Divine sentiment of benevolence, philanthropy and charity in tender accents of compassionate regard in Christian solicitude" (205–206). The give and take of public debate gives way to normative intimacy and representative nationalism, and Blake, named "General-in-Chief of the army of emancipation" (241), has secured his place in both. From that point forward, revolution is a purely literary matter, a conclusion Blake foreshadowed when he proclaimed, early in the novel, "Insurrection shall be my theme!" (44). While this may make him a good leader, it makes him a bad citizen. During all moments of potential insurrection in the novel, Blake remains, as he does during the uprising on board the slave ship *Vulture*, "strangely passive" (236).[40] Not only revolution is paralyzed; so, apparently, are its potential agents.

At the same time, however, *Blake* is a melancholy text, retaining elements of its romantic interruptions—and the alternative models of participation, of "moral responsibility" (101), they represent—right up to its conclusion. Some friends do continue to call Blake back to his revolutionary mission, as when Gofer Gondolier cuttingly uses an older black wisdom—which Blake dismisses as benighted ignorance—to mock the leader's dedication to deferral: " 'if a tiger, hyena, or any other wild beast should attack you, ought you to take its life immediately, or stop to argue the best method of getting rid of danger? "Self-preservation is nature's first law"; an old truth my grandmammy taught me many years ago when a child sitting in the chimney corner' " (310). Gofer pointedly underscores the disciplinary effects of civility, calling whites " 'educated devils that's capable of everything hellish under the name of religion, law, politics, social regulations, and the higher civilization' " (312). This is a lesson Blake once knew, declaring, " 'We want space for action—elbow room; and in order to obtain it, we must shove our oppressors out of the way' " (197). But revolution has become a "novel adventure" (137), more invested in civil identifications, however fictitious, than in romantic disruptions. Even as Blake surrenders to the civil sublime, however, Delany uses characters such as Madame Cordora and Gofer Gondolier to offer alternative models of participatory sociality, and it is in those portraits, perhaps, that the romantic possibilities of *Blake* linger.

Picturing Freedom: Hannah Crafts's The Bondwoman's Narrative

In her afterword to *Black Popular Culture*, Michele Wallace laments the lack of critical attention to "vision, visuality, and visibility" as means by which whites, through "an unrelenting and generally contemptuous objectification," have generated "meaning" for African American bodies.[41] Without an analysis of visual representations of race, Wallace warns, African Americans "are in danger of getting wasted by ghosts . . . , by effusions and visual traces that haunt us because we refuse to study them, to look them in the eye." Exemplifying the "revolution in vision" Wallace calls for,[42] Carrie Mae Weems's photographic exhibition "From Here I Saw What Happened and I Cried" (1995–96) features nineteenth-century and twentieth-century images of African Americans re-photographed, enlarged, and tinted an eerie red. The images are mounted in frames, whose glass is etched with text that calls attention to racial stereo-types, such as "SOME SAID YOU WERE THE SPITTING IMAGE OF EVIL" and "YOU BECAME MAMMIE, MAMA, MOTHER & THEN, YES, CONFIDANT-HA." The texts superimposed on the photos further name the disciplinary knowledges that render contempt "objective" ("YOU BECAME A SCIENTIFIC PROFILE," "A NE-GROID TYPE," "AN ANTHROPOLOGICAL DEBATE," "& A PHOTOGRAPHIC SUB-JECT") and codify race in a hierarchical visual structure (in which, for instance, the anthropologist, as viewer, has authority over the "negroid type," whose image is photographed, named, and given meaning).

At the same time as the superimposed texts saturate the underlying images with meaning (of race, of sexuality, of social position), the faces in Weems's portraits are opaque. Almost any image could be removed from its frame and placed under another text, to similar effect. This is perhaps part of Weems's point: there is no correspondence between the image and the meaning assigned to it, which serves the interests of the viewer rather than objectively naming any quality of the viewed. One label explicitly notes this opacity, stating, "BORN WITH A VEIL YOU BECAME ROOT WORKER JUJU MAMA VOODOO QUEEN HOODOO DOCTOR." The opacity of the face's surface—its veil—serves to rupture the corre-spondence between image and interpretation, between historical experience and the meanings that overtake and manage those experiences. At the same time, Weems, in challenging the power of stereotypes to fix and foreclose visual meaning, authorizes the contemporary viewer to see differently, to imagine other meanings for the photographs and, in the very act of proliferating mean-ing, to challenge the stronghold of singular interpretation over the signifying power of visual representation. Asking questions rather than didactically im-posing answers, Weems invites viewers, in her words, "to refigure and re-introduce the black subject to ourselves."[43] In short, Weems refuses to allow visuality to remain simply a mechanism of racism's control of bodies, insisting instead on the power of interpretation to generate new ways of occupying bodies and social relations.

Beyond refusing the imposition of definitive meaning by white interpretive authorities, the phrase "BORN WITH A VEIL" creates a space of black interiority as well. Behind the stillness of Weems's photographed faces lies a space of desire and rage, ambition and affect, the markers of a humanity denied by objectifying labels. Even Weems's title, "From Here I Saw What Happened and I Cried," insists on the connection between witnessing (seeing) and affect (crying), between vision and interiority, that points to the second absence Wallace names in her essay. "Parallel to the visual void in black discourse," Wallace writes, "and intersecting with it, is the gap around the psychoanalytic."[44] While Wallace leaves the connection unexplored, psychoanalysis's reliance on visual dynamics is clear, from Freud's Oedipal complex, beginning with the child's viewing of the primal scene and ending with the psychic equivalent of Oedipus's self-blinding, to Lacan's mirror stage, predicated on Narcissus's misrecognition of his image in the water. Both the Oedipal complex and the mirror stage are central to psychoanalytic theories of identification, the process through which the subject takes shape in relation to a seen Other (either the sexualized parent for Freud or the differentiated reflection for Lacan). In these conceptions of identification, what you see is what you *are*, vision apparently preexisting the interpellative moment in which spectacle is given meaning. Wallace's formulation of revolutionary vision—looking the traces of history "in the eye"—invokes a moment of identification as well, "history" here taking the form of a pictured face, of portraiture. Revolutionizing visual theory, however, allows viewers control over identification, refusing the "ghost" of identities that white-interpreted representation seeks to name and control.

Expanding Wallace's connection of identification and vision, "From Here I Saw What Happened and I Cried" adds to psychoanalysis an awareness that vision itself is framed by ideological narratives that attempt to determine the outcomes of identification by saturating images with supposedly fixed meaning (the meaning of "mother," of "different," of "self"). Inviting viewers to join in generating multiple interpretations, Weems allows them to reimagine identification as a variable project of creation rather than the foreclosing of imagination by identity's proper names. Drawing the veil between image and interpretation, Weems opens the possibility for transformation in the viewer as well. The opening of identification through a re-conception of visual meaning has particular implications for female viewers, especially in relation to images of black women. (The series begins and ends with the same image of an African woman in profile, arguably establishing her as the "I" of the title and hence the grounds for subjective identification in the series.) The visual theory of the Oedipal complex becomes particularly tricky for women, since their identificatory vision is, according to Freud, of the mother's "lack," granting the daughter a vision of nothing and, therefore, essentially a non-vision. For a woman to insist on vision in the moment of identification, as Weems does, therefore denies the misogynistic construction of womanhood as absence and insists on the material presence of women's experience as and of visual spectacle.

In the remainder of this chapter, I will explore the dynamics of vision and identification in an African American artist who reproduced portraiture not in photography, but in words (the common nineteenth-century practice of *ekphrasis*). In *The Bondwoman's Narrative*, Hannah Crafts, like Carrie Mae Weems, challenges the practices of visual speculation that posit a direct correspondence between outside and inside, what is shown on the surface (of bodies, texts, historical actions) and what those physical traces purport to reveal about obscure "insides" (character, psychology, meaning).[45] Foregrounding and resisting the panoptical regimes underlying slavery, Crafts echoes Frederick Douglass, who told of the overseer who slithered through the fields to spy on the slaves, and Harriet Jacobs, who bore a small hole in the wall of her cramped hiding place to watch her children play as well as to spy on her lecherous master, thereby reversing his scopophilic control of her body. In both narratives, whites justify their ownership of slaves by reading the brutalized actions produced by the deprivations of slavery as evidence of inner, racialized "character."

Crafts undermines the visual economies of slavery by thematizing the ruptures between representation and meaning, outer sign and inner truth. These moments of rupture occur in *The Bondwoman's Narrative* in the depictions of portraits, in which Crafts, appropriating the gothic convention of the portrait that reveals a hidden, usually horrible, truth, rendering the direct correspondence between outer signs and inner truth suddenly unfamiliar and unsettling, slavery's nightmarish uncanny. At the same time, Crafts refuses to abandon vision to the brutal economies of slavery. Rather, as a romantic writer and artist, she reclaims vision as a means for optimistic identifications that generate potentially more enabling, if (because) more fragmentary and patchwork, life narratives. Having troubled the visual economies that assert ownership of bodies in the presumed possession of the inner truth of images, Crafts reinscribes meaning not as a quality of the seen but as a practice of the seer, not as economic investment but as imaginative and often unpredictable identification.

To say that Crafts complicates the apparent correspondence between visual representation and inner truth is not to say that *The Bondwoman's Narrative* is unconcerned with the inner workings of affect and psychology. On the contrary, Crafts's complex affective responses to slavery—fraught with desire and disavowal, guilt and gall—suggest that writing was for her on some level a very personal effort at psychic resolution. *The Bondwoman's Narrative* explores a slave woman's desire for her absent mother and the consequent unpredictable identifications, especially with white women, that, as Jennifer Fleischner argues, characterize the narratives of many slave women.[46] Those narratives assume a natural identification between slave mothers and daughters, making black "identity" the psychic ground for which cross-racial identification is a mis-recognition. Such assumptions ignore not only the ruptures Crafts insists on between vision and meaning, but also the inscription of the oedipal narrative within a bourgeois domesticity forbidden to slaves. The "lack" represented for Freud by the mother's absent penis becomes enlarged in *The Bondwoman's Narrative* into the literal absence *of* a mother, a "lack" that propels Hannah not into psychic blindness, as it does Oedipus, but into a process of inventive identification based precisely in the creative possibilities of sight. At the same time, Crafts's narrative registers rage at the absent biological mother through Hannah's repeated disavowal of other black women and of the heterosexual romance plot that structures "womanhood" and hence the very domestic grounds of oedipal identification. Throughout the narrative, Hannah endeavors to *un*define herself racially through repeated *dis*identifications with other black—and, particularly, other escaped slave—women, giving rise to repeated expressions of rage and grief, which are recuperated only through a reunion with her mother that Crafts codes as fantastic and phantasmagoric.

The Bondwoman's Narrative startlingly depicts black betrayal as the result, not only of systems of distrust and disloyalty fostered by white owners and overseers, but also of the constitutions of a slave's psyche within disavowals of blackness. In these rageful moments, Crafts registers horror not simply at iden-tification with the wrong people, but with the process of identification itself. All identifications, as Crafts suggests in her critique of portraiture's capacity to represent the complexity of human desire and rage, is *mis*identification. At the same time, her narrative is suffused with desire, not for freedom or for a husband and children or even for restored maternity, but for an imaginative intimacy between women, particularly women of undecided racial identity. In this, Crafts seemingly echoes sentimentalism's espousal of "the female world of love and ritual."[47] Yet her desires are more sexual, more violent, and more aesthetic than sentimentalism has been credited with, possibly marking her erotic desire for women, but just as likely pointing to the eroticized drive toward imaginative collective invention that animates *The Bondwoman's Narra-tive* from beginning to end. In narrating these desires and disavowals, Crafts offers what is to my mind the fullest known account of the psychology of race in antebellum America. In *The Bondwoman's Narrative*, "double consciousness" is not simply an ideological schizophrenia imposed *on* blacks, but a prolonged and painful ambivalence toward the uncertainties of identification, which complicates both the heroic disentanglements from slavery characteristic of slave narratives and the purity of sentiment ("right feeling") espoused by fictions such as *Uncle Tom's Cabin*. *The Bondwoman's Narrative* insists, then, on having it both ways: narrating the psychological dynamics of slavery and freedom while simultaneously noting how race and gender block the "truthful" confessions of inner life—of identification, affect, and desire—on which psychology depends. Even while Crafts invites readers to trust in pictures ("I will let the reader picture it all to his imagination," the novel's final sentence declares [239]), she shows how opaque portraits are, especially those that "picture forth" identity's inner truth.

Throughout *The Bondwoman's Narrative*, vision is racialized. From the beginning, Hannah names among the characteristics that mark her as a slave, despite her white skin, her "fancy [for] pictorial illustrations and flaming colors" (6). Among the slaves, she reports, "It was our privilege to look and listen. We loved the music, we loved the show and splendor" (29). An early clue is given to the slave ancestry of Hannah's new mistress when Hannah notes the apparently white woman's "habit . . . of seeming to watch everybody as if she feared them or considered them enemies" (27). While slaves' vision brings them pleasure, the gaze of masters and overseers, scopophilic and panoptic, makes slaves feel "surrounded by watchful prying eyes" (207). Even while their eyes pry, however, whites in *The Bondwoman's Narrative* remain visually inept, exemplified by Hannah's master, who is "not given to habits of observation" (35). Clear racial demarcations arise, then, from visual practices, with pleasure and insight belonging to blacks, invasive prying and metaphoric blindness to whites.

Just as the racial identities of plantation populations were notoriously murky, however, so *The Bondwoman's Narrative* troubles the clear distinctions between blindness and insight, most obviously in Crafts's gothic antagonist, Mr. Trappe, who speculates not only by trading in the bodies of slaves, but also by seeing beyond appearances to the secrets contained in the heart's interior. "He loved to probe the human heart to its inmost depths," Hannah reports, "and watch the manifestations of its living agony" (108). Insight, for Trappe, is a potent means of possession, causing Hannah to feel "that in both soul and body I was indeed a slave" (108). Making it his business to trace the hidden genealogies of wealthy women "far back to a sable son of Africa" (98), Trappe marshals the "hidden" indeterminacies of antebellum race to the detriment not of the slaveholders who insist on the purity of racial identity, but of their creolized victims.

Although Trappe turns insight into a cynical and destructive instrument of possession, his production of interiority and its subsequent mastery are subtly aestheticized, resting on a logic of visual representation that begins with the supposedly direct correspondence between surface and depth, which is then extended to the correlation of appearance and character, action and consent. While his traffic in deceptive appearances might have rendered Trappe skeptical about representation's evidentiary status, on the contrary a portrait's ability to speak the truth of its subject's racial identity grants him his extraordinary power over Hannah's mistress. Showing her a small portrait, Trappe inquires,

> "Do you know it."
> "It resembles me," I answered "though I have never sate [sat] for my likeness to be taken."
> "Probably not, but can't you think of some one else whom it resembles."
> "The slave [Charlotte] Susan."
> "And it was hers, and it is yours, for never did two persons more resemble each other." (47)

The power of visual speculation that gives Trappe the confidence to assert a correspondence between representation and truth, genealogy and identity, robs Hannah's mistress of her power to consent. Her "likeness" is "taken" in both senses. Through visual speculation, she is "seen" to be the equivalent of her representation, a literalness that allows Trappe, in a dynamic of economic speculation, to "take" her for all she has, thereby ending her power of self-determination. At the same time, mirroring the matrilineal logic of slavery (in which children inherit the status of their slave mothers), Trappe asserts a correspondence not only between representation and identity, but also between generations. The over-determined moment of legal and oedipal identification, in which the slave daughter necessarily becomes the "likeness" of her mother, here rests on a representational correspondence that the ambivalent language of only ever proximate equivalence—"likeness," "resembles"—challenges.

The connections Trappe establishes between fixed visual correspondence, generational transmission, and ownership extend far back in the novel's pre-history, costing white as well as black characters their self-determining consent. In the novel's first chapter, Crafts introduces the control masters claim over dynamics of representation and meaning, a control central to the rituals of display underlying the gallery of portraits that is the emotional center of the home of Hannah's master. Having hung his own portrait in the gallery along-side that of his wife, the original owner of the house, Sir Clifford De Vincent,

> denounced a severe malediction against the person who should ever pre-sume to remove them, and against any possessor of the mansion who being of his name and blood should neglect to follow his example. And well had his wishes been obeyed. Generation had succeeded generation, and a long

line of De Vincents occupied the family residence, yet each [one] inheritor had contributed to the adornments of the drawing-room a faithful transcript of his person and lineaments, side by side with that of his Lady. (16)

De Vincent's "malediction" comprises, in effect, three imperatives: first, to "truthful" transcription (the imperative to picture oneself forth); second, to static correspondence between generations (a denial of the possibilities of history producing difference or change); and third, to heterosexuality (a prediction that every master will have a lady who can guarantee the generational transmission of property).

Hannah sets to work undermining the speculative assumptions of the malediction, however, rendering romantic their supposedly "realist" correspondences. Sent to check arrangements before the arrival of the new mistress, she pauses in the gallery before the portraits and muses,

> There is something inexplicably dreary and solemn in passing through the silent rooms of a large house, especially one whence many generations have passed to the grave. Invariably you find yourself thinking of them, and wondering how they looked in life, and how the rooms looked in their possession, and whether or not they would recognize their former habitation if restored once more to earth and them. Then all we have heard or fancied of spiritual existence comes to us. (14–15)

Hannah's meditation seems to credit De Vincent's assumption that future generations will still possess, visually, their belongings, the generational transmission of property carried out reproductively by descendants whose racial purity (i.e., their whiteness) is clearly pictured forth. At the same time, no sooner does Hannah report De Vincent's phantasmagoric prediction than she introduces the possibility of *mis*recognition, that spectacle will not produce clear possession. Here Crafts establishes an important pattern, at once social and aesthetic, that she repeats throughout the novel: beginning with an assertion of exact correspondence (fancied images *are* past generations) tied to possession (members of previous generations gaze on their belongings), Crafts subordinates possession to "fancy" (viewership), giving rise to a moment of failed recognition (the possibility that things might not look the same across time) that in turn generates imaginative speculation ("all we have heard or fancied"). The result is that "inner-ness" is still possible (Hannah uses this scene, after all, to express her own ambivalence about the mistress's arrival and her desire and resentment about the wealth exhibited in the mansion's furnishings), but is separated from direct correspondence to visual "outsides" and is made, instead, the terrain of imagination, now the property of viewers, not of owners. Putting possession in the eye of the beholder, this scene tellingly inverts slavery's usual dynamic, making the owners the viewed, slaves, the viewers. This process, more than "race," "generation" or "possession," Crafts makes instinctual: "a supernatural thrill pervades your frame, and you feel the presence of mysterious beings. It may be foolish and childish, but it is one of the unaccountable things instinctive to the human nature" (15). Slaves' instinctual vision, as Hannah demonstrates, is invested not in finding meaning contained in the spectacle but, rather, in the creation of images to articulate slavery's unspeakable ambivalences, its haunting ghosts.

Slavery is haunted, first and foremost, by its attachment of speculative vision and ownership. Hannah manifests the literalizing gaze of white masters by turning their eyes into cold, unfeeling monuments, attesting to the lack—of imagination, of affect, of compassion—at the heart of white self-representation. "Memories of the dead give at any time a haunting air to a silent room," she says. "How much more this becomes the case when standing face to face with their pictured resemblances and looking into the stony eyes motionless and void of expression as those of an exhumed corpse" (16). Again, however, a slippage between representation and interiority opens the possibility for imaginative transformation on the part of the viewer. "But even as I gazed the golden light of sunset penetrating through the open windows in an oblique direction set each rigid feature in a glow. Movements like those of life came over the line of stolid faces as the shadows of a linden played there" (16). Under Hannah's gaze, the portraits become relaxed, gracious, dimpling with smiles. Relieved of the burden of exerting transparent overlap between appearance and identity, the portraits become, for Hannah, an instrument for imaginative identification, not as a coerced correspondence between inner essence and outer show, but as a moment of creative projection, a wish fulfillment on the part of the spectator rather than a victory of possession on that of the spectacle:

> Though filled with suspicious awe I was in no haste to leave the room; for there surrounded by mysterious associations I seemed suddenly to have grown old, to have entered a new world of thoughts, and feelings and sentiments. I was not a slave with those pictured memories of the past. They could not enforce drudgery, or condemn me on account of my color to a life of servitude. As their companion I could think and speak. In their presence my mind seemed to run riotous and exult in its freedom as a rational being, and one destined for something higher and better than this world can afford. (17)

By turning the presumed reality of representation into mystery, thereby undermining the power of men like Trappe to assert and manage her affective consent, Hannah opens up a world of possibility and entitlement centered on an interiority—"a new world of thoughts, and feelings and sentiments"—asserted without being "pictured forth," a potential now rather than a "nature" and hence a doom.

Whites remain oblivious throughout *The Bondwoman's Narrative* to the visual potential Hannah discovers, as when the head housekeeper, on discovering Hannah gazing at the portraits, scoffs, "Looking at the pictures . . . as if such an ignorant thing as you are would know anything about them" (17). Lacking Hannah's imagination, whites remain haunted by the ambivalence of portraiture, as when her new mistress "passed on to examine beneath a broad chandelier the portrait of Sir Clifford. The image regarded her with its dull leaden eyes. She turns away and covers her eyes" (29). Desiring to pass for white by disguising her own racial indeterminacy, the mistress is terrified by the ambiguity of the portraits, and she can continue her masquerade only by imposing on herself the blindness associated with other whites in the house. The odd shift from past to present verb tense, giving the description the feel of stage direction, invites the reader into a moment of speculation as well, a meta-spectatorship in which, viewing the mistress viewing the portrait, we are invited to see her inability to see life in(to) the portrait as a prediction of her ultimate loss of control over the meanings permitted to her own "likeness." Unlike her mistress, Hannah does not turn away from the portrait or from the potentials of representation; rather, as the household celebrates the new mistress's arrival, "beyond them and over them, and through the mingled sounds of joyous mirth and rain and wind I saw the haughty countenance of Sir Clifford's [frowning] pictured semblance" (29). Crafts here puts the possibility of portraiture's exact correspondence to its subject under erasure, crossing out "frowning" (which would treat the picture as the face itself) and substituting in its place "pictured semblance," a phrase that again inserts representation's only proximate relation to what it pictures forth.

The inability to engage representation creatively particularly haunts Hannah's master, who, rather than subverting the De Vincent imperatives to achieve his imaginative ends, defies them on their own terms. Striving "to obliterate some haunting recollection, or shun from his mental vision the rising shadows of coming events" (29), the master chooses "to dissent from this custom" and has his spouseless portrait hung without "the usual demonstration of mirth and rejoicing" (16). Thinking to kill his ancestor by refusing the imperatives the latter attached to representation, Hannah's master proves as literal as the original De Vincent, with whom he also shares an ignorance of the changes wrought on representation (and hence, on possession) by generational history. When De Vincent's portrait ominously crashes to the floor as the new mistress is welcomed to the house, Hannah speculates:

> Time had been there and solemnly and stealthily spread corrupting canker over the polished surface of the metal that supported it, and crumbled the wall against which it hang. But the stately knight in his armor, who placed it there had taken no consideration of such an event, and while breathing his anathema against the projector of its removal dreamed not of the great leveler who treats the master and slave with the same unceremonious rudeness, and who touches the lowly hut or the lordly palace with the like decay. (30)

Unable to recognize the structure supporting his house—or the labor supporting the wealth represented by that house—the master undermines his benevolent self-representation. Hannah's vision makes his fate clear: while she transforms the portraits of his ancestors into companionable images of mirth and kindness, her master's portrait "seemed to change from its usually kind and placid expression to one of wrath and gloom, and the calm brow . . . wrinkled with passion, the lips turgid with malevolence" (17). In the end, Hannah's master kills himself in the portrait gallery, manifesting the violence of speculation and the inflexible (fated) identifications it produces, while the portraits themselves, in a neat inversion of the slave trade, are "publicly exposed in the market and knocked down to the highest bidder" (194). Refusing to see life in the portraits for similar reasons that they refuse to see humanity in their slaves, white self-representation becomes implicated in the deadening objectifications of economic speculation.

Hannah understands her visual acumen as the result not of biology but of her placement within the social structures of slavery: "I have said that I always had a quiet way of observing things, and this habit grew upon me, sharpened perhaps by the absence of all elemental knowledge. Instead of books I studied faces and characters, and arrived at conclusions by a sort of sagacity that closely approximated to the unerring certainty of animal instinct" (27). Trained by slavery's hypocrisies to question the truth of surfaces, Hannah is able to discern, to her advantage, the distinction between appearances and character. It is in part that Hannah can see through the soft-spoken benevolence of white owners such as Mrs. Wheeler, who "was an adept in the art of dissembling" and whose "countenance would be the smoothest and her words the fairest when she contemplated the greatest injury" (203). Hannah also learns to manipulate appearances to deceive those who would control her, as when a slave trader declares, "'I believe that Hannah can be trusted. I almost know she can. I see it in her countenance, and I've got eyes that [most often] are seldom deceived in the human face'" (110). In the end, Hannah's divorce of character from appearance allows her to form unlikely alliances across lines of race and gender, as when she and her escaped mistress are recaptured and placed in a jail for safekeeping. Hannah quickly begins to form a bond with the ugly and apparently menacing jailor. "Notwithstanding the repulsiveness of his appearance," she reports, "there was something genial and clever in the man" (86), whose looks "concealed a really kind and obliging disposition" (86). Hannah's willingness to see through appearances opens up the possibility that white readers, too, will identify with the jailor's kindly "deeper" self, whatever their previous relation to histories of cruelty and constraint. So confident is she in the skills and advantages of imaginative vision that the last sentence of *The Bondwoman's Narrative* leaves the reader not simply to interpret, but to join Hannah in the act of imaginative creation—interpretation *as* portraiture—that allows identification across time and experience: "I will let the reader picture it all to his imagination and say farewell" (239).

For all Hannah's visual imagination, however, obscuring as it does the correspondence between "race" as maternal history and "race" as fated character, identification necessarily remains as critical to her story as it was for any slave attempting to negotiate between a bondage coded as black and a freedom coded as white. Despite Hannah's challenge to the surface significations that would give access to a slave's psychology, her narrative gives evidence of the often violent conflicts of identification and disavowal that make *The Bondwoman's Narrative* a deeply and disturbingly psychological text.

That conflict is given additional heat by the fact that most of the women with whom Hannah feels maternal identifications are white (or, in the case of her mistress, white-identified): from Aunt Hetty, who teaches Hannah to read; to her mistress, who treats Hannah and her other female slaves "rather as companions than servants" (35); to Mrs. Henry, who nurses Hannah when she is seriously injured in a carriage accident. Her identification with white mother figures complicates Hannah's desires, necessarily conflating the sympathy associated with maternal love and the possessive control associated with whiteness. It is this uneasy conflation that, in large measure, makes identification such a troubled and troubling process for Hannah. Describing her relationship to her fellow slaves, for instance, Hannah reports, "How much love and confidence and affection I won it is impossible to describe. How the rude and boisterous became gentle and obliging, and how ready all were to serve and obey me, not because I exacted the service or obedience, but because their own loving natures prompted them to reciprocate my love. How I longed to become their teacher, and open the door of knowledge to their minds by instructing them to read but it might not be" (12). Obtaining obedience and consensual labor through sympathetic kindness, Hannah echoes white slave owners such as Mr. Trappe, who explains his mastery over slaves in similar terms: " 'I have always found that the simplest request . . . goes farther than the loudest command. If a woman is stubborn or obstinate ask her a favor, coax her, flatter her and my word for it she'll be pliable as wax in your hands' " (89). More disturbing, Hannah's early experience of maternal manipulation seems to necessitate her over-identification with the slave-owning Mrs. Henry, whose "slaves were industrious and obedient, not through fear of punishment, but because [they felt it to be their duty] loved and respected a master and mistress so amiable and good" (123).

Predictably enough, then, Hannah's identification with white women leads her to disavow her association with her fellow slaves, even her supposedly maternal relationship to them. No matter how much power she gains from "mothering" slave children, her desire to *have* a mother predominates, and when her mistress offers her the chance to escape, Hannah quickly declares that, as much as she loves her "children," "I loved my mistress more" (50). Hannah's willingness to place herself under the control of white mothers soon teaches her a painful lesson in the controlling manipulations that underlie disciplinary intimacy. When, after several months of enjoying Mrs. Henry's benevolent care, the kindly white woman tells Hannah her new master is coming to claim her, Hannah begs Mrs. Henry to buy her, but she refuses, holding Hannah's request at bay with a hand "so white and soft and beautiful" (125). Hannah offers to work as a field hand for the Henrys, pleading, " 'all I ask is to feel, and know for a certainty that I have a home, that some one cares for me, and that I am beyond the gripe [grip] of these merciless slave-traders and speculators' " (125). Mrs. Henry shows her so much "sympathy and such an affectionate tenderness" that Hannah goes as far as to consensually surrender complete obedience: " 'You have no idea how good I will be, or how exactly I will conform myself to all your wishes' " (126).

One suspects that, at this point, Hannah is realizing that cold-hearted control is not that different from affectionate sympathy, the translation of power relations into interior states manipulated by whites to gain not only the obedience but the consent of slaves. To drive the point home, Mrs. Henry tells Hannah that on his deathbed, her father commanded his daughter's promise to avoid the slave trade in every form (127): " 'And now dear Hannah, do you wish me to break that vow?' she asked. I could not say that I did, and yet my heart rose against the man, who in a slave-holding country could exact such a promise" (127). Crafts subtly indicts white abolitionists whose benevolence caused increased hardship for slaves and the condition of whose consciences became of more importance than the material well-being of African Americans. Horrendous as its consequences are, the willful control of fathers, being explicit, allows Hannah a space of resistance; the benevolence of Mrs. Henry, by contrast, brooks no opposition, forcing Hannah, mortified when she sees the hurt her pleading has caused Mrs. Henry, to apologize for her desire for even the small comforts that labor on the Henry farm would afford (128). Earlier, when Hannah and her mistress stop during their flight from Trappe to rest in the home of a kindly man and woman who oppose slavery, the fugitives are seduced by their hostess's kindness into a momentary security—until, that is, they realize that the woman is Trappe's sister and that she is also boarding their tormentor in her house (62–63). Kindness and brutality, Hannah discovers, are sometimes kin. Although her experiences with mother figures occasionally work to her advantage, as when Aunt Hetty teaches Hannah to read, hides her in her flight from Trappe, and gives her the money to travel to the North, identification, as Hannah's experience with portraits has shown her, more often involves complicated networks of desire, control, and possession. When the identification is motivated by a need for maternal comfort, the process is all the more complex and disturbing. In opposition to the depiction of sympathetic white mothers in novels such as *Uncle Tom's Cabin*, in *The Bondwoman's Narrative* the hand that rocks the cradle literally rules the plantation, if not the world.

The ambivalence such complexities produce manifests itself in the astonishing violence visited—often by Hannah's narration itself—on potential mother figures. The hypocritical Mrs. Wheeler is transformed by Hannah into "a spoiled child that never cares for what it has, but is always wanting something new" (154). In the end, Mrs. Wheeler is done in by Hannah's "forgetfulness": having purchased for her mistress a face cream that turns Mrs. Wheeler's face black and causes her social ostracism (165–67), Hannah's unconscious (she neglects to inform Mrs. Wheeler of a story she has heard about this transformative cream) effects the "deserved punishment of an act of vanity" (169). Another white mistress who would flatter herself with benevolent self-representations is treated to a similarly violent outcome. Mrs. Cosgrove, whose insistence that her husband's slave mistress and their illegitimate baby be sold to a trader causes the distraught slave to kill the baby and herself, and who later has another of her husband's mistresses driven from the house (177–78), boasts of "'the consolation of having once performed my duty in giving freedom to a poor slave'" (183). In the end, however, Mrs. Cosgrove's suspicions drive her to an accident that leaves her permanently crippled, a violence that transforms her into an impotent "manifestation of love" (192).

Hannah's most ambivalent identification is with her Creole mistress (so ambivalent is Hannah toward this maternal figure that she never even grants her a name), to whom Hannah is bound by kindness, and by her identification with a fellow orphan whose "mother was a slave, then toiling in the cotton fields of Georgia" (44). This bond pulls Hannah into a plot that, due to her mistress's emotional and physical weakness and her attraction for the ubiquitous Trappe, places both women in grave danger. Once again, kindness gives way to a controlling cruelty on the mistress's part and a retributive violence on Hannah's. After living in an abandoned shack for several months, the mistress became "querulous and complaining, upbraided me as a cause of all her difficulties, and heaped the strangest accusations of conspiracy on my head. . . . After a while, my mistress became decidedly insane, and her insanity partook the most painful character. She fancied herself pursued by an invisible being, who sought to devour her flesh and crush her bones" (67). Despite Hannah's representation of her mistress as insane, she *is* being pursued by an "invisible being"—Trappe—and although Hannah bases her charge of insanity on her mistress's hysterical accounts of people devoured by swarms of rats, Hannah herself wakes to find "a huge rat . . . nibbling at my cheek" (79). Horror and desire join in the ambivalent drive toward a precariously ambivalent identification that keeps Hannah tied to a woman she now perceives—or imagines—as dangerously deranged.

The fictional nature of maternal identification, which conjures imagines of a mother she has never seen, allows Hannah the same imaginative control over the process of identification she asserts in relation to the portraits. This control is challenged, however, when Hannah's biological mother appears at the end of the narrative, "aged and venerable, yet so smart and lively and active, and Oh: so fond of me" (237). This largely implausible reconciliation—the two women happen to be living in the same New Jersey community, where the older woman recognizes certain distinctive marks on Hannah's body—is necessary to narrative closure, freedom being coded as successful generational identification, despite what Hannah has realized about the dangerous yoking of that narrative to slavery's possession of black bodies (or, more appropriately, of consensual labor through the management of desire). Perhaps because of this ambivalence, Hannah allows the resolution to occur off-stage, thus blocking the reader's identification with her supposed pleasure:

We met accidentally, where or how it matters not. I thought it strange, but my heart yearned toward her with a deep intense feeling it had never known before. And when we became better acquainted, and fonder of each other's society, and interested in each other's history, I was not half so surprised as pleased and overwhelmed with emotions to which I could find no name, when she suddenly rose one day, came to me, clasped me in her arms, and sobbed out in rapturous joy "child, I am your mother." And then I—but I cannot tell what I did, I was nearly crazy with delight. (238)

The odd phrase "crazy with delight," echoing as it does other moments in the text when maternal identification results in rage and madness, complicates the happy resolution that this reunion nominally signals.

Hannah's ambivalent identification with her biological mother raises a fascinating problem for theories of race and identification.[48] One might well understand Hannah's violent ambivalence toward other maternal figures, as I have suggested, as a result of her cross-racial identifications. This explanation would naturalize, however, her "proper" and already racialized status as "black." That is, the very difficulty Hannah has identifying with white women might seem to naturalize her self-understanding as "really" black. Yet "blackness" itself, as it is defined under slavery, is largely a product of the white imagination, and there is no more reason to assume that Hannah would have any less ambivalence toward the colonized subject position "black" than she does toward the mastering position "white." Her ambivalence toward her mother might therefore be understood not simply as the oedipal struggle endemic to the process of maternal identification, but also as a hesitation before the mirror (stage) of racial identification.

Not surprisingly, therefore, Hannah's relationship to blacks in *The Bondwoman's Narrative* is just as violently ambivalent as is her relationship to white mothers. In addition to what Henry Louis Gates Jr. notes as the house servant's elitist dismissal of field hands—Hannah refers to them as the "vile, foul, filthy inhabitants of the huts" (20–25)—her more subtle and prolonged antagonism seems reserved for figures with whom she *should* identify: other escaped slaves, especially women.[49] This antagonism is notably articulated in relation not to race, but to sexuality. The escaped slaves against whom Hannah expresses the most anger are women who escape in tandem with their husbands (or with men Hannah initially believes to be their husbands). Crafts uses the word "elopement" to describe escapes from slavery, figuring such escapes as movements into a romance plot that, for Hannah, is perilously analogous to slavery. "The slave, if he or she desires to be content," Hannah cautions readers, "should always remain in celibacy" (131). On some level, this may be a gesture toward white female readers, making their domestic imprisonment analogous to slavery and hence inviting sympathetic identification. Or it may be a realization, such as that expressed by Harriet Jacobs, that affectionate bonds become a means to hold women in slavery. However, one may also read this antagonism as another form of Crafts's intervention in generational transmission, as well as a potent exercise in the need to *disidentify* with black *and* white womanhood to open a space of imaginative freedom.

Hannah's ambivalence toward sexualized black women becomes apparent in her response to Charlotte, the slave of the benign Mrs. Henry, whose plot to escape with her husband, William, provokes Hannah's determination "to acquaint Mr. Henry of my suspicions" (135). "How could I acquit my conscience of cruelty and wrong if through discoveries made and information given by me the happiness of Charlotte and her husband should be destroyed, by his subjection for the second time into servitude" (136), Hannah rationalizes, yet it is worth noting that, in these ethical deliberations, Hannah expresses no concern for *Charlotte's* continued subjection under slavery. Hannah, who resolves to betray Charlotte to Mrs. Henry, soon finds that she has *over*-identified with white ownership, expressing more concern for Mrs. Henry's property than the white woman herself. Mrs. Henry tells Hannah, "having eyes we had better not see, and having ears we should not hear. That she hoped and trusted Charlotte's good sense would prevent her taking any rash or precipitous step likely to embarrass either, and that she should make it in her way to give the former a few words of cautious advice" (140). Charlotte, whose resolution to escape is formed by her "dear husband" but who also wants "a female friend to go with us, a good stout-hearted woman who can look danger in the face unblenched, whose counsel could guide us in emergencies, who would be true, and zealous, and faithful; my heart turned to you as the one" (141), hardly exemplifies the wife bound either to slavery or to heteronormative convention. Nevertheless, when Hannah argues with Charlotte's plan, William reprimands her, " 'There, Hannah, now don't dishearten my dear wife,' he said, drawing her affectionately to his bosom. 'Our minds are fixed; they cannot be changed, because we have no alternative. We must either be separated or runaway, and which think you, that an affectionate wife would choose?' " (142). In establishing Charlotte's choice as one between "wife" and "slave," William effectively determines Hannah's choice:

> During this long speech I had time to collect my thoughts, and I answered plainly that however just, or right, or expedient it might be in them to escape my accompanying their flight would be directly the reverse, that I could not lightly sacrifice the good opinion of Mrs. Henry and her family, who had

been so very kind to me, nor seem to participate in a scheme, of which the consummation must be an injury to them no less than a source of disquiet and anxiety. Duty, gratitude and honor forbid it. (142)

Naming the odd nature of her apparent identification—"And so to a strained sense of honor you willingly sacrifice a prospect of freedom" (142)—William fails to recognize how much his own definition of Charlotte as a "wife," hence figuring escape as a romantic "elopement," determines Hannah's distance from the unfortunate other woman.

A similar dynamic occurs when, after she *does* escape, Hannah, wandering in the woods, comes across a man and a woman, the latter sick with a fever. The tenderness between man and woman echoes the relationship between William and Charlotte, producing a similar crisis of identification in Hannah:

Toward morning, however, the paroxysm of her fever subsided, and she sunk into a gentle slumber. Her companion folded her garments closely around her, and then stretching himself by her side seemed to prepare for repose. Presently my thoughts became confused, with that pleasing bewilderment which precedes slumber. I began to lose the consciousness of my identity, and the recollection of where I was. Now it seemed that Lindendale rose before me, then it was the jail and the white towers of Washington, but the scene all faded; for I slept. (215)

Finding that they are brother and sister, not lovers, Hannah befriends Jacob and helps him care for his sister, who soon thereafter dies.

"My dear sister," he said bending his mouth to her ear.
"I hear, but I can't see you. Is the sun arisin?"
"It is, it is."
"It [*sic*] see it now; it is comin, a light, a very bright light."
The sun came, the light arose, the light of righteousness.
Dead.

The ambivalence demonstrated by Hannah's abrupt announcement of the woman's death (and by Crafts's turning her subjective "I" into an objective "It") is detectable, as well, in her defensive digression into the unlikely subject of mourning conventions. Concluding, "We could weep in silence and privacy. Public opinion came not to dictate the outward expression of our grief" (220), Hannah, relieved that no one can see that she mourns *improperly*, opens the possibility that she did not mourn at all.

Hannah's guilt soon gives rise to self-retribution. Left alone with the corpse while Jacob hunts for food, Hannah reports, "I retreated to my hut in which the sad wreck of mortality lay stark, stiff, and immovable. Was it the presence of death, or that my nerves were weak and agitated, but a great and unaccountable terror seized me. I shuddered in every limb, great drops of sweat started to my forehead, and I cowed down in the corner like a guilty thing" (221). Hannah's guilt arises specifically from the unmourned corpse, who "seemed to leer horribly, to gibe and beckon and point its long skinny fingers towards me, and though I knew that this was all fancy, though I had sense enough left to perceive even then the absurdity of my fears I could not overcome them, I could not pray for the protection of Heaven; Heaven seemed to have turned its face against me" (222). Hannah seems to undergo a process not of mourning, but of what Freud describes as melancholia, the subject's inability to surrender a lost love object, aspects of whom the melancholic pulls into herself to preserve the presence of the lost love. While Freud's melancholia is an identification process necessary to the griever who faces disintegration, however, Hannah experiences it as a dynamic of forced merger. "The corpse seemed to rise and stand over me, and press with its cold leaden hand against my heart. In vain I struggled to free myself, by that perversity common to dreams I was unable to move. I could not shriek, but remained spell-bound under the hedious [sic] benumbing influence of a present embodied death" (222). Unable to free herself from enforced identification with a murderous identity, an "other" misunderstood as the "same," Hannah restores her equilibrium only by removing identification from the interior space of her psyche, making it "present embodied death" and thereby allowing her to narrate, and hence gain some interpretive control over, black womanhood.

Having disavowed her identification with black women and recognized the violent control instituted by her identification with white women, Hannah is left with a self-produced and imaginative identity pieced together, like *The Bondwoman's Narrative* itself, from historical events and fictional genres. Hannah learns to treat interior states the way she treats the portraits that are their representational equivalent: she takes a speculative freedom that refuses the direct correspondence between seeming and being. Yet the acts of imaginative freedom that divorce outer show from inner life risk accommodating the historical forces that insist on direct correspondences and clear identifications— the slave economy and the legal apparatus that upholds it—rather than working, materially, to change them. In this regard, Mrs. Wright, one of the most complex figures in the narrative, offers an important caution. Mrs. Wright—a white woman who is arrested when she helps a beloved servant, sent to the slave trader by Mr. Wright, escape—meets Hannah and her mistress when they are imprisoned by Trappe's agents. The aptly named Mrs. Wright seems in many ways a perfect candidate for Hannah's maternal identification. Although identified as white, she is an ideal example of Frye's "tricky slave." Like Hannah, she disrupts the chronological order necessary to generational descent, reporting, "'I cannot recall names and events in their proper places'" (81). Like Hannah, Mrs. Wright favors "habits of intimacy" (82) outside conventional domesticity, leaving her husband and children to help her beloved servant escape. Like slaves in general, she becomes the victim of social death: when, after an epidemic has killed her family and ruined their property, "she ceased to be spoken of even by those who had experienced the most of her kindness" (84). Above all, Mrs. Wright articulates more clearly than any character in *The Bondwoman's Narrative* the destructive hypocrisy that forces subjects "to profess approbation when you cannot feel it, to be hard when most inclined to melt; and to say that all is right, and good, and true when you know that nothing could be more wrong and unjust" (84), thereby rending outward show from inner truth, causing the psychic damage of slavery.

Oddly, Hannah does not identify with Mrs. Wright, however perfect her credentials, for Mrs. Wright offers a sad warning about the dangers of romantic imagination as a practice of freedom. By "constant habit and association," Hannah reports, Mrs. Wright transforms her cell into a luxurious palace, connecting it "with ideas of home, a home that the state with great trouble and expense prepared for her, even as it makes provision for its acknowledged head" (84). In the most perverse maternal identification in the narrative, Mrs. Wright tells Hannah, "'Very motherly and good is the state" (81). As "her eyes [wander] over the rough stone walls, and the high dark ceiling with an admiring and complacent look" (81), Mrs. Wright turns imagination into the most dangerous form of accommodation, the inverse of the white masters who would make it a tool of possession and control.

Despite her imaginative acumen, Mrs. Wright's palace remains haunted by the specter of slavery. Caught between outward show and inner desire, Hannah, however imaginative she is in her romantic interpretations, also remains haunted. Hannah purports not to believe in ghosts, boasting that, unlike other slaves, she rarely "gave way to imaginary terror. I found enough in the stern realities of life to disquiet and perplex, without going beyond the boundaries of time to meet new sources of apprehension" (132). Yet ghosts appear whenever Hannah confronts the violence done to women by men, as when the shack she and her mistress have been living in is haunted by "a beautiful girl" murdered inside (69). Ghosts also rise when Hannah encounters the bodily control of slavery, as when she tells Trappe, "'the thought of you must always be a haunting curse to my memory'" (108). In both cases, Hannah is haunted by the residual traces of identifications with victimhood—with womanhood and with slavery—that she is never able to shake. The association of haunting and identification becomes explicit when Hannah describes her mistress, caught like Hannah between whiteness and blackness, as struck "with horror of what she is" (96). Identifications haunt Hannah because they interiorize the material violence of slavery, individualized in the space of the slave's (un)consciousness. "I am superstitious, I confess it," she says; "people of my race and color usually are, and I fancied then that she was haunted by a shadow or phantom apparent only to herself, and perhaps even the more dreadful for that" (27). It is the inner turmoil of slavery interiorized—the violent splits of desire and disavowal—that is most troubling to Hannah, who, anticipating Franz Fanon's important work on the psychodynamics of race and colonialism, declares, "those who think the greatest evils of slavery are connected with physical suffering possess no just or rational ideas of human nature. The soul, the immortal soul must ever long and yearn for a thousand things inseparable to liberty. Then, too, the fear, the apprehension, the dread and deep anxiety always attending that condition in a greater or less degree" (94). Faced with these tumultuous and conflicting emotions, the slave woman can protect herself only by (over)insisting on the autonomy of interior states, showing, as Hannah does in her interpretation of portraits, that things—and people—are not always what they seem.

* * * * *

As romances, *Blake* and *The Bondwoman's Narrative* use interruption and disjuncture to challenge the inevitable status of both civility and identification. More powerfully, from the resulting moments of rupture both novels explore the imaginative alternatives possible for citizens forced into identities and institutions to which they did not consent and that erode—and often explicitly counter—their participatory agency in creating alliances and ways of life that challenge prevailing systems. In the end, though, romanticism is not enough, for in choosing their battles—civility on the one hand, and identification on the other—both novelists simply switch sides. Delany subverts a faulty civility to identify with white models of leadership, while Crafts subverts structures of identification, only to close her narrative with the most conventional forms of heteronomative civility. This crossing is almost inevitable, given the central place "consciousness" plays in (dis)organizing the lives of black citizens in antebellum America, drawing the seemingly impenetrable borders between interiority and social participation or, in their debased forms, identity and civility. In taking up consciousness, both authors put aside *revolution* in the sense not of a violent uprising, but of a collective self-determination that is, at times, disjointed, disruptive, and contentious. This revolution is precisely what the "tricky slave" promises in the moments when consciousness and civility break apart, when interruptions need no apologies. *Blake* and *The Bond-woman's Narrative* end by implicitly denying the possibility of public and collective democracy, the former by isolating "leaders" from subordinated "followers," and the latter by idealizing conventional privacy as the sole locus of freedom. Perhaps the "tricky slave," who, as Frye writes, is "glimpsed but never seen,"[50] can imagine only isolated and immanent moments of freedom, whose extension, as Hawthorne and Melville also discovered, would seemingly lead back to the fixity of identity or the abstraction of institutionality. In the world of the romance, at least, consciousness and revolution, the interiorizing labor of self-knowledge and the world-changing efforts of imaginative transformation, could rarely, if ever, coexist.

7

"I WANT MY HAPPINESS!" ALIENATED AFFECTIONS, QUEER SOCIALITY, AND THE MARVELOUS INTERIORS OF THE AMERICAN ROMANCE

The history of antebellum interiority is, in important ways, the genealogy of a phantasm. Spaces of bodily "depth," as the previous chapters demonstrate, were imagined through new systems of belief that resulted in fantasies of social relations located—nebulously, variously—inside the body. At the same time, however, fantasy itself became an object of ridicule, characterized as wasteful, impractical, and self-indulgent, the opposite of productive (and reproductive) self-management and civic-mindedness. These paradoxical systems of belief— in which social relations became knowable through fantastic interior states that were discredited precisely because of their basis in fantasy—severed the work of imagination (still available to citizens in interiorized forms of "unconsciousness" such as reverie, mania, melancholy) from institutional authority. Social visions involving the untried or the never before seen—what antebellum authors might have called the *marvelous*—became dismissible *as* fantasy, leaving sociality in the grip of a logic of the already tried and the conventional, codified in the legal system of precedent.[1] Because the imperative force of precedent relies on the implied threat that something untried will lead to anarchy and violence, however, innovation could not be forbidden but was relentlessly produced (as another form of reformability) so as to be discredited, made monstrous or, worse, ridiculous (the soap bubbles blown from the windows of the House of the Seven Gables by the ineffectual aesthete, Clifford Pyncheon).[2]

The denigration of the unprecedented not only limited the power to articulate social alternatives, but it also enabled the dismissive characterization of whole populations *as cultures* through their association with such forms of fictitious, fantastic, or even psychotic imagining: sentimental women, dreamy bachelors, superstitious African Americans, and the drunkards, libertines, or social climbers whose "manias" became symptomatic of addictive appetites. This purported divide between the practical and the marvelous separated particularized "cultures" from "the general public" by asserting strict boundaries between plausibility and implausibility, precedent and possibility, imperative and innovation. Just as dangerous, marvelous populations were characterized as melancholy, nostalgic, and infantile in ways that placed them in the always already un-present region of the vanished past. In contrast, those dedicated to the backward-gazing logic of precedent became, counter-intuitively, credited with the hopes of a productive (and reproductive) future. As institutionality placed agency in an always receding future, then, the denigration of fantasy pushed the demands represented by social vision irretrievably into the past.

What gets lost in this arrangement is the ephemerality and contingency of the present, the conditions that democratic sociality most requires. Only in the present can people interact in ways ungoverned by preconception ("precedent") or by faith in a future when wrongs will be righted by abstracted agency, eliminating the need for cooperative action in the present. A social present built on contingency (rather than precedent) and ephemerality (rather than permanence) might take us beyond the idealization of sameness (of identity or culture) or unity (of comfort or consensus), beyond, that is, institutionalism's demand for permanence, contractual commitment, and agency reduced to reformative self-management. Despite its disparagement as counter-precedent, the contingent, ephemeral, and innovative—the *marvelous*—sociality paradoxically draws on historical precedents, building on models offered by those excluded from public enfranchisement or simply bored by the narrow options provided by domestic interiority: the gossip networks of slaves and servants, the contingent privacies of the licentious, the political demands produced by immigrants in saloons, among others.[3] These systems are rich sources of social theory for those who aspire to relations shaped beyond the image and value of institutions. Of course, fantasy is not, in and of itself, a *social* solution: to believe it is would be to accept the interiorizing logic that moved social relations into the bodily interior, ensuring in the process that fantasy would begin to seem synonymous with sociality. Rather, fantasy is a placeholder, archive, and staging ground in a society where institutional authority is inaccessible to most citizens. Although fantasy may be a poor substitute for social action, the ridiculous, delusional, fantastic, or marvelous persist as important sites of inventive aspirations that take us beyond what *must* and toward what *might* be, a record of what citizens can do—and, indeed, are doing—to maintain inventive sociality despite their location in an institutionalized public and the interior states it mandates.

Perhaps no literary genre stages the struggle between precedent and fantasy as insistently as the romance, rarely credited, in its own day or ours, with *social* innovation. Romances are dismissed because of their traffic in interiority, what

Richard Chase calls the "underside of consciousness." Chase claims that romantic writers show little "command over political theory or, what is more useful to a novelist, the instinct to dramatize politics in action." At the same time, however, he contends that romances have a particular insight into the "inner facts of political life," which "have been better grasped by romance-melodramas" than by more realistic genres. More precisely, romanticism shows how politics began functioning *as* "inner facts"—indeed, as inner laws—through the interiorization of sociality.[4]

Rather than insisting, as Chase does, that the romance simply reflects a naturalized inner "consciousness," however, romanticism challenges the transformation of sociality into consciousness not by refusing interiority, but, rather, by taking it at its word. The "underside of consciousness" imagined by the romance is strategically different from the institutionalized and reformable interiority discussed in the preceding chapters. That interiority is, ironically, hardly interior at all but is repeatedly called to the body's surface to be read by those invested with authority by their knowledge of biological and spiritual precedent (past "proofs" of the transparency between bodily sign and inner truth). Although the logic of precedent made bodily signs into unchanging markers of inner meaning, interiority was necessarily constituted as changeable by the reformative regimes of self-management. Challenging the formative logic of institutionalized interiority, the romance reverses its terms: interiority became constant to the point of obsessive stubbornness, while outer signs submitted to a dizzying range of interpretations that made them anything but historically or socially unchanging. In the romance, the body's outer signs are now in continual flux, and its inner meanings remain purposefully opaque. For Hawthorne and Melville, the supposed transparency between outer signs and inner truth or "nature" was deployed to establish a fiction of institutionalized genealogy (if bodily resemblance establishes family relations, those relations guarantee the passage of family "nature" from the past into the future). Precedent (in the form of family resemblance) was not simply a legal concept, then; it was a restrictive *interior state*, forcing citizens conceived as primarily members of privatized families into patterns of repeated "nature" that thwarted the possibilities of alliance with people outside the class position signified and ensured by family "nature." The romance's challenge to the transparency between external signs and inner truth—the assertion that similar looks do not guarantee similar natures—leads, then, to a challenge to the legal logic of precedent in the form of a genealogical crisis. If outward resemblance cannot determine inner inheritance, the institutional logic of precedent—that the past will pass naturally into the future, whose character it determines—loses its foundational authority.

Freeing the present from the grasp of precedent not by challenging interiority, but by making the interior *so* deep that it becomes unreadable, *so* determinative that it cannot be reformed, the romance opens the innovative potential of the unforeseen, the unprecedented, the marvelous. And while these fantastic imaginings remain largely isolated in the intense privacy of the romantic interior, they also suggest new social arrangements, romanticism's queer sociality. In calling the romance's sociality queer, I do not mean necessarily to suggest anything about the sexuality of its participants, although their desires, affections, and pleasures are anything but heteronormative. Rather, I am contending that romantic sociality, built on contingency, ephemerality, fantasy, and opaque and irredeemable innerness, runs counter to and distorts institutionalized sociality and its supplemental interior states, readable and reformable, that have become synonymous with public civility in the United States.

In examining how the American romance queers hegemonic civility, I intend a corrective to some of the most inventive contemporary theories of democratic sociality. Danielle S. Allen, for example, contends that functional democracy must foster in citizens not a fear of the unknown, but a willingness to treat strangers *as* always potential friends. Returning citizens from frustrated alienation to trustful participation, according to Allen, requires that we acknowledge that all democratic actions require loss on the part of some people and that we clearly articulate the rationale for loss before asking for participants' consent. We must also, Allen argues, ensure that the same citizens are not consistently asked to sacrifice and must compensate loss with acknowledgment and honor.[5] Recognizing and remedying the alienating distrust that arises from the unequal distribution of sacrifice is important to the social vision of the antebellum romance. Hawthorne's *The House of the Seven Gables* builds a sociality based on affection and respect generated among citizens who recognize in each other the extraordinary and unjust sacrifices each has made while also allowing members to remain "strangers," unknown on important levels to each other.

Allen's argument assumes, however, that sacrifice, sometimes quite extraordinary in scope, is an inevitable fact of democracy. If, however, democracy is confined to a context not of scarcity (there will not be enough "rights" for everyone, so someone will have to sacrifice) but of plentitude, of citizens working together to diminish rather than to accommodate sacrifice, then Allen's model risks perpetuating a supposedly inevitable loss and the competition between citizens it generates. Leo Bersani offers a suggestive alternative to scarcity models of sociality. He criticizes psychoanalytic theories of sociality premised on "lack" (in Lacan's mirror stage, the initial lack that prompts the identification with the imago and the second-stage lack that results from the alienation of the imago from the "self"). Instead, Bersani postulates a sociality premised on excess ego, spilling out and flooding those with whom one associates. In his model, rather than pulling others into one's inner hole, "all being moves toward, corresponds with itself outside itself." As a result, we love in others "inaccurate representations of ourselves." Building sociality on the assumption of plenty, of love rather than lack, Bersani usefully diminishes the necessity of loss or sacrifice. At the same time, however, centering sociality on "the extensibility of sameness" in which "we relate to difference by recognizing and longing for sameness," he offers no model for the encounter with difference central to Allen's democracy between strangers.[6] If everyone represents an outpouring of oneself, the very notion of strangeness is eradicated, and we have no feasible account of what causes *change* (especially the important change of self-conception). This problem becomes tragically animated, as the next section demonstrates, in Melville's *Pierre*, in which the desire to move beyond "lack" (which he compulsively experiences in relation to his own "mirror," the portrait of his father) into a broader social world of "love" propels Pierre into a nightmarish tangle of self-extensions. He turns everyone he encounters into a version of himself by generating (fictional) family relations between them and him, the more "strange" the person, the more intimate the connection. In so doing, Pierre never reaches sociality at all but dies in a narcissistic implosion, pulling his beloved into a suicide that reflects his ultimate self-absorption, the flip side of the utopian expansion imagined by Bersani.

Far from endorsing Pierre's efforts to incorporate strangeness into familiar (and familial) versions of the same, the romance remains committed to alienated states that give citizens critical distance from conventional intimacy and the social imperatives of the institutionalized "real." Pierre (the character) is typical of the "social novel," which, Chase reports, privileged "unities and harmonies," absorbing "all maladjustments and contradictions into a normative view of life." As a romance, however, *Pierre, pace* its protagonist, remains fascinated with "oddity, distortion of personality, dislocation of normal life, recklessness of behavior, malignancy of motive."[7] Chase's description suggests something insistently purposeful about the romance's representations of consciousness's perverse and multiform underside, which distorts, dislocates, and maligns. The disruptive contradictions of romanticism preserve social volitions in the form of inner drives, and if those volitions appear "malignant," it is because (un)consciousness has become the interiorized site of social demand. Consciousness is not, therefore, a singular drive that can recognize itself through love of (itself in) others, but a divided and contentious site of contesting demands that is itself a simulacrum of a democracy built not on loving sociality, but on collective—and often conflicting—needs for negotiated differences. Sociality is not a projection of the "self," in other words. The "self" is an introjection of the social.

Yet the interiority imagined by the romance is not simply reflective. As Chase makes clear, it is also inventive. The American romance, he insists, "does not confine itself to what is known, or even what is probable," but "grasps at the possible."[8] The fullness that Bersani suggests as the basis of sociality as plenitude becomes, in the romance, an imaginative (or interpretive) excess, even as the rendition of the marvelous as a blueprint of the possible requires the cooperation of others, whose imaginative participation marks them as distinct, as strangers in a cooperative context. The "penchant for the marvelous" that Chase notes in the romance thus represents not only the estrangement of the "odd," but "the aesthetic possibilities of radical forms of alienation, contradiction, and disorder," which together work toward what Henry James, in his definition of romanticism, calls a "whole possible revolution."[9]

If the romance never quite achieves revolution, it nevertheless releases readers from what James describes as "the inconvenience of a *related*, a measurable state, a state subject to all our vulgar communities."[10] In refusing the "vulgar communities" of precedented relationality, however, the romance opens what Newton Arvin describes as "a strong intuition of human solidarity as a priceless good."[11] In the romance, "human solidarity" consists of not a settled social order of conventional intimacies but, as Chase puts it, a "sharing of the human fate among people temporarily brought together by chance or by a common purpose." Chase rightly notes the contingency ("temporarily brought together") of romantic sociality, ensuring that "the American novel is full of idealized momentary associations."[12] Whereas Chase maintains the distinction between the apparently mutually exclusive options of "chance" *or* "common purpose," however, the romances of Hawthorne and Melville demonstrate that social contingency ("chance") is itself a powerful social fantasy that may be the basis of "common purpose." In relationships made "by chance," the romance imagines the viability of cooperative sociality beyond the framework of institutionality, with its promise of stability, permanence, and futurity, of social or biological reproduction, or of the unified sameness that characterizes national and cultural structures of belonging. Instead, "momentary associations" offer a "common purpose" shot through with difference, brought about by what

Chase astutely identifies as "the instability and mixed motives that characterize united action among Americans." While the resulting sociality barters in universal humanism ("human fate" or a "common cause"), it also preserves a participatory locality, "a deep and narrow, an obsessive, involvement," leaving open the possibility that romantic sociality has meaning only in the contexts created by those brought together, fleetingly, by common purpose *and* mixed motives.[13]

Perhaps rather than the sociality imagined by the American romance being queer, it is the case that contemporary queer sociality is importantly romantic. Generated in cities through networks established informally, often through "momentary associations" formed on streets, in parks, or in bars among people alienated by choice or by force from institutional "normalcy" and yet associated with the most utopian forms of expressive fantasy, contemporary queer sociality operates within the imaginative possibilities generated in antebellum cities by immigrants, workers, sexual deviants, drinkers, and other reformable citizens estranged from the reproductive logics of speculative capital and dedicated to maintaining the vitality of democratic sociality through alternative practices of affiliation and public demand.[14] The conditions of antebellum interiority, as the previous chapters show, gave rise to normative (institutional) citizenry by generating a range of reformable personality types (non-reproductive, uncommitted, socially promiscuous, pleasure addicted, and persistently nostalgic) that, although they cohered in the late-nineteenth-century homosexual, circulated in the antebellum period through a variety of people—slaves, drunkards, bachelors, masturbators, libertines, dreamers, social climbers—who bore the weight of discredited sociality. That homosexuality became characterized by inner states (neuroses, desire, emotionalism, and fancifulness) rather than by the bodily marks that characterize race and gender suggests its emergence at the end of a century in which social distinctions were marked not on but *in* the body. The simultaneous growth of interiority, queerness, and romanticism shows how social abjection is rooted in the history of mitigated public participation and heightened economic speculation, imagined as the erratic appetites and self-managements that formed the interior states of modern citizenship. It is also, however, to remember the investment of abjected populations in (re)deploying interior states—nervousness, desire, and ultimately fantasy—to generate social relations that, predicated on the conditions of ostracized personhood (unregulated appetite, deinstitutionalized contingency, non-reproductive nostalgia), pose democratic alternatives crafted from the stuff of phantasmatic interiority.

As this chapter demonstrates, the romantic socialities imagined in *The House of the Seven Gables*, *Pierre*, and *Clarel*—frail, contingent, alienated, but also richly inventive, respectful of mystery, obliquely eroticized, and persistently un-privatized—exemplify democratic practices maintained in the face of individual self-management and normative intimacy. If interiority turned sociality into the nervous state of desire, queerness turned desire into the public performance of imaginative invention, the most potent form of which, in the nineteenth century and since, is romanticism. Although the social alternatives posed by romanticism, like queer sociality itself, are often dismissed as trivial and self-indulgent, the persistence of the romantic strain in American life, troubling institutional versions of the precedented and the real and allowing citizens to become, as Hawthorne stated, citizens of somewhere else, suggests that this aesthetic phenomenon fills a powerful need for a more participatory, a more contingent, a more *marvelous* sociality in America.

Unprecedented Socialities

The seemingly inevitable struggle between precedent and marvelousness—and its manifestation as the war between inheritance and innovation, law and criminality, realism and fantasy—obsessed both Nathaniel Hawthorne and Herman Melville. In the preface to *The House of the Seven Gables*, Hawthorne, setting out the distinction between novels and romances, associates the former with realism, in which imagination, denied the possibility of fanciful transformation, becomes enslaved to "the probable and ordinary course of man's existence." Romance, on the contrary, need not "rigidly subject itself to laws" but, demonstrating "a very minute feeling" for "the possible," is able "to mingle the Marvelous" (1) with the probable events of everyday life. "Law" functions here for Hawthorne on several levels. Most immediately, he means convention, life lived not as a possibility for invention, but within the comfort of predictable (precedented) pattern. Yet Hawthorne also attaches convention to the legal protection of property "by laying up a street that infringes upon nobody's private rights, and appropriating a lot of land which had no visible owner, and building a house of materials long in use for constructing castles in the air" (3).[15] In the preface, then, Hawthorne attaches the juridical functions of law (the contractual protection of property rights and inheritance) to the conventions of everyday life (the predictable life patterns carried out, presumably, within the privately owned home), both being represented in the plot by the officious, grasping, and literal-minded lawyer Jaffrey Pyncheon.[16]

Throughout *The House of the Seven Gables* and *Pierre*, Hawthorne and Melville challenge the legal principle of precedent through the twinned assault on inherited family nature and on the inevitable conventions precedent imposes on the present through its constructions of a determinative reality that, Hawthorne states, is simply a naturalized fiction. To carry out both critiques, Hawthorne and Melville challenge the imperative demands of interiority by deepening it beyond the reformist scrutiny and regulations that, guaranteeing the continuance of legal precedence *as* social convention, take on the juridical authority of law. The romances of Hawthorne and Melville do not stop at the level of critique, however, but use opaque and wayward interiority to generate unforeseen moments of social alliance predicated on contingency and conflict rather than comfort and consensus. These marvelous moments, in which the invisible and the unprecedented take shape as the demanding visions of the disenfranchised, generate the romance's democratically queer sociality.

The imperative hold of precedent over the ability of citizens to imagine new presents (let alone futures) for themselves is taken to absurd extremes in *The House of the Seven Gables*. One of the oddest features of the plot of that romance is that, over two centuries, with the outcome so doubtful, the Pyncheons continually search for the deed that they believe will give them legal right to Waldo County in Maine, while the Maule descendants equally persistently frustrate the Pyncheons, despite the fact that Waldo County has long since been farmed out, making both families' claims to the land quixotic, at best. Perhaps representatives of both families go on with their customary struggle—the Maules tantalizing the Pyncheons with further mystery, and the Pyncheons responding with frenzied study of dubious evidence—because what both gain from this ritual is more important to them than the land itself. This dynamic sustains the legitimacy of law, which similarly rests on the dialectic of evidence and mystery, of scrutiny and speculation. Despite their different positions in relation to the law (the Pyncheons generally judging while the Maules repeatedly serve as criminals), both families profit from the legitimacy of law. Both are seemingly ensured of their right to inheritance—of family character, if not of property—by the presumed interior transmission of the precedent "nature" established by ancestors and maintained not by legal institutions, but by the interior states that have become their simulacra. The children of both families—Phoebe Pyncheon and Holgrave (a Maule in disguise)—can therefore peacefully wed at the conclusion of the novel. Justifying each other's existence through time, the Pyncheons and the Maules create between them a legal worldview—a cosmic search after evidence that will solve timeless and metaphysical "crimes"—that neither has an interest in ending.

Hawthorne seems to invite readers to share this investment, inviting identification with a host of characters trying to solve some mystery. The formidable Jaffrey Pyncheon seeks to discover the ancient deed to the Maine lands, while his infirm cousin Clifford, recently released from prison, strives to discover Ideal Beauty within the moth-eaten relics of his ancestral home. Sunny Phoebe Pyncheon, come from the country to care for her elderly relatives, attempts to uncover the source of their profound melancholy. Holgrave, a boarder in the Pyncheon home, as a daguerreotypist seeks to bring forth his sitters' inner character through their posed exteriors, as a mesmerist seeks to bring forth historical secrets repressed in the psyches of his impressionable clients, as a suitor seeks to elicit a confession that Phoebe returns his affection, and as a Fourierian reformer attempts to bring forth the socialistic world order obscured by the materialistic scrambling of the modern age. Around these characters struggling to see what lies inside (history, the body, crass materiality, inscrutable sadness) we are invited, like the townspeople who continually hover around the Pyncheon home, gossiping about the centuries of strange goings on within, to muse on the eternal mystery of what makes this odd family tick.

It is important to note, though, that not everyone is looking for evidence in the same place. Some believe that "truth" is discernible from the outside of things, while others look inward, and this difference, which plays out over the course of the romance, signals an important historical relocation of law from exterior actions to interior states. As criminality becomes manifest not in disruptive or violent actions, but in predispositions to action (emotions, affections, and desires), the law takes an inward turn, insisting on inner orders that are the purview not of harsh jurists like Judge Pyncheon, but of benevolent reformers like Holgrave, who, at the novel's conclusion, therefore replaces the judge as patriarchal head of the family.

At the novel's start, the initial faith that external signs will lead to the revelation of Truth is most essential to the legal structure represented by Judge Pyncheon, one of those "ordinary men to whom forms are of paramount importance" (229). Having arranged "clues" to frame his cousin Clifford, who will otherwise inherit the family fortune Jaffrey covets, the judge knows how much the law relies on external signs. His faith that external "facts" will lead invariably to hidden "meaning" leads Judge Pyncheon not only to trust in the evidentiary logic he manipulates to Clifford's detriment, but also to his conviction that the deed to the Maine lands, if discovered, will once and for all establish the Pyncheons' rightful ownership. Contracts—which themselves take signatures as signs of sound character and good faith—are the lawyer's stock in trade, and by insisting that deeds can reverse the course of history, clearing land long settled by independent farmers and returning the Pyncheons to an obsolete aristocratic grandeur, Judge Pyncheon also rationalizes his trust that an outward show will disguise a host of inner blemishes and historical wrongs.

The law's faith in the revelatory power of evidence relies on conventional forms of display. Of the judge, Hawthorne writes, "you could feel just as certain that he was opulent, as if he had exhibited his bank account" (57). So insistently does the judge wear his character—and his wealth, the two being one and the same—on his sleeve that Hawthorne quips, "He would have made a good and massive portrait" (57). The connection between external evidence and social convention becomes most clear, however, in a character with apparently less to gain and who shrinks from the judge at their first meeting: Phoebe Pyncheon, "so orderly and so obedient to common rules" (68) that she "shocked no canon of taste" and works to ensure that she "never jarred against surrounding circumstances" (80). At the same time, Phoebe's faith that all is—and should be—what it seems produces its supplemental excess in the form of nagging doubts and suspicions. Watching the judge in action, Phoebe begins to wonder "whether judges, clergymen, and other characters of that eminent stamp and respectability, could really, in any single instance, be otherwise than just and upright men. A doubt of this nature," Hawthorne concludes, "has a most disturbing influence, and, if shown to be a fact, comes with a fearful and startling effect on minds of the trim, orderly, and limit-loving class" (131). Even as her doubts arise, however, Phoebe, "in order to keep the universe in its old place, was fain to smother, in some degree, her own intuitions as to Judge Pyncheon's character" (131–32). In repressing her "intuitions," then, Phoebe becomes possessed of an unconscious, a broody interiority that, in time, makes her subject to the inward-looking law represented by Holgrave, but also enables her sympathy with her dark and mysterious cousins.

While Phoebe demonstrates the troubled interiority that supplements the conventionalizing of public display, the judge demonstrates the rewards that make the escalating exchanges of troubled insides and reformed outsides worthwhile. As a reformed rake, Jaffrey demonstrates the rewards for reshaping private vices into the image of public virtue. Having learned the material rewards that follow public revelation and reform of inner shame, the judge becomes the foremost instrument of reformative exteriorization and surveillance in the romance:

> "My dear Cousin," said Judge Pyncheon, with a quietude which he had the power of making more formidable than any violence, "since your brother's return, I have taken the precaution (a highly proper one in the near kinsman and natural guardian of an individual so situated) to have his deportment and habits constantly and carefully overlooked. Your neighbors have been eye-witnesses to whatever has passed in the garden. The butcher, the baker,

the fish-monger, some of the customers of your shop, and many a prying old woman, have told me several of the scenes of your interior." (237)

The judge transforms punishment (the imposition of physical force) into the panoptical regimes of discipline (the regulation of "interior" behaviors through the benevolent discourses of health).[17] In doing so, however, he renders his own juridical control over external actions superfluous, replaced by the institutional regulation of interior states. Hawthorne repeatedly shows outward things to be highly unreliable markers of hidden depths. What he states of the Pyncheons' efforts to discover the Maine deed—"Some connecting link had slipt out of the evidence, and could not anywhere be found" (18)—is equally applicable to every effort in the novel to discover truth through external signs. Not only does the evidence leading to the possession of the Maine lands remain elusive, but the material existence of the land itself eludes its external representation, "the natural history of the region being as little known as its geography, which was put down so fantastically awry" (33). The "fantastic" (we might say the "marvelous") here queers the legitimate possession of land, just as Hawthorne's romance satirizes the quest for that possession. "There is something so massive, stable, and almost irresistibly imposing, in the exterior presentment of established rank and great possession," Hawthorne writes, "that their very existence seems to give them a right to exist, at least, so excellent a counterfeit of right, that few poor and humble men have moral force enough to question it, even in their secret mind" (25). The original sin visited on the contemporary inhabitants of the House of the Seven Gables (Colonel Pyncheon's conviction of Matthew Maule as a witch, resulting in the dubious acquisition of Maule's land) highlights from the beginning the dire results of believing that things are as they appear. This original crime sets in play a sequence of disguise, counterfeit, and swindle of which judges—the adjudicators of the Law—are the worst perpetrators.

For Hawthorne, the solution is not a more truthful alignment of surface and depth, of evidence·and truth, but an awareness that surfaces signify only other surfaces. The portrait of Colonel Pyncheon gives way not to the historical personage but to another text—the deed to the lands in Maine—which in turn materializes not into baronial wealth but simply into the narrative of the novel. Unable to recognize this, the characters are driven nearly mad in their desires to break the shell of external signs to reach the kernel of truth within, a process the novel repeatedly figures as "possession." Hawthorne makes this sadistically clear in one of the most bizarre chapters in the novel, "Governor Pyncheon," which describes in detail the atmosphere surrounding Jaffrey's corpse as it sits undiscovered. The narrator circles the body, facetiously giving it various meta-phoric casts and allegorical significances, Hawthorne's macabre delight high-lighting the materiality of death. The judge, who made his life by insisting on his power to make externals speak, has become a lifeless symbol, a mere "coun-terfeit of right" (25).

Having killed off the judge, however, Hawthorne's trouble with the law begins anew. In representing the judge's hypocrisy, his "inward criminality" (312) that belies his public self-regulation, Hawthorne orients the reader to-ward a presumably more recognizably "natural" law based not on external convention but on the inner order of right feeling. Early in the novel, the inno-cent Phoebe, learning that Holgrave associates with "reformers, temperance-lecturers, and all manner of cross-looking philanthropists" (84), is shocked: "'But if Mr. Holgrave is a lawless person!' remonstrated Phoebe, a part of whose essence it was, to keep within the limits of law. 'Oh,' said Hepzibah carelessly—for, formal as she was, still, in her life's experience, she had gnashed her teeth against human law—'I suppose he has a law of his own'" (85). As it turns out, Holgrave has an *inner* law that regulates not public behavior but "deep" emotions (the "confession" he elicits is not of criminal acts but of love). While Phoebe naïvely believes in the mutual dependence of (outward) law and order, Holgrave, even though he challenges conventions and "acknowledge[s] no law" (84), can remain, insofar as he insists on the inner consistency of "identity" (177), an "orderly young man" (84). If Phoebe requires the confor-mity of private anomaly to public order through identification with normative values, Holgrave renders public rituals of conformity obsolete, since affect and consistency of "identity," not Jaffrey's external displays, now guarantee social order. Depicting the transformations of "law" into an interior state, *The House of the Seven Gables* reveals how civil apparatuses such as domesticity and reform (embodied in the betrothal of Phoebe and Holgrave) led citizens to misrecog-nize "the social" as a function not of labor and profit but, rather, of individu-alized and privatized affect.

In addition to being a reformer, Holgrave is a daguerreotypist, a profession that allows him to profit by bringing out his sitters' inner selves. "There is a wonderful insight in heaven's broad and simple sunshine," he says. "While we give it credit only for depicting the merest surface, it actually brings out the secret character with a truth that no painter would ever venture upon, even could he detect it" (91). As a daguerreotypist, Holgrave continues the mesmeric tradition of his Maule ancestors, whose "family eye was said to possess strange powers," including that "of exercising an influence over people's dreams" (26). The Maules' power over human interiority is most clear in the narrative of Alice

Pyncheon, brought first to humiliating servitude and finally to death by Matthew Maules's mesmeric control over the affective dialectic of desire and shame. Just as Matthew brings forth the insecurity and guilt lurking behind Alice's haughty exterior, so the inner "truth" behind generations of Pyncheon counterfeits is brought forth when the Maules work their magic on the family well, making "its inner region all alive with the departed Pyncheons; not as they had shown themselves to the world, nor in their better and happier hours, but as doing over again some deed or sin, or in the crisis of life's bitter sorrow" (21). While the contemporary Maule, Holgrave, shuns such marvelous displays in favor of technological skill, he, too, strategically exhorts confessions of interior states. At the conclusion of the novel, Holgrave cements his place as the head of the Pyncheon family by looking into Phoebe and calling forth her feelings. "'You look into my heart,' replied she, letting her eyes droop. 'You know I love you!'" (307).

While Holgrave's insistence on inner truth apparently supplants the judge's reliance on external conventions, Hawthorne suggests the two men are more similar than they initially appear. While Holgrave's conversation with Phoebe "had generally been playful, the impression left on her mind was one of gravity, and, except as his youth modified it, almost sternness" (94). For all his talk about social reform, furthermore, Holgrave does no more to improve the material conditions of the poor than does the judge, preferring not "to help or hinder; but to look on, to analyze, to explain matters to myself" (216). Hawthorne suggests that reform and conservatism, both serving the interests of middle-class social order, are close kin. "'I have a presentiment,'" Holgrave tells Phoebe, "'that, hereafter, it will be my lot to set out trees, to make fences—perhaps, even, in due time, to build a house for another generation—in a word, to conform myself to laws, and the peaceful practice of society'" (307). "'You find me a conservative already!'" (315), Holgrave happily declares.

What Holgrave "conserves" is, as he acknowledges, the law, especially as a device to maintain family relations and lines of inheritance. The precedent of law is tied, throughout Hawthorne's romance, to that of family character, which ensures the most important inheritance, interior predisposition itself. Possessing nature in the form of land is connected, for these families, to the transmission of nature in the form of natural predisposition, or "character." What Holgrave adds to this mix is a projection not back through history (precedent) but into an unlimited future ("another generation") that will rationalize, retroactively, the corrupt decisions made in the past. He joins, in other words, precedent and institutionalism. To attach precedent to futurity, to redraw the borders ("to make fences") around a family threatening to break apart under the strain of historical dispute, faked documents, and failed resemblances, however, Holgrave must shift from external to interior law, bypassing in the process the historical alterations that mark (or queer) the Pyncheons' present existence. Geographic and economic mobility may introduce outsiders such as Phoebe or Holgrave into the family, and if one believes exclusively in outward resemblances, such "newness" will produce ontological crises. Interiority, however, assures stability in the face of outward change, assuming that sympathy of natures will suture the tears that difference, in the present or the future, may produce. While the romance begins by suggesting that external structures create the "nature" that exits within (the House of the Seven Gables producing the oddities of its inhabitants), by the end the family can move from structure to structure, changing abodes without sacrificing the inner nature that gives meaning to a house and not the other way around. Enabling precedent to travel in a rapidly mobile world, while ensuring the appearance of stable lines of relationality (and hence of inheritance), interiority works its "conservative" magic.

And yet, interiority cannot forestall the question that nags *The House of the Seven Gables*: can a family with a scandalous origin project a glorious future? The same question—fundamental to the modern fusion of legal precedent and institutional futurity through the affective nexus of family "nature"—haunts Herman Melville's 1852 romance *Pierre; or, The Ambiguities*.[18] The story of the young Pierre Glendinning's effort to put right his ill-gotten inheritance born of generations of theft, exploitation, and deception, Melville's romance chronicles his hero's disastrous effort, by pretending to marry a dark stranger he believes to be his abandoned half-sister, to reconcile the precedent of family nature with the socioeconomic changes confronting the aristocratic Glendinnings in the modern world. The family, for Melville, is always already an institution in its modern sense, forming interiorized relations between the past and the future (occluding the present, where history occurs), as well as between the private and the public (occluding the complex middling spaces where everyday life transpires). In *Pierre*, institutions render inconsequential individual mortality, generating an abstract agency that apparently suspends time to envision a better future. "We lived before, and shall live again," Melville writes, expressing succinctly the promise of institutionality, "and as we hope for a fairer world than this to come; so we come from one less fine" (32). The problem becomes, however, that without recognizing differences produced by economic and social exchange, without a space for "private" individuals to interact and a present in which such meetings can occur, institutions suspend the possibility of citizens' working out "fairness" for themselves. Ethical agency has been ceded to institutions, but if institutions are predicated on the "sameness" of participants and the deferral of outcomes, institutional principles will be as severely stunted as the Glendinning family.

The origins of the Glendinnings' wealth are obscured—for the innocent young Pierre, if not for Melville—by the appearance of an uninterrupted transmission across time of a seemingly stable and glorious essence, the mystification, Melville shows, of power and profit. Mary Glendinning, Pierre's mother, "long stood still in her beauty, heedless of the passing years" (5), the embodiment of the "hills and swales [that] seemed as sanctified through their very long uninterrupted possession by his race" (8). The ability to mask the violent disruptions of capital's historical movements with the apparently harmonious time*lessness* of family nature enables Pierre to project his affective satisfaction onto the land and its inhabitants. "Pierre deemed all that part of the earth a love-token," Melville writes, "so that his very horizon was to him as a memorial ring" (8)

The Glendinnings are ultimately undone, however, precisely by their faith that the institution of the family can use affect to equalize the power imbalances that allow them to decide whom to "love" in the first place. If the outward mobility of capital could actually be transformed into the inner stability of family attachment, what would prevent that transformation from reversing, sending sentiment out into the world to erase economic differences in the name of love (the perverse desire of the antebellum politics of sympathy)? In the face of such a reversal, furthermore, if all strangers become family members, how could the prohibition against incest continue to function? This is precisely Pierre's problem, as his faith in familial sentiment produces an increasingly violent series of misnamed relations: mothers and sons pose as brothers and sisters, brothers and sisters pose as husbands and wives, fiancés pose as cousins. In each case, a relationship built on inequalities of power (parents over children, the wealthy over the poor, husbands over wives) is reimagined as a relationship built on equality (sibling equality, affectionate unions). These reworkings of power relations into ties of equitable mutuality are dangerous, Melville suggests, because they disguise as affection and consent the often violent operations of force and theft. More dangerous, these misnamings collapse all social relations into domestic ones, thereby denying social differences in favor of a family model predicated on self-perpetuating sameness. Pierre interacts with few people who are not relations, and when he does, he either absorbs them into the family (making them a sister or a wife), or, as with Charles Millthorpe, simply ignores them. The private relations of domesticity, marriage, and family thus apparently work to stabilize, as in Hawthorne's romance, the inconsistencies, contradictions, and mixings occasioned by social "outsiders." Yet the ridiculous reiteration of Pierre's strategy of collapsing "others" into his familial "same" suggests that something continually exceeds private sentiment's grasp. When an obviously unequal relationship between mother and son (" 'I will manage you yet' " [60], Mary mutters to Pierre) is turned into a supposedly "equal" relation between brother and sister, for instance, the dramatically *unequal* relationship between the siblings, Pierre and Isabel, betrays the dark underside of Mary's and Pierre's "game," prompting Pierre to turn his "sister" into his "wife." Readers have already seen in Pierre's relation to Lucy, however, that men and women in romantic relations are not equal (Pierre dumps Lucy unceremoniously for his new "wife" Isabel), so Lucy is turned from a jilted lover into a "cousin." And yet Pierre's biological cousin, Glen Stanley, has already denied shelter to Pierre and Isabel, charging the former with betraying their childhood intimacy, suggesting that cousins are not always harmonious peers. And on it goes. Hierarchical relationships of manipulation and betrayal, it seems, cannot simply be renamed equality, nor can lack of options be called consent.

Pierre can ignore the violent outcomes of his misnaming because of his faith in precedent. Among his other riches, he "inherited the docile homage to a venerable Father" (7). Believing that an unshakable identification with the Father will produce an institutional relationship between them—that the agency of the father will pass, despite his death, to the son, and so on until an endlessly receding future—Pierre surrenders his capacity for action based on his own principles and becomes paralyzed by what his mother calls "sweet docility" (20). While Mary acknowledges the "most strange inconsistency" of docility and agency (20), she eagerly sacrifices consistency to profit. Pierre also profits (ambivalently) from institutionality, through the inheritance of property and, as an author, from "invitations to lecture before Lyceums, Young Men's Associations, and other Literary and Scientific Societies" (251).

Although literary associations seem innocent enough, Melville shows the more serious consequences of institutionalism when he turns to social reform. The Miss Pennies, a pair of spinsters who cannot encounter the "needy" without putting their proverbial two cents in, have organized "a regular society" (44) to sew for the poor. Most of the work, however, appears to be done by the poor themselves, who, as "the less notable of the rural company," are "voluntarily retired into their humble banishment" (46) at a distance from their wealthier neighbors. The Pennies mask the systematic segregation of the classes, then, through the purported benevolence of reform. Melville challenges such kindness, however, when Isabel, one of the sewing poor, shrieks and faints at the first sight of Pierre, in whom she sees the likeness of the man she believes to be her father. In the wake of Isabel's distress, the company "reminded not the girl of what had passed; noted her scarcely at all" (45). The ability of benevolent reformers to aid the poor while scarcely noting their embodied condition (indeed, while denying them a history—a memory of "what had passed"—that might kindle their sense of having been wronged) takes on a more sinister cast when Melville provides the story of Isabel's conception. When French refugees settle near the Glendinning estate, Pierre's father, "with many other humane gentlemen of the city, provided for the wants of the strangers, for they were very poor" (76). The gentlemen apparently "provided" more than food and clothing, for one of the Frenchwomen, unmarried and reportedly pregnant, hastily returned to France, where her daughter—if Isabel's account can be believed—was abandoned in another "benevolent" institution, an insane asylum.

Such moments of reform might seem ethically superior to the scornful behavior of Mary Glendinning and her minister, who conspire to drive unwed and pregnant Delly Ulster from the community. Unlike his cruel mother, never "had the generous Pierre cherished the heathenish conceit, that even in the general world, Sin is a fair object to be stretched on the cruelest racks by self-complacent Virtue, that self-complacent Virtue may feel her lily-liveredness on the pallor of Sin's anguish" (177). If benevolence and sympathy redeem violent ostracism, if love "is the world's great redeemer and reformer" (34), however, Melville shows, in Isabel's pregnant and abandoned mother and her ignored and mistreated daughter, that sometimes "love" is as cruel as contempt. The latter at least lets its object know the source of her hardship, while "love," in its institutional forms, leaves its object at a double loss: abandoned and degraded but seemingly without any legitimate grounds of complaint or agent against which to rebel.

The institutions supported by "love," therefore, come in for particular criticism in *Pierre*, as they produce what Melville describes as "the dreary heart-vacancies of the conventional life" (90). Conventional life becomes dreary, Melville suggests, precisely because its institutions generate the illusion of interiority—in the shape both of domestic privacy and inner affections and desires—that lets citizens (at least wealthy ones) believe they live in (never quite) secure self-contained units of sameness. Such intimate units supposedly contain the *qualities* of social life (handbooks throughout this period instructed parents on how to raise children to be good citizens by being obedient, self-disciplined family members) while, in fact, isolating inhabitants from interaction with the differences of experience and perspective—including those already existing *within* families and homes—that make social negotiations necessary. The detachment of interiorized intimacy becomes naturalized and disseminated by rhetorics of "love" ("No Propagandist like to Love" [34], the narrator asserts), which ensure that bodily and domestic privacy, rather than seeming drearily isolating, appears as the most important site for exercising consent and deepening one's "inner" life. The ever-loving Pierre, for instance, achieves both interiority and consent when he offers his mother "the voluntary allegiance of his affectionate soul" (15). Producing consent by turning difference into sameness, love, for Melville, has an imperial grasp: "All this Earth is Love's affianced; vainly the demon Principle howls to stay the banns" (34). "For every wedding where true lovers wed," Melville wryly notes, "helps on the march of universal Love."

In particular, love orients citizens toward futurity, transforming sons into (potential) fathers, and therefore reorienting attention away from the past, always burdened with the threat of recognizable injustice and misrepresentation, toward the future, a place of utopian possibility. "Love has more to do with his own possible and probable posterities than with the once living but now impossible ancestries in the past" (32), Melville writes. The shift from past to future seems loaded with promise. But when does the future become the present? When does satisfaction come? Reducing the broad sphere of social interaction and experience to the significantly narrower spheres of institutionalized intimacy (or, indeed, to the interior states of "intimacy") is what makes people less eager to ask that question, turning citizens, as Melville observes, into "jailors all; jailors of themselves," seemingly doomed to "ignorantly hold their noblest part a captive to their vilest" (91).

If his inability to encounter people without turning them into family or lovers leaves Pierre with a "strange feeling of loneliness" (7), however, it is not because there are no other models of sociality open to him. On the contrary, *Pierre* suggests "that the divinest of these emotions, which are incident to the sweetest season of love, is capable of an indefinite translation into many of the less signal relations of our many chequered life" (16). *Pierre* is crammed with such relations, which rival, in the intense satisfactions and communicative freedoms they provide, the romance's institutional intimacies. Melville no sooner introduces the love story of Pierre and Lucy Tartan, for instance, than he offers the tale of Pierre's grandfather's attachment to his horse, a bond so strong that the animal died days after its master's demise. Not long thereafter, Melville introduces Ralph Winwood, with whom Pierre's father "was rather intimate at times" (74). Among his other "curious whimsies" (79), Ralph "much liked to paint his friends, and hang their faces on his walls" (75), a practice that seemingly enables "the ever-elastic regions of evanescent invention" (82). Most dramatically, Isabel, left alone save for her mother's guitar, "made a loving friend of it; a heart friend of it" (125). She tells Pierre, " 'Love is not all on one side with my guitar. All the wonders that are imaginable and unspeakable; all these wonders are translated in the mysterious melodiousness of the guitar. It knows all my past history' " (125). Although these relationships, made with objects and animals, almost laughably suspend human sociality, Melville shields them from ridicule by turning them into placeholders for social values that compete with the plot's "major" intimacies: a horse and its owner can be loyal without demanding sameness; an artist's painted "friends" are companionable without requiring mutual knowledge; intimacy with a guitar can affirm one's history rather than demand an amnesic orientation toward futurity. Above all, made contingently in response to historical need from the ephemeral materials of vastly diminished lives, these relationships provide a queer fullness, in the form of fantasy, daydream, and vision, to refill the "heart vacancies" left by institutionalism's demand for permanence, futurity, and self-management.

While these relationships, made with things rather than people, might suggest intimacy's commodification, they also hold open the possibility that people's need for sociality has not been entirely supplanted but, instead, has moved to strange, unpredictable, even queer outlets. Despite these characters' alienation from family and romance, they maintain the capacity "to respond," which, Melville attests, "is a suspension of all isolation" (291) and an affirmation of "the imaginativeness of the supposed solidest principle of human association" (142). Perhaps institutionalism needs such supplemental alternatives, for apparently fleeting, incomplete, even incoherent experiences make the permanence reportedly provided by institutions seem valuable ("all sweet recollections become marbleized," Melville writes, "so that things which in themselves were evanescent, thus become unchangeable and eternal" [68]). Nevertheless, contingent and ephemeral relationships retain some of their "sweetness" in *Pierre*, providing "that mysterious thing in the soul, which seems to acknowledge no human jurisdiction" (7). Such lawless imaginings are not always pleasant— Melville tells us they often take the forms of "horrid dreams" and "unmentionable thoughts" (71)—but their unsettling qualities are precisely what undo conventional categorizations and make better arrangements thinkable. The relationships at the margins of *Pierre* suggest that "the strongest and fiercest emotions of life defy all analysis" (67), and as long as such emotions are kept vibrant, there is hope that, in Melville's words, "one single, intensified memory's spark shall suffice to enkindle such a blaze of evidence, that all the corners of conviction are as suddenly lighted up as a midnight city by a burning building, which on every side whirls its reddened brands" (71).

Melville's gothic metaphor, suggesting the 1834 burning of the Ursiline convent in Charlestown, Massachusetts, prefigures the most important site of alternative sociality in *Pierre*. The Charlestown incident, in which a mob of sixty disguised workingmen drove twelve nuns and forty-seven female pupils into hiding, robbed the convent, and reduced it to ashes, was part of Melville's family history, as his father-in-law, Lemuel Shaw, was the presiding judge who acquitted the men accused of the attack.[19] There are no nuns in *Pierre*, but the cloistered life makes an important appearance in the form of the Church of the Apostles, where Isabel and Pierre take refuge after fleeing for New York City. In the church, as Wyn Kelley observes, Pierre finds "a community congenial to his newly conceived revolt against house and home."[20] No longer used for religious services, the upper floors of the former church are occupied by the Apostles, "mostly artists of various sorts; painters, or sculptors, or indigent students, or teachers of languages, or poets, or fugitive French politicians, or German philosophers" (267), as well as "well-known Teleological Theorists and Social Reformers, and political propagandists of all manner of heterodoxical tenets" (268). The "heterodoxies" espoused by the Apostles are, on one level, ineffectual, for, despite their revolutionary rhetoric, "yet, to say the truth, was the place, to all appearances, a very quiet and decorous one, and its occupants a company of harmless people" (269). The Apostles nevertheless pose an important alternative to their neighbors. Abandoned by religion, Melville reports, "the building could no longer be devoted to its primitive purpose," but had to be "divided into stores; cut into offices; and given as a roost to the gregarious lawyers" (266), men with "full purses and empty heads" (267). If business replaces faith and law divides human collectivity, other ways of life do not simply vanish but move upstairs, where, like the archival memory whose burning illuminates the corners of conviction, they recall other values than those represented by the lawyers and businessmen below.

Preserving alternative and arguably more generous social values (the Apostles take in the abandoned Pierre and protect him from physical attack), the Apostles become one of the first literary examples of functional queer subculture in the new American cityscape: "Finding themselves thus clannishly and not altogether infelicitously entitled," Melville writes,

> the occupants of the venerable church began to come together out of their various dens, in more social communion; attracted toward each other by a title common to all. By-and-by, from this, they went further, and insensibly, at last became organized in a peculiar society, which, though exceedingly inconspicuous, and hardly perceptible in its public demonstrations, was still secretly suspected to have some mysterious ulterior object, vaguely con-

nected with the absolute overturning of church and State, and the hasty and premature advance of some unknown great political and religious Millennium. (269)

Like queers today, the Apostles turn a shaming appellation into a principle of social organization, one that, like queer culture, often moves unnoticed—obliquely marked yet powerfully flexible—in and around the institutions of public life and the intimacies they sanction. Like modern-day queers, the Apostles generate unpredictable alliances across lines of class or social experience, and therefore compete (and not only comically, as Melville suggests) with the intimacies sanctioned by church and state. Sounding quite queer, indeed, Charles Millthorpe, Pierre's link to the Apostles, declares, " 'By marriage, I might contribute to the population of men, but not to the census of mind. The great men are all bachelors' " (281). The Apostles teach Pierre important lessons about how to build community in ways that do not surrender difference ("heterodoxies") or romanticize it in ways that disable its agents' ability to speak of social—not aesthetic—injustice. Through his childhood friendship with Charles, for instance, Pierre has "some inkling of what it might be, to be old, and poor, and worn, and rheumatic, with shivering death drawing nigh, and present life itself but a dull and a chill!" (277).

The tragic irony of *Pierre* is that at the romance's conclusion its protagonist sits in the midst of a powerful model of counter-sociality, struggling desperately to invent just such an alternative from the frayed materials of his past, never noticing that what he seeks is all around him as his present. Ultimately, Pierre becomes a captive of intimacy because he maintains the sharp division between public and private life that prevents him from seeing that "his own private and individual affection" (49) reflects the institutional values that, in other contexts, he finds abhorrent. Caught within the pastness of intimate precedent and the futurity of institutional intimacy, Pierre never recognizes the "ephemeral inventions" that might produce happiness in the here and now. Careering between an anguished interiority and institutional conventions that turn out to be one and the same, Pierre cannot achieve the queer sociality that permits, on the one hand, an interiority so profound as to disallow either insight or regulation, and, on the other, a liminal space of sociality that is neither private nor public, dedicated neither to the past of precedent nor the future of generation. Only in that space is the present of democracy possible, and only the unlikely queers of romance seem capable of achieving it.

The most striking example of queer sociality comes not in Melville's romances, but in *The House of the Seven Gables*, which turns out to be inhabited by queers. In describing Hawthorne's characters as queer, I do not mean to suggest something about their sexuality, although they do offer glimpses of what, by the late nineteenth century, would emerge as homosexual identities. Hepzibah, who refuses to attend church, becoming in her isolation a comically bad housewife and an Old Maid in whom "the love of children had never been quickened" (39), falls far outside nineteenth-century conventions of femininity, which rested on piety and domestic nurturance. If Hepzibah is a "bad" woman, Clifford's "beautiful infirmity of character" (60) comes from his being *too* feminine, as Hepzibah acknowledges in claiming that the town " 'persecuted his mother in him!' " (60). An "old bachelor" of "an eccentric and melancholy turn of mind" (22), possessed of "gentle and voluptuous emotion" (32), Clifford, in his attraction to Beauty, his obsession with youth, and his "womanly" sensibilities, is, as Neill Matheson argues, a proto-Wildean aesthete.[21] Insofar as modern homosexual identity gained public intelligibility as an inversion of Victorian gender roles, Clifford and Hepzibah, refusing to hold to their "proper" genders, are arguably among American literature's first homosexual characters.

Hawthorne's characters are queer, however, not by virtue of their sexuality but insofar as they deviate from or counterfeit bodily and behavioral norms. Above all, they are queered by their refusal to make interiority publicly visible and to manage its experience and expression by the conventions of future-oriented (re)production. Refusing these imperatives, Hawthorne's characters are queered by excessive and inscrutable emotions, devotion to the past, anti-social reclusiveness, economic and biological non-productivity, and lack of control over bodily functions (Jaffrey's "queer and awkward ingurgulation" [124], Hephzibah's nearsighted frown). While authoritative legal and medical theories of the nineteenth century might have characterized these traits as pathological, predicting their culmination in criminality, misery, illness, and death, they enable Hawthorne's characters to sustain hopes and aspirations, however ill-defined or ill-fated, by mingling (as Hawthorne's preface claims the romance does as a genre) the marvelous and the mundane. Through these minglings, the characters model *queer interiority*, which in turn enables the marvelous sociability that Richard Millington calls "the democratization of the tragic."[22]

As Will Fisher documents, *queer* originally had economic connections, denoting a counterfeit coin or a swindle. The characters who deploy queer interiority to enjoy alternative sociality figure as counterfeits, bad copies of a presumed "original," the precedent that demands and naturalizes self-managing conformity to supposedly unchanging conventions. Denying such precedents through an excess that suggests that all claims to exact reproduction are in effect swindles, Hawthorne's queer characters show identities based on interior states passed (as "nature") from generation to generation to be their own inevitable counterfeits. In so doing, the inhabitants of the House of the Seven Gables anticipate Judith Butler's claim that all performative identities posit an original—the "essence" of "who one really is"—of which subjects are always judged to be incomplete or inadequate reproductions.[23] The suspicion that one has not manifested completely the truth of one's identity drives the compulsive enactment of what can never be gotten right: the manifestation, as identity, of an inner truth that, in the end, is never *inner* at all, but exists in a discursive— and hence *social*—realm that changes historically, as, therefore, will the "identities" it produces. Although Phoebe asserts that conventions have the social force of law, one might well ask who, in her world, lives the "normal" life she strives for?

Phoebe, to a lesser degree than Clifford and Hepzibah but in ways that allow her to sympathize with them, finds herself a not-quite Pyncheon, a bad copy of the family essence. The reiterative performance of the tense nonalignment of originals and (bad) copies is a central plot structure of *The House of the Seven Gables*, played out in repeated ruptures between inheritance and representation. All through the romance, characters comment on the degree to which others do or do not look like "real" Pyncheons. The ur-Pyncheon, in these evaluations, is the founder of the House of the Seven Gables, Colonel Pyncheon, whose disapproving face presides over the inevitable failure of his descendants to measure up to the Pyncheon essence. Hepzibah scowls like her ancestor, but, of course, she is a woman. Clifford is also too much of a woman, favoring his mother to a degree that leads Hepzibah to exclaim, " 'He never was a Pyncheon!' " (60). Jaffrey claims to see a family resemblance in Phoebe's mouth, but she also resembles her mother too much to really be one of the Pyncheon clan. (It is noteworthy—and supports Butler's analysis of "gender trouble" as a potentially disruptive identity performative—that mothers repeatedly get blamed for disrupting identity, and hence inheritance, in the romance.) Even Jaffrey, who most resembles his ancestor, has transformed his appearance in ways his Puritan forefather would condemn (his too benevolent smile, for instance, would ill suit the persecutor of witches). Each descendent, in short, is deemed a bad copy of the ancestral original. Yet the determinations of successful or failed "identity" (their identity as Pyncheons) is made through comparison, not with the original ancestor, but with his portrait, itself an interpretation shaped by historically changeable aesthetic conventions. It is not coincidental that the deed to the Maine lands, obtained through a foundational act of deception, is hidden behind the portrait; Hawthorne thereby suggests (with his usual allegorical finesse) that behind the assertion of origins one will always find a counterfeit, a failed inheritance, a false deed. It is precisely identity's status as counterfeit that must be hidden if what is outside (convention) is to appear as if coming from within, for identification to be misunderstood as identity. The Pyncheons' claim to social superiority rests on the assertion of undeviated and unmediated inheritance, that all subsequent Pyncheons, being the true reflections of the Pyncheon original, are entitled to the same property willed through a direct line of succession (a line Jaffrey, by framing Clifford and hence circumventing his uncle's will, has already undermined). If the generational transmission of property (including one's principal property, "identity") rests on the truthful representation of a representation, a counterfeit of a fake, however, then the law of inheritance is as deceptive as the colonel's justice. Put another way, if the original was already a fake, how can Hepzibah and Clifford possibly be bad copies, failed Pyncheons?

That question becomes unthinkable precisely because of the social authority of those who claim the privilege of normative identity. In declaring his relatives bad copies, the judge makes them socially invisible, disappeared behind the obscuring walls of the family home. He thereby enacts the form of oppression Butler writes about, working "not merely through acts of overt prohibition, but covertly, through the constitution of viable subjects and through the corollary constitution of a domain of unviable (un)subjects—*abjects*, we might call them—who are neither named nor prohibited within the economy of the law."[24] Refusing to acknowledge, much less regulate, the innate "identity" that resides in the body's interior, Clifford and Hepzibah must repeatedly find themselves abjected. But who does not experience this failure? Hawthorne's romance seems to ask. If Hepzibah and Clifford, who felt "mankind's great and terrible eye on them alone" (169), seem extraordinary in their abjection, Hawthorne hastens to remind the reader that the Pyncheon siblings are exemplary in their discordant identification, "a ruin, a failure, as almost everybody is" (158).

Because they do not make common cause in their abjection, however, Hepzibah and Clifford are kept from asserting their presence not by prohibition, but by shame, the characteristic state of those without socially sanctioned identities. When her cent-shop forces her to face the outside world, Hepzibah experiences "overwhelming shame, that strange and unloving eyes should have the privilege of gazing" (46) and later feels "a painful suffusion of shame" (112). When Hepzibah tries to dissuade her brother from going into public, warning him of the townspeople's inevitable judgment, Clifford, whose life has been a series of mortifications, exclaims, " 'What shame can befall me now?' " (113). Shame is a potent force, urging the siblings to stay locked away from the world and preventing them from challenging their cousin's rights to wealth (Clifford might assert his innocence in the murder of his uncle) or respectability (Clifford might publicize Jaffrey's cheating and lying). In contradicting their cousin's rights, Clifford and Hepzibah would challenge the laws of normative social order, both by discrediting the judge's status as representative of public virtue and by showing that *other* forms of social alliance are possible, capable of producing more love, kindness, and creativity than the judge and his laws ever dreamed of. Because shame operates at the level of emotion and results in self-punishment, however, it serves the judge's interests better than any juridical sentence, since his cousins, finding *themselves* lacking and experiencing their punishment not on the outside, where it might elicit sympathy, but on the inside, far from public view, become self-imprisoning subjects. As Hawthorne writes, the couple "could not flee; their jailor had but left the door open, in mockery, and stood behind it, to watch them stealing out. At the threshold, they felt his pitiless gripe upon them. For, what other dungeon is so dark as one's own heart! What jailor so inexorable as one's self!" (169).

While shame works to keep Hepzibah and Clifford, and the challenges they embody, off the streets, it also enables an alternative collective life—a queer sociability—among those sentenced to shame. Creating a world of unpredictable emotions, surprising affinities, and powerful challenge, making the House of the Seven Gables, as Millington notes, "a place of connection as well as coercion,"[25] the errant Pyncheons and their allies turn their failures into what Michael Warner calls an ethics of queer life.

> I call its way of life an ethics not only because it is understood as a better kind of self-relation, but because it is the premise of the special kind of sociability that holds queer culture together. A relation to others, in these contexts, begins in an acknowledgment of all that is most abject and least reputable in oneself. Shame is bedrock. Queers can be abusive, insulting, and vile toward one another, but because abjection is understood to be the shared condition, they also know how to communicate through such camaraderie a moving and unexpected form of generosity.[26]

Warner's formulation of a queer ethics helps explain how what Millington describes as a dissenting "communal consensus" in the romance is shaped by what we today might call "empathy": the ability of more apparently privileged citizens (those extending compassion) to acknowledge (at least to themselves) their own experiences of abjection to imaginatively place themselves in the position of the socially wounded.[27] In such moments ubiquitous experiences of shame are transformed into a potential enactment of fellow feeling. Hawthorne implies as much when he writes that "Clifford saw, it may be, in the mirror of his deeper consciousness, that he was an example and representative of that great chaos of people, whom an inexplicable Providence is continually putting at cross-purposes with the world" (149). Living at cross-purposes, gnashing their teeth on human law, generates Clifford's and Hepzibah's shame, yet shame becomes re-exteriorized as a social connection, a way of life, an ethics.

All who share the ethics of Hawthorne's romance—Clifford, Hepzibah, Phoebe, Uncle Venner, and, at least initially, Holgrave, who possesses "queer and questionable traits" (154)—are at cross-purposes with the world. Describing the elderly jack-of-all-trades, for instance, Hawthorne writes that Venner "was commonly regarded as rather deficient, than otherwise, in his wits. In truth, he had virtually pleaded guilty to the charge, by scarcely aiming at such success as other men seek, and by taking only that humble and modest part in the intercourse of life, which belongs to the alleged deficiency" (61). Casting Venner's social abjection in the language of legal judgment, Hawthorne creates a bond between Clifford and Venner that puts both men at odds with Judge Pyncheon. Hawthorne also places Venner, like Clifford, outside the "common sense" of his social world in part because he refuses the kind of coherent identity associated with the capitalist narratives determining "such successes as other men seek." Venner is "a miscellaneous old gentleman, partly himself, but, in good measure, something else; patched together, too, of different epochs; an epitome of times and fashions" (62). Rather than condemn Venner for his patchwork persona and consign him to the shame his cross-purposeful life would seem to require, Hawthorne credits to it a marvelous counter-wisdom, noting that the old man had "a vein of something like poetry in him" (61).

Venner's romantic "vein of poetry"—the lifeblood of Hawthorne's queer ethics—has a transformative power over even the most apparently "normal" of the Pyncheons. Initially, Phoebe "was not one of those natures which are most attracted by what is strange and exceptional in human character. The path which would best have suited her, was the well-worn track of ordinary life; the companions in whom she would most have delighted, were such as one encounters at every turn" (142–43). Before long, however, Phoebe "grew more thoughtful than heretofore." Finding herself curious about Clifford's past, she "would try to inquire what had been his life" (143). When his history becomes clear to her—partly through what she is told, but also with the help of "her involuntary conjectures," suggesting that Phoebe's imagination contains the stuff of gothic cross-purposefulness—"it had no terrible effect upon her" (144). Phoebe's ability to "conjecture" about Clifford, to place herself imaginatively in his shoes, cements her bonds with her outcast cousins, an outcome Phoebe senses from the start of her visit, when she tells Hepzibah, " 'I really think we may suit one another, much better than you suppose' " (74).

Suiting one another does not require, however, that Phoebe and Hepzibah necessarily *know* each other. Indeed, what is compelling about Hepzibah is precisely how mysterious her emotions remain, existing beyond the scrutiny and self-management that conventionally turn shame into an occasion for reform. Hepzibah's inner states remain so elusive that, as Millington rightly notes, the narrative "can only represent [her] by misrepresenting her."[28] Hawthorne refers repeatedly to her "queer scowl" (50), to "the sad perversity of her scowl" (133), to her "queer and quaint manners" (135), even to her "queer" chickens, who share Hepzibah's "queer, sidelong glances" (89). Hepzibah keeps "the strong passion of her life" in a "secret drawer" (31), never giving it a public name. She is, in this world of confessed inner states, "a queer anomaly" (37). Although her passions are one of the most persistent, if understated, mysteries of the romance, Hepzibah, refusing to acknowledge that she even *has* a secret, resists the public orders of domestic self-sacrifice and commercial competition. For all its opacity, Hepzibah's passionate interiority—"the vivid life and reality, assumed by her emotions" (66)—becomes a pointed commentary on the "realities" of the external world, making "all outward occurrences unsubstantial, like the teasing phantoms of a half-conscious slumber" (66).

Hepzibah thus represents what might be the romance's most promising insight: the "interior" contains nothing at all, no "essence" to validate the public scrutiny of shameful secrets. If, as Hawthorne claims, "the reader must needs be let into the secret" (28), the secret may turn out to be that there *are* no secrets—at least, none that can be brought forth by public law and reconciled with its nominal orders. As Hepzibah defiantly claims in answer to the judge's demands for her brother's confession, " 'Clifford has no secret!' " (237). In the face of such emptiness, one finds in oneself only one's desire to know, as Hawthorne suggests in one of his first descriptions of the House of the Seven Gables: "As regards its interior life, a large, dim looking-glass used to hang in one of the rooms, and was fabled to contain within its depths all the shapes that had ever been reflected there" (20). In the end, *The House of the Seven Gables* shows us what the mirror reveals: the desires of those who would look, the law's dim gaze. Emotions, passions, melancholy all become, in Hawthorne's romance, not interior states but the external means to a more sustainable, if more provisional, social affinity. "Mellow, melancholy, yet not mournful," Hawthorne writes, "the tone seemed to gush up out of the deep well of Hepzibah's heart, all steeped in its profoundest emotion. There was a tremor in it, too, that—as all strong emotion is electric—partly communicated itself to Phoebe" (96).

Queer sociality requires more than an "electric" bond of sympathy, however; it requires a location, one that exists apart from the conventional division of public and private life. Every Sunday, Hawthorne relates, his "oddly composed little social party" (155) gathered in the garden, a site that anthropomorphizes the characters' queer transformation of shame into sociability. Made up of "such rank weeds (symbolic of the transmitted vices of society)" (86), the garden becomes, like those who enjoy its at first unapparent beauties, a haven from social abjection, where "Nature, elsewhere overwhelmed, and driven out of the dusty town, had here been able to retain a breathing space" (87). Generating a space outside the shameful interior of the house yet making "an interior of verdant seclusion" (145), the garden fosters "the sympathy of this little circle of not unkindly souls" (157).

Just as the garden's "vagrant and lawless plants" (86) bring forth a marvelous sociability, so do the queer passions of its inhabitants bring forth, through what Millington calls "the shared risks of transformative interchange," remarkable testimonies of hopefulness and perseverance.[29] Uncle Venner voices the group's characteristic optimism, defiantly claiming, " 'I'm not going to give up this one scheme of my own, even if I never bring it really to pass' " (155–56). Although Hawthorne asserts that croaky voices like Hepzibah's "have put on mourning for dead hopes" (135), the old woman, left for thirty years to long for her brother, keeps alive "in the dungeon of her heart . . . the imprisoned joy, that was afraid to be enfranchised" (102) but that maintains "her undying faith and trust, her fresh remembrance, and continual devotedness" (32). Similarly, "Clifford had willfully hid from himself the consciousness of being stricken in years, and cherished visions of an earthly future still before him, visions, however, too indistinctly drawn to be followed by disappointment" (155). "Individuals, whose affairs have reached an utterly desperate crisis," Hawthorne writes, "almost invariably keep themselves alive with hope, so much the more airily magnificent, as they have the less of solid matter within their grasp, whereof to mould any judicious and moderate expectation of good" (64). This becomes evident in one of the most poignant scenes in the novel. Having sat quietly in his half-somnolent state while his companions socialize in the garden, Clifford suddenly announces, " 'Many, many years have I waited for it! It is late! It is late! I want my happiness!' " (157).

Ironically, Clifford's happiness, like Pierre Glendinning's, is already around him, in the hopeful imagination, the faithful devotion, the caring compassion—

in the queer sociability—of his companions. If the public world is full of citizens whose "judicious . . . expectation of good" renders them continually confronted by disappointment and shame, if public paradise is lost through the duplicitous snake of sanctioned, but counterfeit, identity, Hawthorne holds out a garden where one can find, in queer inscrutability and unruly passion, what Robert S. Levine has called "the regenerative and redemptive possibilities of reconstituted family."[30] Does the sociability shared by his queer characters, Hawthorne asks, "deserve to be called happiness?" His answer whimsically appropriates the language of counterfeit, not to adjudicate shameful failure, but to reveal the marvelous fantasies that permit the continued life of hope. "Why not? If not the thing itself, it is marvellously like it, and the more so for that ethereal and intangible quality, which causes it all to vanish, at too close an introspection" (158). If Clifford laments to his sister, " 'We are ghosts!' " (169), referring to the civil death that characterizes the socially abject, Hepzibah, for her part, knows all too well that, supported by queer sociality, " 'dead people are very apt to come back again!' " (76). Finding that they " 'belong nowhere' " (168), Hawthorne's characters demonstrate that happiness is all around us, if only we had their ability to embrace our shame and, recognizing with Clifford how late it is, demand its marvelous outcomes *now*.

Alienated Affections and Queer Transnationalism

Soon after Hawthorne created the marvelously queer garden of *The House of the Seven Gables*, he found a somewhat analogous intimacy that also took shape in a liminal space between the interior and the fully revealed. On August 5, 1850, Hawthorne was invited to join a group of his literary neighbors on a hike in the Berkshires, during which he met Herman Melville. The younger Melville engaged the often reclusive Hawthorne in conversation, and the two men commenced a friendship solidified later that evening at a dinner at the home of local historian, David Dudley Fields. Over dinner, Oliver Wendell Holmes held forth on the superiority of British gentlemen to their American counterparts, to which Melville strenuously objected, and Hawthorne, usually detached from such debates, vigorously joined Melville's defense of his countrymen. In retrospect, it seems possible that Evert Duyckinck, friend and publisher of both writers, set up their meeting to establish a distinctly American literary movement, an aspiration he made explicit not long after when he asked Melville to review Hawthorne's *Mosses from an Old Manse*. Duyckinck published the review, in which Melville employed an uncharacteristically nationalist rhetoric to establish Hawthorne as an American Shakespeare, in his *Literary World* on

August 17 and 24, 1850, under the title, "Hawthorne and His Mosses, by a Virginian Spending July in Vermont."[31] The review, which one biographer has characterized as Melville's "love letter" to his literary idol, made its author a favorite of the Hawthorne family, and the friendship grew until November 1851, when Hawthorne moved his family back to eastern Massachusetts. The two men corresponded periodically over the following years and met twice in Liverpool, where Hawthorne served as American consul.

Most critics have read the Hawthorne–Melville relationship as a failure, blaming its short span on Hawthorne's cold detachment or Melville's hot passions. Based largely on evidence drawn from Melville's semiautobiographical poem *Clarel*, some have assumed that Melville made physical advances on Hawthorne who, in a moment of homosexual panic, precipitously fled Lenox, disavowing the friendship in the process. There is scant—if any—evidence, however, that either man considered the relationship a failure and a good deal of evidence that, between them, they established an intimacy built on the principles both experimented with in the fictions they composed during this period. When critics read the relationship as failed, they draw on criteria of success derived from the institutional logics of antebellum nationalism: a full reciprocal revelation of interior states that permits a mutual knowledge and hence a lasting relationship extending, through continued mutual production, into the future. By these standards, the Melville–Hawthorne relationship— which lasted only fifteen months, in which both men remained largely mysterious to each other, and in which mutual production in the form of epistolary correspondence or literary collaboration ended abruptly—may be a failure. It is especially tempting to read the relationship by these standards, given its framing, by Duyckinck and by Melville himself, in nationalist terms. Having established the friendship as an instance of federal affect, such terms invite us to judge intimacy as we would judge nations (and, as I have implied, the institutions that do the civic work that has often been mistakenly attributed to nationalism).

If, however, we reverse these evaluative standards—if, that is, we stop judging relationships by the standards of institutionalism and start building institutions on the basis of experimental intimacy—then we might see the Melville– Hawthorne relationship as a successful experiment in queer sociality, in which the two men collaborated on an intimacy without interiority, forming an alliance that relied not on mutual knowledge and contractual commitment, nor on shared nature or complementary personality, but on the local and historical contingency of confluence and need. Seen in this light, the Melville– Hawthorne relationship *became* romance, taking sociality across the borders of knowingness and predictability into an inventive mobility that turned Melville in particular into what Chase calls "a kind of alien wanderer in the world of imagination."[32] Alienated affections become, in this light, not a sign of loss and failure, but a queer kind of homecoming.

Images of migration, wandering, and border crossing characterized the relationship from the start as a register not of loss but of both men's efforts to move beyond the limits of federalized affect, to become, as Hawthorne wrote in "The Custom House," citizens of someplace else. Responding to *The House of the Seven Gables*, Melville characterized Hawthorne as saying "NO! in thunder," and thereby crossing "the frontiers into Eternity with nothing but a carpet-bag,— that is to say, the Ego."[33] Melville described his review of *Mosses* as a "poor fugitive scrawl" (225), and offered to engage Hawthorne in "some little bit of vagabondism."[34] More comically, on August 1, 1851, Hawthorne reported that, while sitting with his son Julian in a field, they were approached by a "cavalier" on horseback who greeted them in Spanish. The "cavalier," of course, was Melville.[35] Together, these references suggest that border crossing was less a matter of literal travel than of imaginative companionship, working to transform, rather than reinforce, the ontological conventions of institutional intimacy. Melville described his all-night conversations with Hawthorne as "ontological heroics."[36] Hawthorne's claim that those same conversations concerned "possible and impossible matters" suggests that the movement between the possible and the impossible, the here and the somewhere else, the real and the marvelous allowed assumptions of what should constitute the intimate "real" ("ontology") to be, heroically, transgressed.

Sociality, for these authors, was neither here nor there, then, but in the imaginative efforts, not to make difference into a version of the same, but to allow it to *change* one's conception of "sameness," to see how life might be under another sense of normalcy, to recognize that morals, desires, conversations are not *things* in space (even the deep interior space of the individual), but that they take on significance in the give and take *between* the known and the unknown, the self and the beloved. That model of sociality characterizes one of the most perplexing episodes of the Hawthorne–Melville relationship. On August 13, 1852, after Hawthorne had left Lenox, Melville wrote to tell him about a story he had heard concerning a woman, Agatha, who had nursed a shipwrecked sailor, Robertson (whom Melville renamed Robinson), back to health and married him, only to be deserted when her beloved again took to the sea. After seventeen years of awaiting his return, Agatha learned that her husband had married again. The story, Melville cryptically tells Hawthorne, "lies very much in a vein, with which you are peculiarly familiar" (Wilson, 234).

Brenda Wineapple has speculated that Melville, left behind by his beloved Hawthorne, identified with the abandoned Agatha and passed this story on to his former friend as a passive aggressive articulation of his hurt.[37] Yet Melville's subsequent gloss on the story suggests a different interpretation. On October 25, Melville again wrote to Hawthorne, "In his previous sailor life Robinson had found a wife (for a night) in every port. The sense of the obligation of the marriage-vow to Agatha had little weight with him at first. It was only when some years of life ashore had passed that his moral sense on that point became developed."[38] Apparently, Melville identified not with abandonment, but with a kind of intimate relativism, rendering the constitutive terms of intimacy—commitments, loyalty, betrayal—contingent on social practices and therefore open to comparative re-inscription. Such intimate revisionism is possible, as Agatha's story makes clear, only in movement *between* commitments, beyond the borders of home(land)s. Melville notes that Robinson never fully "abandon[ed]" Agatha but kept coming back to her, offering companionship and financial support. What is missing in this story, then, is not intimacy but continuity and permanence, an abstract (institutionalized) commitment that exists when neither party is actively engaged. Perhaps Melville was drawn to Robinson because he seemed to offer a model of intimacy built on the crossings—physical but, more important, *ontological*—to which Melville repeatedly returned in his accounts of his friendship with Hawthorne. Despite the nationalist rhetoric of "Hawthorne and His Mosses," then, for Melville the best metaphor for intimacy was itinerancy, not institutionalism.

Like Agatha and Robinson, Melville and Hawthorne never quite abandoned each other, although their meetings became less frequent. The two met for the last time in the pages of Melville's 1876 poem *Clarel*, in which the writer supposedly memorialized his troubled relationship with Hawthorne.[39] Often read as a melancholy lament, *Clarel* demonstrates how to recover alienated affections by making them, ironically, *more* alien. In so doing, *Clarel* becomes Melville's masterpiece of a post-interior romanticism.

In the poem, an American student, Clarel, travels to the Holy Land in a vain effort to resolve his spiritual doubts, discovering along the way that truth exists beyond the narrow provincialism of his upbringing in the United States. He can shake his "cultivated narrowness," Clarel understands, only when he "rove[s] / At last abroad among mankind" to "Forgo the state / Of local minds inveterate" (6). At first, Clarel attempts to reduce difference to a harmonious sameness, as when, hearing "polyglot" voices at prayer, he imagines the different creeds "Tingling with kinship through and through—/ Faith childlike and the tried humanity" (14–15). Clarel can answer his urgent question, "What profound /

Impulsion makes these tribes to range?" only by reducing historical difference to affective similitude: "Stable in time's incessant change / Now first he marks, now awed he heeds / The intersympathy of creeds / Alien or hostile tho' they seem—" (23).

Ultimately, however, Clarel, abandoning the fantasy of "inter-sympathetic" harmony, allows himself to be "confronted so / By the true genius, friend or foe, / And actual visage of a place / Before but dreamed of in the glow / Of fancy's spiritual grace" (6). This is not a replication of "sameness" in others but a shattering confrontation of such universalizing projections ("fancy's spiritual grace") by local encounters with difference. Neither peaceful nor comforting, such encounters remind Clarel of the "wrangles . . . which oft befall: / Contention for each holy place, / And jealousies how far from grace." He bitterly asks the polyglot pilgrims, "O bickering family bereft, / Was feud the heritage He left?" (24). "Disturbed and troubled" by the discord he encounters in the Holy Land, where pilgrim faces seem "a book / Of disappointment" (8), Clarel undergoes a process of fantastic and (because) disruptive incorporation: "took, / In way but little modified, / Part to himself; then stood in dream / Of all which yet might hap to them" (20). The future, while (because) disconcertingly alien, shocks him out of the familiar belief in sympathy and universal love that he had brought with him from his homeland.

While Clarel's search is initially spatial—"Some other world to find. But where?" (38)—the pilgrim, like his creator, realizes that geographic metaphors, imposing a choice between projection and incorporation, harmony and discord, must be abandoned. Instead, he seeks "solacement in mate" (8): only in other people does Clarel find the promise of a world "re-imparadised" (28). Thinking about Luke's encounter with the resurrected Christ, Clarel imagines a "novel sympathy, which said—/ I too, I too; could *I* but meet / Some stranger of a lore replete, / Who, marking how my looks betray / The dumb thoughts clogging here my feet / Would question me, expound and prove, / And make my heart to burn with love—" (26). The move from "inter-sympathy," seemingly natural and universal, to "novel" sympathy, unique, contingent, and perhaps imaginary, corresponds with the shift from projection to encounter in which the love-inspiring stranger's challenging questions cause the lover to think, to grow, and to change.

The strangers Clarel meets in the Holy Land possess inviolable interiorities, refusing love's prying eyes. Mystery is what prevents the American Clarel from gaining knowledge of the strangers who would allow him to hierarchize cultures into an imperial order, while his traffic in the universalizing terms of humanism (sympathy, solace, love) forestalls the orientalizing abjection that puts an absolute distance between self and others. Beginning with the epigrammatic pilgrim, Nehemiah, a "flitting tract-dispensing man" (28) who invites Clarel, "'With me divide the scrip of love'" (30), the young American encounters a series of men who excite his love without ever disclosing the secrets of their inner selves. Melville describes the first such encounter: "mutely for moment, face met face: / But more perhaps between the two / Was interchanged than e'en may pass / In many a worded interview" (35). While this exchange feels deeply meaningful ("A novel sympathy impressed"), Clarel resolves not to "renew" the encounter (35), allowing contingency to override his desire for continuation. Soon thereafter, Clarel meets another dark stranger, Celio, whose "reserve," disrupting Clarel's "habitual Past" (40), performs the task Clarel first expected of the landscape. As the "unexpected supervenes," Celio produces in Clarel "an upstart element" (40) while remaining "Unpledged, unhampered" (37). These encounters climax when Clarel meets Vine, the supposed stand-in for Hawthorne. At his prayers, Vine suddenly "looked up, and Clarel viewed, / And they exchanged quick sympathies / Though but in glace, moved by that act / Of one whose faith transfigured fact. / A bond seemed made between them there" (90). One might expect Vine's "manner shy," his "Ambiguous elfishness" and "austere control of self," to form "A clog, a hindrance" to connection, but once again the opposite proves true (91). Although Vine remains "shrunk / In privity," between the two men an "excess of feeling pressed / Til ache to apathy was won" (94).

Despite this intense exchange of feeling, which leads Clarel to question the stories other pilgrims tell him and his prior beliefs about the Bible, the young student is plagued by self-doubts arising from impossible expectations of full disclosure and permanent attachment. Asking himself, "Would Vine disclaim / All sympathy the youth might share?" or consent to "communion true / And close; let go each alien theme; / Give me thyself!" (95), Clarel discovers in Vine a man all too typically self-occupied: "Vine, at will / Dwelling upon his wayward dream, / Nor as suspecting Clarel's thrill / Of personal longing, rambled still" (226). Caught within his conventional expectations, Clarel talks himself into immanent disappointment.

> Divided mind knew Clarel here;
> The heart's desire did interfere.
> Thought he, How pleasant in another
> Such sallies, or in thee, if said
> After confidings that should wed
> Our souls in one:—Ah, call me *brother!*

So feminine his passionate mood
Which, long as hungering unfed,
All else rejected or withstood.
Some inkling he let fall. But no:
Here over Vine there slid a change—
A shadow, such as thin may show. (226–27)

Although some read this passage as proof of Hawthorne's rebuff of Melville's physical advances, Vine never rejects Clarel, if only because the young American never moves from fantasy to action. Rather, Clarel *imagines* Vine responding, "But for thy fonder dream of love / In man toward man—the soul's caress— / The negatives of flesh should prove / Analogies of non-cordialness / In spirit. —E'en such conceits could cling / To Clarel's dream of vain surmise / And imputation full of sting" (227). The "sting" is not Vine's rebuke but Clarel's own inability to let go of his desire—similar to Pierre's—to make from contingent encounters a presumably permanent familial relation ("call me *brother*").

Are short-lived relationships necessary failures? Are friends disloyal because they move on? When two ships pass in the night, does anything of value pass between them? If we assume, as Clarel initially does, that because intimacies refuse the standards of institutional commitment, they are doomed to bad feeling, then we cannot help seeing contingency, conflict, or mystery as signs of wasted time. Moments of queer sociality between people who share their *un*-knowability in ways that provoke imagination and change demonstrate, however, that intimacy and wandering are opposites only in an institutional logic that equates continuity with fulfillment. If continuity is the sine qua non of institutional meaning, however, ephemerality is the moving experience of intimacy. If institutionalism grounds sociality, sociality keeps citizenship uprooted, contingent, moving. Perhaps few would choose to live as perpetual pilgrims— emotionally or physically—and certainly fewer want our most rewarding relationships to exist solely in the realm of fantasy. In the modern world, however, in which affect is largely federalized into the logics of institutional commitment, fantasy may be the only space for a post-interior intimacy, and as such, it is an archive we cannot afford to discredit. Only in the marvelous queer sociality of romanticism can we learn, as Melville writes in *Clarel*, "to realise the unreal!" (86) and hence to bring the social alternatives abjected by their association with fantasy back into play not as the circular deferrals of desire, but as the material practices of everyday relations. Melville asked Hawthorne, "Is love appreciated?"[40] If we judge love as we judge institutions, by the standards of disclosed and self-regulated interiority, then the answer is probably no. But if we judge institutions as we might judge social relationships, the ones that give us *real* pleasure, asking for the same give and take, the same imaginative responses to *not* knowing, the same growth through encounters with difference and often uncomfortable conflict, the same influx of the seemingly impossible into the imperative probable, then perhaps our answers will change.

Sophia's Choice?

While we wait for those changes, however, interiority continues to limit ethical deliberation and transformative participation. The marvelous queerness of the American romance offers valuable options for reconfigured sociality but never dares to imagine that sociality as a mode of *public* life. Until the individual (and largely psycho-affective) mobilities of pilgrimage or the collective formations of semi-reclusive subculture can claim their status *as public*, agency and consent will continue to tremble nervously at the limits of democracy, becoming ever more estranged by the institutional logics of modern mediation. The evisceration of public citizenship goes unresisted, however, because its bones appear sufficiently alive, animated by the dense and nervous affect that makes a dead interior the simulacrum of a living democracy.

Hawthorne's Concord offers a poignant example of interiority's power to appropriate the consensual participation not only of the living but of the dead. On June 26, 2006, the remains of Sophia Peabody Hawthorne and her daughter Una were interred in Concord's Sleepy Hollow Cemetery alongside those of her husband, Nathaniel. Both women's remains had previously rested in a British cemetery operated by the order of nuns founded by the Hawthornes' other daughter, Rose. The event raised strong feelings in Concord. A horse-drawn cortege followed the coffin to the gravesite, where the interment was witnessed by a gathering of Hawthorne descendants. Great-great-granddaughter Imogen Howe reported, "It's very emotional. They know now in spirit that everyone is reunited." Another descendant, Alison Hawthorne Deming, claimed, "From all accounts they adored and inspired one another for the duration of their marriage, which was not a marriage of convenience, but one of deep interconnection," adding, "It's so great that suddenly they're at their real home, here."[41]

These remarks animate Sophia Hawthorne's remains with the expressive power of interiority. Loving, contented, and grateful, Hawthorne's remains continue to possess deep interiority that her descendants can apparently discern. In return, the descendants gain their identities *as* Hawthornes, inheritors of a family nature that gives them, presumably, insights into their ancestors' feelings and desires. In an ironic imitation of the Pyncheons, these latter-day

Hawthornes generate a sentimental portrait of Sophia against which they measure their Hawthorneness, performing the loyalty—to Nathaniel, to Concord, to the United States—that they imagined as Sophia's.

While the Pyncheon descendants are queer copies of their ancestral original, abandoning the desire to embody interiorized precedents to enjoy the benefits of queer sociality, the Hawthorne ancestors prove less marvelous, strenuously insisting on the durability of the Hawthornes' marriage as a sign of their national allegiance, and vice versa. More troubling, the assertion of Sophia's interiority allows the descendants to override her own arrangements, returning Sophia to a home(land) she chose to leave. Like her husband, Sophia Hawthorne chose to be a citizen of somewhere else, but her great-grandchildren decided otherwise. Allowing the descendants to imagine an unbroken line of desire and consent, interiority overrides Sophia's choice, leaving only a skeletal parody of living consent.

As I read the story of the re-interment, I remembered a visit to the Old Manse in Concord, where the tour guide pointed out the scratching Sophia Hawthorne made in the window with her diamond ring. On a winter afternoon, Sophia wrote on the window an account of her daughter romping in the snowy yard behind the house. It is tempting to construct from this recollection a romance of Sophia Hawthorne that might contradict her descendants' portrait of their contentedly domestic and heteronormative ancestor. Trapped, isolated, Sophia inscribed on the liminal pane the movement of her sight beyond the limits of the interior realm of home and fantasy, identifying with the active daughter (with whom, significantly, she later traveled Europe). The meeting of ring and glass— suggestive symbols of commitment and vision—did not set Sophia free to wander promiscuously, as it did her husband and his friend Melville, but kept her in the interior, recording her musing in ways that, two centuries later, remain on display, making her the object, not the subject, of vision.

In either version of Sophia Hawthorne, however, affect sets the limits of and compensates for the loss of action, fantasy for the absence of consent. We cannot know whether Sophia Hawthorne yearned to be in Concord because of deeply nostalgic attachments or longed to get out because of equally romantic cravings. We do know that she left Concord, traveled to Europe, and became, like Clarel, a wanderer, without limiting her wanderings to the fantasies of romance. Whatever we might imagine today, that was Sophia's choice, unmade retroactively in the name of interiority, which reclaimed the remains of consent for less-than-marvelous fantasies of deep love, nostalgic attachment, and emotional homecoming that become the only options—the only precedent—in the institutionalized sociality of modern interior states.

Epilogue. HUMANISM WITHOUT HUMANS:

THE POSSIBILITIES OF POST-INTERIOR DEMOCRACY

In our mass-mediated, pervasively psychological, and insistently institutional-ized world, attempting to imagine a sociality free of interiority may be the most extravagant form of fantasy. Given that public testimonials of interiority (con-fessions of pain, remorse, or faith) remain one of the few options for public speech, perhaps life without interiority is not only unthinkable but undesirable. As each of the preceding chapters has shown, interior states are not only the means through which conflict is sacrificed to comfort, relationality turned to nervousness, and social demand transformed into toxic appetite and shameful predisposition, they have also been citizens' last resort in a world with less and less properly social life. Whether through Eliza Wharton's melancholy, Maria Monk's ambivalent Catholicism, Devil-Bug's nervous mania, Mary Arlington's weird fascinations, Hannah's visual speculations, or Clarel's wandering inti-macies, nineteenth-century authors have repeatedly transformed interior states into haunting articulations of dissatisfaction, aspiration, and demand. The twentieth-century deployments of interiority in calls for civil rights—from Martin Luther King's articulation of his dream to the performance of the AIDS Coalition to Unleash Power (ACT UP) of its melancholic rage—are the modern manifestations of these antebellum deployments of an otherwise debilitating interiority.

While it has been put to progressive ends, however, interiority has gained a monopoly over public discourse, making alternative structures of sociality—based, for instance, on conflict rather than comfort, pleasures rather than desire, action rather than anxiety—appear quixotic, dreamy, out of touch. As I have argued, the appearance of interiority corresponds with an estrangement of human agency into the social simulacra of institutions and their corollary interior states. This relationship is circular: as institutions appropriate agency, citizens are compensated with the self-management of interior states. As citi-zens in turn become more preoccupied and self-characterized by emotional, psychological, and spiritual states, they become more easily labeled as partisan, self-interested, and biased in ways that make the estrangement of their agency by supposedly impartial (because abstracted beyond the contingent interests of temporal location, of history) institutions appear more necessary. This cycle, as Hannah Arendt warned, produces the violence born of frustration, which in our day has reached world-history proportions, casting politics in the global drama of spiritual excess and terror, rage, and grief, which render the institutional operations of global capital nearly indiscernible. In such a world, we would do well to deploy interiority more judiciously, making it just one epistemology among many. In so doing, we might make the terms and conditions of interiority publicly debatable, rather than making them the adjudicating principles and self-managing substitutes for such debates.

Effective efforts to de-center interiority as public discourse may have to begin, as Ernesto Laclau has encouraged, by appropriating the values of liberal humanism, which is one of the strongholds—along with neo-Christian fundamentalism, its unlikely corollary—of civic interiority in the United States. Leftist academics, among whom I proudly count myself, have spent decades battling with humanism's abstract vocabulary ("equality," "liberty," "consent," "rights," and "happiness," to name a few), taking the ontological vacuity of these terms as proof of at best their political inefficacy and at worst their function as a disciplinary apparatus. As an alternative, such critics often offer either the psychic disruption of the "death drive" or of desire, or the supposedly individualizing particularity of multiculturalism, ignoring the ways both psychology and culture reproduce the interior logics that make psychological or cultural personhood and humanist institutions corollaries, rather than antagonists, of one another. While humanism's vocabulary is groundless, however, it is not arbitrary and, hence, should not be abandoned but debated and refined. In so doing, a humanist vocabulary might become not the grounds of a nebulous and anxiety-producing interiority, but the occasion for collaborative and at times fantastic invention. Again, the romance provides a model for how to put the humanist lexicon up for debate. When in *The Scarlet Letter* the townspeople see an "A" miraculously framed in the sky, they begin to interpret. The results are as various as the social interests represented by the citizens and cannot ultimately be adjudicated through appeals to spirit (the authority of the Puritan elders fails to determine the meaning of Hester's "A"), affect (Dimmesdale's heart-ringing confession fails to determine its reception by his congregants), or psychology (the "maternal bond" between Hester and Pearl fails to fix the meaning of the errant child as embodiment of the scarlet letter).[1] The conflict between universal (divine) and particular (emotional or psychological) meanings generates an irresolvable difference of interpretation that empties the signifier and, in the process, enables debate *as* democracy's "meaning." Out of this interpretive debate emerges a new sociality, built among the sympathetic strangers who gather in Hester's cottage, despite the stigma imposed by the Puritan fathers.

To make public debate work as social invention, however, we need to challenge not the vocabulary of post-Enlightenment humanism, but the interiorizing lexicon that has become its predominant sphere of operation and, more dangerously, the adjudicative basis for shutting down debate.[2] It is its tendency to predicate its assertions on appeals to human interiority in place of public debate, thereby foreclosing the very processes of democracy it promises, that makes humanism a subjective fundamentalism (as shown by the triadic foundation of current political discourse: desire, shame, and political-spiritual rebirth). The project I am suggesting, insisting on the *invented and inventive* status of the interior, has no such foundations, not even psychic ones. It involves a sociality rich in debate over the terms of relational justice and collective fulfillment, while also understanding the "self" not as a foundational and autonomous ground that settles or—worse—closes such debates but as a shifting nexus of the material and the marvelous, neither of which resists ultimately *in* the self. Public debate might occur, under such terms, without recourse to the inner states that have become synonymous in modernity with humanness itself. In offering the terms of liberal humanism for public contestation while withholding the interior states that have become the basis of modern humanity (even "drives" or "desires"), we might produce a radically democratic state of collaborative and deliberative sociality that might be called humanism without humans.

To enact such a de-humanized humanism, we must try, on the most basic level, to avoid making interiority the ground of adjudication, the truth that settles uncomfortable debates. In other words, conflict cannot be settled by appeals to an interior state ("Well, that's just how I feel" or "Deep down, I just know that to be wrong" or "You can't understand because you're not like me"). Nor can grievances be rectified through tearful apologies or appeals to psychological distress or spiritual exuberance. To claim any of these interior states as a ground of adjudication is to remove social debate from the collaborative realm and to relocate it in what may *appear* social (in the way that interiority functions as a simulacrum of relationality) but, in fact, empties the social of its deliberative function. Without the conflict provided by divergent experiences, interpretations, and demands, in other words, sociality is mooted.

The content of such debates or actions is not my concern here, nor should the content be predetermined, for such decisions, made by participants, will set the boundaries of collective deliberation and establish the trust necessary for its successful execution. This is why the relationality I imagine here is contingent and, quite probably, ephemeral, changing with the conditions of aspiration and demand. Instead of determining content, I want to trace the pitfalls that, by establishing false criteria for sociality or by misconstruing the potential outcomes of debate, preclude collective deliberation. Alternatives to such pitfalls have been suggested, in the texts analyzed in *Interior States*, by the melancholic, monstrous, addicted, and dreamy who do the hard work of archiving abjected social possibilities in the face of interiority's normative rule. These characters tell us several important things about post-interior sociality. First, it does not require full mutual disclosure, not only because the "inner life" that forms the content of disclosure is only ever fictitious, but also because anonymity and mystery are the condition of mutual invention that is the basis of romantic sociality. As I have suggested, moreover, a post-interior sociality avoids permanence, for three crucial reasons. First, permanence requires the abstraction of relationality to some transcendent entity that continues past—but also dangerously surrogates—the commitment of embodied members (one can think of a marriage contract, for instance, as such an entity). Second, such entities deny the historical contingency that makes human sociality both necessary and changeable. And third, attempts to suture the (mitigated) human commitment and the (abstracted) contractual entity require a perpetual (and necessarily unsuccessful) labor that robs energy from other forms of social invention. Finally, post-interior sociality privileges rational deliberation and pleasure over feelings and desire. For while desire separates the psyche from its object(s) before the moment of social connection, feelings mediate (again, in the self-contained circuit of the individual psyche) the aftereffects of that connection. Both states, in other words, are profoundly antisocial, while both pleasure and conflict require the presence of others—of material bodies and their differing experiences—within the *present* of social exchange.

Let me be more precise. In much contemporary cultural criticism, agency has taken the almost exclusive form of desire. Social structures are subverted, and counter-publics are built purely through the agency of desire. As I show in chapter 5, however, our modern notion of desire is predicated on a speculative economy that values deferral, and, indeed, desire can go on "acting" only insofar as it is not gratified. Judith Butler, for example, defines fantasy as "the very scene which *suspends* action" precisely because it is predicated on desire, a "closed circuit of a polymorphous auto-eroticism" that makes fantasy "always and only its own object of desire."[3] This is the antebellum neurologists' notion of the nerve system and its "auto-erotic" productions of a desire that, never extending beyond the body to reach an object, produce not agency but neurosis. Predicated on desire, our agency, paradoxically, is generated by the perpetual incommensurability between our want and its object, short-circuiting what most of us would think of as agency. We must stop thinking about desire as an end in itself and think of it instead as a means of achieving *pleasure*, erotic or otherwise. At the very least, however, the first step in evolving a post-interior sociality would involve articulating modes of agency other than those predicated on desire.

As important as conceiving agency without desire is, it is less urgent—and less difficult—than imagining pubic discourse without feelings. Yet as Ann Douglas famously observed, the sentimentalism of public life erodes the possibility of clearly defined and well-thought-through positions, reducing public discourse to the middle-ground emotionalism that characterizes mass consumption. Moving beyond the middle-ground comforts of mass-mediated popular culture to take the rigorously and often disruptive positions that make public debate possible requires a re-privileging not of the "isolated and reified" rationality of patriarchal authority, but of the principled and ethical deliberations needed to preserve "all virtues, even those of gentleness and generosity." Sentimentalism need not be reduced to interior states, of course, and no rationality can—or should—be divorced from the affective states of compassion, conviction, or optimism. When affect becomes the lowest-common-denominator of mass culture, however, it risks short-circuiting the clear and conflicting positions that make democratic debate possible. Intellectual rigor, as Douglas rightly notes, does not oppose but enables the "imaginative precision difficult to achieve without collective effort." That imaginative effort, as I have argued, comes most effectively through "a fully humanistic, historically minded romanticism," which sought to counter modern culture's "intense self-consciousness," or what I have described as self *as* consciousness, characteristic of sentimental interiority.[4]

Other revisions will prove necessary, and they offer possibilities for more discussion and debate. For now, the revisions I have named here—that desire is not synonymous with agency, that feelings are not the deliberative "real," that the longevity of commitment and the full mutual disclosure of inner life do not good relationships make—seem hard enough, perhaps because they are so local, so embodied, and so entrenched within contemporary life. American citizens may be willing to undertake such efforts, not through dissatisfaction with interiority, but with its abstract corollary in the forward-deferring, inward-directing, agency-supplanting imperatives of institutionalism. Even while promising unprecedented power to bring global order and ensure "homeland" security and prosperity, institutions in the United States have become visibly powerless to predict or prevent terrorist attacks, to discover weapons of mass destruction at home or abroad, to end an extraordinarily bloody and destructive foreign occupation, to protect globally sanctioned humanitarian standards, to enforce business ethics (or, for that matter, legal strictures), or even to guarantee federal elections by vote rather than court intervention. As Hurricane Katrina proved in September 2005, protecting Americans from devastation or providing humanitarian relief has proved beyond the will or capacity of "domestic" institutions. Superimposing the headline "System Failure" over the face of a weeping African American, *Time* expressed the inability of institutions ("systems") to ensure a future, particularly for poor Americans, while simultaneously rendering citizens incapable of helping themselves. After what the *New York Times* columnist David Brooks calls "a string of confidence-shaking institutional failures that have completely changed the nation's psyche," a new time of public debate about the value of institutions may be here. That debate, however, will need, as I have suggested, to move beyond figurations of public life as interiority: demand as anxiety, agency as desire, or a localized public as "the national psyche."

Until such debates begin, the erosion of associational life in the United States is likely to continue, along with the increasing incapacity of citizens to exert social agency collectively rather than deferring, abstracting, or interiorizing that agency through institutionality. If the ubiquitous depression and loneliness (what the sociologist Robert Putnam calls "bowling alone") plaguing Americans is caused by isolation, skepticism, and perceived powerlessness, the solution may lie in reconceiving and reanimating the inventive agency of democratic association. Defining associations as "networks of civic engagement [that] foster sturdy norms of generalized reciprocity and encourage the emergence of social trust," Putnam argues that when "economic and political negotiation is embedded in dense networks of social interaction, incentives for opportunism are reduced" and participants gain an enhanced " 'taste' for collective benefits."[5] Building on Putnam's definition of association, Amy Gutmann argues that "intimate relationships of love and friendship, which are valuable for their own sake," produce "camaraderie, cooperation, dialogue, deliberation, negotiation, competition, creativity, and the kinds of self-expression and self-sacrifice that are possible only in association with others." The "viability and vibrancy of liberal democracy," she concludes, "depend in many morally important ways on the associational activity of its citizens."[6]

Such accounts of associations as powerful sites for the generation of democratic values, of humanism without humans, underscore the need to re-localize sociality, to foster the participatory (even, at times, conflictual) give and take of local association as an antidote to the surrogated agency of institutionality. It is equally important, however, to conceive associations as sites of inventive alternatives, as my discussion of the romances of Hawthorne and Melville shows, and not simply as reflections of preexisting or predetermined values or, worse, interior states. At stake, then, is not simply perpetuating social ideals through associations, but also providing occasions—even from within institutions—for the collaborative negotiation of those ideals themselves.

Such local associations existed in the nineteenth-century United States, represented as the "reformable" socialities shared by immigrants, working people, sexual deviants, nuns, urbanites, criminals, all targeted by reform efforts to normalize a middle-class interior state. Despite reform's best efforts, such socialities persist in our own day, although we are often reluctant, because of their discredited status as partisan, divisive, or just trivial, to take them as social models. I would like to conclude, however, by offering two such associations and their productions of humanism without humans. The first example is affinity groups within ACT UP, an association of activists who, beginning in 1987 in New York City, worked to alter research, treatment, social policy, and public representation related to HIV/AIDS. In its heyday, ACT UP organized and carried out public demonstrations that attracted media attention to the AIDS epidemic, publicized accurate information through the media, and displayed forms of public activism for people hitherto represented as isolated, sick, and helpless. These demonstrations, powerful interventions in the operations of public institutions (the National Institutes of Health, the New York Stock Exchange, the Catholic church), were facilitated by self-organized "affinity" groups with specific tasks within a larger demonstration (videotaping the demonstration for publicity purposes, for instance, or blocking traffic to create a public space for other protesters). Before each demonstration, affinity-group members underwent training in nonviolent resistance, in legal rights and responsibilities, and in the data related to the overall demonstration. Members collaboratively planned their actions, assigning functions (holding medications for the larger membership, photographing the action in case of politic violence, alerting media representatives). What bound these groups together was not the sameness of identity (they were often diverse in race, age, class, gender, and sexuality) or personal history (members could participate in affinity groups without any prior knowledge of other members), but a specific goal, and while affinity groups sometimes acted together in a number of demonstrations, they might disband at any point. Forming permanent communities was not the goal of affinity groups, in other words, although collective action was instrumental in achieving the task at hand. In the act of planning and executing its goal, the groups generated their specific values, although those values oriented toward the humanist terms (rights, value of life, equality of opportunity, etc.) set by the demonstration and by ACT UP's mission generally. From the first discussions where ideas and information were shared (effective self-presentation and listening), to establishing actions, often involving disagreements that had to be worked out collaboratively (negotiation), through everyone's eventual agreement to the action (advised consent), the assignment of functions (mutual responsibility), and, finally the action itself, the collectively negotiated values ("affinity"), not sameness of identity and culture or continuity of relationship, motivated the group. ACT UP affinity groups were anti-institutional associations, not only in their explicit confrontation of public institutions, but, more important, in their refusal to defer justice to the horizon of futurity (chants declared, "What do we want? Health care! When do we want it? NOW!"); their refusal to act on the basis of interiority (unlike "pride" movements, ACT UP's goals could not be met by rectifying the interior states of shame and "right feeling"); and their refusal to abstract or surrogate agency, insisting on direct, contingent, and local action.

Of course, associations need not be as explicitly or confrontationally political as ACT UP affinity groups to enact a post-interior humanism. Another brief—admittedly parochial—example will suffice. The English Department at Loyola is housed in a building with maze-like hallways and few common spaces, with little opportunity for social interaction. In response to this isolation, several colleagues appropriated a room and began meeting daily for lunch. While we share an institutional location (all members of the same department) and professional interest (all teachers of literature), the "lunch group" shares very little else in regard to literary field, methodological interest, politics, social background, or rank. Over time, colleagues come and go, depending on schedules and the need for interaction. Few political, social, intellectual, or (most commonly) institutional issues fail to find their way to the table. Rarely does everyone agree (indeed, conversation can be quite heated), but we all experience the pleasures—along with the frustrations—of debate, deliberation, negotiation. Though the "lunch group," unlike ACT UP affinity groups, has no mission or political agenda, it arose no less from an institutional lacuna: desiring the space of sociality denied by the institutional culture in which we worked, we made it for ourselves.

Our differences are not a threat to our association but are what make association pleasurable. Our disagreements over a shared set of values (ones without fixed definitions) form an occasion for social invention, and hence for mutual trust. And while the occasional disagreements and flared tempers may cause members to withdraw temporarily, the trust that arises from reasonable and respectful debate draws us back. When members return to a group from which they have dissented, they know they have done so voluntarily, from a will to continue with the mutual task of the group, from a commitment to the values the group generates. "A community kept in existence by the need for community itself," the political theorist Samuel Fleischacker argues, "must require a conformity that eventually erodes its members' sense that they have individually chosen to be part of it." Dissent, however, "allows for *community itself* to occur," enabling members to remain free.[7] The flexibility of dissent comes most easily, Fleischacker shows, in trivial and undervalued associations accessible to most citizens in their everyday lives. "Sociability under such circumstances," he argues, "is often the most pleasant kind of sociability, and also a sociability where people are willing to open up, temporarily at least, to hearing about other ways of living, to receiving criticism of their political, or moral, or religious positions, to playing with other ends they might take on, ends they might adopt but have so far resisted adopting, ways of life they might regard as reasonable alternatives to their own."[8] While ACT UP was an extraordinary association—drawing wide public attention and finding its ways into history books—the lunch group is common, everyday, local. While such associations disappear in most accounts of public belonging, they are nevertheless sites where alternative social imaginaries are developed and progressive change takes root, where essential democratic values are generated and perpetuated. As such, they are essential antidotes to deferment, interiorization, and abstraction. Quite possibly, we undertake that work in much of everyday life, although we fail to recognize the significance of our actions. If we did recognize the significance of "insignificant communities," perhaps groups like ACT UP would become less extraordinary.

If generating more occasions for humanism without humans is a theoretical daydream, I can only second Hawthorne's narrator, who muses, "I know not justly, if it be a weakness or a sin to create these phantoms that we love and to group them into a paradise—soul-created. But if it is a sin, it is a sweet and enchanting sin, and if it is a weakness, it is a strong and stirring weakness."[9] The narrator poignantly concludes, "Much as hope may lean toward the intoxicating joy of distinction, there is another leaning in the soul, deeper, and stronger, toward the pleasures which the heart pants for, and in whose atmosphere, the affections bloom and ripen."[10] And yet, given that interiority has become the precondition of public personhood (perhaps of personhood generally), to postulate a democracy *without* interiority is not only to suggest the end of disciplined subjectivity as theorized by Foucault, but to open up new—more collective, more reasoned, and more fantastic—constructions of democratic collaboration. It is to imagine the end, perhaps, of humanity so as to imagine the (re)vitalization of humanism, of people who are citizens of somewhere other than an interior state.

NOTES

Introduction

1 See, e.g., Crenson and Ginsberg, *Downsizing Democracy*; Frank, *One Market under God*; Lummis, *Radical Democracy*; Smith, *The Politics of Deceit*.

2 "Democracy means that the people rule," writes C. Douglas Lummis. "To do so, the people must form itself into a body by which power can in principle be held." Democracy "is not a kind of government, but an end of government; not a historically existing institution, but a historical project." Today, Lummis warns, we risk becoming "a people that has lost its political memory" due to social reform, which encourages people to accept "the basic conditions of competition and of work in the capitalist economy as unalterable." While reform may seek "only to make things 'a bit more pleasant,'" thereby conceding defeat from the beginning, democratic power "does not fall from above, it is generated by a people in a democratic state of mind, and by the actions they take in accordance with that state of mind. It is the possibility of this change of state that is the power of the powerless." For Lummis, democracy is not a product but a process, as the people achieve, in the process of striving for democracy, "the full development of the intellectual and moral powers," enabling them to make "the choice between faith and cynicism." When Lummis claims that "power cannot be held by *any* collection of persons, but held only by persons who have formed themselves into 'a people' through their public commitment to political virtue," he lays the groundwork for what, in the conclusion to this book, I call humanism without humans: see Lummis, *Radical Democracy*, 21–22, 26, 33, 35, 39, 42–43.

3 Putnam, "Bowling Alone." Tocqueville reports, "In no country in the world has the principle of association been more successfully used or applied to a greater multitude of objects than in America. Besides the permanent associations which are established by law under the names of townships, cities, and counties, a vast number of others are formed and maintained by the agency of private individuals": Tocqueville, *Democracy in America*, chap. 12.

4 The seventy years between the ratification of the Constitution and the beginning of the Civil War brought profound change in the United States. With the incorporation of territories acquired in the 1803 Louisiana Purchase and the Mexican War (1846–48), the United States grew from thirteen to thirty-four states, while the population increased from 3.9 million in 1790 to nearly 31.5 million in 1860. The statehood of territories with large populations of Spanish, French, and Native American inhabi-

tants diversified the American population, as did unprecedented immigration, which jumped from five thousand annually at the start of the nineteenth century to six hundred thousand during the 1830s, 1.7 million in the 1840s, and 2.6 million in the 1850s. Immigrants settled the western territories, but they also pioneered new ways of life in America's growing cities. By 1860, the United States had eight cities with populations greater than 150,000, and immigrants formed 40 percent of the populations of the nation's fifty largest cities. Consequently, urban citizens interacted with diverse cultures with varying mores and conventions, making belief in a single, "natural" way of life harder to maintain. At the same time, the anonymity, mobility, and new forms of association and leisure within cities made conventional forms of surveillance and moral regulation more difficult to enforce. By 1835, there were nearly three thousand licensed drinking places in New York, for instance, nearly one for every fifty persons over fifteen, and an estimated two hundred brothels: see Mintz, *Moralists and Modernizers*, 4, 7.

5 In claiming that "ideology has no history" but is "endowed with a structure and a functioning such as to make it a non-historical reality, i.e. an *omni-historical* reality," Louis Althusser states that this claim may be "related directly to Freud's claim that *the unconscious is eternal*, i.e. that it has no history": Althusser, *Lenin*, 160–61.

6 Jameson, *Political Unconscious*, 22

7 Butler, *Gender Trouble*, viii.

8 In distinguishing between government and governmentality, I am drawing on new work in political theory that takes Michel Foucault's insights from *Discipline and Punish* to a range of activities through which government purports to empower and protect citizens by regulating citizens' subjectivity. See esp. Cruikshank, *The Will to Empower*, 123, who argues that "the will to empower is a strategy of government, one that seeks solutions to political problems in the governmentalization of the everyday lives of citizen-subjects," and Thomas Dumm, *Michel Foucault and the Politics of Freedom*, who traces the moves from disciplinarily to security, from the control of individual subjects to that of subject populations though modifications in popular conceptions of "freedom."

9 See, e.g., Barker, *The Tremulous Private Body*; Lynch, *The Economy of Character*; Rosenwein, *Anger's Past*.

10 For an extended critique of generational futurity, see Edelman, *No Future*.

11 Marx, *The Marx-Engels Reader*, 160–61.

12 For an excellent account of the rise and popularity of social reform in antebellum America, see Mintz, *Moralists and Modernizers*. On Fourier's influence on utopian communitarians in the United States, see Guarneri, *The Utopian Alternative*.

13 Emerson, "Man the Reformer," 132–33.

14 Michael Warner refers to the emergence of a mass public in antebellum America from "partial nonidentification with the object of address in public speech," particularly in public-reform speeches popularized by temperance meetings: Warner, "Whitman Drunk," 78.

15 Mintz, *Moralists and Modernizers*, 73, 127.

16 Thoreau, "Reform and the Reformers," 186.

17 Mintz, *Moralists and Modernizers*, 10.

18 For a full analysis of the "Cetology" chapter in the context of nineteenth-century racial ethnography, see Otter, *Melville's Anatomies*, 132–59. I am indebted to Otter's thoughtful and richly contextualized study of Melville's "material analysis of consciousness": ibid., 5.

19 Melville, *Moby-Dick*, 116, 122, 127, 135.

20 Rogin, *Subversive Genealogy*.

21 White, "The Politics of Historical Interpretation,"115.

22 Emerson, "Experience," 295, 297, 311.

23 Quoted in Clinton, *Tocqueville, Lieber, and Bagehot*, 5.

1. *"Matters of Internal Concern"*

1 Findley, "Reply to Wilson's Speech," 98.

2 Hamilton, in "Articles of Confederation," 176.

3 Ibid.

4 Warner argues that the "We" of the U.S. Constitution authorizes a "sovereign interpellation" through which "the people are always coming across themselves in the act of consenting to their own coercion": Warner, *The Letters of the Republic*, 112. Warner's notion that the Constitution's sovereign control—what Jay Fliegelman (*Declaring Independence*, 35) calls its "soft compulsion"—comes about by making citizens "the site where all lesser collectivities are evacuated" (Warner, *The Letters of the Republic*, 12) is foundational to my argument in this chapter.

5 On melancholy in the early American novel, see Stern, *The Plight of Feeling*. I am also grateful to Frank Shuffelton, who shared with me his conference paper "Melancholy and the Constitution of the Federal Ego: Loss and Repression in the Early American Novel." In that paper, Shuffelton argues that, for Americans who enjoyed connections to British civility, history, and empire, the end of the Revolution brought a profound loss. While "many were able to acquire an American subjectivity by working through their mourning for lost connections and in the process embraced, cathected to, an imagined American community and landscape," Shuffelton contends, "others were unable to accept the loss of what had meant most to them." Shuffelton's argument can be profitably applied to *The Coquette*, which begins with the death of Eliza's father, a figure who, like the fathers Shuffelton describes in William Hill Brown's *The Power of Sympathy*, represents both comfort and loss. It is important to note, however, the Eliza does not grieve the loss of British civility. In fact, her friends embody a continued form of that civility, deployed as a mirror to instill in Eliza precisely the kinds of national ego formations that Shuffelton claims were lost with the supposed end of British manners in America.

6 Warner, *The Letters of the Republic*, 104, 108.

7 "Articles of Confederation," 85–86.

8 Warner, *The Letters of the Republic*, 114.

9 Cox, *Four Pillars of Constitutionalism*, 62.

10 Rossiter, *Federalist Papers*, 294–95.

11 Ibid., 456.

12 See, e.g., the work of Elizabeth Barnes, Lauren Berlant, Caleb Crain, Peter Coviello, Elizabeth Dillon, Julie Ellison, and Glenn Hendler.

13 Blanchard, "On the Importance and Means of Cultivating the Social Affections among Pupils," 24. Page numbers cited in the text are from this edition.

14 The structuring of democracy around an endlessly deferred promise of future fulfillment that diminishes citizens' capacity to make democracy in the here and now has been cogently theorized by Dana D. Nelson, to whose *National Manhood* I am deeply indebted.

15 The phenomenon I am describing is close to what Arjun Appadurai calls "locality," which he defines as "primarily relational and contextual rather than as scalar or spatial": Appadurai, *Modernity at Large*, 178. Appadurai contrasts locality to neighborhoods, which, he contends, necessarily define themselves in opposition to some other context they themselves produce. Although neighborhoods are prerequisites to the production of locality and of localized subjects, "as these subjects engage in the social activities of production, representation, and reproduction (as in the work of culture), they contribute, generally unwittingly, to the creation of contexts that might exceed the existing material and conceptual boundaries of the neighborhood": ibid., 185. We might say that Eliza's vision of friendship marks a transition from neighborhood to locality, since it defines itself in opposition to the context of mobility and heteronormative privacy yet has not fully exceeded the boundaries of space to incorporate a larger social network than that of near neighbors.

16 Russ Castronovo argues that "citizens adhere to a lexicon that governs without regard to 'irregular conditions' that particularize subjects such as institutional location or racial ancestry. U.S. democracy deploys a freedom that operates above culture, or, better yet, that makes culture a hindrance to citizenship": Castronovo, "Political Necrophilia," 117. The quest for a democracy without culture, as Castronovo demonstrates, proves suicidal to citizens forced to bear the burden of embodied particularity.

17 "Articles of Confederation," 86.

18 I draw here on Nelson's analysis of "managerial democracy," in which citizens are encouraged to cede their participation in the making of democracy to distant authority and deferred promise: Nelson, *National Manhood*, 204–37. In thinking about modes of counter-democracy, I am also indebted to Michael Warner's description of queer ethics, arising "where the most heterogeneous people are brought into great intimacy by their common experience of being despised and rejected in a world of norms that they now recognize as false morality": Warner, *The Trouble with Normal*, 36.

19 See Foucault, "Friendship as a Way of Life."

20 Fliegelman notes the interiorization of civic order in the rhetorical practices of the Revolutionary era, in which public speaking became "an occasion for the public revelation of a private self" conceived and judged by "private rather than public

virtues: prudence, temperance, self-control, honesty, and, most problematically, sincerity." In what he calls "the elocutionary revolution," individuals were put "beyond themselves and their own self-interest into the realm of a mutuality of feelings." Given the normative policing of those "feelings," this process of generating national belonging constitutes a potent form of what Fliegelman calls "soft compulsion": Fliegelman, *Declaring Independence*, 24, 35, 40.

21 My thinking here is influenced by *The German Ideology*, in which Marx calls "estrangement" the transformation of "what we ourselves produce into an objective power above us, growing out of our control, thwarting our expectations, bringing to naught our calculations." Estrangement describes the emergence of the state, "divorced from the real interests of individual and community," yet serving "as an illusory communal life, always based, however, on the real ties existing in every family and tribal conglomeration": Marx, *The Marx-Engels Reader*, 160.

22 Philip Hamburger makes a powerful case for the ways "liberality" choreographed civic order in the new republic. Writing that Federalists "assumed that freedom could be preserved only if a people were willing to sacrifice their individual interests for the sake of their republic as a whole and that this 'civic virtue' or devotion to the common wealth was unlikely beyond the relatively cohesive circumstances of small, homogeneous societies," Hamburger shows how local attachments were transferred to abstract "virtues" that with "a distinction compatible with the equality of mankind" allowed for a faith in equal access to virtue that compensated (or repressed) the increasing inequalities of economic opportunity: Hamburger, "Liberality," 1219, 1241.

23 As Hamburger notes, "Liberality had the potential to condemn all that stood in its path as narrow interest and prejudice and therefore was already becoming an ideal so far-reaching as to stimulate, both among the liberal and the less liberal, a sense of the incompatibility between general principles and particular practices, affiliations or attachments": ibid., 1252. While Hamburger contends that liberality arises in response to social fragmentation in America (ibid., 1225), I am arguing that liberality produced fragmentation, detaching people from their local allegiances in order to reattach them to more abstract entities. As Hamburger writes, "Refracted through their liberalized lives and liberal sentiments, any number of things, including the aspirations and bonds of a close-knit locality, could come to seem burdensome and illiberal, and, in this way, liberality and the liberalization with which it was connected probably stimulated the social fragmentation amid which Americans found liberality appealing": ibid., 1270.

24 Without strict communal standards, citizens turned to etiquette books for education in liberal virtues, increasing Americans' dependence on print. Hamburger argues that liberality was increasingly tied to law, which was elevated above public opinion as "a legitimate sanction in a republic": ibid., 1251. But the very print circulations that substituted for local convention necessitated that citizens be dependent on print, which in antebellum America was also a principal tool of public opinion. Because of this, I would argue that liberality became much more closely bound to print than to law, which was often seen as the domain of the state rather than of the civil sphere,

which is liberality's proper location. Karen Haltunen argues that the wide practice of reading etiquette books in antebellum America created a conflict between "sentimental sincerity and genteel self-restraint" that became resolved in what she calls "the genteel performance, a system of polite conduct that demanded a flawless self-discipline practiced with an apparently easy, natural sincere manner": Haltunen, *Confidence Men and Painted Women*, 93, see also 92–123.

25 Widely distributed at the time of its initial publication in 1846, a second edition of the speech appeared in 1847, and a third, in the form of a volume, in 1847. Page numbers cited in the text are from Lieber, "The Character of the Gentleman," in *The Miscellaneous Writings of Francis Lieber*.

26 I am in agreement here with Bruce Burgett, who reads "Rip Van Winkle" as an allegory of "the rise of extra-political means of social control": Burgett, "America's Nationalism—R.I.P.," 318.

27 On Irving's reluctance to participate in the federal project of turning myth into history, see Jeffrey Rubin-Dorsky, *Adrift in the Old World*, who argues that Irving's tales, by insisting that the nation's "past" be recognized as a mythic creation, maintained the importance of imagination in a society increasingly dedicated to commercial competitiveness and "useful" labor. Christopher Looby extends this argument, showing how the "allegorization of historical practice as semiotic substitution," a repetitious "substitution of one 'sign' for another," turns the expectation of a terminus in national "meaning" into an endless deferral: Looby, *Voicing America*, 95. Michael Gilmore notes, "The age palmed off fictions as truthful narratives; Irving reversed the process by turning history into fiction and so jumbling actual events and sources with invented ones that it seems impossible to disentangle them." Gilmore concludes, "laughter and confusion deflate history's authority as the realm of truth": Gilmore, "Washington Irving," 665.

28 Even in their movement into print, as Gilmore notes, Irving's narrators express a melancholy attachment to an older and more local way of life. "Avoiding the novel, the genre of a modernizing civilization," Gilmore observes, Irving "worked in forms—the essay serial, the sketch, the history—that now seemed old-fashioned" and that perpetuate "an understanding of literature as a communal possession." Through these print forms, then, Irving presented "a conservative challenge to the emergent liberal consensus" in regard to "the putative advancements and moral authority of middle-class civilization." At the same time, Irving's trade in print commodities cannot fully avoid the dispersed conditions of modern life, and Gilmore astutely notes that "Irving's narratives make a fetish of mediation. To read the story is to be made aware of one's removal from a departed or inaccessibly point of origin": Gilmore, "Washington Irving," 661, 666–67, 674.

29 This is one of the most remarked on details in Irving's tale. See, e.g., Burgett, "America's Nationalism—R.I.P.," 317; Gilmore, "Washington Irving," 672; Looby, *Voicing America*, 43; Rubin-Dorsky, *Adrift in the Old World*, 114.

30 Looby, *Voicing America*, 47. Outlining "the rapid migration of large parts of the population" in Irving's day, in which communities "were left behind, new ones begun

and then abandoned for the promise of still greater opportunities," Rubin-Dorsky notes "an undertow of anxiety about the breakdown and loss of community" in tales such as "Rip Van Winkle." For Irving, time, which, as Rubin-Dorsky argues, "meant loss—loss of expectation, loss of identity, and the loss that had a special poignancy for his generation, loss of home," could be countered only by works of imagination that constitute "a compensation for unsettling change": Rubin-Dorsky, *Adrift in the Old World*, 4–5, 13, 113.

31 See Anderson, *Imagined Communities*. I am building on Castronovo's important insight that "political necrophilia seeks to put to rest conditions that force human actors to play a political fort/da game, in which historical, material, legal, and institutional circumstances restrict access to the pleasures of abstract liberty": Castronovo, "Political Necrophilia," 137.

32 Stern, *The Plight of Feeling*.

33 Freud, "Mourning and Melancholia," 170–73.

34 Ibid., 166.

35 Freud traces the relationship of character and melancholy in the opposite manner. As Judith Butler argues, Freud asserts in *The Ego and the Id* that "character" is the residue of melancholic incorporations in which the grieving ego pieces itself together from aspects of the lost love object. Melancholic identification, according to Freud, is central in ego formation and " 'makes an essential contribution toward building up what is called its "character": quoted in Butler, *The Psychic Life of Power*, 133. If the abstract "character" collectively constructed by Eliza's survivors is predicated on their identification with and incorporation of her "error," then Eliza might be said to be a disruptive psychic contradiction within the normative ego of federal America.

36 In reading Eliza's removal as a willful gesture, I want to resist assessments of her last days as a failure and forfeiture. "Eliza Wharton's protoliberal impulses are ultimately stillborn," Stern writes, "and her rebellious nature recontained because she cannot imagine a life beyond the very republican cohort that would stifle and bury alive her powerful desire for freedom." While Stern at first presents Eliza as the victim of conspiratorial republicanism, she soon makes her the victim of her own imaginative failures: "The heroine's tragedy finally involves her failure to function as the sympathetic spectator of her own plight," Stern asserts; "once she loses the capacity to see her dissent from the majority's tyranny as a valid desire, her interpellation into the ideology of republican fellow feeling becomes complete" (Stern, *The Plight of Feeling*, 75). Both the individualization of social failure and the inevitability of normative interpellation require that Eliza's story end in a death figured as irremediable interpellation: "Eliza Wharton is destined to suffer an unrelenting fate, one that . . . involves erasure, invisibility, and, finally, death" (ibid., 140). Burgett similarly assumes that Eliza is fated by her own failure of imagination: "Eliza lacks the desire (and the structures) that would enable her to differentiate personal (sexual or gender) identity from publication" (Burgett, *Sentimental Bodies*, 107). David Waldstreicher, too, declares Eliza's absolute defeat: "From obsession with signs and public personae, an abandoned Eliza moves to a preoccupation with her own heart—and melancholia"

(Waldstreicher, "Fallen under My Observation," 214). I would agree that Eliza is melancholic, but I do not think she "moves" there only at the end of the novel as a result of her own "failure to regulate the signs of sentiment" (ibid., 216). "Having failed," Waldstreicher contends, "Eliza seeks to know her own heart better" (ibid., 214), a conclusion that implies that Eliza has failed to "know her own heart" in the first place.

37 Freud, "Mourning and Melancholia," 165.

38 Ibid., 172, 176.

39 Berlant, "Intimacy," 5–6. Arguing that "Foster demonstrates that freedom exists even within the limits that curtail the experience of and scope of freedom," Gillian Brown deconstructs the opposition structuring most critical treatments of *The Coquette*. Brown argues that, in freeing consent from the tedious debates about marriage and child raising in which her friends engage, Foster presents "a charge to society that it separate consent from the contradictions in which it has operated." Ultimately, Brown's argument raises troubling questions about the relationship of restriction and freedom, as when Brown writes, "Foster's novel displays the populousness of consent and the prominent role of witnesses in defining consent. The goal of the interests competing for Eliza's consent is to reduce this crowded state: to make consent represent one voice, one direct line of cause and effect." How reducing the inventiveness of intimacy to one form of representation ("voice") and of narrative ("direct line of cause and effect") could do anything other than jeopardize freedom is a question left unaddressed in Brown's will "to bring the coquette to consequences." At the same time, Brown's argument importantly allows that one may consent to something other than federal affect: for Brown, freedom might reside elsewhere than in the electoral processes to which citizens ostensibly consent or in the forms of public judgment that normalized intimacy requires: Brown, "Consent, Coquetry, and Consequences," 627, 638–39, 640, 643.

40 Teute and Shields, "The Confederation Court." I am grateful to Fredrika Teute and David Shields for sharing their unpublished essay.

41 Quoted ibid., 4.

42 Ibid., 11, 14–16.

43 Ibid., 123.

44 Berlant, "Intimacy," 6.

45 Butler, revising Freud's theories of melancholy, argues that gender identity is the incorporated trace of a disavowed desire for people of the same sex. Coercive heterosexuality, Butler contends, demands that people disavow both their same-sex desire and the resulting grief, generating a melancholic disquietude illusorily resolved by the incorporation of gender as the interiorized preservation of the disavowed object of desire. This theory of double disavowal, of what Butler calls "the 'never-never' that supports the naturalized surface of heterosexual life as well as its pervasive melancholia" (Butler, *The Psychic Life of Power*, 138), may account for why the bonds of friendship in both Foster's novel and Dall's are chiefly among women, whose friendships are most perilously threatened by conventional marriage. At the same time, these novels help us historicize and consequently expand Butler's reading of melancholy,

suggesting that U.S. culture is haunted by a historical disavowal of association more broadly. Keeping in view these macro- and micro-processes of disavowal as mutually reinforcing dynamics in early America, we might speculate that the constitution of gender identity as an outgrowth of the disavowal of same-sex love is a paradigmatic example of the prior interiorization of social order, whereby citizens were encouraged to replace intimate attachments with managed privacy, with strict gender roles and heteronormativity interiorized as personal virtue.

46 Whitman, *Leaves of Grass*, 35.

47 As Cathy Davidson argues, many of the early American sentimental novels provide "an education in the value of playing the proper sexual roles available to women who were thereby seduced by the sentimental plot as well as in it." She notes that such novels paradoxically affirm "the need to educate women and the uselessness of any such education in a society that has no place for educated women" and contends that, set "within a specific context of limiting marriage laws and restrictive social mores," *The Coquette* "is less a story of the wages of sin, than a study of the wages of marriage": Davidson, *Revolution and the Word*, 110–11, 143. Carroll Smith-Rosenberg seconds Davidson's argument, contending that Foster warned against romances "not because they taught women sexual passion for men, but because they taught women to renounce their own reason and independence." As such, Foster's warning was not only to female readers but to *all* Americans, since the wayward coquette, Smith-Rosenberg demonstrates, was a gendered projection of the attributes—the speculative desire for greater opportunity gained through the acquisitiveness taken on through the trade in paper (currency rather than novels)—more properly characterizing middle-class men in the market economy of post-Revolutionary America: Smith-Rosenberg, "Domesticating 'Virtue,'" 177.

48 Foster, *The Coquette*, 107. Page numbers cited in the text are from this edition.

49 Waldstreicher makes the case for an "economy of vision" in *The Coquette* operating by "a new system of exchanged signs of sentiment governed by particular rules for viewing and interpretation. The rhetoric of sentimental display assured readers that, despite mistaken perceptions and repeated transgressions, vision and virtue are always restored to reality." Having entered this exchange in sentimental signs, Eliza, Waldstreicher rightly notes, is "less free, for in virtue's marketplace she is a defined commodity: not allowed to change, to be various, or even have an interior will that differs from the true feelings she must show." In Waldstreicher's reading, Eliza is the victim of "the gaze that searches for yet denies a veiled interiority": Waldstreicher, "Fallen under My Observation," 206–207, 212.

50 "The only resolution is beyond the gaze of monitors," Waldstreicher argues, "where a physically abused Eliza can stand in for the idea of virtue, apart from vision and the evaluation of virtue." Waldstreicher seems close to what I am suggesting here about the disruptive power of silence, but in the end he declares, "Eliza is finally what Boyer wanted her to be: an idea held close to the heart." While it is true that, having taken possession of the text of virtue, Boyer, like Eliza's friends, can declare her fully interpellated into visible character, it is not true that Eliza's silence has no declaratory power.

Waldstreicher suggests as much when he writes, "In an economy of gazes, freedom can only mean control of who watches and what they see." Eliza has no control over the former (her friends circulate her texts promiscuously), but she does have a limited control over the latter, not through visibility (always registered in the language of intelligible sentiment) but, rather, through what is made invisible. Although Waldstreicher minimizes this power, claiming, "Eliza . . . has lost control over signs and now can only avoid them," given the powers he attributes to the monitory regimes of modern sentiment, Eliza's removal from the economy of signs may be the subject's insistence on a different relation to language, to the intersubjective, and hence to sociality itself: ibid., 210, 215–16.

51 Although "print" may seem too formal a term for the circulation of private correspondence described in *The Coquette*, I use it to convey the ways in which Eliza's letters, circulating promiscuously to shape groups of distant friends into a supposedly coherent "group" through their imagined identification with discourses of value. Epistolarity thus parallels the uses of print in eighteenth-century America to create the imagined community of the nation, in which every citizen felt an affective identification with an abstract public sphere. Warner describes this dual function of eighteenth-century print—as "a republican paradigm of public virtue" and as "categories of private appropriation such as politeness, fame, and luxury" (Warner, *The Letters of the Republic*, 151)—as being central to the rise of the novel in early America. Davidson suggests the potential usefulness for women readers of such fictionalized identifications, writing, "As the community of women within the novel exchange views and ideas on such crucial subjects as friendship, marriage, and economic security, their letters constitute a dialogic discourse in which the reader was also invited to participate if only vicariously": Davidson, *Revolution and the Word*, 144. But I am inclined to agree with Warner's conclusion that such identifications, which he describes as "the reflective management of esteem," are ultimately deadening to democracy: "You can be a member of the nation, attributing its agency to yourself in imaginary identification, without being a freeholder or exercising any agency in the public sphere. Nationalism makes no distinction between such imaginary participation and the active participation of citizens": Warner, *The Letters of the Republic*, 173–74.

At the same time, I would suggest that if print identifications leave citizens bereft of democratic agency, some, like Eliza, pursue the gaps in fictional citizenship that the novel only apparently sutures. The reader's imagination can thereby become a space of compensatory mediation within the necessary language of sensibility—a sensibility that is not always pulled into the realm of public interpretation but, rather, that appropriates elements of the social into an imaginative reordering. Ian Finseth argues as much when he writes that, "despite the novel's socially responsible frame," *The Coquette* "could engage imaginative possibilities and explore ambitious human realities in ways that public discourse could not." Finseth claims, "Just as individual self-interest in Eliza's world must be subordinated to the common weal, so must the irregularities, impieties, and improprieties of real human existence be subsumed by the print language of group cohesion." Finseth adds that Eliza's exchanges with her friends "illustrate an inability to agree upon the identity of certain core words and point to a fundamental difference regarding the nature of language itself." I agree with Finseth's conclusion that Eliza in the end moves into "an eloquent silence" that bespeaks "a faith that language may yet be renewed and regenerated, and thus provide a richer understanding of that larger world." Yet I would resist Finseth's effort to turn Eliza into a proto-Romantic who represents "feelings" as personal expression, rather than as registers of broader social imaginaries: see Finseth, "A Melancholy Tale," 7, 13–15.

52 The ultimate text is the gravestone her friends erect at the end of the novel. As Finseth writes, "Translating into words the identity of the woman in the grave," Eliza's friends "create a textual version of Eliza which will enter the public domain much as a book would, and which must therefore conform to the same standards of moral propriety": ibid., 17. They also create, as Stern notes, a fetish fully divorced from that body: Stern, *The Plight of Feeling*. By showing how the majority comes together over a tombstone, Foster suggests the fictive nature of their identifications. What "dies" at the end of *The Coquette*, then, is not so much Eliza and the possibility for sensational dissent she represents, but the illusion of correspondence between "character" as a circulating text and as the "nature" contained by individual bodies. Eliza's withdrawal, driving a wedge between sensation and fantasy on the one hand and public circulations of "character" on the other, troubles the assertion that the name (whether it is the etched name on the tombstone or the "good name" restored by her friends' postmortem moralizing) is, to put it simply, who one is.

53 Although Boyer tells Eliza, "Your own heart must be your monitor," Eliza makes this literally true in a way that Boyer, of course, does not intend. The fusion of judgmental vision and internalized scrutiny can never be successfully completed or there is no rationale for the continued mechanism of observation. Boyer uses "monitor" more in the sense of a technology of display than of judgment. That Eliza takes this literally proves ultimately disruptive to her friends' monitorial prerogative, since it short-circuits the conduit of internalization and externalization at the critical suture of the confessional narration and the affective body. Having professed to want an utter fusion of the two, her friends now have it: Eliza's affective body can be fully surmised from her postmortem confessions.

54 There are five references to confession in the last pages of the novel (Foster, *The Coquette*, 184, 191, 212, 220, 229) and nine to criminality (ibid., 222, 226, 229, 230 [two references], 231, 234 [three references]).

55 Stern argues that Eliza's expressive independence is betrayed by her female friends who, turning their backs on her requests for sympathetic companionship, become visible as a moral community only when her death allows them to inscribe the moral of her story in terms of normative republican (and gendered) values. See the astute analysis of fetishism and monumentality in the creation of fictive community in Stern, *The Plight of Feeling*, 138–51.

56 Pettengill, "Sisterhood in a Separate Sphere," 198.

57 To read the novel's close in this way is to attempt to raise the dead, which, as Sharon

Holland asserts, is simultaneously an effort to articulate alternative constructions of national character. Holland notes that Benedict Anderson rests the birth of nationalism on a figure of death and mourning: the Tomb of the Unknown Soldier. For Anderson, a dead body signals both the loss of particular identity and the rebirth into a collective memory supporting the shared identity of citizenship. The fact that this body is "unknown" is necessary to its resurrection into national unity, since it allows for the abstraction of those particularities that might unsettle the national identity it supposedly registers. Answers to the questions that a soldier's particular body would present trouble the assertions of "sameness" that make national belonging believable to discreet citizens encouraged, in acts of mourning, to similarly identify with the abstract national body. Holland evocatively builds on this theory to explore the relationship of death and mourning in the creation of black subjectivity. African Americans experience a "social death" (in the lingering national imaginary no less than during historical slavery), Holland argues, in ways that attempt to silence the particularities of black experience and give rise to a notion of national health figured as whiteness. Yet the black body, if dead, is never forgotten: to serve as a prop to national identity, the specter of black undeath must be kept always alive. Mourning as a state of white citizenship, then, maintains the memory of black (not quite complete) death at the center of its self-imaginings. If the dead can never be allowed to vanish, they also maintain the potential to speak those truths not only of injustice but also of alternative formations of communal life and genealogical connection that are (never quite successfully) silenced at the scene of nation formation: Anderson, *Imagined Communities*; Holland, *Raising the Dead*.

58 Foucault, "Friendship as a Way of Life," 204–5, 207.

59 Although the subtitle of Dall's novel refers to Susanna Rowson's *Charlotte Temple*, the plot entirely concerns Eliza Wharton.

60 Dall, *The Romance of the Association*, 111. Page numbers cited in the text are from this edition. In 1841, at the encouragement of Elizabeth Peabody, Dall attended Margaret Fuller's "Conversations," which led Dall later to write *Margaret and Her Friends* (1885) and *Transcendentalism in New England* (1897), one of the earliest considerations of the relationship between Transcendentalism and feminism. Fuller's influence can also be seen in Dall's characterization of Eliza Wharton. Like Fuller, who married the younger Italian Marquis Angelo Ossoli, with whom she had a son (all three died in a shipwreck off Fire Island, New York), Dall's Eliza marries a European aristocrat of whom she fears her friends will not approve and dies with her son while attempting to prove her devotion to her husband.

2. Bad Associations

1 Gladwell, "Institutional Health," 35.

2 Ibid.

3 Ibid.

4 Rios is quoted in Lithwick, "Holy Matrimony."

5 I am building here on Amy Kaplan's provocative insight that metaphors of expansive domestic order in antebellum America enabled the imperial spread of U.S. interests beyond the national border. If, as Kaplan has compellingly argued, the nineteenth century used the home to expand the nation's global reach, the violent dissent brought about by that imperial project came home to roost in the late twentieth century, both in the form of domestic terrorism and in the institutional panics expressed by Rios and other neo-conservatives: Kaplan, "Manifest Domesticity."

6 Edelman argues that the heteronormativity of public discourse relies on a "reproductive futurism" with the power to "impose an ideological limit on political discourse as such, preserving in the process the absolute privilege of heteronormativity by rendering unthinkable, by casting outside the political domain, the possibility of a queer resistance to this organizing principle of communal relations": Edelman, *No Future*, 2. While Edelman is correct in his analysis of contemporary culture, the discourse of "reproductive futurism," my argument shows, has a longer history in which the relational resistance of citizens in general—and not only of "queer" citizens—was limited by a deferred futurity that made "unthinkable" the possibility of social demand in the present. Edelman, like many other queer theorists, resolves the tension between futurism and dissent by locating "queerness" in the psyche (the "death drive") of the individual subject, thereby eliding the possibility of "communal relations" as a resistant intersubjective presence/present.

7 Habermas, *The Structural Transformation of the Public Sphere*, 24.

8 Mintz has observed the institutionalization brought about by antebellum reform, which involved the founding of penitentiaries, reformatories, mental hospitals, and residential schools for the deaf and the blind by men such as Samuel Gridley Howe, who in 1863 told the Massachusetts Board of State Charities, "Institutions . . . so strongly build, so richly endowed, ... cannot be gotten rid of easily." It is "a pointed historical irony that the period of growing laissez-faire also marked the beginning of a new public paternalism," Mintz writes, "in which public institutions took on the moral prerogatives, presumed benevolence, and good will invested in kinship and local communities": Mintz, *Moralists and Modernizers*, 82, 85, 116.

9 Arendt, "Reflections on Violence," 99.

10 Ibid.

11 Marx, *The Marx-Engels Reader*, 160–61.

12 Arendt, "Reflections on Violence," 99.

13 Ibid.

14 Beecher, *A Plea for the West*, 12. Page numbers cited in the text are from this edition.

15 For details of the Amory Hall lectures, including the sequence of lectures and the press coverage, see Johnson, "Reforming the Reformers."

16 Garrison, *Liberator*, vol. 13, no. 5 (April 26, 1844), 67.

17 Emerson, "New England Reformers," 15. Page numbers cited in the text are from this edition.

18 Thoreau, "Reform and the Reformers," 181. Page numbers cited in the text are from this edition.

19 Emerson, "Self-Reliance," 32.

20 Ibid., 37.

21 Attempting to correct the psychoanalytic construction of desire as generated by "lack," which necessitates a model of relationality "grounded in antagonism and misapprehension," Leo Bersani offers a model very close to Emerson's. Proposing that the psyche recognizes in the other not a lack in itself but its own superabundant replication in the world, the psyche "evokes what we might call inaccurate representations, or a modified sameness, of itself. That which is external to it is included in that which identifies or individuates it." The psyche, as Emerson would almost certainly have agreed, "corresponds with itself outside of itself." While Bersani's desire to rescue relationality from the antagonisms born of lack is valuable, the end result, for Bersani as for Emerson, is to leave no room for relationality at all. That is, if all relations are only inaccurate replications of the psyche, then all we are left with—here, as in Emerson—is individualism writ large. Concluding, "We love, in other words, inaccurate representations of ourselves," Bersani echoes Emerson's formulation of love as an extension of the self-same (same-self) set of virtues onto formerly independent others (although Emerson, unlike Bersani, does not concede that our representations are "inaccurate"). In removing antagonism, for instance, Bersani also eliminates the need for negotiations of difference that allow for psychic change, and not simply for suspended or misapprehended difference. Bersani is right to claim that his theory is not another version of Freudian narcissism, but it comes close to another version of Freudian melancholy, which, as I argued in the first chapter, carries on a hope for a relationality in the face of absence—now a relational rather than a psychic lack—of social interaction: Bersani, "Sociality and Sexuality," 648–49, 651, 656.

22 Ripley, "Letter to the Church in Purchase Street," 257.

23 Emerson, "Love," 98. Page numbers cited in the text are from this edition.

24 Foucault describes how the circular incitements of self-exploration, confession, and a normalization always undone by the "implantation" of more perversion produces "power that lets itself be invaded by the pleasure it is pursuing; and opposite it, power asserting itself in the pleasure of showing off, scandalizing, or resisting": Foucault, *History of Sexuality*, 45.

25 Born in Prussia in 1807, Lieber volunteered in the army and fought against Napoleon at Waterloo, where he was wounded in 1815. After being persecuted at a number of German schools for his politics, he immigrated to Greece, England, and finally, in 1827, the United States, where he edited the *Encyclopedia America* in Boston from 1829 to 1833, before becoming professor of history and political economy at South Carolina College, a position he held for nearly twenty years. Lieber's anti-slavery and pro-Union politics were unpopular in the South, however, and he left for New York to teach political science and legal ethics at Columbia College, where he taught from 1857 until his death in 1872. Lieber's eminence as a political theorist is indicated by the adaptation of his work as textbooks in law schools and universities throughout the United States (earning him the reputation of having founded the field of academic political science in the United States); by the eminence of his numerous correspon-

dents (Henry Clay, Alexis de Tocqueville, Dorothea Dix, Henry Wadsworth Long-fellow, Charles Sumner, and Edgar Allan Poe, among others); and by the important political positions to which he was appointed. In addition to writing the Codes of War for the American Civil War (later used in the Hague and Geneva Conventions), Lieber drafted the Plans for Education for Girard College (1834) and was appointed curator of the Confederate Archives in 1865 and final arbiter of claims between Mexico and the United States in 1870. For details of Lieber's biography, see Clinton, *Tocqueville, Lieber, and Bagehot*.

26 Samson, "Francis Lieber and the Sources of Civil Liberty."

27 Lieber, *On Civil Liberty and Self-Government*, 253. Page numbers cited in the text are from this edition.

28 Steven Alan Samson credits Lieber with changing the definition of "self-government" as he popularized the term in nineteenth-century social theory. Originally, Samson writes, the terms, a literal translation of the Greek *autonomeia* (autonomy), described a non-colonial autonomy of one state from rule by another. As the term came into theological usage, Samson notes, it took an inward sense, describing the self's control over its own moral condition. Combining the two usages, Samson argues, Lieber defined "self-government" as an individual's autonomy from other people and an institution's autonomy from other institutions. Clinton expands Lieber's theories of individual and institutional autonomy to account for why Lieber refuted claims for international governing bodies (such as a World Court), as he granted nation-states the same self-governing independence he granted to the individuals who, according to Lieber, authorize nation-states and their institutions: Samson, "Francis Lieber and the Sources of Civil Liberty."

29 "In national manhood," Nelson writes, "civic identification *split* men, requiring them to manage 'their' competing desires not through a paradigm of equality but rank-order: to 'master' themselves." Encouraged to surrender their particular interests vertically to the nation, male citizens were given in return the imagined "fraternity" of presumably shared race (white) and gender (male): Nelson, *National Manhood*, 22.

30 Lieber briefly notes that "American liberty" is based on race. "I believe I may state as a fact," he writes, "that the staunchest abolitionist, who insists upon immediate manu-mission of all slaves, does not likewise insist upon an immediate admission of the whole manumitted population to a perfect political equality": Lieber, *On Civil Liberty and Self-Government*, 265.

31 While print publicity has become, in recent accounts, the foremost mode for rational contestation of the state, Lieber, aligning publicity and institutionalism, shows the former to be a potent mechanism for naturalizing self-regulation. He first draws a predictable distinction between unhindered communication ("orality") and cor-rupted forms of "official" communication ("writing"), to which the former is far superior. "I do not believe," Lieber writes, "that a high degree of liberty can be imagined without widely pervading orality," which he goes so far as to call "the aesthetics of liberty." By contrast, "writing," governed by rules and conventions, lacks speech's apparent spontaneity. "Modern centralized absolutism has developed a sys-

tem of writing and secrecy," Lieber notes, "and consequent formalism, abhorrent to free citizens who exist and feed upon the living word of liberty. Bureaucracy is formed upon writing, liberty on the breathing word." While praising oral communication for its directness, however, its ties to the body also make it prone to the subjectivism Lieber presents as destructive of liberty. Just as institutions mediate between an abstract federalism and the spasmodic bodies of citizens, so must a third term—"epistolary communion"—settle the supposed dispute between writing and speech: ibid., 90, 132, 136.

In *On Civil Liberty and Self-Government*, as in *The Coquette*, epistolarity seemingly sutures the widening tears in intimacy brought about by geographical and ideological distance. Like speech, letter-writing stands outside and counter to the "bureaucracies" of the state, ensuring the future of "adhesiveness" in a social network quickly coming unglued. Yet like institutions, which occupy a corollary position between embodiment and abstraction, letters serve a disciplinary, as well as a curatorial, function in relation to social relations. Letters are, of course, a form of writing, similarly governed by form and convention, and therefore also distinct from "personal observation and experience." If letters preserve traces of intimacy in the face of bureaucratic secrecy, they also impose shape on what might otherwise be idiosyncratic (even spasmodic) expression. Publicity, Lieber writes, "is the great process by which public opinion passes over into public will, which is legislation; and publicity in the elaboration of the opinion of the public, as well as in the process of ascertaining or enouncing it by elections": ibid., 131. Tellingly, "public opinion" becomes the vehicle through which "will," far from contesting centralized government, serves the interests of law ("legislation") and federalism ("elections"), both of which Lieber has elsewhere in his text blamed for eroding citizens' agency.

32 Lieber here works in tandem with Adam Smith, who similarly argued in *The Theory of Moral Sentiments* that members of communities put a necessary pressure on other members to conform to moral conventions. On Smith and social regulation, see Fleischacker, "Insignificant Communities," 282–86, and chap. 3 in this volume.

33 Warner describes how temperance literature generated a division of will and desire. Whereas for eighteenth-century temperance writers, alcohol consumption and its temperate control were both effects of will, for nineteenth-century reformers, he argues, "addiction" broke free of will and became the autonomous force of desire. The more reformers insisted on the utopian possibilities of will (signing the temperance pledge would make one permanently abstinent), Warner argues, the stronger became the addictive power of desire, perpetually locked in what he calls "a dialectic between self-mastery and self-abandonment": Warner, "Whitman Drunk," 32. For more on Warner's argument in relation to the temperance movement, see chap 4. in this volume.

34 On Lieber and the Mormons, see Burgett, "On the Mormon Question."

35 Emerson, "New England Reformers," 17.

36 Associated by many Protestants with "the violent, the exotic, and the hidden," the confessional, according to Franchot, was "a mysterious architectural interior closed

off from public surveillance, a place where secret dialogue transpired beyond the alleged democratizing influence of print." This suspicion of the confessional's irresistible power, Franchot observes, allowed Protestant nativists to represent themselves as relatively "powerless in an electoral system increasingly afflicted by fraud and greed": Franchot, *Roads to Rome*, 99–100.

37 *Liberator*, April 26, 1844, 67.

38 Ibid., 67.

39 Franchot, *Roads to Rome*, 106

40 Beecher, *A Plea for the West*, 64–65. Page numbers cited in the text are to this edition.

41 Protestant nativists were often shockingly anti-immigrant, as when Beecher accused Rome of "paying of the passage and emptying out upon our shores such floods of paupers, emigrants—the content of the poor-house and the sweepings of the streets—multiplying tumults and violence, filling our prisons and crowding our poor-houses, and quadrupling our taxation": Beecher, *A Plea for the West*, 54. Lieber warned of the "danger from uneducated minds" brought about "by the rapid influx of foreign emigrants, the greatest part unacquainted with the institutions, unaccustomed to self-government, inaccessible to education, and easily accessible to prepossession, and inveterate credulity, and intrigue, and easily embodied and wielded by sinister design": Lieber, *On Civil Liberty and Self-Government*, 51. Particularly dangerous are Catholic immigrants, who, as Lieber charged, "are generally of the class least enlightened, and most implicit in their religious subjection to the priesthood, who are able, by their spiritual ascendancy, to direct easily and infallibly the exercise of their civil rights and political action." Only American institutions, according to Lieber, could keep immigrants from continuing "to clog and perplex," allowing a "perverse religious power" to establish "a distinct nation of their own subjects, organized and wielded by them, in the midst of us": ibid., 138–40. The virulent anti-Catholicism of men like Beecher and Lieber cannot be attributed solely to their xenophobic response to the influx of Irish and Germans, however, since Beecher distinguished between individual Catholics, who are blameless, and the "system" that manipulates those individuals. Anti-immigrant sentiment also does not explain why anti-Catholicism flourished at the same historical moment in countries that did not experience increased immigration, such as England, where the Gordon Riots anticipated the burning of the Charlestown convent in Massachusetts.

42 For a fuller account of Beecher's anti-Catholicism, see Franchot, *Roads to Rome*, 99–125.

43 Ibid., 100.

44 Reed, "Six Months in a Convent," 11. Page numbers cited in the text are to this edition.

45 Emerson, "New England Reformers," 12–13.

46 Colton, *Protestant Jesuitism*, 94. Pages cited in the text are from this edition.

47 Like Emerson and Thoreau, Colton blamed reform on the ungovernable appetites of reformers themselves. "Unhappy himself," Colton writes, "he cannot endure that others should be happy. His uneasiness impels him to overstep the bounds of common civility, and he cannot allow his neighbour to eat a beefsteak, or drink a glass of wine,

without inflicting upon him a lecture that shall take away the agreeable gust thereof. It is true he will have the pretense of a benevolent aim; but the secret impulse lies in the envious cravings of his own stomach, though he may not be aware of it" (93).

48 Monk, *Awful Disclosures of the Hotel Dieu Nunnery in Montreal*, 150. Pages cited in the text are from this edition.

49 Monk's first-person narrative was quickly discredited by investigations of the convent, which did not support her architectural descriptions. Her veracity was further challenged by rumors that she had spent the years she claimed to be in the convent confined in the Magdalen Asylum for Wayward Girls. Maria Monk, according to Ray Allen Billington, moved to Philadelphia as "Jane Howard," where she sought employment as a domestic servant in a Catholic asylum. In 1838, she gave birth to a second child out of wedlock, and in 1849 was arrested in a whorehouse in New York's notorious Five Points district, after picking the pocket of a customer. She is rumored to have died destitute in prison. Billington reports that *Awful Disclosures* was written by J. J. Slocum and George Bourne, with little or no input from Monk herself. Given the detailed descriptions of institutional life, whether witnessed in the Magdalen Asylum or the Hotel Dieu convent, I am inclined to believe, however, that Monk had some role in the writing of her narrative.

50 I am grateful to Carina Pasquesi for this important insight.

51 Foucault, *Discipline and Punish*.

52 According to Levander, "Though Jane criticizes repressive Catholic practices, she also serves an important function in ensuring the nuns' compliance. Jane's verbal antics disrupt the linguistic rituals of the convent, but they also maintain the nuns' spirits and so complicity in those rituals": Levander, *Voices of the Nation*, 73.

3. Abolition's Racial Interiors

1 Steven Mintz's *Moralists and Modernizers* is an interesting case in point. Mintz notes that antebellum reform not only "arose in a millennialist sense of possibilities," but that it also "believed the only way to stabilize the social order was to internalize self-restraints within the depth of individual character." Mintz further observes that antebellum reform's "efforts to replace physical coercion resulted in less visible, but no less potent psychological forms of discipline." Despite his insight that these forms of discipline were essentially psychological, centered on the creation of a "sober, educated, self-disciplining citizenry," Mintz quickly shifts to the institutional sites of social discipline, claiming that "reformers effectively created new institutions of social control and confinement, ranging from poorhouses and prisons to reformatories and asylums." Perhaps because he eliminates the psychological effects of reformist discipline on those *not* confined to such institutions, Mintz is able to imagine an unambivalently progressive contemporary inheritance from antebellum reform, stripped of its "internalize[d] self-restraints." Antebellum reforms, according to Mintz, "reinvigorated American ideals and reinforced the nation's commitment to equality and social

justice. If Americans today recognize the various forms that oppression, inequality, exploitation, and tyranny can take, this is largely on account of past reformers who stuck thorns in the side of indifference and dared to dream of a new world." Mintz is right to claim that antebellum reformers reinvigorated America's commitments to justice, especially at a moment when the ideals of the Declaration of Independence were beginning to seem cynically rhetorical. In formulating this inheritance, however, he ignores his own insight that reform resulted in self-mastery and psychological control as much as in justice, much less "equality." His optimistic claim that Americans today—who continue to elect politicians who have dismantled affirmative action and welfare, fought initiatives for universal health care, deregulated the "free market," defined "marriage" legally in relation solely to heterosexual couples—can "recognize the various forms that oppression, inequality, exploitation, and tyranny can take," though qualified by the conditional "if," suspends the self-managing disciplines at work not only on the criminal and the abject but on the normative middle-class citizen. Those self-managements, too, are antebellum reform's legacy: see Mintz, *Moralists and Modernizers*, xiii–xv.

2 In addition to Morrison, *Playing in the Dark*, see Berlant, *The Queen of America Goes to Washington City*.

3 On the history of the American Colonization Society, see Staudenraus, *The African Colonization Movement*.

4 While many Northern supporters, including Finley, expected colonization to bring gradual emancipation, the society's predominantly Southern board of trustees ensured that the organization took no strong abolitionist position. By the mid-1830s, an assault on the American Colonization Society, headed by William Lloyd Garrison, was under way, charging that colonization increased the value of slaves by decreasing the labor force of free blacks; by removing the threat of slave revolt, real or imagined, through the transport of the free blacks who many Southerners believed were agitators; and by affirming the unalterably degraded character of African Americans that, according to men such as George Fitzhugh, particularly suited them to slavery. This last point in particular became a lever against colonization's popular appeal. Garrison launched the American Anti-Slavery Society, which became the most powerful abolition organization in America, with the charge that colonization's supporters were hypocrites who asserted, on the one hand, that slaves could never be uplifted into full citizenship and, on the other, that they should be sent to Africa as teachers and missionaries: see Garrison, *Thoughts on African Colonization*.

5 Morrison, *Playing in the Dark*, 8

6 In tying knowledges of the body to the operations of state power, I am building on Foucault's analysis of the eighteenth-century shift from public spectacles of torture and punishment toward apparently more humane modes of disciplining the bodies of subjects and extracting their voluntary labors. Foucault shows how knowledges taken as bodily "truths" demarcate the borders between the sane and the insane, the criminal and the law-abiding, the healthy and the sick. While apparently benevolent, these

discourses constitute the normative subject by identifying its imagined deviations, thereby prescribing and delimiting the subjectivities of those who receive and those who offer "care": Foucault, *Discipline and Punish*.

7 Foucault, "Politics and Reason," 60.

8 I am arguing here that Finley primarily offers pastoral care, in both its religious and, following Foucault, its ideological sense. Yet in centralizing whiteness through an act of international border drawing, Finley also, in his colonization scheme, engaged state power. His move from pastoral to state power in the course of his career challenges the state's consolidated existence prior to the interpellation of individual citizens and supports Foucault's broader assertions about the local operations of discursive power, assertions noted even by nineteenth-century critics of colonization such as Calvin Colton. Noting the dependency of the state on pastoral power, Colton charged that benevolent societies "sought to create a 'dynasty of opinion' by manipulating 'the two capital conservative elements indispensable to the permanency of the American Government and its institutions—education and religion'": Colton, *Protestant Jesuitism*, in Staudenraus, *The African Colonization Movement*, 15.

9 Brodhead, *Cultures of Letters*, 16.

10 Witherspoon, *Works*, 141. All page numbers cited in the text are to this edition.

11 Brown, *Memoirs of the Reverend Robert Finley*, v. Page numbers cited in the text are from this edition.

12 Although Brown was much more forceful in his deployment of Enlightenment doctrines of reason and free will than Finley and argued more directly for the need to abolish slavery, he followed Finley's lead in arguing against immediate abolition in favor of the gradual ending of slavery through colonization. Like Finley, Brown argued that free blacks were doomed by white prejudice to perpetual unhappiness in the United States. Brown also took Finley's side against his mentor's nemesis, William Lloyd Garrison, whose followers used "severe strictures and harsh invectives against those who were connected with the slaveholding system" and thereby "entirely failed to aid the cause of freedom: Finley, *Thoughts on the Colonization of Free Blacks*, 126.

13 Education in early modern Europe, as Bernard Bailyn has argued, served to transmit traditional knowledge intact from one generation to the next. Carried on primarily in the extended family, education was moral as well as vocational, serving as a seamless threshold between private and public worlds, between unquestioning loyalty and obedience to the father and the same obedience to the father's extended agency in communal government. The colonial migration changed this social model, however, and altered its educational systems. The availability of land and relative cheapness of establishing households caused widespread migration that broke the extended family into its conjugal nuclei, which no longer resembled the broader social network. Children worked and even lived away from their parents, who could no longer be counted on to instill loyalty and obedience as *moral* duties. Consequently, the state began to support and regulate other sites of instruction, especially the church. The effect of education under denominational control became, as Bailyn notes, not simply the transmission of culture but the formation of "character": "controversial, conscious,

constructed: a matter of decision, will, and effort." Denominational churches became invaluable instructional institutions for the nation-state, Bailyn argues, for they reconciled individual will to group loyalty by making submission to a communal order an *effect of*, not a threat to, individual will and by tying both to abstract concepts of goodness and rightness. Once obedience became a function of willed choice, the state could no longer demand loyalty through force without appearing tyrannical. In place of such obvious demands, the work of order was carried out in the classroom through programs of pedagogical discipline such as the ones I am tracing here: Bailyn, *Education in the Forming of American Society*, 98.

14 Several of Finley's students became leaders in early Republican politics, including Samuel Southard, secretary of the Navy and governor of New Jersey; Theodore Frelinghuysen, New Jersey senator, vice-presidential candidate in 1844, and president of Rutgers; and Robert Field Stockton, who captured Los Angeles in the Mexican War: Staudenraus, *The African Colonization Movement*, 16.

15 It is reasonable to assume that "poor and ignorant" stands here partly as a euphemism for African American, since in the great migration of African Americans North in this period (from 60,000 free blacks in 1790 to 250,000 in 1820), the largest population of free blacks (1,500) in New Jersey resided in Somerset County, the home of Finley's parish: ibid., 15.

16 Fliegelman, *Declaring Independence*, 24.

17 Ibid., 35–36.

18 Ibid., 38, 40.

19 According to Brown, Finley acquired his hatred of slavery from John Witherspoon. Witherspoon's lessons in the evils of slavery are ironic, given that he solicited funds from slaveholders in Jamaica and the West Indies to support professorships at Princeton. In his "Address to the Inhabitants of Jamaica, and other West-India Islands, on Behalf of the College of New Jersey" (March 21, 1772), Witherspoon solicited funds to support Princeton based in part on the university's ability to make the sons of slaveholders masters of his art of pedagogical discipline (in addition to the fact that Princeton was closer in climate to the islands than was Great Britain!). "As to the governance of the college," Witherspoon assured potential donors, "no correction by stripes is permitted. Such as cannot be governed by reason and the principles of honor and shame, are reckoned unfit for residence in a college." Of additional importance to the operation and teaching of discipline, he said, is the smallness of the village, which assures "that any irregularity is immediately and certainly discovered, and therefore easily corrected." In conclusion, he asked, "Could their esteem and friendship be expected in return for an austere and rigorous confinement, out of which they had escaped as birds out of the snare of the fowler?" Under Witherspoon's tutelage, the sons of slaveholders would learn the value of obedient labor performed under constant surveillance, thereby translating into broader cultural discipline the structures of slavery: Witherspoon, *Works*, 194, 199.

20 Finley, *Thoughts on the Colonization of Free Blacks*, 4. Page numbers cited in the text are from this edition.

21 Here Finley anticipates the use in the late nineteenth century and early twentieth century of race and racism to control the labor of immigrant whites. He argued that whites, in the presence of free blacks, would always imagine themselves "masters" and therefore would resist "habits of industry, and along with it a love of order and religion." Only by removing blacks from the United States could poor whites be persuaded to take up "the more humble and toilsome pursuits of life": ibid., 5.

22 Finley won the early support of Paul Cuffee, a free black resident of Philadelphia who had generated plans for establishing an African colony for free blacks. Assuming that Cuffee spoke for the entire black population of Philadelphia, Finley was alarmed, on his return from Washington in 1817, to discover that several African American leaders —most notably, James Forten, Richard Allen, Absalom Jones, and Robert Douglass— had organized against the scheme. Finley quickly called a meeting of those leaders and convinced them that colonization was the best hope for ending slavery and for improving the status of African Americans.

23 "The country itself did not present to him an interesting and pleasing aspect," Brown reported, adding, "The place of his future abode did not afford a prospect of so much convenience and comfort to him and his family, as he had been accustomed to enjoy and induced to anticipate": Brown, *Memoirs of the Reverend Robert Finley*, 187. Finley found that a great deal of college lands had been sold off to invest in a bank that had failed, leaving the university in dire financial straits, and he, as the new president, traveled around Georgia to solicit funds. In so doing, he fatally exhausted himself and died from a fever.

24 Birney, *Letter on Colonization*, 3. Page numbers cited in the text are from this edition.

25 Walter Jackson Bate was among the first critics to note the social function of sympathy in choreographing civic morality in eighteenth-century England. Bate documents the rise of a specific mode of sympathy that linked classic conceptions of civic order to an early Romantic focus on states of feelings, giving rise to a distinctively modern individualism. At the center of this philosophic development, according to Bate, was Adam Smith's *Theory of Moral Sentiments*: Bate, *From Classic to Romantic*.

26 See, for example, Clark, "The Sacred Rights of the Weak."

27 See Barnes, *States of Sympathy*; Marshall, *The Surprising Effects of Sympathy*; Stern, *The Plight of Feeling*.

28 Smith, *The Theory of Moral Sentiments*, 26. Page numbers cited in the text are from this edition.

29 In a move that anticipates Foucault's study of modern disciplinary forms, Barnes persuasively argues that "sympathy is revealed to be a self-regulating practice," one of the key "affective forms of disciplinary control" in early America. She argues that post-Revolutionary women were encouraged to form sympathetic relations to sentimental novels in which wayward daughters learn to subject themselves to the authoritative if arbitrary rule of fathers, thereby rationalizing the "consensual" subjection of citizens to the founding fathers of the national family. Demonstrating "early national culture's attempts to reconcile conservative republican values of duty to others with a liberal agenda of self-possession," she writes, sentimental fiction is the logical outgrowth of

Smith's theory of sympathy, in which "imagining oneself under the constant scrutiny of others, one eventually comes to internalize that perspective. What follows is Smith's vision of an individual conscience that takes shape as a separate subject, [who] by temporarily adopting the other's perspective, manages to teach us the 'most complete lesson of *self*-command.'" Through her focus on sympathy's regulation of the gendered subject (in both senses of the word), Barnes poses a compelling critique of antebellum reform when she wryly asks, "Why reform social and political structures when you can reform the woman herself?" While Barnes suggests that under such disciplinary reform "difference is to be negated rather than understood," however, I argue that the goal of racial discipline is neither negation nor understanding, but internalization. To Barnes's assertion that "to read sympathetically is to read like an American," I would add that it is to read like a *white* American, since the end result of racial sympathy, I am contending, is not the subsuming of difference into a national sameness, but the reification of white citizenship through the manufacture of racial character. Gender is made to produce a fantasy of sameness in post-Revolutionary America, in other words, while race is made to produce difference: Barnes, *States of Sympathy*, 2, 8, 10, 12, 18, 21–22.

30 In Bentham's model, prisoners are visible to guards who are not themselves visible to the prisoners. The result is that prisoners, who are always potentially watched (but are never assuredly so) begin to act continually *as if* they are under guard. Having internalized surveillance, then, prisoners lose the ability to distinguish between coercion (what is imposed from outside) and consent (behavior produced, under internalized scrutiny, as if from free will). Modes of self-regulation produced under internalized cultural scrutiny Foucault, following Bentham, called "panoptical," which became the basis of the shift from punishment (force exerted by external authority) to discipline (force produced through self-regulation based on the self's desire to conform to norms produced by new "knowledges of the body," natural and social science taking the place of the guards in Bentham's prison): Bentham, *The Panopticon Writings*; Foucault, *Discipline and Punish*.

31 Lott describes the "pale gaze" as "a ferocious investment in demystifying and domesticating black power in white fantasy by projecting vulgar black types as spectacular objects of white men's looking": Lott, *Love and Theft*, 153.

32 "The retributive justice of God was never more strikingly manifested than in this all-pervading negrophobia, the dreadful consequence of chattel slavery," Garrison observed: Garrison, "The 'Infidelity' of Abolition," in *Selections from the Writings and Speeches of William Lloyd Garrison*, 6.

33 Garrisonian abolition emerged during a period when, as Habermas has shown, the "public" became a place where critical debate, animated by private, autonomous conviction, was increasingly directed at—rather than animated by—collective institutions. To the degree that one challenged church and state, one gained status as a moral individual, privately suited for public authority: Habermas, *The Structural Transformation of the Public Sphere*.

34 See, e.g., Garrison, *Thoughts on African Colonization*.

35 For Balibar, the "nation form" operates as an ideological structure by generating a twofold illusion. In the first, "the generations which succeed one another over centuries on a reasonably stable territory, under a reasonably univocal designation, have handed on to each other an invariant substance." Joined to this is the illusion that "the process of development from which we select aspects retrospectively, so as to see ourselves as the culmination of that process, was the only one possible, this is, it represented a destiny." The nation form thereby resolves "the interminable conflict between theological universalism and the universality of nationalism": Balibar and Wallerstein, *Race, Nation, Class*, 86, 95.

36 Garrison, "Declaration of Sentiments," in idem, *Selections from the Writings and Speeches of William Lloyd Garrison*, 69. Titles of essays and page numbers cited in the text are from this edition, unless noted otherwise.

37 His position at the heart of public controversy yet outside its relativist jurisdiction required that Garrison deny the source of his successes in the opinion-saturated domain of print. "Now, on what are right and wrong dependent?" he asked. "On recorded declarations? On ancient parchments or modern manuscripts? on sacred books? No. Though every parchment, manuscript, and book in the world were given to the consuming fire, the loss would not in the least affect the right or wrong of moral actions. Truth and duty, the principles of justice and equality, the obligations of mercy and brotherly kindness, are older than all books, and more enduring than tablets of stone": Garrison, "War essentially Wrong." Garrison's repeated denial of his reliance on print reveals an anxiety about his relation to public opinion and, therefore, to the very organizational vogues, distributional markets, and national public formations— in short, to ideology—he criticized in others. Throughout Garrison's writings, the agency of print was always subsumed on the one hand by providential wisdom, and on the other by the affective response of readers, who are constructed as embodied consumers of the print commodity and its ideology. That the readership of the *Liberator* was mostly black sets the stage in disturbing ways for the economic incorporation of African Americans within the nationally "inclusive" utopia set forth by the newspaper. African Americans would become citizens simultaneously with their interpellation as consumers, both functions merging in the consumption of "identities" such as "black" and "virtuous citizen." At the same time, the newspaper's editor, insofar as he was also the public (white, male) voice of authority, could eclipse his own situation within the economic market. Given the role of newspapers in generating the imagined national community, it is not surprising that the ambivalence Garrison expressed about print is similar to his ambivalence about the nation as a social institution. My argument attempts to introduce the question of racial triangulation (between Garrison as exemplary, racially mobile citizen, prejudiced white citizens at large, and suffering blacks) into Robert Fanuzzi's analysis of Garrison's use of print to create a triangulation between Garrison as private citizen, the market public for the *Liberator*, and a "political subject conceived and refined through the political economy of newspaper publishing": Fanuzzi, "The Organ of an Individual," 123. Compelling as that argument is, to leave "race" out of an analysis of the print public generated by the

Liberator is to miss the extent to which Garrison's political subject exemplifies white Republican citizenship at the threshold between radical individualism and market democracy.

38 Garrison, *Thoughts on African Colonization*, 37.

39 Just as disturbing, however, is the connection Garrison drew between African and North American expansion, which he exalted as precisely the kind of voluntary displacement of citizens that African colonization could ideally become: ibid., 15–17. In making such a claim, Garrison bracketed the role of westward expansion in extending and strengthening slavery in the United States (a connection he elsewhere acknowledged and condemned, but only at the level of federal agency, as when the government admitted Texas as a slave state). In bracketing that connection, Garrison sidestepped as well the consistency of his fantasy of citizenship without nations with the imperialist rhetorics of Manifest Destiny: both relied on divine injunction; both freed the citizen form from specific national borders to generate a universal, imperialist "mission"; both justified their universalism through claims to "uplift" benighted people of color; and both, as Alexander Saxton notes, rely on "an intermediate language by which rational and moral ideas—self-evident to the intellect or logically deducible— could be transposed into emotional, metaphorical, even sensual images, comprehensible at the inferior levels of the social order" (Saxton, *The Rise and Fall of the White Republic*, 46); both, that is, having freed citizenship from its national borders sought to map it onto—and into—the bodies of unwilling people of color.

40 On Douglass's battles with Garrison, see Cain, "Introduction."

41 Garrison, *Thoughts on African Colonization*, 7.

42 Garrison, "Address," 21.

43 Ibid., 13.

44 Ibid.

45 Ibid.

46 Ibid.

47 Ibid., 4.

48 Ibid., 23.

49 Ibid., 12.

4. Ardent Spirits

1 Karen Sanchez-Eppler rightly encourages readers to "recognize the violence and sensuality embedded within even the most angelic and sentimental generic conceit" of temperance fiction, especially since, as she reminds us, the premise of this fiction— that the incestuous love of fathers and daughters can redeem family order—had dire real-life consequences for wives and children. While Sanchez-Eppler's point is well taken, and her conception of how love and law converge in temperance fiction through the ethos of "moral suasion" is exactly right, I diverge from her reading in my contention that novels such as *Ten Nights in a Bar-Room* do not reinforce patriarchal authority. Rather, the irredeemable erosion of that authority by capital, not domestic

feminization, means that both daughter and father are trapped in a bad bargain (although, as I acknowledge, Joe Morgan is enfranchised at the novel's end, although arguably not as a "patriarch" but as a "consumer," a role opened to and embodied by nineteenth-century women as well). If the novel "reconfigures trauma into the possibility of moral triumph," as Sanchez-Eppler asserts, that triumph, retaining the trauma of commodified reputation, is precisely what prevents restoration of patriarchy: Sanchez-Eppler, "Temperance in the Bed of a Child," 61, 66.

2 Arthur, *Ten Nights in a Bar-Room*, 92. Page numbers cited in the text are from this edition.

3 Sellers, *The Market Revolution*, 260.

4 Eve Kosofsky Sedgwick argues that, "in any male-dominated society, there is a special relationship between male homosocial (*including* homosexual) desire and the structures for maintaining and transmitting patriarchal power: a relationship founded on an inherent and potentially active structural congruence." To obscure the role of desire in the production of patriarchal power, Sedgwick argues, the continuity of homosocial and homosexual bonds must be "radically disrupted." Triangulated erotic relations threaten to reveal the congruence that, Sedgwick argues, is only illusorily broken: Sedgwick, *Between Men*, 2, 25.

5 Quoted in Sellers, *The Market Revolution*, 251.

6 Ibid., 238–39.

7 While my analysis is indebted to Charles Sellers's account of the relationship between temperance reform and economic change in Jacksonian America, I disagree with his reliance on "self-repression" as the central psychological dynamic of an emerging middle-class ideology. His premise that the middle class forged itself by conquering its "own inclinations" is prone to Foucault's critique of the "repressive hypothesis" underlying conventional historiography of Victorian sexual mores. Discourses of sexuality, Foucault shows, sought to produce, not repress sexuality, albeit in managed ways, to generate norms of acceptable behavior and thereby to characterize other sexual mores (which were simultaneously produced, disseminated, and popularized until they characterized the majority of sexual practices) as abnormal, degraded, and perverse. In the same vein, we can argue that, rather than seeking to "repress" the appetite for drink, temperance publicized the pleasures, even the thrills, of alcohol consumption, to produce the need for vigilant self-examination and habitual correction: ibid., 261.

8 Ibid., 245–46.

9 Ibid., 239.

10 Ibid., 259.

11 Ibid.

12 James Hart reports that more than 12 percent of American novels published during the 1830s were temperance fictions, which circulated widely among working-class readers: Hart, *The Popular Book*, 108.

13 Sellers, *The Market Revolution*, 267–68.

14 Ibid.

15 Kingsdale, "The 'Poor Man's Club,'" 258–62.

16 Ibid., 259.

17 Stott, *Workers in the Metropolis*, 239.

18 Gilfoyle, *City of Eros*, 81.

19 Stott, *Workers in the Metropolis*, 239.

20 Wilentz, *Chants Democratic*, 309.

21 Sellers, *The Market Revolution*, 241–42, 259.

22 Griffin, "The 'Washingtonian Revival,'" 70–73.

23 Ibid., 71.

24 Brasher, *Walt Whitman*, 124.

25 Claims that Whitman disavowed both temperance and *Franklin Evans* are based on largely apocryphal accounts given by the author himself, beginning in 1888, when Whitman reported to Horace Traubel:

> I doubt if there is a copy in existence: I have none and have not had one for years; it was a pamphlet. Parke Godwin and another somebody (who was it?) came to see me about writing it. Their offer of cash payment was so tempting—I was so hard up at the time—that I set to work at once ardently on it (with the help of a bottle of port or what not). In three days of constant work I finished the book. Finished the book? Finished myself. It was damned rot—rot of the worst sort—not insincere, perhaps, but rot, nevertheless: it was not the business for me to be up to. I stopped right there: I never cut a chip off that kind of timber again. (Traubel, *With Walt Whitman in Camden*, 3:93)

Later in the same year, Whitman claimed to Traubel that he "never was in" the temperance movement and wrote *Franklin Evans* solely for profit: ibid., 4:323. Whitman did, of course, express reservations about social reform movements, as when he declared, "we would not be considered one of those bigots that think there is no good in humanity, except what resides in some favorite school of faith—we believe in a *general average* of good": Whitman, *Journalism*, 338. In regard to the temperance movement, Whitman expressed similar hesitation, remarking in 1840, "I am not one of those who would deny people any sense of delight, because I think it is a sin to be happy, and to take pleasure in the good things of this life. On the contrary, I am disposed to allow every rational gratification, both to the palate, and the other senses": ibid., 20. At the same time, Whitman held in contempt any anti-reform politician who was "averse to innovation, loves the old rather than the new, and will not favor any 'experiment'" and therefore was "the very opposite of reform": ibid., 338. He declared himself committed—"as who, sincere with his own heart, can fail to be?"—to "the great salutary *truth* of the temperance doctrine—of the mighty evils of drink, spreading like a deadly thing wherever it flows—or the salutary effects of the *pledge*, the charm that has reformed hundreds, and as a precautionary measure, saved thousands": ibid., 365. As early as 1840, Whitman used his journalism to inveigh against all forms of intemperance, including tobacco consumption. "Our young men," Whitman wrote, "entertain an idea that there is something very manly in having a segar stuck in the corner of their lips; or a round ball of sickening weed that a dog would not touch rolling in their mouths." Whitman warned, "Custom may, and does, enable some people to become so habituated to these things, that they produce no evident evil. But it is still not less the case that they *do* produce evil. They weaken the strength of the nervous system; they alternately excite and depress the powers of the brain; and they act with constant and insidious attacks upon the health": ibid., 19. Whitman reflects his conflicted attitudes toward reform in his ambivalent relation to his own novel, of which he remained proud enough, his disavowal to Traubel notwithstanding, to re-publish it in the *Brooklyn Eagle* when he became the paper's editor in 1846.

26 I am following here Michael Denning's insight that in literature of the 1840s addressed, as *Franklin Evans* explicitly is, to the "masses," "questions about the sincerity of their purported beliefs or the adequacy of their political proposals are less interesting than questions about the narrative embodiment of their political ideologies": Denning, *Mechanic Accents*, 103.

27 Cowie, *The Rise of the American Novel*, 208.

28 Emory Holloway astutely observes, "Passionate desires which are under conscious control" in waking hours "come tumbling forth under pressure of time and the stimulation of alcohol, but in disguise": Holloway, *Free and Lonesome Heart*, 30. Saloons, as Leslie Fiedler notes, were distinctly homosocial space, "for a long time felt as the anti-type of the home, a refuge for escaping males nearly as archetypal as the wilderness and the sea": Fiedler, *Love and Death*, 258.

29 The "halving" Franklin describes in himself is typical of the pattern Warner describes as "selfing" in *Franklin Evans*. Warner analyzes the inner contradiction between will and desire, each unmaking the other and rendering the fiction of coherent selfhood implausible. For Warner, this tension is endemic to a mass public predicated on voluntary association, which relied both on a willful subject (able to make choices) who is simultaneously "addicted" (incapable of choice): see Warner, "Whitman Drunk."

30 Warner reads this scene as making "reference to the emergent same-sex subculture of New York": Warner, "Whitman Drunk," 281.

31 Benjamin, *Charles Baudelaire*, 55.

32 Ibid.

33 Turner, *Backward Glances*.

34 In Nelson's germinal formulation, "national manhood" is an illusory "fraternity" of white men whose self-identity as benevolent and rational is constructed in relation to women and people of color, even as the abstract status of citizenship occludes the investment of national subjectivity in codified systems of racialized and gendered power: Nelson, *National Manhood*.

35 Whitman's characterization of Margaret may have come from his visits to minstrel shows in New York. Whitman reports, "I often saw Rice, the original 'Jim Crow' at the old Park Theatre filling up the gap in some show bill—and the wild chants and dances were admirable—probably ahead of anything since": Whitman, *Collected Writings*, 4:53. Performing racial "mixing," blackface minstrels bring forth, in Whitman's imagination, not essential racial difference, but the theatricality of race. Margaret, too, is a

skillful actress, able to disguise her unruly passions with the appearance of temperate calm. This aspect of her character makes Margaret, for Frances Winwar, "the most complete and satisfactory portrait [Whitman] had so far painted of a woman": Winwar, *American Giant*, 78.

36 *Brooklyn Eagle and Kings Country Democrat*, March 18, 1846, in Whitman, *Journalism*, 288.

37 Holloway, *Free and Lonesome Heart*, 30.

38 Ibid., 29.

5. The Nervous State

1 On postbellum psychology, see Lutz, *American Nervousness, 1903*; Pfister and Shnog, *Inventing the Psychological*.

2 On nineteenth-century nerve science, see Drinka, *The Birth of Neurosis*; Lutz, *American Nervousness, 1903*.

3 Drinka, *The Birth of Neurosis*, 32–34.

4 Ibid., 40–42.

5 Ibid., 35.

6 Ibid., 34.

7 Beecher, *The American Woman's Home*, 24, 89. Page numbers cited in the text are from this edition.

8 Thomas Lutz, *American Nervousness*, situates the "economic plot" of nerve science in the turn-of-the-century work of George Beard and Weir Mitchell.

9 Butler, "The Force of Fantasy," 185.

10 Orson Fowler sought to deny the mutually enforcing relation of effort and desire, however. In his theory of habitual motion and "earnest speech," he created the unconscious as the psychic barrier between labor and perversion:

> Thus, as the gestures of a carpenter, when talking earnestly, will be back and forth, as if shaving the jack-plane, or with a striking motion, as if driving a nail—as those of the blacksmith will be as if swinging his hammer, those of the farmer, often circular, as if turning the grindstone; and all because they severally make these repetitive motions so often as to assume them involuntarily—so, and for a similar reason, those who indulge much with the opposite sex, when they laugh, or gesticulate earnestly, will carry their hips and their organs forward, because so much accustomed to this motion; *forward* while those who abuse themselves will have a similar motion, only that this apparatus is directed a little upward, as well as thrown forward, because they assume this position so often in self-pollution. (Orson Fowler, *Amativeness*, 51)

While Fowler established labor and perversion as parallel performatives, they remain in a state of tension. Unless one is unusually ambidextrous, one can embody one's work or one's perversion, but not both. The body, for Fowler, thus becomes indexical of a necessary—if only ever illusory—border between perversion and labor, desire and capital.

11 If the "animal propensities" are "duly governed," Orson Fowler asserts, "the more the better, for they impart force": Fowler, *Intemperance and Tight-Lacing*, 19). The struggle between the animal propensities stimulated by desire and the moral judgments executed by self-restraint thus produce the "force" that generates bodily volition.

12 Quoted in Robson, "Francis Lieber's Theories," 241.

13 I am grateful to the special collections librarian John Lancaster at the Robert Frost Library, Amherst College, for making the manuscript available to me.

14 Orson Fowler, "Temptation—Its Influence on Guilt."

15 The contemporary debate about universality and particularity is grounded in concerns about political efficacy. Advocates of "particularity" argue in favor of the multiplicity of experience, which presumably exceeds and challenges the interpellative abstractions structuring the nation-state. Robyn Wiegman, *American Anatomies*, argues against the universalizing gestures that conflate blacks and women into an abstract generality that obscures the reality of oppression. Russ Castronovo, "Political Necrophilia," similarly contends that the consequences of a nation with an abstracted citizenry are not only dire but deadly and force us to alienate or eliminate those elements of our lives that place us outside the purview of those abstractions. And Lauren Berlant, "Diva Citizenship," asserts that the nation's enfranchised citizens have much to learn from those moments when the "subaltern" subjects speak from the particularity of their experiences, an articulation Berlant calls "diva citizenship."

More recently, critics have begun to reconsider the efficacy of the abstractions previously viewed as intrinsically silencing, confining, and mortifying. Eric Lott figures this interest in universalism as "what one gets 'after' identity politics: a politics of *participatory discrepancy* that comes about as a congeries of new social movements jostle, collide, and sometimes collude in broad, transmovement desires": Lott, "After Identity, Politics," 666. In agreement with Linda Zerilli, "This Universalism which Is Not One," and building on Ernesto Laclau (who claims in *Emancipation[s]* that identity movements logically always already contain some ideal of the universal), Lott contends that universalism seems to many a politically efficacious alternative to postmodern theory's perceived failure to produce an effectively unified political movement. In her critical exchange with Laclau and Slavoj Žižek, Judith Butler uses Hegel to expound on the problems arising from political projects that seek to move beyond "the particular" by merely including minoritized subjects. "There is no way to bring the excluded particularity into the universal," Butler writes, "without first negating that particularity. And that negation would only confirm once again that universality cannot proceed without destroying that which it purports to include": Butler et al., *Contingency, Hegemony, Universality*, 24. Later, however, she explains that viable political movements must engage in a "translative project" in which there is "an active engagement with forms of multiculturalism" that one cannot "reduce . . . to the politics of particularity": ibid., 168–69. For Butler, "universalism" represents the potential for a plurality of "competing universalities," of truths drawn from the particular but shown to be common beyond it through a program of "translation," creating an enlarged and empowered united political front. But not everyone has been so optimistic. Discussing the potential for a globalized sexual liberation movement, Inderpal Grewal and Caren Kaplan worry that "universalized models of resistance with idealized tropes or politics of identity obscure rather than elucidate the terrain of subjectivity in postmodernity," emphasizing that the postmodern deconstruction of identity, in their view, serves a political end: Grewal and Kaplan, "Global Identities," 670. Walter Benn Michaels is suspicious of the basic logic directing new models of universality. Using Butler's "translation" model as an example, he contends that "the commitment to translation is a commitment to establishing the connections between the languages without destroying the difference between them . . . Butler's universalism is thus a form of the identitarianism she imagines herself to critique": Michaels, *The Shape of the Signifier*, 179. Wiegman notes what she calls the "paradox of particularity," calling into question the goal of focusing on the particularity of "whiteness" within the emerging field of whiteness studies. She explains her idealized version of the field, writing, "The political project for the study of whiteness [should entail] not simply rendering whiteness particular but engaging with the ways that being particular will not divest whiteness of its universal epistemological power": Wiegman, "Whiteness Studies and the Paradox of Particularity," 150. For Wiegman, universality and particularity both prove threatening, as neither seems fully, in her view, to do away with the existence of privilege. In fact, both can work to reinforce it.

16 Wells, *A Manual of Etiquette*, 57. Page numbers cited in the text are from this edition.

17 On the attendance of Beecher and Fowler at Spurzheim's lecture, see Albertson, "Phrenology in the Nineteenth Century," 66. Details of the Beecher–Fowler debate are from an unattributed report in the Fowler file, Robert Frost Library Special Collection.

18 The account of the fire at "Fowler's Folly" comes from an unattributed newspaper clipping in the Fowler file, Robert Frost Library Special Collection.

19 Orson Fowler, *Intemperance and Tight-Lacing*, 13.

20 In a fascinating article in the *Harvard Law Review*, Pierre Schlag argues that the structures of American law may in fact be derived from phrenology. "In an era in which religious beliefs were rapidly eroding," he observes, "phrenology promised to restore order and meaning to the universe," which it did primarily by organizing folk beliefs into a system of horizontally oriented abstractions (the "propensities" of the brain). Both phrenology and law, Schlag notes,

> emerged as disciplinary knowledges through attempts to cast them in the form of sciences. Both "sciences" were aesthetically organized around a fundamental ontology of reification and animism—"faculties" in the case of phrenology, "doctrines" and "principles" in the case of law. Each discipline developed into an extremely intricate production of self-referential complexity. In both cases, the disciplinary edifice was maintained by practitioners who sought confirming evidence of the truth (and later the normative value) of the disciplinary enterprise and who went to great lengths to avoid disconfirming evidence and disenchanting encounters. In law in particular, the legitimation of the enterprise has been understood to be an essential aspect of the enterprise itself. Finally, the surface plau-

sibility of both enterprises—phrenology and law—was maintained through tacit dependence on folk beliefs (folk-frames and folk-ontologies) that were re-cast in a professionalizing jargon (Schlag, "Law and Phrenology," 895–96).

In the end, however, phrenology was done in by its own empiricism, Schlag argues, whereas the law, generating a self-referential structure of abstractions, became "well positioned to proliferate" and to assert its jurisdiction "with ever more intensity in ever more precincts": ibid., 917–18.

21 Orson Fowler, *Education and Self-Improvement*, 3.

22 Idem, *Intemperance and Tight-Lacing*, 11.

23 Noyes Wheeler defines "marvelousness" in the following manner: "*Use*: Wonder; credulity; belief in prophetic writing and miraculous interpositions of Divine Providence. *Abuse*—Belief in phantoms; ghosts; fortune-telling; dread of omens; eager to relate or listen to improbably or marvellous stories. Larger in women than in men": Wheeler, *The Phrenological Characters and Talents of Henry Clay, Daniel Webster, John Quincy Adams, William Henry Harrison, and Andrew Jackson*, 29.

24 Cecilia Tichi notes that phrenology's "popularity is in large part attributable to its scientized validation of received opinion codified along lines of racial hierarchy and nationalism": Tichi, *Embodiment of a Nation*, 28.

25 Orson Fowler, *Education and Self-Improvement*, 135.

26 Caldwell, *New Views on Penitentiary Discipline, and Moral Education and Reform*, 48.

27 Lorenzo Fowler, *The Principles of Phrenology and Physiology Applied to Man's Social Relations*, 42.

28 Orson Fowler, *Education and Self-Improvement*, 135.

29 Ibid., 132.

30 Ibid., 133.

31 Lorenzo Fowler, *The Principles of Phrenology and Physiology Applied to Man's Social Relations*, 132–33.

32 On the class interests of phrenology, see Roger Cooter's astute analysis of how European phrenologists such as George Combe and F. J. Gall provided the means to secure "consent to bourgeois liberal rule." Initially taken up by the middle-class bourgeois class opposed to working-class independence, phrenology popularized "the rational (antianarchistic and nonegalitarian) reflection necessary to fit these otherwise 'brutal and ignorant' workers 'for the friendly intercourse with their superiors.'" Without appearing to be "direct apologist[s] for industrial capitalism," Combe and Gall provided "a practical means to the self-help/self-serving ideology upon which the system flourished," naturalizing the "self-interest necessary for success in the competitive capitalist society." Taken up by "useful knowledge" societies and study groups, phrenology became so widespread among all classes that, as Harriet Martineau observed, "No power on earth could stop it." Because of its central strategy of "internalization," Cooter observes, phrenology was especially popular among the workers who were disciplined by its inculcation of orderly self-interest. "Without usually being conscious of the fact," he writes, "they pursued the philosophy that the way to effect 'real'

subordination (as distinct from merely 'formal' or shop-floor subordination) was to remake people's 'images of reality,' thereby to mystify domination in the minds of he dominated": Cooter, *The Cultural Meaning of Popular Science*, 135, 137, 144, 165.

33　Lydia Fowler, *Familiar Lessons on Phrenology*, 198–99.

34　Ibid., 200.

35　Ibid.

36　Ibid., 201–202.

37　Orson Fowler, *Education and Self-Improvement*, 4, 138, 157, 159–60.

38　Lorenzo Fowler, *The Principles of Phrenology and Physiology Applied to Man's Social Relations*, 43; Orson Fowler, *Education and Self-Improvement*, 149.

39　Lydia Fowler, *Familiar Lessons on Phrenology*, vi.

40　Orson Fowler, *Education and Self-Improvement*, 32. "The only true source of saving this country from dismemberment, decreasing influence, and from being a nation of hospitals," Lorenzo Fowler contended, "is by contriving at once a great SOCIAL RE-FORM," which could be accomplished only by using habitual discipline to stem the "uprising, loosening, and stirring up of every principle and institution, moral, social, political, and intellectual": Lorenzo Fowler, *The Principles of Phrenology and Physiology Applied to Man's Social Relations*, 84.

41　Orson Fowler, *Education and Self-Improvement*, 32.

42　On the changes in Freud's theories of anxiety, see Salecl, *On Anxiety*. Valerie Traub, writing about early modern culture, describes desire and anxiety as inextricable counterparts that are mediated not by a perceived notion of normalcy but through other cultural commitments that delimit lived possibilities, such as social and familial alliance. Traub sees the anxious individual afflicted with a disorganization of selfhood that derives not from the psyche but from ideological constraints that remove the individual's sense of self-cohesion: Traub, *Desire and Anxiety*.

43　In rethinking Freud's theory of anxiety in this way, I am following Butler's lead in rethinking Freudian melancholy to produce a theory of *productive* libidinal drive. Whereas Butler leaves "desire" as a causal state, making it therefore the underpinning of identity categories (even highly "performative" ones such as "the homosexual"), however, I am suggesting that desire itself is an after-effect of a thwarted relationality built not on desire, but on pleasure. Because Freud's theories of desire are predicated on *frustration*, desire leads Butler to found a politics of instability and incompleteness. While that politics has an important role in the postmodern civil sphere, it also leaves unanswered the sources of reconstructive community, which Butler leaves open to the ethical deliberation of individuals. Only when desire is removed as the *foundation* of agency, however, can that ethical deliberation produce anything but more frustration and, as Freud warns, more anxiety: Butler, *Psychic Life of Power*.

44　Lydia Fowler, *Familiar Lessons on Phrenology*, 21, 195.

45　Orson Fowler, *Love and Parentage*, 13.

46　Lorenzo Fowler, *The Principles of Phrenology and Physiology Applied to Man's Social Relations*, 29.

47　Ibid., 63.

48 Ibid., 10.

49 Orson Fowler, *Love and Parentage*, 14.

50 Lorenzo Fowler, *The Principles of Phrenology and Physiology Applied to Man's Social Relations*, 16.

51 Ibid., 13.

52 Ibid.

53 Lydia Fowler, *Familiar Lessons on Phrenology*, 36.

54 Lorenzo Fowler, *The Principles of Phrenology and Physiology Applied to Man's Social Relations*, 32.

55 Orson Fowler, *Love and Parentage*, v.

56 Lorenzo Fowler, *The Principles of Phrenology and Physiology Applied to Man's Social Relations*, 30–31.

57 Orson Fowler, *Love and Parentage*, vii–viii.

58 Idem, 50, 53, 55–56, 72.

59 Lydia Fowler, *Familiar Lessons on Phrenology*, 15.

60 Ibid.

61 Williams, *Marxism and Literature*, 121–27.

62 In his groundbreaking 1983 essay "Capitalism and Gay Identity," John D'Emilio makes the important argument that the rise of capitalism moved the labor force out of the home and made leisure activities such as sex, loosened from the necessities of reproduction, the basis for "private" identities. Although capitalism is responsible for the breakdown of tight family structures, D'Emilio argues, gays, lesbians, and feminists, all themselves the products of a new privatized leisure, have been made capitalism's scapegoats. Yet tracing the economic forces that allowed "homosexual desire to coalesce into a personal identity," D'Emilio leaves the sources of *desire* unaddressed. Indeed, D'Emilio takes "homosexual desire" as a given, a natural force simply freed up by social changes brought about by capitalism: D'Emilio, "Capitalism and Gay Identity," 8.

  Building on D'Emilio, we might speculate that capitalism, in producing the logic of the commodity, does not liberate but produces desire and, if desires are only deceptively multiform, that "homosexual desire" is in fact a misnaming of the state of dissatisfied interiority that is the supplement of capital. More than a mere chickenand-egg problem, these questions formulate a challenge for the radical potential of desire "itself," which in much queer theory has taken on the power to disrupt the coherence of the subject (thereby enhancing the dissatisfactions that are, I would argue, the desired and desiring state of capital to begin with) or to oppose the statedriven regulation of sexual culture (a culture repeatedly located, in these manifestos, in the marketplace of gay capital, thereby presenting the questionable hypothesis that capital can disrupt the state). In short, queer theory has accepted the natural(ized) separation of sexual and economic desire, the former disruptive and radicalized, the latter restrictive and hierarchical, in ways that obscure the historical kinship—the simultaneity and perhaps even the *identity*—of these two "desires."

63 Marx, *The Marx–Engels Reader*, 52. Page numbers cited in the text are from this edition.

64 The historian Thomas L. Haskell has argued that developments in late-eighteenth-century capitalism enabled the humanitarianism that imagined social change as a matter of good hearts and virtuous character. A new contractual market, where investors were often unknown to each other, required widespread agreement to abstract virtues aimed at creating economic subjects who felt bound by their "human nature" to keep promises. At the same time, the speculative nature of contractual investment required that citizens possess a sense of causality and an ability to imagine the consequences of their actions farther into the future than people had before. Haskell treats humanitarianism as a variation on the social contract, in which reformers saw their everyday actions as producing broad consequences, based on virtues necessary to the fulfillment of contracts: Haskell, "Capitalism and the Origins of the Humanitarian Sensibility, Part 2."

65 Orson Fowler's commencement address, "Temptation," is from Amherst College, Robert Frost Library, Special Collections.

66 In the reading of the novel that follows, I take issue with Shelley Streeby's privileging of the democratic potential of "particularity" in *The Quaker City*. "Although an emphasis on the body can work at times to naturalize distinctions of class, race, sexuality and gender, or to provide footholds for normalizing projects," Streeby argues, "an in-your-face body politics can also unsettle such distinctions and provide perverse sensations which stimulate different constructions of collective identity." In Lippard's "republican gothics," she contends, "uncanny bodies are enmired in fleshly particularities that resist universalizing abstractions. They are deeply marked by gender, class, and race, and their appearance signals the return of what was repressed or abjected by republican constructions of personhood and citizenship: the particularities of persons and the material histories of different kinds of bodies": Streeby, "Haunted Houses," 450–51. While it is certainly true, as Streeby contends, that resistance must ultimately be embodied, Lippard's novel shows the opposition of particularity and universality to be twinned productions of modern capital working in tandem, not necessarily in opposition.

67 Ibid., 451, 454. In the labor newspaper he edited, the *Quaker City* weekly, Streeby argues, Lippard "foregrounded the disparity between certain radical democratic ideals —such as economic equality and participatory democracy—and the harsh inequalities produced by the breaking of the artisan system and the long, uneven process of industrialization": Streeby, "Opening Up the Story Paper," 182. In so doing, however, Lippard "problematically associates nonreproductive sexualities and nonreproductive modes of work with evil-class Others." I am more inclined to agree with Streeby's later argument that "Lippard tries to align these inequalities so as to transform republican ideology in the service of a different, national popular collective will." In particular, Streeby notes, "sadomasochistic, hypercharged, homosocial relationships expose social crises and different, even conflicting masculinities instead of reinforcing an over-

arching, homogenous mode of manhood": Streeby, "Opening Up the Story Paper," 182, 183, 197. I am arguing that, rather than attributing non-reproductive sexualities to these Others, Lippard charts the coalescing of "reproductive sexualities" around the professional-class interests that are the real evil—and hence the real Other—of the novel.

68 Streeby argues that Lippard's paralleling of seduction and exploitation plots "may suggest that sexual desire is inherently evil, that only men experience it, and that women should remain in the private sphere rather than venture out into 'dangerous' public spaces": Streeby, "Haunted Houses," 202. Although I disagree with her contention that only men in *The Quaker City* express desire, I agree with Streeby that, "for Lippard, the exploitation of 'free' laborers and the seduction or rape of women are analogous forms of oppression that betray revolutionary ideals and contradict republican principles": Streeby, "Opening Up the Story Paper," 199.

69 Streeby documents Lippard's opposition to middle-class life, writing, "If Lippard rejected New England Puritanism as the source of an American self, neither did he embrace a middle-class identity. In fact, he was quite hostile to the very idea, as he understood it, of such an identity. 'In every age, the classes improperly styled by this title,' Lippard agued in the *Quaker City* weekly, 'have been the veriest lick-spittles of Power' (2 June 1849). Far from simply reinforcing an emerging middle-class consensus, Lippard tried to articulate a kind of early working-class position that emphasized the material underpinnings of both spiritual and republican virtue—the importance of attention to the body as well as to the individual soul": Streeby, "Haunted Houses," 447.

70 Nelson, *National Manhood*, 148.

71 Ibid.

72 Castronovo, *Necro-Citizenship*.

73 Foucault, "Power/Knowledge."

74 I am building on Fredric Jameson's insight that "ideology is not something which informs or invests production; rather, the aesthetic act is itself ideological, and the production of aesthetic or narrative form is to be seen as an ideological act in its own right, with the function of inventing imaginary or formal 'solutions' to unresolvable social contradictions": Jameson, *The Political Unconscious*, 79.

75 Elizabeth Maddock Dillon has persuasively argued for the emergence of aesthetic theory in the eighteenth century as a post–Revolutionary attempt to restore social order without challenging—indeed, while strengthening—the autonomy of self-governing citizens. "Lodging new authority in the individual," Dillon writes, "in every instance, required developing an account of the individual's right to that authority and the capacity to exercise it with responsibility. Aesthetic theory offered precisely such a description of the 'moral law within' the individual or what Kant would famously call a 'conformity to law without a law' ": Dillon, "Sentimental Aesthetics," 498. Dillon's account of how aesthetic theory interiorized obedience to the laws (now the law of "taste" rather than the coercive laws of the state) helps explain the relationship, for

Lippard, between the aesthetic power exercised by Ravoni and other forms of inner force—desire and anxiety, chief among them—that aesthetics supplant and refine.

76 Mitchell, *Reveries of a Bachelor*, 478; Berlant and Warner, "Sex in Public," 322.

77 Admiring in Mitchell's *Reveries of a Bachelor* the ways fantasy permits "a public voice for private values," Lisa Spiro suggestively contends that Mitchell provides readers with a safe distance from those fantasies while simultaneously inviting them to become collaborators in dreaming (rather than to be appropriated by *his* dreams), through a repeated narrative technique that she calls "detached intimacy": Spiro, "Reading with a Tender Rapture," 71.

78 Jameson defines the "political unconscious" as "Necessity" or "what hurts." Refusing to be turned into the content of a new political "vision," the political unconscious, for Jameson, "refuses desire and sets inexorable limits to individual as well as collective praxis, which its 'ruses' turn into grisly and ironic reversals of their overt intention." Thus, history can be reached "only through its effects, and never directly as some reified force": Jameson, *The Political Unconscious*, 102.

79 Butler, "Force of Fantasy," 185–86, 192.

80 Butler, *The Psychic Life of Power*, 249.

81 Ibid., 265–66.

82 Ibid., 272.

83 Ibid.

84 Hawthorne, *The House of the Seven Gables*, 157.

6. Romanticism and Racial Interiority

1 Delany, *Blake*. Page numbers cited in the text are from this edition.

2 Reid-Pharr, "Violent Ambiguity," 89–92.

3 Ibid.

4 Du Bois, *The Souls of Black Folks*, 8

5 On "illocutionary" and "perlocutionary" significance, see Austin, *How to Do Things with Words*.

6 On the connections between the gothic novel and slavery, see Goddu, *Gothic America*. On juridical innovation in the African American novel, see Clymer, "Martin Delany's *Blake* and the Transnational Politics of Property"; Crane, "The Lexicon of Rights, Power, and Community in *Blake*." On transnational globalism, see Gilroy, *The Black Atlantic*; Levine, *Martin Delany, Frederick Douglass, and the Politics of Representative Identity*; Powell, "Postcolonial Theory in an American Context"; Sundquist, *To Wake the Nations*.

7 Surprisingly little has been said about the relationship between romanticism and race, even in the United States, where the age of romanticism coincided with fierce debates over chattel slavery. There are, of course, exceptions. Robert Levine devotes a chapter of his *Conspiracy and Romance* to the "conspiratorial discourse" of slave revolt and mutiny, explaining that such "melodramatic discourse" provided the opportunity to

delve into the contradictions that gird "the vaguely defined social space of the American republic." He contends that "there was no escape for white Americans from insurrectionary nightmares," and their admixture of dread and desire produced romances in which racialized Others are shown to be both the white man's inferior and yet capable of the sort of large-scale conspiracy required to undertake planning a highly organized revolt or mutiny: Levine, *Conspiracy and Romance*, 12, 166–67.

Joan Dayan claims, "The development of romance in the United States was linked in unsettling ways to the business of race. Out of the ground of bondage, the curse of slavery, and the fear of 'servile war' came a twisted sentimentality, a cruel analytic of 'love' in the New World: a conceit of counterfeit intimacy." For Dayan, the art of the American romantics—Poe and Melville in particular—depended on a civilizing mechanism of "human bondage" in which the "civilized" man could define himself against the subjugated and subhuman slave. This made the slave, defined as the romanticist's racial other, a prime target for the terrorizing and eroticizing fantasies of white male authors. "Out of the ground of bondage, the curse of slavery, and the fear of 'servile war,' " she writes, "came a twisted sentimentality, a cruel analytic of 'love' in the New World: a conceit of counterfeit of intimacy." While turning "negroes into matter for idealization" served the needs of abolition, generating an apparently benevolent refutation of images of black brutes, the transformation of black Americans "into superlatives" nevertheless resulted in "a reduction into generalities," leaving slaves and free blacks without the possibility of making particular or divergent "real human claims" and, hence, "deprived of the possibility of significant action." Dayan concludes, "The black fugitives turned hero or heroine" found their stories "embellished or made to serve the often demeaning fantasies about the 'African character' ": Dayan, "Romance and Race," 90–91, 93, 95, 98, 105.

Two other studies that include extended considerations of slavery are Ellis, *The Theory of the American Romance*, and Gravil, *Romantic Dialogues*. Both consider the effects of slavery on various writers of the romance tradition. Ellis explains how the "conservative and aristocratic" critical tradition has obfuscated slavery and plantation culture generally and the significance of both to the antebellum romance: Ellis, *The Theory of the American Romance*, 131–33. Gravil discusses Wordsworth's influence on Whitman and their ambivalence on questions of slavery and revolution: Gravil, *Romantic Dialogues*, 178–84.

Goddu explains the racially motivated critical turn away from discussions of "the gothic" in favor of "the romance." Because "the American gothic is haunted by race," rather than obfuscating race within the romance's symbolic universe, reading for the gothic requires us to connect physical blackness to looming racial anxieties that haunt both the texts and the society that produced them: Goddu, *Gothic America*, 7.

8 Dayan, "Romance and Race," 95.

9 Ibid., 105.

10 Ibid., 95.

11 Frye, *Anatomy of Criticism*, 186.

12 See Butler, "The Force of Fantasy."

13 Frye, *Anatomy of Criticism*, 193.

14 Ibid., 196–97.

15 Jameson, "Magical Narratives," 139, 143–44.

16 "Consciousness" is typically given a more liberating connotation in criticism of *Blake*. Levine deftly articulates Blake's belief "that a black revolution would fail if it should occur *before* blacks attain the consciousness of freemen" (210), understanding that "'blackness' is as much a matter of politics as biology" (210): Levine, *Martin Delany, Frederick Douglass, and the Politics of Representative Identity*, 210. Similarly, Sundquist argues that *Blake* is "a work in which radicalism is first of all an act of consciousness": Sundquist, *To Wake the Nations*, 198.

17 Butler, "The Force of Fantasy."

18 Jameson, "Magical Narratives," 138. Although Jameson attributes the language of white and black magic to Frye, in fact Frye resists such terminology. While he does describe the antagonism of heroes and villains in terms of the white and black pieces on a chessboard, he never attributes whiteness or blackness to forms of magic.

19 Ibid., 158, 161.

20 Sundquist dates the composition of *Blake* between 1852 and 1858, the height of the Romantic period: Sundquist, *To Wake the Nations*, 183.

21 On the publication history of *Blake*, see Levine, *Martin Delany, Frederick Douglass, and the Politics of Representative Identity*, 178–80. On the historical conflations in Delany's novel, see Sundquist, *To Wake the Nations*, 184. Sundquist writes that Delany's craft "is rudimentary," a fact compensated for by his "compelling portrait of a revolutionary ethos."

22 Levine, *Martin Delany, Frederick Douglass, and the Politics of Representative Identity*, 216.

23 Ibid. Levine argues persuasively that "Blake is less interested in fomenting an immediate revolution than in finding leaders who can help him to develop in Cuba what Delany hoped to develop in Africa: a 'progressive negro nationality'": ibid., 209. Sundquist similarly argues that *Blake* "is among the most compelling statements of black transnationalist ideology in the nineteenth century": Sundquist, *To Wake the Nations*, 206.

24 Levine, *Martin Delany, Frederick Douglass, and the Politics of Representative Identity*, 195.

25 For a thorough account of how *Blake* formulates a black "ruling element," see ibid., 208–23.

26 On the conflation of historical events in *Blake*, see Sundquist, *To Wake the Nations*, 184.

27 Levine, *Martin Delany, Frederick Douglass, and the Politics of Representative Identity*, 190.

28 Gregg Crane notes that, in Blake's vision of revitalized nationalism, "any power to ensure the freedom or inherent rights of minority members of the community" lies

with those members themselves, who "must aspire to majoritarian power of their own for the precognition and protection of their rights": Crane, "The Lexicon of Rights, Power, and Community in *Blake*," 546.

29 Levine, *Martin Delany, Frederick Douglass, and the Politics of Representative Identity*, 192.

30 Allen, *Talking to Strangers*, 17.

31 Levine touches on Blake's imitation of structures of mastery when, in response to the question "What is it that makes Blake not simply another foreign intruder but the embodiment of Cuba?" he answers, "Oddly enough, it is the fact of his implication in mastery": Levine, *Martin Delany, Frederick Douglass, and the Politics of Representative Identity*, 204. Robert Reid-Pharr goes even further, arguing that Blake's program of black nationalism relies on the sadomasochistic structures of mastery and submission derived from slavery: Reid-Pharr, "Violent Ambiguity," 89–92.

32 I am building here on Balibar's crucial insight into "second position racism" (22), "whose dominant theme is not biological heredity but the insurmountability of cultural difference, a racism which, at first sight, does not postulate the superiority of certain groups or peoples in relation to others but 'only' the harmfulness of abolishing frontiers." Blood thus gives way to culture, biology to social psychology and anthropology, but in the transformation arises ever greater aggressiveness. All group antagonisms, for Balibar, are therefore always already racialized, even (especially) those that "celebrate" cultural "difference": Balibar and Wallerstein, *Race, Nation, Class*, 21–23. Timothy Powell gets at something like this double bind of culture—to not have one is to be pre-social, but to have one is to be racialized in a set system of antagonistic differences—when he reports that *Blake* "captures with startling accuracy the historical tension within the African American community between an ever present impulse to cultural independence and the disturbingly persistent plight of being contained as a nation within a nation by a form of internal colonization that the dominant white society refuses to acknowledge": Powell, "Postcolonial Theory in an American Context," 363. Whereas Powell would see "cultural independence" as a liberating conclusion to this tension, however, Balibar shows it to be the cause.

33 Glenn Hendler contends that "Delany's nationalism was part of his lifelong effort to give public and institutional form to the racialized sentiments at the affective core of his political thought," in the process pushing "at the limits of the actually existing public sphere" and revising "hegemonic norms of civility in order to reveal them as merely national norms": Hendler, *Public Sentiments*, 81. While I am skeptical about some of Hendler's assumptions—that one can form public institutions innocent of the "norms" that are "merely" national, that "racialized sentiments" preexist their inscription through such institutional norms—I am convinced by Hendler's rich reading of the counter-knowledge productions in *Blake* and in the nineteenth-century public sphere generally.

34 On Blake's renunciation of the conjurers, see Levine, *Martin Delany, Frederick Douglass, and the Politics of Representative Identity*, 198.

35 Reid-Pharr, "Violent Ambiguity."

36 Sundquist, *To Wake the Nations*, 184.

37 On the perpetuation of desire, see Reid-Pharr, "Violent Ambiguity," 91.

38 Ibid. "It does not take too great a conceptual leap to recognize that the condition of 'The Black Family' acts in Delany's political economy as a barometer of the condition of 'The Black Nation,'" Reid-Pharr argues. "One might argue, in fact, that as both a nationalist and a bourgeois, Delany understood the maintenance of the autonomous and 'respectable' household as absolutely necessary to the production of 'New Africa,'" "a symbol of one's loyalty to the 'race'" that simultaneously preserves the "gender, economic, and ideological hierarchies" of slavery: ibid., 75, 77, 92.

39 Most critics agree with Levine's assessment that the "spirit of resistance (to the slaveholder, the spirit of terror) portrayed in *Blake* is most effectively embodied in the suggestion left behind by its hero that local units have been inspired and prepared to act with independent force on their own." For Levine, the truncated novel "keeps in perpetual suspension the threat of black insurrection, making the creation of white paranoia the potent end product of Blake's plotting." Even without its conclusion, then, "the novel can be said to have achieved a satisfying sense of completion": ibid., 198, 215.

40 During the revolt on the *Vulture*, Levine writes, Blake "assumes a spectatorial role appropriate more to an evaluator of talents than a fellow revolutionary." Through this, Delany might be expressing his fears "that uncontrolled revolution could erupt as a form of intemperance": ibid., 208.

41 Wallace, "Afterword," 335.

42 Ibid., 344.

43 Quoted in Pickle, "Reading Carrie Mae Weems," 11.

44 Wallace, "Afterword," 344.

45 Crafts, *The Bondwoman's Narrative*. Pages cited in the text are from this edition.

46 Fleischner, *Mastering Slavery*.

47 The phrase is from *Disorderly Conduct*, in which Carroll Smith-Rosenberg describes a vast network of affective, physical, and erotic intimacy between middle-class women in antebellum America.

48 My thinking on racial identification draws on Diana Fuss's elaboration of Franz Fanon's project in *Black Skin, White Masks*. "'Fixed' by the violence of the racist interpellation in an imaginary relation of fractured specularity," Fuss writes, "the black man, Fanon concludes, 'is forever in combat with his own image'": Fuss, *Identification Papers*, 143. For Hannah Crafts, vision is not only fractured by the racial power knowledges produced through slavery, but it is put under erasure by the visual "lacks" imposed by structures of gender identification. From both vantages, Hannah learns that, "by imposing upon the colonial other the burden of identification (the command to become a mimic Anglo-European), the Imperial Subject inadvertently places himself in the perilous position of object—object of the Other's aggressive, hostile, and rivalrous acts of incorporation": ibid., 146. Hannah exemplifies what Fuss, through

Fanon, names as a principal psychic weapon of the weak: the power "to identify and disidentify simultaneously with the same object, to assimilate but not to incorporate, to approximate but not to displace": ibid., 146.

49 Henry Louis Gates Jr., "Introduction," in Crafts, *The Bondwoman's Narrative*, lxv–lxvii.

50 Frye, *Anatomy of Criticism*.

7. "I Want My Happiness!"

1 The term "marvelous" comes from phrenology handbooks, which define it as "wonder; credulity; belief in prophetic writing and miraculous interpositions of Divine Providence" or as "Belief in phantoms; ghosts; fortune-telling; dread of omens; eager to relate or listen to improbably or marvellous stories. Larger in women than in men": Wheeler, *The Phrenological Characters and Talents of Henry Clay, Daniel Webster, John Quincy Adams, William Henry Harrison, and Andrew Jackson*, 29.

2 I am building here on Butler's definition of the real as "an installation and foreclosure of fantasy, a phantasmatic construction which receives a certain legitimation after which it is called the real and disavowed as the phantasmatic." This construction of reality, she argues, relies on a "set of exclusionary and constitutive principles" that amount to a simple pointing at an external world that presumably represents reality's referent. Efforts to sanction and police alternative versions of the real necessarily produce "certain forms of exclusion that return, like insistent ghosts, to undermine those very efforts." While fantasy "postures *as* the real," establishing "through a repeated and insistent posturing" its empirically verifiable status, the fantastic origins of the real persist as "the possibility of suspending and interrogating the ontological claim itself, of reviewing its own production, as it were, and contesting their claim to the real." As a result, Butler argues, "fantasy is not equated with what is not real, but rather with what is not *yet* real, what is possible or futural, or what belongs to a different version of the real": Butler, "The Force of Fantasy," 185–87.

3 On Hawthorne's experiments with homosociality, which produced a "defamiliarization" of conventional domesticity anticipating both the perspectival shifts and sexual non-normativity that became associated with queer modernity, see Romero, *Home Fronts*, 88–105.

4 Chase, *The American Novel and Its Tradition*, ix, xi, 74.

5 Allen, *Talking to Strangers*.

6 Bersani, "Sociality and Sexuality," 656.

7 Chase, *The American Novel and Its Tradition*, 1–2.

8 Ibid., 17.

9 Ibid., 2, 21, 31; James, *The Art of the Novel*, 31.

10 James, *The Art of the Novel*, 33.

11 Arvin, *Herman Melville*, 181.

12 Chase, *The American Novel and Its Tradition*, 106.

13 Ibid., 13, 106.

14 My thinking on queer sociality has been shaped by the work of Lauren Berlant and Michael Warner, who describe the range of relationships typical of queer world making:

> Queer culture has learned not only how to sexualize these and other relations, but also to use them as a context for witnessing intense and personal affect while elaborating a public world of belonging and transformation. Making a queer world has required the development of kinds of intimacy that bear no necessary relation to domestic space, to kinship, to the couple form, to property, or to the nation. These intimacies *do* bear a necessary relation to a counterpublic—and indefinitely accessible world conscious of its subordinate relation. They are typical both of the inventiveness of queer world making and of the queer world's fragility. (Berlant and Warner, "Sex in Public," 322)

In this manner, Berlant and Warner show how queer world making manifests the promise of unpredictable alliance and redrawn lines of power Foucault, in "Friendship as a Way of Life," claimed arises from queer friendship.

15 On Hawthorne and property law, see Michaels, "Romance and Real Estate."

16 On the contractual nature of Hawthorne's preface, see Jameson, "Magical Narratives."

17. I am drawing on Foucault's distinction in *Discipline and Punish* between physical coercion and systematized installations of interior order, productivity, and consent.

18 Melville, *Pierre*. Pages cited in the text are from this edition.

19 Franchot, *Roads to Rome*, 140.

20 Kelley, "*Pierre*'s Domestic Ambiguities," 106.

21 Matheson, "Clifford's Dim, Unsatisfactory Elegance."

22 Millington, *Practicing Romance*, 113.

23 Butler, "Imitation and Gender Insubordination," 18.

24 Ibid., 20.

25 Millington, *Practicing Romance*, 110.

26 Warner, *The Trouble with Normal*, 35.

27 On sympathy in Hawthorne's romances, see Hutner, *Secrets and Sympathy*.

28 Millington, *Practicing Romance*, 111.

29 Ibid., 139. On Hawthorne's hopefulness, see also Thomas, "Reading the Romances of America."

30 Levine, *Conspiracy and Romance*, 159.

31 In the review, Melville helped establish an American literary tradition with Hawthorne at its head. Challenging his countrymen's belief in the unparalleled genius of Shakespeare, Melville asked, "What sort of belief is this for an American, a man who is bound to carry republican progressiveness into Literature, as well as into Life?" Against charges that the United States had not yet produced writers of genius, Melville asserted that "Shakespeares are being born on the banks of the Ohio." Not only are American authors born *on* the national landscape, they *embody* that landscape, as Melville's characterization of Hawthorne seems to demonstrate: "He is one of the new, and far better generation of your writers. The smell of your beeches and hemlocks is upon him; your own broad prairies are in his soul; and if you travel away inland into

his deep and noble nature, you will hear the far roar of his Niagara." While America "has good kith and kin of her own to take to her bosom," Melville enjoined, "let her not lavish her embraces upon the household of an alien." Melville resisted claiming "that all American writers should studiously cleave to nationality in their writing," but he did contend that "no American writer should write like an Englishman, or a Frenchman": Melville, "Hawthorne and His Mosses," 221–24.

32 Chase, *The American Novel and Its Tradition*, 90.

33 Wilson, *The Hawthorne and Melville Friendship*, 186.

34 Melville, "Hawthorne and His Mosses," 225; Wilson, *The Hawthorne and Melville Friendship*, 199.

35 Wilson, *The Hawthorne and Melville Friendship*, 4.

36 Ibid., 196.

37 Wineapple, "Hawthorne and Melville."

38 Wilson, *The Hawthorne and Melville Friendship*, 240.

39 Melville, *Clarel*. Pages cited in the text are from this edition.

40 Wilson, *The Hawthorne and Melville Friendship*, 212.

41 I take the details of the re-interment from Katie Zezima, "Historic Married Couple of Letters Are Reunited after 142 Years," *New York Times*, June 27, 2006.

Epilogue

1 My reading of *The Scarlet Letter* builds on Sacvan Bercovitch's advocacy of "oppositionalism," a conflict that "assumes a dialectical form." Arising "from historical contradiction," Bercovitch contends, oppositionalism "expresses a partiality we associate with ideological partisanship; the oppositions it makes visible reflect fundamental differences that force us to take positions, rather than to mediate . . . between them." While I agree with Bercovitch about the desirability of such opposition, he is less sanguine about its results in *The Scarlet Letter*, which, he contends, "seeks to eliminate" real opposition by substituting symbolic opposition, which "transmutes opposition into complementarity" and makes Hester's cottage community "a counseling center for patience and faith." Given that we never learn the content of what transpires in this "counseling center," I suspect Bercovitch is projecting more consent than is warranted by the text, which, far from using "the prospect of certain meanings" as a "form of closure and control," frustrates the choice between "the reasons of the heart and the claims of institutions" precisely by rendering content inscrutable and speculations such as Bercovitch's groundless: Bercovitch, *The Rites of Assent*, 194–95, 200.

2 Jonathan Culler has recently noted that the "crisis" in the humanities arises, in great measure, from the fact that "the term *humanities* seems to have tied a set of academic disciplines to a particular ideology of the human," thereby foreclosing investigations of a humanist lexicon—"madness, justice, discipline, sexuality, the self"—that arrive at counter-hegemonic articulations of subjectivity, humanity, or history: Culler, "In Need of a Name?" 40. While I wholly agree with Culler's analysis of the "crisis" faced by the contemporary humanities—and I would extend that crisis beyond the limits of

the academy—I disagree with his conclusion that the solution might come from abandoning the term "humanities" to its hegemonic constructions. In developing the concept of humanism without humans, on the contrary, I am positing a way to reappropriate the terms of humanism without surrendering the critique of the subject (especially the manifestation of subjectivity as "consciousness") that, as Culler rightly notes, has been the most important intellectual development of the past half-century.

3 Butler, "The Force of Fantasy," 189, 192.
4 Douglas, *The Feminization of American Culture*, 5, 8, 11–13.
5 Putnam, "Bowling Alone," 67.
6 Gutmann, "Freedom of Association," 3–4, 18.
7 Fleischacker, "Insignificant Communities," 289.
8 Ibid., 293.
9 Hawthorne, *The House of the Seven Gables*, 502.
10 Ibid., 568.

REFERENCES

Abbott, W. W., ed. *Papers of George Washington: Confederation Series I*. Charlottesville: University of Virginia Press, 1992.

Albertson, Karla Klein. "Phrenology in the Nineteenth Century." *Early American Life* 26, no. 3 (1995): 52–55, 66.

Allen, Danielle S. *Talking to Strangers: Anxieties of Citizenship since* Brown v. Board of Education. Chicago: University of Chicago Press, 2004.

Althusser, Louis. *Lenin and Philosophy and Other Essays*. New York: Monthly Review Press, 1971.

Anderson, Benedict. *Imagined Communities: Reflections on the Origin and Spread of Nationalism*. London: Verso, 1991.

Appadurai, Arjun. *Modernity at Large: Cultural Dimensions of Globalization*. Minneapolis: University of Minnesota Press, 1996.

Arendt, Hannah. "Reflections on Violence." Pp. 69–101 in *The First Anthology: Thirty Years of the New York Review of Books*, eds. Robert B. Silvers, Barbara Epstein, and Rea S. Hederman. New York: New York Review of Books, 1993.

Arvin, Newton. *Herman Melville*. New York: Grove Press, 1950.

Arthur, Timothy Shay. *Ten Nights in a Bar-Room, and What I Saw There* (1854). Bedford, Mass.: Applewood Books, 2000.

"Articles of Confederation" (1777). Pp. 84–96 in *Four Pillars of Constitutionalism*, ed. Richard H. Cox. Amherst, N.Y.: Prometheus Books, 1998.

Austin, J. L. *How to Do Things with Words*. Cambridge, Mass.: Harvard University Press, 1975.

Bailyn, Bernard. *Education in the Forming of American Society*. New York: W. W. Norton, 1972.

Balibar, Etienne, and Immanuel Wallerstein, *Race, Nation, Class: Ambiguous Identities*. New York: Verso, 1991.

Barker, Francis. *The Tremulous Private Body: Essays on Subjectivity*. Ann Arbor: University of Michigan Press, 1995.

Barnes, Elizabeth. *States of Sympathy: Seduction and Domesticity in the American Novel*. New York: Columbia University Press, 1997.

Bate, Walter Jackson. *From Classic to Romantic: Premises of Taste in Eighteenth Century England*. New York: Harper, 1946.

Baym, Nina., "The Erotic Motif in Melville's *Clarel*." *Texas Studies in Literature and Language* 16, no. 2 (1974): 315–28.

Beecher, Catharine. *The American Woman's Home* (1869), ed. Nicole Tonkovich. Hartford, Conn.: Harriet Beecher Stowe Center, 2002.

Beecher, Lyman. *A Plea for the West*, 2d ed. Cincinnati: Truman and Smith, 1835.

Benjamin, Walter. *Charles Baudelaire: A Lyric Poet in the Era of High Capitalism*. London: Verso, 1983.

Bentham, Jeremy. *The Panopticon Writings*, ed. Miran Boxovic. London: Verso, 1995.

Bercovitch, Sacvan. *The Rites of Assent: Transformations in the Symbolic Construction of America*. New York: Routledge, 1993.

Berlant, Lauren. *The Queen of America Goes to Washington City: Essays on Sex and Citizenship*. Durham: Duke University Press, 1997.

——. "Poor Eliza." *American Literature* 70, no. 3 (September 1998): 635–68.

——. "Intimacy: A Special Issue." Pp. 3–8 in *Intimacy*, ed. Lauren Berlant. Chicago: University of Chicago Press, 2000.

——. "The Subject of True Feeling: Pain, Privacy, and Politics." Pp. 42–62 in *Cultural Studies and Political Theory*, ed. Jodi Dean. Ithaca, N.Y.: Cornell University Press, 2000.

Berlant, Lauren, and Michael Warner. "Sex in Public." Pp. 311–30 in *Intimacy*, ed. Lauren Berlant. Chicago: University of Chicago Press, 2000.

Bersani, Leo. "Sociality and Sexuality." *Critical Inquiry* 26 (Summer 2000): 641–56.

Billington, Ray Allen. "Introduction." In Maria Monk, *Awful Disclosures of the Hotel Dieu Nunnery*. Facsimile ed. Hamden, Conn.: Archon Books, 1962.

Birney, James, *Letter on Colonization*. Boston: Garrison and Knapp, 1834.

Blanchard, Jonathan. "On the Importance and Means of Cultivating the Social Affections among Pupils, Delivered at the American Institute of Instruction at Its Annual Meeting." Boston: n.p., 1835.

Bomine, Walter. *Collaborative Psychoanalysis: Anxiety, Depression, Dreams, and Personality Change*. Rutherford, N.J.: Farleigh Dickinson University Press, 1989.

Brasher, Thomas L., ed. *Walt Whitman: The Early Poems and the Fiction*. New York: New York University Press, 1963.

Brodhead, Richard H. *Cultures of Letters: Scenes of Reading and Writing in Nineteenth-Century America*. Chicago: University of Chicago Press, 1993.

Brooks, David. "The Bursting Point." *New York Times*, September 4, available online at http://www.nytimes.com/2005/09/04/opinion/04brooks.html.

Brown, Gillian. *Domestic Individualism: Imagining Self in Nineteenth-Century America*. Berkeley: University of California Press, 1990.

——. "Consent, Coquetry, and Consequences." *American Literary History* 9, no. 4 (1997): 625–52.

Brown, Isaac V. *Memoirs of the Reverend Robert Finley, D.D., Late Pastor of the Presbyterian Congregation at Basking Ridge, New-Jersey, and President of Franklin College, Located at Athens, in the State of Georgia*. New Brunswick, N.J.: Terhune and Lutson, 1819.

——. *Slavery Irreconcilable with Christianity and Sound Reason; or, An Anti-Slavery Argument*. New Brunswick, N.J.: Charles Scott, 1858.

Burgett, Bruce. *Sentimental Bodies: Sex, Gender, and Citizenship in the Early Republic*. Princeton, N.J.: Princeton University Press, 1998.

——. "American Nationalism—R.I.P." *American Literary History* 13, no. 2 (2001): 317–28.

——. "On the Mormon Question: Race, Sex, and Polygamy in the 1850s and 1990s." *American Quarterly* 57, no. 1 (2005): 75–102.

Butler, Judith. *Gender Trouble: Feminism and the Subversion of Identity*. New York: Routledge, 1990.

——. "Imitation and Gender Insubordination." Pp. 13–31 in *Inside/Out: Lesbian Theories, Gay Theories*, ed. Diana Fuss. New York: Routledge, 1991.

——. *The Psychic Life of Power*. Stanford, Calif.: Stanford University Press, 1997.

——. "The Force of Fantasy: Mapplethorpe, Feminism, and Discursive Excess" (1990). Pp. 183–303 in *The Judith Butler Reader*, ed. Sara Salih. Oxford: Blackwell, 2004.

Butler, Judith, Ernesto Laclau, and Slavoj Žižek. *Contingency, Hegemony, Universality: Contemporary Dialogues on the Left*. London: Verso, 2000.

Cain, William. "Introduction." Pp. 1–57 in *William Lloyd Garrison and the Fight against Slavery: Selections from "The Liberator."* New York: St. Martin's Press, 1995.

Caldwell, Charles. *New Views on Penitentiary Discipline, and Moral Education and Reform*. Philadelphia: William Brown, 1829.

Castronovo, Russ. *Necro-Citizenship: Death, Eroticism, and the Public Sphere in the Nineteenth-Century United States*. Durham: Duke University Press, 2001.

——. "Political Necrophilia." *boundary 2* 27, no. 2 (Summer 2000): 113–48.

Chase, Richard. *The American Novel and Its Tradition*. Garden City, N.Y.: Doubleday, 1957.

Clark, Elizabeth B. " 'The Sacred Rights of the Weak': Pain, Sympathy, and the Culture of Individual Rights in Antebellum America." *Journal of American History* (September 1995): 463–93.

Clayton, John J. *Gestures of Healing: Anxiety and the Modern Novel*. Amherst: University of Massachusetts Press, 1991.

Clinton, David. *Tocqueville, Lieber, and Bagehot: Liberalism Confronts the World*. New York: Palgrave Macmillan, 2003.

Clymer, Jeffory A. "Martin Delany's *Blake* and the Transnational Politics of Property." *American Literary History* 15, no. 4 (2003): 709–31.

Colton, Calvin. *Protestant Jesuitism*. New York: Harper and Brothers, 1836.

Cooter, Roger. *The Cultural Meaning of Popular Science: Phrenology and the Organization of Consent in Nineteenth-Century Britain*. Cambridge: Cambridge University Press, 1984.

Coviello, Peter. *Intimacy in America: Dreams of Affiliation in Antebellum Literature*. Minneapolis: University of Minnesota Press, 2005.

Cowie, Alexander. *The Rise of the American Novel*. New York: American Books, 1948.

Cox, Richard H., ed. *Four Pillars of Constitutionalism*. Amherst, N.Y.: Prometheus Books, 1998.

Crafts, Hannah. *The Bondwoman's Narrative* (c. 1855–1859), ed. Henry Louis Gates Jr. New York: Warner Books, 2002.

Crane, Gregg. "The Lexicon of Rights, Power, and Community in *Blake*: Martin R. Delany's Dissent from *Dred Scott*." *American Literature* 68, no. 3 (1996): 527–53.

Crenson, Matthew A., and Benjamin Ginsberg. *Downsizing Democracy: How America*

Sidelined Its Citizens and Privatized Its Public. Baltimore: Johns Hopkins University Press, 2004.

Cruikshank, Barbara. *The Will to Empower: Democratic Citizens and Other Subjects*. Ithaca, N.Y.: Cornell University Press, 1999.

Culler, Jonathan. "In Need of a Name? A Response to Geoffrey Harpham." *New Literary History* 36 (2005): 37–42.

Dall, Caroline. *The Romance of the Association; or, One Last Glimpse of Charlotte Temple and Eliza Wharton*. Cambridge, Mass.: John Wilson and Son, 1875.

Davidson, Cathy N. *Revolution and the Word: The Rise of the Novel in America*. New York: Oxford University Press, 1986.

Davis, David Brion. "Reflections on Abolitionism and Ideological Hegemony." *American Historical Review* 92, no. 4 (October 1987): 797–812.

Dayan, Joan. "Romance and Race." Pp. 89–109 in *The Columbia History of the American Novel*, ed. Emory Elliott. New York: Columbia University Press, 1991.

Delany, Martin R. *Blake; or, The Huts of America* (1859). Boston: Beacon Press, 1970.

Deleuze, Gilles, and Félix Guattari. *A Thousand Plateaus: Capitalism and Schizophrenia*, trans. and foreword by Brian Massumi. Minneapolis: University of Minnesota Press, 1988.

D'Emilio, John. "Capitalism and Gay Identity." Pp. 3–16 in *Making Trouble: Essays on Gay History, Politics, and the University*. New York: Routledge, 1992.

Denning, Michael. *Mechanic Accents: Dime Novels and Working-Class Culture in America*. New York: Verso, 1987.

Dillon, Elizabeth Maddock. "Sentimental Aesthetics." *American Literature* 76, no. 3 (2004): 495–523.

Douglas, Ann. *The Feminization of American Culture*. New York: Avon, 1977.

Downey, Jean, ed. *Walt Whitman, Franklin Evans or The Inebriate: A Tale of the Times*. New Haven, Conn.: College and University Press, 1967.

Drinka, George Frederick. *The Birth of Neurosis: Myth, Malady, and the Victorians*. New York: Simon and Schuster, 1984.

Du Bois, W. E. B. *The Souls of Black Folk*. New York: Library of America, 1987.

Duggan, Lisa. *The Twilight of Equality? Neoliberalism, Cultural Politics, and the Attack on Democracy*. Boston: Beacon Press, 2004.

Dumm, Thomas. *Michel Foucault and the Politics of Freedom*. Thousand Oaks, Calif.: Sage, 1996.

Eagleton, Terry. *The Ideology of the Aesthetic*. London: Blackwell, 1990.

Edelman, Lee. *No Future: Queer Theory and the Death Drive*. Durham: Duke University Press, 2004.

Ellis, William. *The Theory of American Romance: An Ideology in American Intellectual History*. Ann Arbor: University of Michigan Research Press, 1989.

Ellison, Julie. *Cato's Tears and the Making of Anglo-American Emotion*. Chicago: University of Chicago Press, 1999.

Emerson, Ralph Waldo. "Experience." Pp. 285–311. *Selected Essays*, ed. Larzer Ziff. New York: Penguin, 1982.

———. "Love." Pp. 97–107 in *Essays: First and Second Series* (1841). New York: Library of America, 1990.

———. "Man the Reformer." Pp. 129–47. *Selected Essays*, ed. Larzer Ziff. New York: Penguin, 1982.

———. "New England Reformers." Pp. 11–18 in *Antebellum Reform*, ed. David Brion Davis. New York: Harper and Row, 1967.

———. "Self-Reliance." Pp. 29–52 in *Essays: First and Second Series*. New York: Library of America, 1990.

Fanuzzi, Robert A. " 'The Organ of an Individual': William Lloyd Garrison and the Liberator." *Prospects* 23 (1998): 107–23.

Fiedler, Leslie A. *Love and Death in the American Novel*. New York: Dell, 1960.

Findley, William. "Reply to Wilson's Speech: 'An Officer of the Late Continental Army.' " Pp. 97–104 in *The Debate on the Constitution, Part One*, ed. Bernard Bailyn. New York: Library of America, 1993.

Finley, Robert. *Thoughts on the Colonization of Free Blacks*. Washington, D.C.: n.p., 1816.

Finseth, Ian. " 'A Melancholy Tale': Rhetoric, Fiction, and Passion in *The Coquette*." *Studies in the Novel* 33, no. 2 (2001): 125–59.

Fisher, Will. "Queer Money." *English Literary History* 66 (1999): 1–23.

Fleischacker, Samuel. "Insignificant Communities." Pp. 273–313 in *Freedom of Association*, ed. Amy Gutmann. Princeton, N.J.: Princeton University Press, 1998.

Fleischner, Jennifer. *Mastering Slavery: Memory, Family, and Identity in Women's Slave Narratives*. New York: New York University Press, 1996.

Fliegelman, Jay. 1993. *Declaring Independence: Jefferson, Natural Language, and the Culture of Performance*. Stanford, Calif.: Stanford University Press, 1993.

Foster, Hannah Webster. *The Coquette* (1797). New York: Penguin, 1996.

Foucault, Michel. *Discipline and Punish: The Birth of the Prison*, trans. Alan Sheridan. New York: Vintage, 1979.

———. "Friendship as a Way of Life." Pp. 203–9 in *Foucault Live: Collected Interviews, 1961–1984*. New York: Semiotext(e), 1989.

———. *The History of Sexuality, Volume 1: An Introduction*, trans. Robert Hurley. New York: Random House, 1978.

———. "Politics and Reason." Pp. 57–85 in *Politics, Philosophy, Culture: Interviews and Other Writings, 1977–1984*, ed. Lawrence D. Kritzman. New York: Routledge, 1988.

———. *Power/Knowledge: Selected Interviews and Other Writings, 1972–1977*, ed. Colin Gordon. New York: Pantheon Books, 1980.

Fournier, Ron. "Rhetoric Not Matching Reality." Associated Press, September 2, 2005, available online at http://customwire.ap.org/dynamic/stories/K/KATRINA.HAPPY.

Fowler, Lorenzo N. *The Principles of Phrenology and Physiology Applied to Man's Social Relations*. Boston: Saxton and Pierce, 1842.

Fowler, Lydia. *Familiar Lessons on Phrenology, Devised for the Use of Children and Youth in Schools and Families*. New York: Fowler and Wells, 1848.

Fowler, Orson S. *Amativeness*. New York: Fowler and Wells, 1854.

———. *Education and Self-Improvement*. New York: O. S. and L. N. Fowler, 1844.

——. *Intemperance and Tight-Lacing, Considered in Relation to the Laws of Life*. New York: Fowler and Wells, 1847.

——. *Love and Parentage, Applied to the Improvement of Offspring*. New York: Fowler and Wells, 1852.

——. "Temptation—Its Influence on Guilt." Unpublished ms., 1834, in Robert Frost Library Special Collections, Amherst College, Amherst, Massachusetts.

Franchot, Jenny. *Roads to Rome: The Antebellum Protestant Encounter with Catholicism*. Berkeley: University of California Press, 1994.

Frank, Thomas. *One Market under God: Extreme Capitalism, Market Populism, and the End of Economic Democracy*. New York: Anchor, 2001.

Freud, Sigmund. "Mourning and Melancholia." Pp. 164–79 in *General Psychological Theory*. New York: Simon and Schuster, 1991.

Frye, Northrop. *Anatomy of Criticism: Four Essays*. Princeton, N.J.: Princeton University Press, 1957.

Fuss, Diana. *Identification Papers*. New York: Routledge, 1995.

Garrison, William Lloyd. *Address Delivered in Boston, New-York, and Philadelphia before the Free People of Color*. New York: Free People of Color, 1833.

——. *Selections from the Writings and Speeches of William Lloyd Garrison*. Boston: R. F. Walcutt, 1852.

——. *Thoughts on African Colonization; or, An Impartial Exhibition of the Doctrines, Principles, and Purposes of the American Colonization Society*. Boston: Garrison and Knapp, 1832.

Gilfoyle, Timothy J. *City of Eros: New York City, Prostitution, and the Commercialization of Sex, 1790–1920*. New York: W. W. Norton, 1992.

Gilmore, Michael T. "Washington Irving." Pp. 661–75 in *The Cambridge History of American Literature*. Volume I: *1590–1820*, ed. Sacvan Bercovitch. Cambridge: Cambridge University Press, 1994.

Gilroy, Paul. *The Black Atlantic: Modernity and Double Consciousness*. Cambridge, Mass.: Harvard University Press, 1993.

Gladwell, Malcolm. "Institutional Health." *New Yorker*, December 1, 2003, 35, 38.

Goddu, Teresa A. *Gothic America: Narrative, History, and Nation*. New York: Columbia University Press, 1997.

Gravil, Richard. *Romantic Dialogues: Anglo-American Continuities, 1776–1862*. New York: St. Martin's Press, 2000.

Grewal, Inderpal, and Caren Kaplan. "Global Identities: Theorizing Transnational Studies of Sexuality." *GLQ* 7, no. 4 (2001): 663–79.

Griffin, Charles J. G. "The 'Washingtonian Revival': Narrative and the Transformation of Temperance Reform in Antebellum America." *Southern Communication Journal* 66, no. 1 (Fall 2000): 67–78.

Guarneri, Carl J. *The Utopian Alternative: Fourierism in Nineteenth-Century America*. Ithaca, N.Y.: Cornell University Press, 1994.

Gutmann, Amy. "Freedom of Association: An Introductory Essay." Pp. 3–32 in *Freedom of Association*, ed. Amy Gutmann. Princeton, N.J.: Princeton University Press, 1998.

Habermas, Jürgen. *The Structural Transformation of the Public Sphere: An Inquiry into a Category of Bourgeois Society*, trans. Thomas Burger. Cambridge, Mass.: MIT Press, 1991.

Haltunen, Karen. *Confidence Men and Painted Women: A Study of Middle-Class Culture in America, 1830–1870*. New Haven, Conn.: Yale University Press, 1982.

Hamburger, Philip. "Liberality." *Texas Law Review* 78, no. 6 (May 2000): 1215–85.

Hart, James. *The Popular Book: A History of America's Literary Taste*. New York: Oxford University Press, 1950.

Haskell, Thomas L. "Capitalism and the Origins of the Humanitarian Sensibility, Part 2." *American Historical Review* 90, no. 3 (1985): 547–66.

Hawthorne, Nathaniel. "The Custom House" (1850). Pp. 3–45 in *The Centenary Edition of the Works of Nathaniel Hawthorne*, Vol. 1, eds. William Charvat et al. Columbus: Ohio State University Press, 1964.

———. *The House of the Seven Gables* (1851), ed. Milton R. Stern. New York: Penguin, 1986.

Hendler, Glenn. *Public Sentiments: Structures of Feeling in Nineteenth-Century American Literature*. Chapel Hill: University of North Carolina Press, 2001.

Holland, Sharon Patricia. *Raising the Dead: Readings of Death and (Black) Subjectivity*. Durham: Duke University Press, 2000.

Holloway, Emory. *Free and Lonesome Heart: The Secret of Walt Whitman*. New York: Vantage, 1960.

Hutner, Gordon. *Secrets and Sympathy: Forms of Disclosure in Hawthorne's Novels*. Atlanta: University of Georgia Press, 1989.

Irving, Washington. *The Sketch Book* (1819). New York: Signet, 1961.

Jacobs, Harriet. *Incidents in the Life of a Slave Girl* (1861), ed. Jean Fagan Yellin. Cambridge, Mass.: Harvard University Press, 2000.

James, Henry. *The Art of the Novel*. New York: Charles Scribner's Sons, 1934.

Jameson, Fredric. *Archaeologies of the Future: The Desire Called Utopia and Other Science Fictions*. London: Verso, 2005.

———. "Magical Narratives: Romance as Genre." *New Literary History* 7, no. 1 (1975): 135–63.

———. *The Political Unconscious: Narrative as a Socially Symbolic Act*. Rev. ed. Ithaca, N.Y.: Cornell University Press, 1982.

Jehlen, Myra. *American Incarnation: The Individual, the Nation, and the Continent*. Cambridge, Mass.: Harvard University Press, 1986.

Johnson, Linck C. "Reforming the Reformers: Emerson, Thoreau, and the Sunday Lectures at Amory Hall, Boston." *ESQ* 37 (1991): 235–89.

Kaplan, Amy. "Manifest Domesticity." Pp. 581–606 in *No More Separate Spheres! A Special Issue of* American Literature, ed. Cathy N. Davison. Durham: Duke University Press, 1998.

Kelley, Wyn. "*Pierre*'s Domestic Ambiguities." Pp. 91–113 in *The Cambridge Companion to Herman Melville*, ed. Robert S. Levine. Cambridge: Cambridge University Press, 1998.

Kingsdale, Jon M. "The 'Poor Man's Club': Social Functions of the Urban Working-Class Saloon." *American Quarterly* 25 (December 1973): 472–89.

Knoper, Randall. "American Literary Realism and Nervous 'Relaxation.'" *American Literature* 74, no. 4 (December 2002): 715–45.

Laclau, Ernesto. *Emancipation(s)*. London: Verso, 1996.

Levander, Caroline F. *Voices of the Nation: Women and Public Speech in Nineteenth-Century American Literature and Culture*. Cambridge: Cambridge University Press, 1998.

Levine, Robert S. *Conspiracy and Romance: Studies in Brockden Brown, Cooper, Hawthorne, and Melville*. Cambridge: Cambridge University Press, 1989.

——. *Martin Delany, Frederick Douglass, and the Politics of Representative Identity*. Chapel Hill: University of North Carolina Press, 1997.

Lieber, Francis. "The Character of the Gentleman." Pp. 225–79 in *The Miscellaneous Writings of Francis Lieber*. Volume 1: *Reminiscences, Addresses, and Essays*. Philadelphia: J. B. Lippincott, 1880.

——. *On Civil Liberty and Self-Government*. Philadelphia: J. B. Lippincott, 1859.

Lippard, George. *The Quaker City, or The Monks of Monk Hall: A Romance of Philadelphia Life, Mystery, and Crime* (1844), ed. David S. Reynolds. Amherst: University of Massachusetts Press, 1995.

Lithwick, Dahlia. "Holy Matrimony: What's Really Undermining the Sanctity of Marriage?" *Slate Magazine*. 20 November 2003. Http://www.slate.com/id/2091475/.

Looby, Christopher. *Voicing America: Language, Literary Form, and the Origins of the United States*. Chicago: University of Chicago Press, 1996.

Lott, Eric. "After Identity, Politics: The Return of Universalism." *New Literary History* 31, no. 4 (2000): 665–78.

——. *Love and Theft: Blackface Minstrelsy and the American Working Class*. New York: Oxford University Press, 1993.

Lummis, C. Douglas. *Radical Democracy*. Ithaca, N.Y.: Cornell University Press, 1997.

Lutz, Thomas. *American Nervousness, 1903: An Anecdotal History*. Ithaca, N.Y.: Cornell University Press, 1991.

Lynch, Deidre. *The Economy of Character: Novels, Market Culture, and the Business of Inner Meaning*. Chicago: University of Chicago Press, 1998.

Marshall, David. *The Surprising Effects of Sympathy*. Chicago: University of Chicago Press, 1988.

Martin, Robert K., and Leland S. Person. "Missing Letters: Hawthorne, Melville, and Scholarly Desire." *ESQ* 46, nos. 1–2 (2000): 99–122.

Marx, Karl. *The Marx–Engels Reader*, ed. Robert C. Tucker. New York: W. W. Norton, 1978.

Matheson, Neill. "Clifford's Dim, Unsatisfactory Elegance." Paper presented at the Modern Language Association Convention, Washington, D.C., December 2000.

McGowan, Philip. "The Intemperate Irish in American Reform Literature." *Irish Journal of American Studies* 4 (1995); 49–66.

Melville, Herman. *Clarel* (1876). In *The Writings of Herman Melville*, Vol. 12, eds. Harrison Hayford, Hershel Parker, and G. Thomas Tanselle. Evanston, Ill.: Northwestern University Press, 1984

——. *Correspondence*. In *The Writings of Herman Melville*, Vol. 14, eds. Harrison Hayford, Hershel Parker, and G. Thomas Tanselle. Evanston, Ill.: Northwestern University Press, 1984.

——. "Hawthorne and His Mosses" (1850). Pp. 215–29 in *The Hawthorne and Melville Friendship*, ed. James C. Wilson. Jefferson, N.C.: McFarland, 1991.

——. *Moby-Dick; or, The Whale* (1851). In *The Writings of Herman Melville*, Vol. 6, eds. Harrison Hayford, Hershel Parker, and G. Thomas Tanselle. Evanston, Ill.: Northwestern University Press, 1984.

——. *Pierre; or, The Ambiguities* (1852). In *The Writings of Herman Melville*, Vol. 7, eds. Harrison Hayford, Hershel Parker, and G. Thomas Tanselle. Evanston, Ill.: Northwestern University Press, 1984.

Michaels, Walter Benn. "Romance and Real Estate." Pp. 156–82 in *The American Renaissance Reconsidered: Selected Papers from the English Institute*, eds. Walter Benn Michaels and Donald E. Pease. Baltimore: Johns Hopkins University Press, 1985.

——. *The Shape of the Signifier: 1967 to the End of History*. Princeton, N.J.: Princeton University Press, 2004.

Miller, Edwin Haviland. *Salem Is My Dwelling Place: A Life of Nathaniel Hawthorne*. Iowa City: University of Iowa Press, 1991.

Millington, Richard H. *Practicing Romance: Narrative Form and Cultural Engagement in Hawthorne's Fiction*. Princeton, N.J.: Princeton University Press, 1992.

Mintz, Steven. *Moralists and Modernizers: America's Pre–Civil War Reformers*. Baltimore: Johns Hopkins University Press, 1995.

Mitchell, Donald Grant. *Reveries of a Bachelor, or, a Book of the Heart* (1850). Pp. 474–584 in *Popular American Literature of the Nineteenth Century*, ed. Paul C. Gutjahr. New York: Oxford University Press, 2001.

Monk, Maria. *Awful Disclosures of the Hotel Dieu Nunnery in Montreal* (1836). Pp. 187–330 in *Veil of Fear: Nineteenth-Century Convent Tales*, ed. Nancy Lusignan Schultz. West Lafayette, Ind.: Purdue University Press, 1999.

Morrison, Toni. *Playing in the Dark: Whiteness and the Literary Imagination*. New York: Vantage Books, 1992.

Mott, Frank Luther. *A History of American Magazines, 1741–1850*. Cambridge, Mass.: Harvard University Press, 1957.

Nelson, Dana D. *National Manhood: Capitalist Citizenship and the Imagined Fraternity of White Men*. Durham: Duke University Press, 1998.

Otter, Samuel. *Melville's Anatomies*. Berkeley: University of California Press, 1999.

Pettengill, Claire C. "Sisterhood in a Separate Sphere: Female Friendship in Hannah Webster Foster's *The Coquette* and *The Boarding School*." *Early American Literature* 27, no. 3 (1992): 185–283.

Pfister, Joel, and Nancy Schnog, eds. *Inventing the Psychological: Toward a Cultural History of Emotional Life in America*. New Haven, Conn.: Yale University Press, 1997.

Piché, Thomas, Jr. "Reading Carrie Mae Weems." Pp. 9–27 in *Carrie Mae Weems: Recent Work, 1992–1998*. New York: George Braziller and Everson Museum of Art, 1998.

Powell, Timothy. "Postcolonial Theory in an American Context: A Reading of Martin Delany's *Blake*." Pp. 347–65 in *The Pre-Occupation of Postcolonial Studies*, eds. Fawzia Afzal-Khan and Kalpana Seshadri-Crooks. Durham: Duke University Press, 2000.

Putnam, Robert. "Bowling Alone: Democracy in America at the End of the Twentieth Century." *Journal of Democracy* 6, no. 1 (January 1995): 65–78.

Reed, Rebecca. *Six Months in a Convent* (1835). Pp. 1–186 in *Veil of Fears: Nineteenth-Century Convent Tales*, ed. Nancy Lusignan Schultz. West Lafayette, Ind.: Purdue University Press, 1999.

Reid-Pharr, Robert. "Violent Ambiguity: Martin Delany, Bourgeois Sadomasochism, and the Production of a Black National Masculinity." Pp. 73–94 in *Representing Black Men*, eds. Marcellus Blount and George P. Cunningham. New York: Routledge, 1996.

Ripley, George. "Letter to the Church in Purchase Street." Pp. 251–57 in *The Transcendentalists*, ed. Perry Miller. Cambridge, Mass.: Harvard University Press, 1971.

Robson, C. B. "Francis Lieber's Theories of Society, Government, and Liberty." *Journal of Politics* 4 (1942): 227–49.

Rogin, Michael Paul. *Subversive Genealogy: The Politics and Art of Herman Melville*. New York: Alfred A. Knopf, 1983.

Romero, Lora. *Home Fronts: Domesticity and Its Critics in the Antebellum United States*. Durham: Duke University Press, 1997.

Rosenwein, Barbara. *Anger's Past: The Social Uses of Emotion in the Middle Ages*. Ithaca, N.Y.: Cornell University Press, 1998.

Rossiter, Clinton, ed. *Federalist Papers* (1788). New York: New American Library, 1961.

Rubin-Dorsky, Jeffrey. 1988. *Adrift in the Old World: The Psychological Pilgrimage of Washington Irving*. Chicago: University of Chicago Press, 1988.

Salecl, Renata. 2004. *On Anxiety*. London: Routledge, 2004.

Samson, Steven Alan. "Francis Lieber and the Sources of Civil Liberty." *Humanitas* 9, no. 2, (1996): 40–62.

Sanborn, Geoffrey. "Whence Come You, Queequeg?" *American Literature* 77, no. 2 (2005): 227–57.

Sanchez-Eppler, Karen. "Temperance in the Bed of a Child: Incest and Social Order in Nineteenth-Century America." Pp. 60–92 in *The Serpent in the Cup: Temperance in American Literature*, eds. David S. Reynolds and Debra J. Rosenthal. Amherst: University of Massachusetts Press, 1997.

Sandler, Joseph. *From Safety to Superego*. New York: Guilford, 1987.

Saxton, Alexander. *The Rise and Fall of the White Republic: Class Politics and Mass Culture in Nineteenth-Century America*. New York: Verso, 1990.

Schlag, Pierre. "Law and Phrenology." *Harvard Law Review* (February 1997): 877–922.

Sedgwick, Eve Kosofsky. *Between Men: English Literature and Male Homosocial Desire*. New York: Columbia University Press, 1985.

Sellers, Charles. *The Market Revolution: Jacksonian America, 1815–1846*. New York: Oxford University Press, 1991.

Shuffelton, Frank. "Melancholy and the Constitution of the Federal Ego: Loss and Repression in the Early American Novel." Paper delivered to the Group for Early Modern Cultural Studies, Newport, R.I., 1998.

Smith, Adam. *The Theory of Moral Sentiments* (1759). London: A. Millar, 1761.

Smith, Glenn W. *The Politics of Deceit: Saving Freedom and Democracy from Extinction.* Hoboken, N.J.: John Wiley and Sons, 2004.

Smith-Rosenberg, Carroll. *Disorderly Conduct: Visions of Gender in Victorian America.* New York: Alfred A. Knopf, 1985.

——. "Domesticating 'Virtue.'" Pp. 160–84 in *Literature and the Body: Essays on Populations and Persons, Selected Papers from the English Institute, 1986,* ed. Elaine Scarry. Baltimore: Johns Hopkins University Press, 1988.

Spiro, Lisa. "Reading with a Tender Rapture: *Reveries of a Bachelor* and the Rhetoric of Detached Intimacy." *Book History* 6 (2003): 57–93.

Staudenraus, P. J. *The African Colonization Movement: 1816–1865.* New York: Columbia University Press, 1961.

Stern, Julia. *The Plight of Feeling: Sympathy and Dissent in the Early American Novel.* Chicago: University of Chicago Press, 1997.

Stott, Richard Briggs. *Workers in the Metropolis: Class, Ethnicity, and Youth in Antebellum New York City.* Ithaca, N.Y.: Cornell University Press, 1990.

Streeby, Shelley. "Haunted Houses: George Lippard, Nathaniel Hawthorne, and Middle-Class America." *Criticism* 38, no. 3 (1996): 443–72.

——. "Opening Up the Story Paper: George Lippard and the Construction of Class." *boundary 2* 24, no. 1 (1997): 177–203.

Sundquist, Eric J. *To Wake the Nations: Race in the Making of American Literature.* Cambridge, Mass.: Harvard University Press, 1993.

Taussig, Michael. *The Nervous System.* New York: Routledge, 1992.

Teute, Fredrika J., and David S. Shields. "The Confederation Court." Paper presented at Court without Kings: The International Court Studies Association, Boston, September 2001.

Thomas, Brook. "*The House of the Seven Gables*: Reading the Romance of America." *PMLA* 97, no. 2 (1982): 195–211.

Thomas, Calvin. *Male Matters: Masculinity, Anxiety, and the Male Body on the Line.* Urbana: University of Illinois Press, 1996.

Thomas, John L. "Romantic Reform in America, 1815–1865." *American Quarterly* 17 no. 4 (1965): 656–81.

Thoreau, Henry David. "Reform and the Reformers." Pp. 181–97 in *Reform Papers,* ed. Wendell Glick. Princeton, N.J.: Princeton University Press, 1973.

Tichi, Cecila. *Embodiment of a Nation: Human Form in American Places.* Cambridge, Mass.: Harvard University Press, 2001.

Tocqueville, Alexis de. *Democracy in America* (1835), ed. Phillips Bradley. New York: Random House, 1945.

Traub, Valerie. *Desire and Anxiety: Circulations of Sexuality in Shakespearean Drama.* London: Routledge, 1992.

Traubel, Horace. *With Walt Whitman in Camden.* Volume 3: *March 28–July 14, 1888.* New York: D. Appleton, 1908.

——. *With Walt Whitman in Camden.* Volume 4: *July 16–October 31, 1888.* New York: D. Appleton, 1908.

Turner, Mark. *Backward Glances: Cruising Queer Streets in London and New York*. London: Reaktion Books, 2004.

Veblen, Thorsten. *The Theory of the Leisure Class*. New York: Penguin, 1953.

Waldstreicher, David. "'Fallen under My Observation': Vision and Virtue in *The Coquette*." *Early American Literature* 27, no. 3 (1992): 204–18.

Wallace, Michele. "Afterword: 'Why Are There No Great Black Artists?' The Problem of Visuality in African-American Culture." Pp. 333–46 in *Black Popular Culture*, ed. Gina Dent. Seattle: Bay Press, 1992.

Warner, Michael. *The Letters of the Republic: Publication and the Public Sphere in Eighteenth-Century America*. Cambridge, Mass.: Harvard University Press, 1990.

——. *The Trouble with Normal: Sex, Politics, and the Ethics of Queer Life*. New York: Free Press, 1999.

——. "Whitman Drunk." Pp. 269–89 in Michael Warner, *Publics and Counterpublics*. New York: Zone, 2002.

Wells, Samuel. *A Manual of Etiquette; or, How to Behave: A Pocket Manual of Republican Etiquette*. New York: Fowler and Wells, 1857.

Wheeler, Noyes. *The Phrenological Characters and Talents of Henry Clay, Daniel Webster, John Quincy Adams, William Henry Harrison, and Andrew Jackson*. Boston: Dow and Jackson, 1844.

White, Hayden. "The Politics of Historical Interpretation: Discipline and De-Sublimation." *Critical Inquiry* 9 (September 1982): 113–37.

Whitman, Walt. *Collected Writings*, Vol. 3. New York: G. P. Putnam's Sons, 1902.

——. *Collected Writings*, Vol. 4. New York: G. P. Putnam's Sons, 1902.

——. *Franklin Evans; or, The Inebriate: A Tale of the Times* (1842), ed. Jean Downey. New Haven, Conn.: College and University Press, 1967.

——. *Journalism*, vol. 1, eds. Herbert Bergman, Douglas A. Noverr, Edward J. Recchia. New York: Peter Lang, 1998.

——. *Leaves of Grass* (1855), eds. Sculley Bradley and Harold W. Blodgett. New York: W. W. Norton, 1973.

Wiegman, Robyn. *American Anatomies: Theorizing Race and Gender*. Durham: Duke University Press, 1995.

——. "Whiteness Studies and the Paradox of Particularity." *boundary 2* 26, no. 3 (1999): 115–50.

Wilentz, Sean. *Chants Democratic: New York City and the Rise of the American Working Class, 1788–1850*. New York: Oxford University Press, 1984.

Williams, Raymond. *Marxism and Literature*. New York: Oxford University Press, 1977.

Wilson, James C., ed. *The Hawthorne and Melville Friendship*. Jefferson, N.C.: McFarland, 1991.

Wineapple, Brenda, "Hawthorne and Melville; or, The Ambiguities." *ESQ* 46, nos. 1–2 (2000): 75–98.

Winwar, Frances. *American Giant: Walt Whitman and His Times*. New York: Harper Brothers, 1941.

Witherspoon, John. *Works*, vol. 4. Philadelphia: William Woodward, 1802.

Zerilli, Linda M. G. "This Universalism which Is Not One." *diacritics* 28, no. 2 (1998): 3–20.

Cowie, Alexander, 159

Crafts, Hannah, 13, 15. See also *Bondwoman's Narrative, The*

Crane, Gregg, 343–44 n. 28

Cullen, William, 169

Culler, Jonathan, 348–49 n. 1

Dall, Caroline, 19, 56–59

Davidson, Cathy, 46, 313 n. 47, 314–15 n. 51

Dayan, Joan, 218–20, 341–42 n. 7

Delany, Martin, 13, 15. See also *Blake; or, the Huts of America*

Deleuze, Giles, 2, 173–74

D'Emilio, John, 338 n. 62

democracy, 1; disciplinary role of, 3; humanism and, 16; imagination and, 12; mobility and, 4–5, 24, 35

Denning, Michael, 332 n. 26

desire, 190–201; capital and, 338 n. 62

Dillon, Elizabeth Maddock, 340–41 n. 75

Douglas, Ann, 298

Douglass, Frederick, 130

Dred Scott decision, 79

Edelman, Lee, 317 n. 6

Emerson, Ralph Waldo, 7, 15, 68–69, 71–76, 85, 90

Fanuzzi, Robert, 328–29 n. 37

Federalist Papers, 21

Findley, William, 17

Finley, Robert, 102–6, 111–22, 326 nn. 22–23; labor and, 326 n. 21

Finseth, Ian, 314–15 nn. 51–52

Fisher, Will, 278

Fleischacker, Samuel, 302

Fleischner, Jennifer, 238

Fliegelman, Jay, 115–16, 308–9 n. 20

Foster, Hannah Webster, 64. See also *Coquette, The*

Foucault, Michel, 2–3, 25, 55, 73, 75, 94, 96, 101, 105–6, 208, 224, 318 n. 24, 323–24 n. 6, 324 n. 8, 327 n. 30, 330 n. 7

Fourier, Charles, 7

Fowler, Lorenzo (L. N.), 179, 181, 185–87, 337 n. 40

Fowler, Lydia, 169, 172, 181, 183, 185, 187, 189

Fowler, Orson (O. S.), 170, 171–75, 183, 185–86, 188

Franchot, Jenny, 86–87, 320–21 n. 36

Freud, Sigmund: on anxiety and desire, 184; on mourning and melancholy, 39–44; on Oedipal complex, 236, 238

friendship, 20–22, 24–26, 96; in *The Coquette*, 46–49, 51, 54–55; Emerson on, 73; Foucault on, 55

Frye, Northrop, 220–21

Fuss, Diana, 345–46 n. 48

Garrison, William Lloyd, 68, 76, 102–3, 118, 125–35; imperialism and, 329 n. 39; *The Liberator* and, 62, 86, 126, 328–29 n. 37

Gilfoyle, Timothy, 143–44

Gilmore, Michael, 310 nn. 27–28

Gladwell, Malcolm, 60

Goddu, Teresa, 341–42 n. 7

Grewal, Inderpal, and Caren Kaplan, 334–35 n. 15

Guattari, Félix, 173–74

Gutmann, Amy, 299

Habermas, Jurgen, 62–63, 102, 128, 231, 327 n. 33

Haltumen, Karen, 309–10 n. 24

Hamburger, Philip, 309–10 nn. 22–24

Hamilton, Alexander, 17–18, 20–23

Haskell, Thomas L., 339 n. 64

Hawthorne, Nathaniel, 15, 35, 77; friendship of, with Melville, 285–88. See also *House of the Seven Gables, The*; *Scarlet Letter, The*

Hawthorne, Sophia Peabody, 292–93

Hendler, Glenn, 344 n. 33

Holland, Sharon Patricia, 316 n. 57

Holloway, Emory, 166, 322 n. 28

homoeroticism, 140–41, 156; in *Franklin*

CHRISTOPHER CASTIGLIA is professor of American Literature and senior scholar at the Center for American Literary Study at the Pennsylvania State University. He is the author of *Bound and Determined: Captivity, Culture-Crossing, and White Womanhood from Mary Rowlandson to Patty Hearst* and the coeditor of Walt Whitman's *Franklin Evans, or The Inebriate: A Tale of the Times* (Duke, 2007).

Library of Congress Cataloging-in-Publication Data
Castiglia, Christopher.
Interior states : institutional consciousness and the inner life of democracy in the antebellum United States / Christopher Castiglia.
p. cm. — (New Americanists)
Includes bibliographical references and index.
ISBN 978-0-8223-4244-1 (cloth : alk. paper)
ISBN 978-0-8223-4267-0 (pbk. : alk. paper)
1. American literature—19th century—History and criticism.
2. Politics and literature—United States—History—19th century.
3. Democracy in literature. 4. Self in literature. 5. Democracy—Psychological aspects. 6. Democracy—Philosophy. 7. Affect (Psychology)—Social aspects—United States—History—19th century. 8. Emotions—Social aspects—United States—History—19th century. 9. Affect (Psychology)—Political aspects—United States—History—19th century. 10. Emotions—Political aspects—United States—History—19th century. I. Title.
PS217.P64C37 2008
810.9'358—dc22   2008023165